PEOPLE OF THE VOLCANO

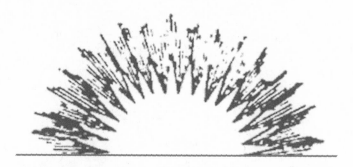

PEOPLE OF THE VOLCANO

ANDEAN COUNTERPOINT IN THE COLCA VALLEY OF PERU

NOBLE DAVID COOK, *with Alexandra Parma Cook*

DUKE UNIVERSITY PRESS *Durham and London* 2007

© 2007 Duke University Press

All rights reserved

Printed in the United States

of America on acid-free paper ∞

Designed by Amy Ruth Buchanan

Typeset in Dante by Tseng

Information Systems, Inc.

Library of Congress Cataloging-in-

Publication Data appear on the last

printed page of this book.

This book is for the present peoples of the Colca Valley,
the survivors of conquest and colonization

CONTENTS

ILLUSTRATIONS AND TABLES

Illustrations

Tables

PREFACE

Peru's richly terraced Colca Valley first came to the attention of the outside world with the stunning aerial photographs taken in the early 1930s by the Johnson-Shippee expedition to South America. Published in a series of lavishly illustrated articles in the *National Geographic*, the valley, dominated by glaciated volcanic peaks, intrigued viewers. But it was not until the early 1970s, with the massive irrigation project to channel water from the highlands to the Majes coastal desert, that a road was constructed, breaking the valley's isolation. Almost overnight the valley's people had access to the outside world, to the not far-distant city of Arequipa, and the nation's capital of Lima well beyond. At last the valley's wonders—the great canyon, the flocks of wild vicuña grazing on the puna lands, the richly decorated colonial churches, and the people—were opened to outsiders, simultaneously accelerating the process of change.

My hope is to provide a guide for those who, moved by their experience in the valley, may wish to understand better how its people transformed their landscape, making it what we see today. The work is historical, with an eye fixed on place, the environment. Much of what one views in the valley is the result of what the outsiders, the Spanish, took in the sixteenth century and the way they modified Inca and pre-Inca foundations. The foundations are not just material: not just the waterworks, the households, or the crops that were planted and harvested. Foundations are also social: the way in which human relationships—religious, economic, and social—are constructed to permit survival in a difficult environment. These structures, alien to the "modern" mind, are those that I wish to explore. They are not static but are constantly changing.

I learned of the Colca Valley in 1974, during my tenure as Visiting Fulbright Professor at the Pontificia Universidad Católica del Perú. The late Dr. Franklin Pease, then director of the Museo Nacional de la Historia, asked me to codirect a group of his students in analysis of a late sixteenth-century census document. That *visita*, or inspection of the *urinsaya* section of Yanque Collaguas for 1591, provides detailed information on all native inhabitants of the middle Colca Valley, including their names, age, and societal position; their marital status; their condition as tributary; and whether or not they were orphans, widows, or widowers. Their physical condition is noted (blind or deaf, or lame), as well as their occupation and political role. Each person is listed by village and household, under societal categories (upper or lower halves), and *ayllu* (kinship unit). Landholdings are provided by toponym and crop type; even the numbers of llamas and alpacas are given. The possibilities for detailed analysis of demography, society, and economy are rich.

With travel money from the Peruvian office of the Ford Foundation, and after completing preliminary research on the census and supplementary investigations in Lima's National Archive and Library, we set out for Arequipa in August 1974. Our initial mornings were spent in search of other information on the Colca Valley in the Provincial Archive in Yanahuara. In the afternoons some researchers worked in Arequipa's Municipal Archive, while Alexandra Parma Cook and I worked in Yanahuara's parish records. During afternoons we also purchased supplies of food, water, and "camping equipment," and searched for a reliable way to reach the valley. Although it had been recently improved, the gravel road leading to our destination was still an adventurous ten- to twelve-hour trip, requiring a steep climb up the flanks of the volcanic cone of Misti, then across the high puna toward the town of Chivay, the district capital. Rising to 15,000 feet in some spots, the road challenges sufferers of *soroche*, or altitude sickness. Our research design was to establish a base at the village of Yanque, the colonial administrative capital for the province. From there we would conduct a reconnaissance of the valley in search of both material remains worthy of future investigation, and documentary evidence that might remain in local churches, municipal offices, or in private hands. Fortunately, Max Neira Avendaño, a team member from Arequipa's Universidad Nacional de San Antonio, had conducted archaeological research in the valley earlier. He, Eusebio Quiroz, the late Alejandro Malaga Medina, and others in the Arequipa group were indispensable for the project's success.

Critical help in the valley came from the late Maryknoll father Pablo Hagen, who was the resident priest, and from the Maryknoll sister Antonia Kayser. Both served the spiritual needs of the Yanque community, and they operated a first-resort clinic, medical dispensary, and emergency food bank. They were also strong advocates for the villagers. Both held a profound appreciation and respect for the history of the valley's people. They offered "space" in one of the structures that had been part of the original Franciscan convent, simultaneously providing "status" for the team of outsiders. And they opened the "Yanque Parish Archive" for our investigation. Not only did we find original parish registers—for Yanque they are fairly complete from 1685 to the present—but even more important, we found colonial censuses for various parts of the valley, comparable in quality to that of Yanque urinsaya of 1591. There was ample information on the valley for many future investigators. Sister Antonia shared selflessly with us and others her hospitality and love of the people of Yanque. Her support during several weeks of archival and field research while we resided in the convent in 1977 remain forever imprinted in our memory.

Over the years numerous institutions have provided assistance. The Fulbright Commission in Lima extended fellowships as Visiting Professor at the Universidad Católica in 1974 and 1984. Marcia Koth de Paredes of the commission enthusiastically supported the opening of the valley to both scholars and the general public. The Ford Foundation provided travel funds for the first expedition in 1974. The National Endowment for the Humanities via the Summer Seminar Program for College teachers in 1976 facilitated readings in anthropological theory at the University of Illinois, helping me probe the complexities of ayllu and moiety. The Wenner-Gren Foundation for Anthropological Research aided direct investigation in the Colca Valley in early 1977. A Fulbright for Spain in 1985 allowed for tracking down colonial documents in various archives. Mellon Foundation Summer Grants during my tenure at the University of Bridgeport, as well as a year's sabbatical in 1988–89, permitted sustained research in Spanish collections. Various appointments as Visiting Fellow at Yale University, through the kind intercession of History Department chairs Jonathan Spence, Connie Tottman, and the late John Boswell, gave unlimited access to one of the finest libraries in the United States. Additional related material appeared during research for other books: a John Simon Guggenheim Fellowship in 1991–92, and an American Council of Learned Societies Fellowship for 1998–99, both for investigations in Spanish archives.

We thank the staffs of various libraries and archives who invariably went out of their way to assist us. In Peru we consulted the Archivo Parroquial de Yanque, Archivo Histórico Provincial de Arequipa, Archivo Municipal de Arequipa, Archivo Nacional del Perú, Biblioteca Nacional del Perú, Museo Nacional de la Historia, and the Archivo del Monasterio de San Francisco de Lima. In Spain we used the Archivo General de Indias in Seville; and the Archivo Histórico Nacional, Biblioteca del Palacio Real, Biblioteca de la Real Academia de la Historia, and the Biblioteca Nacional, all in Madrid. In the United States we worked in the Library of Congress, the New York Public Library, Yale University's Sterling and Beinecke Rare Book Libraries, the Rosenbach Museum and Library in Philadelphia, and the P. K. Younge Collection of the University of Florida.

In Miami I thank the staff of the Green Library and interlibrary loan department of Florida International University (FIU). Ivan E. Santiago, coordinator of Educational Technology Resource Center at FIU, along with Haig Durant and Rocío González, provided valuable assistance in preparing the illustrations.

The late Antonine Tibesar, O.F.M. (Order of Friars Minor), an expert on the Franciscan Order in the Andes, graciously provided valuable leads, contacts, and photocopies of important material in Rome. Thanks to the generous introduction of Father Tibesar, Father Lobatón, then Franciscan general commissioner in Peru, graciously allowed access to the Franciscan Archive in Lima in 1984. More recently Father Julián Heras, O.F.M., shared fresh insight into the order's history in Peru. A brief notice of the results of our team's efforts in the valley was published in the *Latin American Research Review* in 1975. Within ten years numerous Peruvian academics had conducted research on various aspects of the valley's past and present, all the way from students preparing their baccalaureate theses, to well-established scholars. Outsiders entered the scene; geographer William M. Denevan of the University of Wisconsin secured significant funding to mount an interdisciplinary team with primary focus on agricultural terrace abandonment and restoration. Numerous dissertations, books, and scientific treatises have resulted. David J. Robinson has continued publication of the series of visitas that Franklin Pease initiated in 1977. I thank many specialists for leads, suggestions, and friendly advice: Tom Abercrombie, María Benavides, the late Woodrow Borah, W. George Lovell, Mariana Mould de Pease, María Rostworowski de Diez Canseco, Eldi Flores Nájar, Frederick Schwaller, Margarita Suárez, John TePaske, the late Theodore de la Torre-Bueno, Nancy van Deusen, Rafael Varón, Steven A. Wernke, and Anne Wightman. And I thank my students who have listened to my musings about the valley's people, and who invariably pressed for more. I especially appreciate the efforts of the La Católica student cohort of 1974, those who have done such excellent work on Andean studies, among others: Amalia Castelli, Guillermo Cock, David Cunza, Ximena Fernández, Elias Mujica, José Luis Rénique, and Efraín Trelles.

Susan Ramírez and Lyman Johnson read and extensively commented on a longer version of the text, and I appreciate their suggestions. The geographer and Colca Valley specialist David J. Robinson provided critical insight as he reviewed both versions. Maps were prepared thanks to the expertise of cartographer Joe Stoll at Syracuse University under the direction of David Robinson. I thank especially my editor at Duke, Valerie Millholland, whose insistent prodding did result in the reduction of the manuscript by more than a third. Its copyeditor, Sonya Manes, did an exceptional job, as did the assistant managing editor, Mark Mastromarino. All photographs were taken by the authors, or by

Greg Cook. Many thanks to Lydia Garibay of the Siglo XXI Editores in Mexico for permission to duplicate illustrations from their edition of the Felipe Guaman Poma de Ayala text. The debt to Franklin Pease is incalculable; without his towering intellectual curiosity and enthusiastic prodding, as well as support, the present study might never have been attempted. Alexandra Parma Cook has collaborated from the beginning. She was in the initial group entering the valley in 1974, and she returned in 1977 to share in the tedious collection of parish register data required for demographic and social analysis. She culled the documents for answers to questions we posed during almost continuous discussions. And we shared in research in archives and libraries in Peru, Spain, and the United States. Along the way I completed a monographic examination of the valley's population history, and we jointly authored a microhistory that centered on Francisco Noguerol de Ulloa, one of the valley's early settlers. Her critical insight and probing questions have helped shape both past and present arguments. The third part of our Colca Valley trilogy will focus on the endeavors of a Franciscan friar, Luis Jerónimo de Oré.

PART I. FOUNDATIONS

CHAPTER ONE

BENEATH THE SOARING CONDOR

They have come from a *huaca* or ancient shrine that is situated within the confines of the neighboring province of Vellilli, which is a snow-capped peak in the shape of a volcano, set out from the other peaks of the area, and which they call Collaguata. They say that from this mountain or from within it many people departed, and they descended to this province and its valley, and that they have settled in this riverbed. They conquered those who were the natives, ousted them by force, and then remained. . . . Because the volcano from which they have come is called Collaguata, they are called the Collaguas.
—Testimony of valley residents, 20 January 1586, from Juan de Ulloa Mogollón, "Relación de la provincia de los Collaguas."

The first Europeans to view the Colca Valley in the 1530s surely marveled at its natural beauty. Either descending from the desolate high-elevation grasslands or climbing from the desert Pacific strip, one is impressed by the massive patchwork of irrigated terraces blanketing the river's slopes. The dense multicolored crops testify to the fecundity of the volcanic soil, and stand in stark contrast to the frigid glaciated peaks towering above the valley and the canyon's rocky riverbed below. High in the crystal sky a solitary condor soars, spreading its wings, catching the rays of the brilliant sun. Fields, hamlets, and cottages with wisps of smoke wafting upward complete the picture.[1]

The source of water and life for the Colca Valley's people is the moisture absorbed by the air as it flows over the Pacific Ocean. The prevailing southwesterly winds push humid sea air upward against the barrier of the Andean cordillera. As the elevation increases the temperature plummets, and humidity is squeezed from the atmosphere to create rain or, in the lofty mountains, sleet and snow. During the wet season, from late November to March, heavy afternoon showers regularly drench the valley, while on the puna violent thunderstorms assault pastoralists and occasional travelers. The force of the elements, especially thunder and lightning, which the Quechua called Llapta, was feared and propitiated by Andeans long after foreigners introduced Christianity.[2]

In the dry season the snowcapped peaks above the puna bestow life-giving water. The sun, venerated as a spiritual force, has ample power midday to melt snow and ice at the edge of stone and rock, creating trickles, then rivulets. And groundwater emerges from springs, which are also venerated. From melting snow at the edges of the region's volcanic cones and the Patacapuquio, or hundred springs of water found toward nearby Lampa, the Colca River is born. After meandering in the puna behind the peaks of Chachani and Misti the river cuts a valley through the highland mass and flows westerly, falling from 3,300 to 2,700 meters before cascading downward, creating a precipitous gorge, deeper than North America's Grand Canyon. Near the end of the profound canyon the Colca joins a river originating in Condesuyos, creating the Majes, before emptying at Camaná into the Pacific. It is not just the Colca that provides life-giving water. Upper irrigation channels bring water from other glaciated peaks. Water for Achoma is taken from both melting ice near the base of Hualca Hualca from where it is channeled into the upper Sepina, and from nearby springs. On the south side of the Colca, water is channeled from the summits of Huarancante, Ampato, and Sabancaya; while on the north side, Quehuisha, Mismi, and Huillcaya are the main sources. The longest of the irrigation canals reaches thirty kilometers![3]

It is in the middle valley, stretching east to west for fifty kilometers, that the bulk of the population is concentrated. The volcanic soil provides a rich foundation for a variety of crops. As early as 2400 BC, inhabitants terraced accessible valley slopes, creating *andenes*, and they constructed irrigation channels to provide water from mountain streams and springs during the long dry season. At higher valley elevations, they grew the grain *quinua* (quinoa) and tubers, especially potatoes and *olluco*; while prized maize was cultivated in intermediate elevations, and squash, beans, gourds, *ají* (chili peppers), fruits, and nuts were produced at lower levels. Autochthonous farmers planted dozens of varieties of grains and vegetables, a diversity lost by contemporary agriculturalists. On the puna vast flocks of llamas and alpacas grazed. They provided wool, meat, and other products; the larger of the camelids transported goods. On the high flat plateaus native straw, called *ichu*, was cut for thatching cottage roofs. Game and fowl as well as fish were abundant.[4]

The Colca Valley's idyllic rural setting has its darker side. Earthquakes pose a constant threat. Two-story stone residences often collapsed and killed dur-

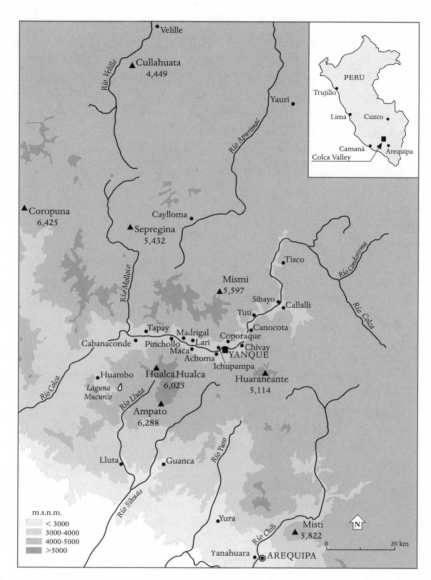

Map 1. The southern region of Peru, from Caylloma to Arequipa
(m.s.n.m. = "meters above sea level")

ing earthquakes. Infants and the elderly were especially vulnerable. Landslides buried or swept away entire villages. Furthermore, the quaking earth often devastated agricultural terraces and irrigation channels. More dangerous were volcanic eruptions. Although such events were rare they caused massive destruction, as on 19 February 1600, when Huaynaputina, in nearby Ubinas province, exploded. A dense cloud of volcanic ash drifted northward, sweeping beyond Cuzco into the Amazon basin. Valley crops were covered and destroyed; the only compensation following such tragedies is soil enrichment. A more gradual tectonic upward shift over several generations likely disrupted the natural flow of water, ruining irrigation systems. Floods do major damage during periods of excessive rainfall; mudslides are as destructive as earthquakes, erasing irrigation channels, even hamlets. And there is the gradual impact of longer-term climatic variations.[5]

In Inca times the territory was the home of two ethnic groups: the Collaguas lived in the upper valley, the Cabanas the lower. Smaller ethnicities shared the valley. The Spanish conquerors created a single administrative unit, calling it the province or the *corregimiento* of Los Collaguas. The confines of the colonial province were supposedly precise; European boundaries were expected to be. But peoples of the valley had kin and, via kin, access to resources in distant locales, even on the desert coastal strip. Andeans viewed basic socioeconomic units as "people," not "place." Controversies between conquerors and colonized erupted throughout the colonial era, the result of fundamentally different views of the relationship between people and land. After conquest, the Spanish toiled to make native practice conform to their own preconception that Collaguas could be defined as inhabiting a land with fixed boundaries; they were only partially successful. Colonial bureaucrats delimited the province of the Collaguas on the south by Camaná and Arequipa, on the west by Condesuyos, on the north by Canas y Canchis, and on the east by Urcosuyo. By the Bourbon reforms of the late colonial period, the name was changed to the intendancy of Caylloma, celebrating the silver mines discovered in the northern part of the district in the early 1600s.[6]

The homeland of the Collaguas and Cabanas is vast: the post-Independence district of Caylloma, roughly equivalent in size to the colonial province of Los Collaguas, contains 14,780 square kilometers. Although half the size of Belgium, or three-quarters that of El Salvador, most land is useless for agriculture. Glaciated peaks and rugged mountains constitute much of the province. The relatively level puna, although too frigid for most forms of agriculture, is ideal for herding alpacas and llamas. Exact estimations of the amount of land useful for agriculture is virtually impossible. A 1961 Peruvian agricultural census provides a figure of 25.95 percent, a little less than 4,000 square kilometers.[7] By careful analysis of aerial photographs in the 1980s, the Denevan and Treacy interdisciplinary team calculated that the cultivated area in fields in the twelve communities of the middle valley, including both abandoned and terraces, was approximately 14,356 hectares. Of those about 42 percent were abandoned; their estimate does not include the extensive grazing lands of the puna.[8]

Descent from the Volcano

We are unsure if the first people entering the Colca Valley ascended from the coast, clambering into the intermountain valley, or if they descended from the puna, where they might have been hunting. In either case what lay before them was vastly different from the valley's present scenery, and from what the Europeans saw in the sixteenth century. Climatic variations are imperfectly delineated, but specialists believe that the area was then warmer and more humid, with a denser natural vegetation. The agricultural terraces, the distinctive feature of the recent landscape, were absent.[9] The cultural sequence in the Colca parallels that of nearby highland valleys. Groups evolved from simple hunters, fishers, and gatherers, to sophisticated agriculturalists over the millennia. Two to three millennia before our era, the domestication of plants and animals in Andean America occurred. Centuries before the Inca conquered the region, the basic elements—the irrigation channels, agricultural terraces, and richly varied domesticated crops—were part of the cultural landscape. The advanced socioeconomic organization permitted surplus production of diverse crops, supporting a dense native population.[10]

A reconnaissance of the major archaeological sites in the Colca Valley reveals several important ruins that merit careful excavation. Some of the sites consist of large storage facilities for excess agricultural production. The very name by which the valley is now known, q'olqa, means "deposit" in Quechua. There were storehouses at Huacallua, near Chivay, and Uscallacta, between Chivay and Yanque. There were extensive storage deposits at Achoma, and others have been catalogued in lower zones at Alto de Betancur (between Lluta and Siguas) and the Pampa de Timiran. Furthermore, traces of fortresslike structures on some of the hilltops overlooking the valley floor remain, including two above Achoma. Burial chambers abound, usually in niches in agricultural terraces or in the more inaccessible parts of the canyon wall and the rocky cliffs above the valley.[11]

A number of imposing population clusters attract attention. Ullo Ullo, the original home for many subsequently settled in Yanque under the orders of Viceroy Francisco de Toledo, is a large site with many two-story structures. It is divided into halves by a stream running through the middle, and the sectors are surrounded by walls. Agricultural plots, Yanque Viejo, as the abandoned settlement is called by present villagers, abound with surface potsherds with Inca designs. Ullo Ullo—Ludovico Bertonio in 1612 defined the Aymara word *uyu* as a livestock corral, and *uyu uyu* as "when there are many [corrals] together"—was abandoned around 1572. Viceroy Toledo's new Yanque on the canyon's south side was founded on the site of a preexisting hamlet. The Spanish called it La Brota, appropriately meaning "bud" or "sprout." Several preconquest structures at Yanque are easily identified because of their finely worked stone doorways—with serpents, llamas, and circular patterns resembling snails carved on the surface. Some portals sport solidly carved foundation and corner stones. Lower in the valley, Cabanaconde was the home of the Cabanas.[12]

Archaeological evidence for prehistory of the Colca Valley is abundant, and although much remains to be done, substantial investigation has been conducted during recent decades. The dating and study of likely methods of construction of early terraces, the feature that most informs our vision of the Colca Valley, have been completed. The rough outlines of the ceramic and cultural sequence of the valley are in place. Yet much systematic scientific evaluation lies ahead. Unfortunately, many of the questions we wish to ask about the valley's past are not amenable to archaeological probing. When and why did the Inca penetrate the valley? Who were their leaders, and how did the locals respond to their intrusion? How did the Inca incorporate valley peoples into their system? What role did religious belief play in this process? What of economic relationships between the Inca and locals? The written record is absent, for the Andeans lacked writing. Yet records were kept in other ways. Quantities were recorded then manipulated by trained accountants, using colored knotted string memory devices called *quipus*. Some Spanish chroniclers report that the skilled *quipucamayo* could "record" chronologies, even recalling numbers of warriors during battles. Also, pictorial "histories" were painted on a variety of surfaces. Such information is difficult to interpret, and much was lost during the shock of Spanish conquest.

Fortuitously through oral history, transferred to writing, the collective memory of the Colca Valley's peoples persists. "From the information that is passed from parents to children,"[13] the valley's past was transmitted from one generation to the next. Oral history can be remarkably accurate in preliterate societies for three generations, approximately a century. It can in broad outline if not in exact chronology be valid longer. European administrators made their first systematic attempt to collect information on the valley and its history in the village of Yanque on 20 January 1586, a half century after Spanish penetration. A handful of the respondents were born before the arrival of the outsiders. Most who participated in the inquest belonged to the second generation, the children of the conquered. Their testimony stresses the history of the Collaguas ethnic unit, providing tantalizing glimpses of "Incaization" of the valley preceding European conquest.[14]

The inquiry stemmed from Philip II's desire for detailed information on his realm's resources, both in the Old World and the New. Philip's representatives diligently compiled many geographical reports in the Indies beginning in the 1570s, asking about the people and their products, their history, and the nature of local society and religion. The *corregidor* (the royal official who governed a district) Juan de Ulloa Mogollón with the scribe Juan Durán oversaw the questioning of Colca Valley residents in the village of Yanque. Over twenty native leaders and outsiders gathered in the plaza to answer thirty-seven questions prepared by officials of the Council of the Indies. It was a short one-day session, and it seems unlikely there were disputes. The questioning was preceded by Mass in the parish church; celebrations with food and drink followed. If there were variations in individual answers, they are imperceptible in the final report. Customarily younger men deferred to community elders. One of the oldest witnesses was García Checa, principal *kuraka* (chieftain, cacique) of Yanque's *urinsaya* section. Born around 1521 he was old enough to remember life in the valley before the Europeans' arrival, and he provided insight into his people's past. Other principal and secondary kurakas, from both the upper and lower halves of the various communities that composed the valley, also spoke. Kurakas were not the only natives contributing. The interpreter Diego Coro Inga, born in Coporaque, provided important testimony. It is unclear where Diego was educated; Franciscans may have taught him in Coporaque's monastery, established a quarter century earlier. He was both a translator and Coporaque's notary and teacher of reading, writing, and counting. Select Spaniards also contributed their perceptions of the valley.

Three witnesses were priests: Father Diego Hernández Talavera, curate of Guambo and Pinchollo, arrived in the region around 1561. Father Amado González of Yanque was also questioned, although he had not resided in the Collaguas long. For six years Father Hernando Medel de la Feria attended to the religious needs of Lari, a village downstream from Yanque. He had replaced a Franciscan friar, and his testimony may have been tainted; he was involved in a long conflict with the order and was finally expelled from his parish. The timing of the report was inopportune. Had the inquest been conducted a few years earlier, when the Franciscans ministered in the valley, or later, when they were reinstated in their *doctrinas* (Indian parishes), they might have provided richer testimony, given their deeper knowledge of the region. The presence of secular clergy in the valley was generally unwelcome, and many locals were petitioning for the restoration of the friars. The mestizo Gonzalo Gómez de Buitrón, who lived in the province for more than twelve years, likewise participated in the inquiry. He knew the valley's kurakas well, but was mistrusted because he was immersed in illegal economic activities. All witnesses were biased in one way or another.[15]

The genesis of the valley's peoples was probed first. Witnesses testified that the Collaguas originated in the highlands to the north and east. In the province of Velille in the direction of Cuzco rises a great mountain, an extinct volcano called Collaguata. The witnesses affirmed that their ancestors emerged from it and subsequently settled the Colca Valley. Their origin myth affirms it was not a peaceful settlement; they faced resistance from native residents and succeeded only by warfare. Following fighting the original inhabitants were expelled, and the Collaguas took their lands. The newcomers built strongholds or forts in the direction of the region from which they migrated. "They prove this by some forts, that they call *pucara* in their own language, that are constructed on some of the hilltops that overlook the valley from which they descend to conduct warfare." Intermittent warfare characterized life in the region prior to the Inca conquest. Writing a decade after the Ulloa Mogollón inquest, Coporaque's Franciscan friar Luis Jerónimo de Oré related that "in the province of the Collaguas I knew an Indian who had saved a cloak over which he had sewn the fingernails of the Indians that his ancestors killed, and by memory would boast of having many proofs of lives which had been taken, all to defend the lands of that province."[16] At the local level, skirmishes and battles over both water rights and plots of land were frequent, continuing into the twentieth century.

Informants quickly pointed out there were "two types of people of different language and dress" in the province. The Collaguas venerated the mountain that gave them birth, "and because the volcano from which they have come is called Collaguata, they are called the Collaguas."[17] Similar to the Collaguas, the Cabanas descended from a mountain to populate the valley, but their place of origin was the nearby spectacular snowcapped peak of Hualca Hualca (6,025 m), which thrusts its majestic summit above the village of Cabanaconde. Hualca Hualca's melting snow provides water for the southern side of the lower valley. Similar to the Collaguas, the Cabanas conquered and dislodged earlier inhabitants. The Cabanas genesis myth suggests primacy; they probably entered the valley before the Collaguas. How much earlier is unclear, but enough so they identified their origins locally rather than in a distant place. The key cultural difference between the Collaguas and Cabanas was linguistic: the Collaguas spoke Aymara. The Cabanas, informants said, "speak in the general language of Cuzco [Quechua], although corrupt and very debased." Informants noted that in some villages other languages were spoken. Perhaps some were descendants of the valley's original inhabitants. Observers reported that among the Aymara Collaguas several dialects existed, especially in Pinchollo, Calo, and Tapay.[18]

Andean settlement patterns are markedly different from the sixteenth-century Spanish ones, and are difficult to discern from the meager historical record. Ethnic entities needed to secure as complete a set of resources as possible, and sent kin, usually for temporary periods, to access natural resources beyond their primary subsistence base. In the vertical world of the Andes, with many microenvironmental zones lying in close proximity, it was possible to organize the economic structure of society so that each ethnic unit had access to virtually all products necessary for sustenance. Since other groups followed the same survival strategy, a patchwork of ethnic units often shared the same space. Generally, but not always, ethnic interaction was peaceful. Sharing by rotation—for example, a salt mine or fishing site—was normally successful. Production of special crops, such as ají or coca, could have the result that several ethnic units were cultivating in the same general area in a more permanent fashion. With this settlement pattern in mind, the linguistic and cultural variations described in 1586 are comprehensible. The small ethnic-linguistic enclaves still visible in 1586 maintained permanent links with people beyond the confines of the valley. The Cabanas probably had ties with peoples in the direction of Cuzco, perhaps toward Condesuyos, or in the province of Cabanas situated between Cuzco and Lake Titicaca. But they had lived in the valley long enough to associate their origins locally. It is unlikely that the Cabanas were Inca *mitimaes* (migrants) who had been settled in the valley, for had this been the case it would have been reported in the 1586 testimony.[19]

The oral report of 1586 tells little of religious practices in the valley prior to Inca expansion. We know their principal *huacas*—anything of spiritual power—were the mountain peaks of Collaguata, Hualca Hualca, Suquilpa, Apoqico, and Omascota. Veneration involved display of respect and awe. There were no trappings of a priesthood with formal ceremony or elaborate ritual cult. Valley witnesses informed Europeans "the custom was adoration, by stopping and bringing the hands together with a demonstration of great humility." Various types of sacrifices were made. Guinea pigs, the intestines of llamas, small statues or objects of gold and silver, and often corn beer (*chicha*) and coca were offered to appease the mountain huacas. Rarely a young person was left on a temple platform at the summit of a mountain, as at Ampato.[20] The great peaks continue to be respected by valley dwellers. Today Pumach'iri is considered sacred, an Apu, or protector, of the people of the village of Coporaque. Nearby Chumpiña Huito and Yurac Ccocca receive similar devotion.

At a more personal level are the ubiquitous *apachitas*, rock piles surviving alongside major foot trails. Weary sojourners after a challenging crossing, perhaps a mountain pass or river, place a small stone in a spot to symbolize the successful passage and to express thanks to the forces that will permit continuation of the journey. After time a rock cluster swells into a large pile, an apachita. Contemporary travelers continue to place gifts that keep apachitas alive as spiritual forces. Stone objects are powerful symbols in the Andean world, from massive mountain peaks to small pebbles.[21] Worked stone holds an even more powerful meaning. Not mentioned in the 1586 valley report, but evident in the archaeological and ethnological record, are the *conopas*, carefully crafted stone objects the size of the palm of the hand, depicting fields, houses, corrals, and herds. Conopas were and continue to be placed in niches in the walls of homes or hidden by owners and are used to assist in rewarding the family's agricultural efforts with fertility.

Little is known of the pre-Inca political structure of the valley. The Cabanas and the Collaguas were independent *señorios* (kingdoms), or states in European terminology, each under the leadership of a local lord. In the area under Collaguas control described in the 1586 report, two kurakas competed for leadership: one was based in Yanque, the other Lari. The informants' Yanque might even be "Yanque Viejo," or Ullo Ullo, above the river's north bank, not the new Yanque of "La Brota" on the canyon's south side. The north bank prior to Inca expansion was largely Aymara speaking, and was divided into *sayu* (halves). Yanque Viejo lay at the upper end, and downstream was Lari in the middle valley. Informants reported that Yanque was the "village in which the leaders reside." They confided that Lari means "uncle" or "relative," and that "between the Laris and Yanquis, who are brothers that have issued from Collaguata the mountain, they say that they established these two principal pueblos, the one named Yanque, where the most important lords reside, and the other Lari, where the lords that follow stay, and they are as uncles and nephews." This brief passage illustrates key elements of Andean kinship. In Quechua and Aymara the same term is used for father and uncle; your uncle is also your father. Political succession of the *kurakazgo* passed from brother to brother before falling to the subsequent generation. If one's brother died, the surviving sibling took the widow as wife. The children were already classified in Quechua and Aymara terminology as offspring.

At another level the entire valley can be viewed as divided into larger ethnic halves, the Aymara Collaguas on the north side of the river and the Quechua Cabanas on the south. Such a division fits within the framework of Andean cosmology. Another division needs to be considered: a celestial one. The night sky is crystal clear in the high Andes, and native astronomers carefully plotted and discussed patterns in the heavens. They believed the Milky Way split the heavens into halves. Here the Colca River seems to connect with the heavenly star river on the eastern horizon, and the two flow together in the west in the direction of the Pacific Ocean, unifying heaven and earth. The star cluster the Europeans named the Pleiades is called the q'olqa in Quechua. The cluster is closely associated with the agricultural cycle in the southern Andes and is used to predict rainfall and indicate when it is time to plant certain crops. Q'olqa means "granary" as well, and implies agricultural fertility. The celestial q'olqa unites with the terrestrial river to provide precious water for the fertility of annual crops in the valley.[22]

There were marked cultural differences between Cabanas and Collaguas. In addition to the linguistic distinction, the two groups wore unique clothing and practiced differing forms of skull deformation. The Collaguas wore special cloth bands called chucos on their heads. The chuco was placed on infants almost immediately after birth in order to compress, thin, and lengthen the skull as much as possible. Pressure continued to shape the head until the age of four or five, when the binding was removed. Informants explained that the purpose of the custom was to mold the skull to match the shape of the volcano from where their ancestors emerged. The ideal was the perfect "cone head." The Cabanas, in contrast, strove to flatten and widen their heads. The great mountain of Hualca Hualca is not a cone at all; instead it takes the shape of rugged blocks. Not surprisingly the Collaguas told the Spaniards that they believed that their Cabanas neighbors, by widening their skulls, were "very ugly and disproportionate."[23] The Mercedarian friar Martín de Murúa, witnessing results around 1590, vividly described Collaguas and Cabanas skull deformation: "The Collas and Puquinas and other nations of Indians still use the practice of forming the heads of children in diverse manners or figures with much superstition, and in some places make them very long that they call cayto uma, making them thin, and making them come to the form of a narrow and long bonnet that they call chucu; in other places they make the heads flat and wide in the front. That is called paltauma; of these they are all generally from Cabanaconde, because all, young and old, are dressed thusly." Early clergy disapproved of such idolatries and attempted to eradicate them. In the 1570s Viceroy Toledo, shocked at finding that skull deformation continued, issued an ordinance prohibiting the custom within the region. The practice had serious consequences. The Jesuit observer Bernabé Cobo complained of the risks when describing skull deformation among the Collas around Lake Titicaca. The binding process was painful, at times deadly, and he lamented that "many children died of the pain that they suffered, and it was not uncommon for their brains to be squeezed out or for them to remain sick and crippled for life." He related "the Collas made their heads long and pointed. They took this to such an extreme that it is amazing to see the old men that I observed with that fashion from their pagan times."[24] For the Collaguas and Cabanas the principal purpose of skull deformation was spiritual; heads of the infants were molded to resemble the principal huaca of their ancestors, the ethnic entity's place of genesis. Spanish clergy believed it was one of the most hideous native practices, yet in the Colca Valley the custom persisted decades following conversion.[25]

The Rule of Tawantinsuyu

Tawantinsuyu, the "land of the fours quarters," pre-Columbian America's largest state, extended from today's southern Colombia into central Chile, 5,000 kilometers distant. The polity was formed in the century before the arrival of the Europeans by an ethnic group, the Incas, whose homeland was in or near the Cuzco Valley. The Inca state was not the first created in the central Andes; its growth was based on a fully evolved material and political structure. Although there is debate over the nature and chronological evolution of the Inca state and the "official" list of rulers, it is clear that the principal expansion commenced the same century the Europeans sailed westward in search of the Indies. Pachacutec (ca. 1438–71) was the chief figure in the conquest and political integration of the Andean region into a single Inca polity.[26]

Inca penetration into the Colca Valley is rarely mentioned by early Spanish chroniclers. Our two most thorough yet disappointing descriptions of the region date from the mid-1550s. Both were penned by soldier-bureaucrats with wide experience in Peru. Pedro de Cieza de León related (ca. 1553), "the Hubinas and Chiquiguanita and Quimistaca and Collaguas are among the peoples subject to this city [Arequipa]; they were once very populous and possessed many herds of sheep [llamas]. The war of the Spaniards destroyed part of the one and the other." Beyond this tantalizing glimpse, Cieza provided little insight into the lives of the Collaguas or their conquest by the Inca.[27] Juan de Betanzos, a notary with excellent linguistic abilities, settled in Cuzco in the early 1540s. Betanzos married the Inca *ñusta* (princess) Cuxirimay Occlo, baptized Doña

Angelina Yupanqui, thus securing a unique insight into the Andean past. Living in Cuzco, he had ample opportunity to listen to and question elders, especially his wife's relatives, as he prepared his narrative. He compiled a Quechua Christian doctrine and dictionary prior to 1551; both are lost. Betanzos's wife was a daughter of Yanque Yupanqui, thus directly related to the conqueror Pachacutec. Betanzos's narrative is very much a history of his wife's lineage. Juan de Betanzos related that the Inca conquest of the Collaguas occurred under the Inca Yupanqui Pachacutec. "The captains that he sent to the province of Condesuyo conquered and subjugated until Arequipa, and from there they ascended toward Cuzco, subduing the peoples and provinces of the Collaguas and Canas and those of Urocache, and from there they went to the city of Cuzco."[28]

It took several years before a more complete understanding of the history of Inca expansion into the Colca Valley would emerge. Knowledge required someone to live among the valley's people, one who knew their language and was interested in all aspects of their past and present. That person was Friar Luis Jerónimo de Oré, a Creole born in Guamanga (modern Ayacucho) around 1554. His father, Antonio de Oré y Río, was a wealthy *encomendero* (holder of an Indian grant) and silver miner. Luis Jerónimo grew up in a large household where education, especially religious, was emphasized. His siblings read and wrote Spanish and Latin, and they were fluent in Quechua and probably Aymara. Their wet nurses and family servants were *encomienda* (grant of tribute-paying Indians) Indians. Luis Jerónimo became a novitiate in Cuzco's Franciscan monastery, then continued training in Lima where he was ordained by Archbishop Toribio de Mogrovejo on 23 September 1581. Oré was named to serve in the Collaguas in 1590, and as the curate of Coporaque he assisted in preparation of a detailed 1591 census of the region. He spent several years working in the valley, an experience that influenced his later writing. In more than one manuscript Oré mentioned his stay in the Collaguas and recounted the stories he heard about the valley's history.[29] His 1598 *Symbolo catholico indiano* includes a geographical and historical description of Peru; the section on the Collaguas is noteworthy: "In the service of Mayta Capac, who had as a wife Mama Yacchi, native of the Collaguas, the Indians of that province made a great building all of copper as the residence for the Inca and his wife, who came to visit her homeland." Oré's work was read widely in Peru in the seventeenth century; his *Symbolo* and later *Ritvale, sev manvale* were required texts for clergy in the Indian parishes in the diocese of Cuzco for decades. The historian Garcilaso de la Vega received a personal copy of the *Symbolo* from Oré while in Spain and mined it in his history of the Incas. Bernabé Cobo borrowed the account to embellish his narrative of Inca control in the Colca Valley.[30]

In his *Royal Commentaries of the Incas* (1609) Garcilaso de la Vega described in poetic detail the Arequipa district conquests of Inca Mayta Capac. "From Parihuana Cocha the Inca advanced and crossed the desert of Coropuna, where there is a most beautiful and lofty pyramid of snow that the Indians reverently call huaca, for the meanings of this word include that of 'wonderful,' which it certainly is. In their ancient simplicity the natives worshiped it for its height and beauty, which are remarkable. Passing the desert, he entered the province called Aruni. Thence he passed to another called Collahua which stretches to the valley of Arequipa." Garcilaso reported that the Incas experienced no difficulty conquering the region, for the locals were very impressed by the invaders' ease in crossing the mountains, and believed they must be "invincible and children of the Sun."[31]

Although Bernabé Cobo's history was not completed until 1653, the author spent much of the first three decades of the seventeenth century researching. Cobo presented an account of Inca penetration of the Colca Valley that paralleled Oré's.

> When the prince (Mayta Capac) came of age, he took the fringe and the government of the kingdom, and married a lady named Mama Tancaray Yacchi, daughter of the cacique from Collaguas; and for this reason, the Indians of that province, as a service to this king, made a house all of copper in which to accommodate them when they went to visit the queen's kinsmen. Some of the copper was found due to the diligence of the Franciscan friars who teach in that province; from it they made four large bells. The Indians said that the rest of the copper that was missing had been given to Gonzalo Pizarro and his army during the time of the civil wars.

Here Bernabé Cobo borrowed directly from Jerónimo de Oré, without citing his source, a common practice at the time. But Cobo adds information: Mayta Capac had two sons by his legitimate Collagua wife, Capac Yupanqui and Tarco Huaman.[32]

The evidence provided by the early Spanish chroniclers is of questionable reliability and limited in scope; at best Inca expansion into the Colca Valley was modestly resisted, if at all. Had there been major resistance — as in the case of the Chanca, Conchuco, Cañari, Chachapoya, Huanca, and Lupaca — both Oré and Ulloa Mogollón's informants would have been quick to note it. We are less certain of the chronology. In the Oré version, the movement of the Incas into the region comes early, for Mayta Capac is one of the earlier Incas, third or fourth in a chain that extends to the twelfth Inca Huayna Capac, who died victim of disease on the eve (ca. 1525–1527) of Spanish conquest. In Garcilaso de la Vega's account Mayta Capac was responsible for completion of the conquest of the Collas of Lake Titicaca. He also reputedly moved Inca forces southwest into coastal Moquegua, and late in the reign expanded west and southward. Leading an army of about 20,000 warriors he marched through Velilli, Allca, and Taurisma. Moving further the Inca invaders encountered resistance in Cotahuasi, Pumatampu, and Parihuana-cochca. It took substantial effort to defeat and incorporate these people into Tawantinsuyu. The forces of Mayta Capac continued southward, and took over Aruni, Coropuna, Collagua, and Arequipa. The second narrative tradition, provided by Cieza de León, limits the successes of Mayta Capac to the immediate area around Cuzco, and dates the expansion of the Incas to the time of the ninth ruler, Pachacuti, about the third decade of the fifteenth century. Some historians argue that Mayta Capac is purely a mythical figure.[33]

According to oral tradition Inca control of the Collaguas was cemented by marriage of the daughter of a Collagua kuraka to the Inca, thus integrating the Collaguas into the "state" political structure. This type of arrangement was a common device of the Inca during their expansion, with marriages linking the elite of conquered provinces to members of the Inca ayllu. But what of the historical authenticity of a bond between the Inca Mayta Capac and the Collagua Mama Yacchi? In the earliest chronicles outlining the history of the empire, the wife of Mayta Capac was not Mama Yacchi. Cieza de León stated simply: "And because he had no sister he could marry, he took as a wife a daughter of a *señorete*, or captain, of the village of Oma, that was about two leagues from Cuzco, whose name was Mamaca Guapata." Cobo, perhaps trying to rectify disparate traditions—those of Cieza de León and of Garcilaso de la Vega—in his rendering, decided to combine the two and reported that the Inca married "Mama Tancaray Yacchi, daughter of the cacique from Collaguas." Cobo created a fictitious person, thus solving the inconsistency in his sources. Cobo also suggested that the marriage was celebrated at the beginning of Mayta Capac's rule, when he "came of age, took the fringe and government of the kingdom." In Cieza de León's version, the conquest was already complete when he married.[34]

The oral history Oré recorded was not always based on fact, but on Collagua myths surrounding Inca conquest of the valley, legends that were embellished over several generations after the actual events. Valley residents later believed the Incas conquered the area during the rule of Mayta Capac. The Incas themselves would have encouraged such a view of the events, which would create a longer-standing tie between the two. The real conquest of the Collaguas likely occurred under the Inca Pachacutec, but not by the Inca himself, rather by one of his "generals." The general was most certainly of the Inca ayllu or lineage. The war leader, or the first governor appointed to administer the province, may have been named Mayta Capac. In keeping with Inca policy, he would have married one or more of the daughters of the kuraka of the Collaguas. With the passage of time, the Collaguas believed that the conquest and marriage were under Inca ruler Mayta Capac. Both Inca rulers and local kurakas would have approved the story as reported by Oré. The legend, after all, enhances the reality of the bond between Collagua and Inca in the popular mind. The belief furthermore promotes the idea that the Collaguas held an important place in Tawantinsuyu. Oré's report of a warrior in the valley who had a cloak that was passed down from his ancestors with the fingernails of enemies sewn on it also suggests that Inca control of the Collaguas was a relatively recent event in the valley's past.[35]

The evidence is also fragmentary regarding the nature of the Cabana and Collagua under Inca domination. Clearly Inca power in the valley was absolute. The Collaguas were subservient, and by various actions they demonstrated their obedience to their overlords. They were required to send male children of the elite to train in Cuzco. Some young women, selected for beauty and skill, often daughters of kurakas, were reserved for marriage to the Inca or the Inca ruling elite. Local warriors served in Inca expansion. Colonies of loyal Collagua tribesmen could be called on to settle elsewhere in the empire, as *mitimaes*. In addition to contributing finished cloth, the *runa* (adult working males) were expected to serve on construction projects, such as bridges, roads, *tambos* (way stations, often described by the Spanish as inns), or on the estates set aside for the Inca or state cult. This draft labor was carefully regulated, and theoretically was not excessive.[36]

Inca social structure in the valley was complex: the ayllu and suyu categorizations are outside sixteenth-century European norms, and foreign observers had difficulty in defining them. The informants of 1586 provided an idealized notion that in Inca times there were three ayllus: Collana, Pasana, and Cayao. Each ayllu was under the leadership of a headman, with a primary chieftain over all. The informants reported that under the Inca there were 300 Indians, probably adult married male heads of household, in each ayllu. The head kuraka possessed military and juridical authority in the village. According to the information gathered by Ulloa Mogollón, the kuraka was placed in office by the Inca and was succeeded by his sons. If a kuraka died without sons, he was succeeded by his brothers and their male children. It must be emphasized that the idealized ayllu and line of succession were precisely what the 1580s kurakas, desirous to maintain their position, wanted Spanish officials to believe. The reality was far more complex.[37]

The ayllu is the key unit of Andean social and economic organization, and it predates the Inca. In spite of its significance the earliest Europeans found it difficult to concisely define what it was. One of the earliest writers, the Dominican friar Domingo de Santo Tomás, composing his Quechua-Spanish dictionary before 1560, reported that the "ayllo, or villca" is a lineage, generation, or family. The term *lineage* implies the descendants of a common ancestor. But the word *family* could refer to a nuclear or an extended family which might include several generations of variously related people. His definition of a generation poses a greater problem. Did he mean that all of the same "generation" belonged to the same ayllu? Separately he defines *parentesco*, or *sangre* (blood relatives), as ayllu. For Santo Tomás, lineage seemed to most closely define ayllu. He probably believed it had other meanings related to family, and even place, but was unable to be more precise.[38]

Definitions of ayllu by colonial chroniclers parallel those of the dictionary compilers. Cieza de León, collecting information for his multivolume chronicle of Peru before 1551, referred to ayllu as lineage. Betanzos (1551) suggested that the ancestors of the members of an ayllu came from a specific locality. The jurist Polo Ondegardo, in a treatise finished around 1560, took a similar approach. Cristóbal de Castro and Diego Ortega Morejón, in their brief 1558 description of the coastal Chincha Valley, equated ayllu with *parcialidad* or section. Cristóbal de Molina, who around 1579 composed a treatise on Inca religion and society, concurred. The high coincidence of Andean origin myths which describe the emergence of ancestors from mountains, lakes, and stones, and which have concrete existence in a geographical spot, provides corroborative evidence.[39] Most likely the ayllu was a lineage, a group tracing descent from a common ancestor or place. The ayllu comprised all people who were related, by marriage or consanguineously. Since preconquest settlements were generally small hamlets, the term *ayllu* could refer to the entire community. In a broader sense, the ayllu could be a separate cultural and linguistic group. The word *ayllu* has another, suggestive meaning: the ayllu is a hunting weapon made of three long animal skin cords, with "heavy copper balls connected at the end of each string." Twirled above the head, then slung great distances, the cords entangled the legs of animals or enemy warriors. The symbolism is revealing: ayllus provide protection for the entire community.[40]

The ayllu played a central role in the Andean economy. Exchange based on a monetary system did not exist. The economy was based on local self-sufficiency, preceding and following creation of the Inca state. Self-sufficiency occurred at several levels. Land was a collective resource of the ayllu, and access was not limited by age, sex, or physical condition; it was even bestowed upon infants.[41] Felipe Guaman Poma de Ayala reported that at the time of birth, a girl "was given land and fields." The Andean norm was one of parallel descent; men and women had access to basic material resources. In sharp contrast to the European system, even Andean orphans received plots, which, according to Guaman Poma, "were planted by the ayllus." Nor was distribution of land limited to able-bodied workers. Under Inca dominion, fields were cultivated by ayllu members for the warriors absent on campaigns. The blind and crippled had access to plots. There was also land cultivated in common by the ayllu for the entire group. Provision was made for letting land lie fallow, at times for several years, and rotated following an established pattern. In annual ceremonies local officials "distributed" this land to individuals who had usufruct. In the native system, individually assigned land could always be redistributed as conditions demanded. The concept of the "sale" of land was alien. After the conquest many Spaniards mistakenly assumed that fallow land was vacant (*tierras baldías*), and attempted to appropriate it. Along the Pacific coast, where demographic collapse depopulated entire sections, Europeans were successful in securing control of vacant native fields.[42]

Economic self-sufficiency was achieved by ayllu access to lands or other resources in different ecological zones. In the Andean region the type of crops that can be produced is largely based on the variables of elevation; sunlight, which influences temperature; soil quality; and water availability. One side of a mountain spur might be shaded from sunshine more than the opposite side, and thus sustain a different crop, even at the same elevation above sea level. Significant variation in the amount of rainfall occurs, contingent largely on the rain shadow effect. The early agricultural and population censuses of the Colca Valley provide a clear portrait of the system as it operated in the sixteenth and seventeenth centuries. An ayllu member living in Yanque might have a plot of corn in Ullo Ullo; a nearby section for the raising of quinua; a medium-sized plot of potatoes in Tuti; and the use of grazing lands in the puna above Chivay. It is obvious that if lands were scattered over too great a distance, production would be inefficient. Not all individuals were able to achieve an ideal balance of resources, but by sharing resources among members of the same ayllu, sufficiency was secured. Some people engaged in specialized activities: potters, metalsmiths, quipucamayos. Alpaca and llama herding also called for specialization of labor.[43]

Ayllu families could live scattered over a wide expanse of territory. Although the exact method of exchange in pre-Spanish times is unclear, certain products and labor service continue to be exchanged outside the money economy. Ayllu members producing wool might transfer it to someone cultivating maize or chili peppers. Exchange was not barter in the European sense, and there seem to have been no large market cities in the Colca Valley or the southern Andes during the Inca period. There were flourishing pre-Spanish markets in other places; in the Chincha Valley of central coastal Peru, wide interchange of goods occurred with the participation of a "merchant" group.[44] In order to facilitate interchange of goods within the ayllu, it is possible that products had assigned "values." For example a certain amount and quality of woolen cloth could be exchanged for a specific amount and type of coca leaves. During set times each year, one group of ayllu members could travel to the Pacific coast and catch and dry fish, then transport them back to the highlands for other ayllu members. Other families might take a turn each year producing salt at a site near Guambo or Lluta. Ayllus grew and declined with the natural rhythm of the expansion and contraction of their populations. As ayllus grew in size they might split into two or more. But if the population became too small, ayllus joined to create a new unit.[45]

Another principal characteristic of south Andean society is the division into halves (*saya*). The Quechua designate the halves as upper (*anan*) and lower (*urin*). This dual structure played an important function. Archaeological evidence, especially the canal systems, suggests that Colca Valley peoples were divided into upper and lower halves prior to the Inca conquest. There is little doubt the Inca used a dual structure in the valley to strengthen and perpetuate their domination. Early colonial descriptions of the dual organization usually refer to the Cuzco example, Anan and Urin Cuzco. The word for a division in Quechua is *suyu*. Santo Tomás defined *suyu* as simply a part of something which had been divided, and he listed the related Quechua verbs, but he furnished no information about the division of society into sections.[46] In the 1586 dictionary published by the Lima printer Ricardo the compiler called *suyu* a faction, and discussed upper and lower groups. An important clue to the ritual meaning is found in the verb *suyuchani*: to appoint men by their factions (*parcialidades*) for games or skirmishes. *Suyuchanacuni* means "to put in order" or "to practice in order to play or skirmish." It is possible to recognize in these definitions the dual nature of the structure: there are upper and lower sections with members competing in labor, games, or mock battles.[47] Bertonio described parallel Aymara divisions in his 1612 vocabulary and reported that factions existed in all villages, indicating the strength of suyu in the southern Andes.[48] In the early 1570s Pedro Sarmiento de Gamboa consulted living elders of the Cuzco elite and quipucamayos. He learned that "before the Incas, . . . in each tribe there were two divisions. One was called Hanansaya, which means the upper division, and the other Hurinsaya, which is the lower division, a custom which continues to this day. These divisions do not mean anything more than a way to count each other, for their satisfaction, though afterwards it served a more useful purpose." Sarmiento de Gamboa stressed the importance the divisions had in administration, for they facilitated territorial organization and frequent Inca censuses.[49]

Cristóbal de Molina arrived in Cuzco around 1556. Tenure as priest in the Indian Hospital and the parish of Los Remedios, coupled with an excellent command of Quechua, provided him with the tools necessary to investigate Inca history and religion. Molina provides excellent insight into the function of saya ceremony in the city. On the first day of the month of Camayquilla (December), young men of opposing halves who had reached maturity faced each other in the great square. Armed with slings, they hurled thistles. Their test of strength often ended in hand-to-hand combat, but if the situation became too tense order was restored when the Inca, who presided, stood up. Here the division into sections played an important role in the rites of passage of young men into adulthood. "Afterward, they all sat, according to their lineages." Following the ceremonies they banqueted, joined by the huacas and mummified ancestors of the Incas who were carried into the square, those of Hanan Cuzco on one side, Hurin Cuzco on the other. Both the living and the living dead were given food and drink.[50]

Alonso Ramos Gavilán, whose perceptive insight on duality is largely overlooked, suggested, around 1621, that the Inca not only divided existing settlements throughout the empire into sections, but also introduced new groups into a region, which then became a faction. "Among the Urinsayas, who are the natives of a place, the Inca was accustomed to sending trustworthy Indians in order to better amalgamate them into the customs of the Empire and to watch over the fidelity of the newly conquered; these foreigners were called Anansayas: two factions which looked at each other with distrust and many times came to blows, as Jews and Samaritans. . . . The Urinsayas said to the Anansayas that they were poor newcomers without fields or their own homeland."[51] The halves were "equal" according to most eyewitnesses. The difference was one of precedence, a prestige in entering first, in sitting on the right, in being referred to as "upper." After the arrival of the outsiders and the subsequent impact of a market economy based on Old World currency and the drive to acquire riches, a class distinction based on wealth, which had no previous place in Andean society, was introduced.

Beyond the issue of "class," there is general agreement among the colonial sources regarding the chief characteristics of Inca duality. The division became widespread, partly the consequence of a conscious effort by Inca administrators to neutralize potential opposition to the regime. In many cases mitimaes loyal to the Inca were transferred to a new location within the realm and settled into the local community as a saya. They competed for area resources, but competition was ritualized. Members of each faction interacted in various festivities during the year. These included ceremonial drinking bouts, competition in games and mock battle, and joking and boasting contests. Groups were equal, although in joint ceremonies the "upper" half preceded in order of activity. Ayllus existed within that dual structure; each saya was composed of one or several ayllus. Debate continues among anthropologists about whether the halves constituted moieties. One of the key points in the definition of moiety is moiety exogamy. But colonial censuses and parish registers of the Colca Valley document strong saya endogamy. Thus the term *moiety* is probably inappropriate for the Andean dual structure.[52] It is also apparent from parish records of the village of Yanque that by 1700 the anansaya enjoyed a higher status than the urinsaya, based on social and economic differences which would make a marriage between the two factions undesirable, although not impossible.[53]

Direct information on religious practices in the valley during Inca domination is limited. Inca religion did not require orthodoxy or unitary adherence; hence earlier religious practices in the valley continued. With Tawantinsuyu's expansion, major regional religious forces and deities were absorbed under the umbrella of "Inca" religion. Loose polytheistic concepts permitted much assimilation, and tolerance reduced the possibility of insurrection. The sun, Inti, came to be regarded as the divine ancestor of the Inca lineage. Inti had a special relationship to agriculture and was sometimes depicted as a golden disk. Concurrent with Tawantinsuyu's rise, the veneration of Inti approached a state cult. Sun temples were constructed throughout Tawantinsuyu, and local fields were assigned to support a priesthood, as at Coporaque. The moon, Mama Quilla, was the wife of Inti the sun. Associated with silver, she was important for celebrations involving the calendar, or measurements of time, and had her own temples and priestesses. For agriculture, Earth Mother, or Pachamama, was venerated. A counterpart, the sea mother, or Mama-qoca, was an important spiritual force for coastal dwellers and fishermen. The Andean concept of a general "creator god," Viracocha, a sky divinity, believed to intervene in times of crisis and also envisioned as a culture hero, was quickly utilized by Spanish priests in their efforts to explain Christianity. Local beliefs and customs persisted under Inca rule.[54] Major ceremonies were conducted by practitioners, usually on open squares or plazas in village centers. Mention is made of many practices in Ulloa Mogollón's Colca Valley report. Sacrifices of food, chicha, coca, maize flour, and llama fat, as well as gold and silver, were offered to huacas and mummies of dead ancestors. Llamas and guinea pigs were frequently sacrificed; human offerings were rare, except during times of famine or pestilence, natural disasters, or warfare. In some places male or female "priests" acted as confessors, a practice that surprised Spanish observers. The existence of the symbol of the cross in the Andean world also intrigued Europeans. Another parallel with Christianity was the requirement to confess before participating in religious ceremonies, in order to purify. Penance might be required, perhaps a period of fasting, or prayer at a huaca. The penitent often washed in water.[55] External similarities with Christianity initially confounded European clergy. A priesthood, women resembling nuns, confession, penance, fasting, and ritual washing all made conversion to the faith of the conquerors easier; yet similarities made it difficult to prevent vestiges of native beliefs from infiltrating into Christian practice at the local level.

Some sites had religious significance and attracted "pilgrims." The pyramid of coastal Pachacamac in the valley south of Lima was one such shrine. More important for the Cabanas and Collaguas of the Colca was a temple on the edge of Lake Titicaca. Ramos Gavilán reported that the Inca sent Collagua natives to the shrine of Copacabana, which under Christian domination became associated with an appearance of the Virgin. The force of thunder, Llapta, was feared and propitiated. Andeans, impressed by the Europeans and their noisy weapons, came to identify thunder and lightening with the patron saint of Spain, Saint James the Greater, or Santiago. European firearms, which flashed brightly, belched smoke, and emitted a sound resembling thunder, were called *illapa*. The spiritual force of lightning is highlighted in colonial parish registers. Cause of death is rarely mentioned in burial records; this is not true for those killed by lightning. The night heavens were also significant for valley people under the Inca, and before. The star group called the q'olqa was commonly venerated, and its movement in the heavens was linked to the agricultural calendar. Other star groups were important. Even the reverse, the absence of stars in part of the night sky, was discerned, and dark constellations were identified.[56]

Opposite: Religious practices in the southern Andes as depicted by Felipe Guaman Poma de Ayala, from his ca. 1613 *El primer nueva corónica y buen gobierno*, edited by John V. Murra and Rolena Adorno (3 vols., Mexico City: Siglo Veintiuno, 1980); numbers refer to the illustrations. Permissions thanks to Licenciada Lydia Garibay V. of Siglo XXI's editorial offices in Mexico City, 3 February 2006.

Veneration and sacrifice to the volcanic cone of Coropuna (272 [274])

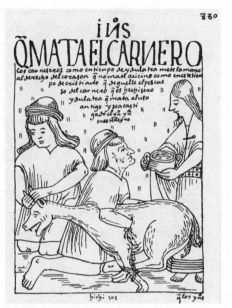

Persistence of rituals involving sacrifice of llamas (880 [894])

Dancing and singing in Condesuyo's festivals (326 [328])

Burial practices in Condesuyos (295 [297])

The Collaguas and Cabanas continued to venerate their principal huacas during the rule of Tawantinsuyu: Collaguata, Suquilpa, Apoqico, Omascota, and Hualca Hualca. Local religious functionaries continued to serve the peaks, with offerings of small objects of gold and silver, and at times called for human sacrifice. But under Tawantinsuyu no human sacrifices could be made without the Inca's authorization. The huacas were ubiquitous; they could be almost anything with supernatural powers. In addition to mountain peaks, they could be springs, caves, stones, tombs, or mummies, even constructions such as temples or bridges. Local huacas in the valley were serviced by either the family or the ayllu, either male or female but preferably an elder. Local religious functionaries continued to perform their rituals under Inca domination.[57] Devotees might prepare food or chicha to be offered in the traditional fashion. At the "state" level, a local Inca "temple" was tended by priests who had a variety of tasks. The cult had livestock with local herders assigned for its support. But far more important to the valley's villagers were the forces of the volcanic cones, the springs and caves, the apachitas and conopas, which continued to be appeased long after the disappearance of the Inca state in the Andes.[58]

Inca control over the Colca was direct and total; the ruling elite did not tolerate independence. Yet there is little reason to believe valley peoples resisted Cuzco domination. Inca demands were tempered by Andean traditions of reciprocity, and state requirements consisted primarily of labor drafts. Much of the work was local and did not disrupt the agricultural cycle. Indeed, imposed tasks often helped improve productivity. Terrace agriculture may have reached its apogee in the valley under the Incas. Substantial terrace construction took place under the Incas, as we know from recent archaeological findings. The extensive q'olqas, predating Inca control of the valley, were also expanded. The storehouses contained goods that could be distributed elsewhere in reciprocal form, or used during local emergencies. The population of the valley grew in the millennium preceding arrival of the Spaniards as new technologies and improvement of crops led to expanded agricultural production. Irrigation, better seed stocks, application of fertilizer, crop rotation and fallowing, and careful breeding of native livestock ultimately resulted in increased carrying capacity of the valley and puna ecosystems. We are unsure if the population of the valley reached its apogee concurrently with the European invasion, or before and had already started a decline. Regardless of what occurred in the region before 1532, the population was substantial in the 1520s; as many as 71,000 could have been sustained by the mature agricultural system.[59] Labor relating to the cult of Inti was limited and carefully regulated. Demands for soldiers to support Inca militarism were less significant than demands made on others, such as on the

Lupaca Collas on the shores of Lake Titicaca. The annual transfer of a handful of young women to serve the Inca did not alter demographic and social patterns in the valley, nor did the few kurakas or their sons who traveled to the imperial capital of Cuzco. The valley's people may not have risen up to assist in defense of Tawantinsuyu when it fell under Spanish attack, but they did not find it worthwhile to attempt to overthrow the yoke of Inca domination when under its sway.

Centuries later, as the people of the Colca Valley, similar to others in the Andean world, suffered under the harsh demands of an alien people, some came to reflect on Tawantinsuyu with nostalgia, and dreamed of a more perfect era that had existed before the arrival of the Europeans. In the last quarter of the twentieth century, one valley resident related to outsiders that some villagers remembered an Inca ruler who had come, bringing order, terraces, corn, and civilization to the valley's residents.[60] Why this collective memory of a prior, perhaps better world? What happened to the peoples of the Colca Valley in the generations following contact with Old World invaders? Is there any validity to a belief that they were better off then, in the time of the Inca rulers, or before? One can learn much from the stilled voices of the ancestors of present valley residents that now speak to us through scattered bundles of papers guarded in disperse archives. Even though most did not write, they fell under the scrutiny and control of colonial bureaucrats who did record in pen and ink the activities of commoners and the local elite, their hardships, complaints, and at times their celebrations.

CHAPTER TWO

RETURN OF THE VIRACOCHA

Those Indians had many huacas and idols which were worshiped, and taken as gods. Fathers Friar Juan de Monzón and Friar Juan de Chaves, who were the first in that province, discovered a great number of these huacas and idols and burned them and threw the ashes into a river. . . . In a pueblo called Lari Father Juan de Chaves had them carry the huacas that they had collected in order to burn them, and fifty or sixty Indians were loaded with them.

—Franciscan report of 1585 to Friar Gonzaga, for *"De origine ordinis Seraphici."*

The Pachacuti

During the contested rule of the Inca Atahualpa, curious and confounding news began to filter into the Colca Valley. Coming by word of mouth, perhaps from the children of Collagua and Cabana kurakas sent to Cuzco for training, or local Inca administrators, or mitimaes, they heard of strange outsiders, reminiscent of ancient legend. The Inca Atahualpa received three messengers from north coastal Tangarará. They described the appearance of "white and bearded people": "they bring a type of sheep [llama] on which they . . . ride, and [the animals] are very large, much more so than ours." The Inca asked what they were called, and the emissaries replied they were uncertain but called them "Viracocha cuna," meaning "the gods."[1] The legendary Contiti Viracocha created humanity, then departed by sea, traveling in the direction of the setting sun. Europeans quickly seized on the myth and encouraged Andeans to call them Viracocha. The ploy briefly worked as they attempted to conquer and settle

Tawantinsuyu. A decade earlier the Spaniards exploited a similar tale as they subjugated Aztec Mexico.[2]

Some saw a more ominous threat with the arrival of the outsiders. A generation later Juan de Santa Cruz Pachacuti Yamqui, who lived near the Colca Valley, wrote that the newcomers carried disease and death. While the Inca ruler Huayna Capac, father of Atahualpa, was engaged in the conquests in the north, he had a vision of "his headquarters surrounded by a thousand million men, and they did not know them nor understand who they were. At this they say that he said they were the souls of the living, that God had given a sign signifying that so many had to die in the pestilence. The souls said that they came against the Inca, from which the Inca understood that it [pestilence] was his enemy."[3] Pestilence did reach far inland, sweeping ahead of the small force of Spanish explorers along the Pacific coast. Huayna Capac fell ill and died, near Quito. His body was embalmed with his wife and child, and their mummy bundles were carried by litter to Imperial Cuzco. The Mercedarian friar Martín de Murúa, active several years in Indian parishes (*doctrinas*) between the Colca Valley and Lake Titicaca, noted that even before the ruler sickened, he received news of "pestilence in Cuzco, and that Auqui Topa Ynga, his brother, and Apo Hilaquita, his uncle, and his sister Mama Coca, and a number of lords of his lineage" had perished. Huayna Capac attempted to escape by hiding underground, but sickened with fevers, while "others say that a great pestilence of smallpox was occurring." Murúa reported, "He could not escape it [death], and upon dying, infinite thousands of common people died of smallpox that had fallen upon them."[4] The date the epidemic began is disputed; clearly it struck between late 1524 and 1528.[5] Although there are no written eyewitness accounts of disease in the Colca Valley during the conquest of Tawantinsuyu, there is indirect evidence in later valley censuses. A discerning demographer can see in the results of the 1591 Yanque Collaguas count a sharp deficit in the group that would have been infants to young teenagers during the critical 1524–31 years.[6] The missing succumbed to the ravages of the initial shock of conquest.

Strongly etched in the mind of Andean peoples is the concept of a succession of worlds or epochs. The ages are delimited by great upheavals, *pachacuti*, that mark the transition from one to the next. After two or three generations, Colca Valley people viewed the arrival of the outsiders as a time of a destructive pachacuti and longed for the coming age, when the invaders would be overthrown. Juan de Betanzos highlighted the concept, pointing out that the arrival of the foreigners had been predicted. At that time there "would be a pachacuti, that means a reversal of the world, and the lords asked him [Huayna Capac's grandfather] if this universal upheaval would be by water or by fire or by pestilence, and he told them that it would not be by any of those things, rather there would come a white bearded and very tall people with whom there would be a war."[7] Juan de Santa Cruz Pachacuti Yamqui also made the crisis clear when contrasting the sharp distinction between the period of the Incas, and the "turning of the times" occasioned as the Europeans replaced Tawantinsuyu's true rulers.[8]

The initial events of Spain's conquest of Andean America centered on Cajamarca, where in 1533 the Inca Atahualpa was taken prisoner and held for ransom; then Jauja in the central highlands, where the Europeans established temporary headquarters; and finally Cuzco, the Inca capital and goal of the conquerors. Cuzco was "founded" as a Spanish city on 23 March 1534. The primary phase of conquest was completed quickly, with amazing ease. There is no direct record of what role the Collaguas and Cabanas played in Tawantinsuyu's destruction. Certainly, the two groups were not yet foes of the Europeans; nor did they fight to protect Tawantinsuyu. No single factor explains this complex historical process of Spain's rapid subjugation of the Inca empire. A variety of influences played their respective roles: internal strife over succession; ethnic animosities; the weakening of the population with the onslaught of Old World epidemics; the factor of surprise; the Europeans' use of native allies; initial failure of the Inca leadership following Atahualpa's capture; superior weapons and military technology; and confusion as to the intentions of the outsiders. The Incas ruled a complex empire, composed of diverse ethnic groups, relatively recently colonized and integrated. The arrival of the foreigners disrupted the carefully assembled blocks of Tawantinsuyu, like an earthquake that weakens a faulty structure, causing it to collapse.[9]

Cuzco was occupied by the Spaniards; houses, lands, and Andeans were distributed to Francisco Pizarro's stalwart supporters. When the Europeans arrived, some natives of the Colca Valley—either workers, retainers, or children of the valley's elite who had gone to Cuzco for training—saw the invaders for the first time and suffered the impact. It was in Cuzco that the Cabanas of the Colca Valley first shouldered the yoke of foreign domination and recognized what the unfolding new order held in store. In a colorful ceremony, on 1 August 1535, Francisco Pizarro gave the Cabanas, about 1,500 people "in the province of Condesuyo," at the lower end of the Colca Valley, to Cristóbal Pérez and his son, Juan de Arbes. Cristóbal Pérez was not with Pizarro at Cajamarca, but arrived shortly after, bringing important reinforcements from Hispaniola. In addition to his encomienda grant, Pizarro appointed Pérez sheriff of Cuzco. According to the vague terms of the grant, the Cabanas lived scattered in hamlets: Ayomarca, Tirpa, Pascya, and Api in the eastern part of the grant; and Guanca, Marco, Guambo, and Yura to the west. Mitimaes were also included. Under the grant's terms, Cristóbal Pérez was required to introduce missionaries to indoctrinate his charges in Christianity and was in turn authorized to collect their tribute and exploit their labor in various activities, including gold mining.[10]

The grant was followed several days later by an official "Act of Possession." On 12 August 1535 Pérez and some of his Cabanas appeared before the *alcalde* (chief executive officer, similar in function to magistrates) of Cuzco. The alcalde took the Indians, and handed them back to the encomendero in a brief ceremony of possession, a practice that was regularly repeated in the Andean world as the outsiders assumed political control of native ethnic groups. Ampire, the principal kuraka along with other resident Cabanas, and the kuraka Yanquinicho, were duly transferred. This relatively simple ceremony was followed by a bout of drinking and eating in the encomendero's residence. The kurakas Ampire and Yanquinicho along with their subordinates probably viewed the ceremony and subsequent banqueting as a new version of the ritual cementing of the relationship of the local elite with the center of authority. They expected a continuation of reciprocity, the foundation on which their relationship with the Inca had been based. The kurakas expected to be treated as they had been during the rule of Tawantinsuyu: with respect and the reality of shared authority. The Spanish encomendero expected something else: labor and tribute.[11]

The kurakas Ampire and Yanquinicho, who acknowledged the control of Cristóbal Pérez in the ceremony, were resident Cabanas living in Cuzco and were part of the governing class of Tawantinsuyu. It was impossible for the Spanish to rely on firsthand information about the riches of the Colca Valley in August 1535; they had to accept testimony of the kurakas and other Indians residing in Cuzco. The reported population size and resources bore only superficial relation to the valley's social and economic realities. It is unlikely that Cristóbal Pérez had visited the valley before Pizarro made the grant, and the Collaguas in the upper part of the valley still were not distributed. Perhaps they had slipped out of Cuzco as the Europeans entered, for their links with Tawantinsuyu were tenuous. But the Cabanas with closer ties to the Quechua-speaking Cuzco elite remained in the city and were available for Pizarro's distribution. Firmly established as an important and powerful *vecino* (legal resident with political rights) of Cuzco, Cristóbal Pérez sent his son, Juan de Arbes, back to Hispaniola to collect his mother and new reinforcements for their Peruvian venture.[12]

The Cabanas were about to find themselves on the unfortunate receiving end of the first wave swept by the new pachacuti. The duty of Cristóbal Pérez and his son was to "civilize" the Cabanas, which implied that they were expected to make the natives as European as possible, especially to guarantee conversion. Legally Cabanas tributaries were neither serfs nor slaves, rather subjects of the

Spanish monarch, although they were considered minors, temporary wards of the encomenderos. For the next decade the Cabanas' principal contact with the Europeans was the encomendero's majordomo and catechist, if available. The Spanish gravitated into newly founded cities, where they received appointments to office, town lots, and nearby agricultural fields. They tended to stay in urban centers, leaving others to travel to the distant Colca to enforce the tribute regime. The first Cabana encomenderos to visit their charges ruled the natives as medieval lords, providing undesirable examples of Christianity. Spanish officials were soon plagued by so many complaints about the less-than-Christian lifestyles of encomenderos that the king decreed that their primary residence after 1563 must be the European city.[13] The privileges of Cristóbal Pérez and his son were far more significant than their responsibilities for education and conversion of their charges. If Pérez was similar to many of his compatriots, the Cabanas suffered severely in their first months under European domination. Elsewhere in Peru abuses were perpetrated by Spaniards intent on getting rich quickly, then returning home to enjoy their wealth and status. At first little was done by officials to check abuses of the new regime. Pizarro, having awarded Indians to his fellow conquerors, had little inclination to rein in their rapacious demands.

Andean Americans did take stock of their rapidly disintegrating world and struck back. The first uprising was led by Manco Inca. The young Manco had been recognized by Pizarro in Jauja, and he returned to Cuzco in late July 1534. Relations were at first harmonious; he was able to reinitiate some elements of Inca administration and helped the Spanish collect tribute. As was customary for new Incas, he began construction of his own palace. In 1535 he directed the festival of Inti Raymi. In the meantime the Spanish were having their own difficulties. The partnership between Pizarro and Diego de Almagro had long been unraveling, and news of Charles V's bestowal of the southern part of Peru to Almagro that reached Cuzco in early 1535 did not solve the problem, especially because it was unclear if Cuzco was in Pizarro's jurisdiction, or in Almagro's. In May they reached a truce whereby Almagro departed Cuzco to explore the reputedly wealthy land of Chile, which was clearly in his jurisdiction. Meanwhile Manco's position became more tenuous, for his strongest supporters were Almagro and Hernando de Soto. That month Manco provided Almagro with 12,000 Indian retainers, including his sibling Paullo and the high priest Villac Umu, for the Chile venture.

Some Cabanas and Collaguas may have participated in the expedition, for their lands were near the route. Meantime Francisco Pizarro departed for Lima, leaving Cuzco under his brothers Juan and Gonzalo, who further insulted

Manco and his subjects. The natives who began the Chilean expedition, facing the wrath of frustrated conquerors, broke ranks at Copiapó in today's Bolivia and returned to their homes. Late in 1535, Manco's situation worsened. The priest Villac Umu, returning from the Chilean march, and other elders easily convinced Manco that the outsiders intended to establish an alien Andean dynasty and that the time to resist and expel them had arrived. He escaped the city with a small group, but was captured by Juan and Gonzalo Pizarro just before leaving the valley. Later Pedro Pizarro wrote that had he "not been captured at this juncture all of us Spaniards in Cuzco would have perished, for the greater part of the Christians had gone out to inspect their encomiendas." Although we lack corroborative evidence, it is possible that the kurakas Ampire and Yanquinicho returned to the Colca Valley with either Cristóbal Pérez or his majordomo for a first inspection of the grant. If so, the reconnaissance was rapid.[14]

Now captive, Manco Inca suffered worse treatment. Some leaders, including his principal war captain, Tiso, escaped Cuzco and initiated a movement against the Spanish in the north, centering on the Jauja district. There were similar uprisings in the south and Condesuyo, the general quarter in which the Colca Valley was located. About thirty Spaniards, including encomenderos, were killed in the countryside, including one surnamed Becerril in Condesuyo. But at this point Hernando Pizarro, one of Francisco Pizarro's siblings, who had returned to Peru after delivering to Spain a portion of the ransom for the release of Atahualpa, appeared. Francisco then sent him from Lima to Cuzco in early January 1536 to replace his younger sibling Juan as governor, and at once Hernando began to ingratiate himself with Manco, in part due to instructions from Charles V to give Manco Inca the respect due to a monarch. Manco was "released" from arrest. Unknown to the Spaniards, he now began to plan the uprising systematically. It was to commence at the end of the rainy season. In Condesuyo, the leaders Surandaman, Curi-Hualpa, and Quilcana were charged with bringing warriors to join the campaign. Manco convinced an entirely gullible Hernando Pizarro to permit him to leave the city with Villac Umu to conduct rituals in the nearby Yucay Valley, promising to deliver a life-size gold statue of his father, Huayna Capac. The departure from Cuzco on 18 April 1536 marks the beginning of the final preparations for the great rebellion.

Cuzco was soon surrounded by 100,000 to 200,000 native warriors, according to most accounts, and after several skirmishes the principal attack began on 6 May. There were about 180 Spaniards, 90 of them on horse, plus native allies. Manco's forces set fire to the city, retaking the city block by block, leaving the Spanish only the houses in the immediate vicinity of the main square. The situation was dire, and the Spanish concluded their only chance lay in captur- ing the great fortress of Sacsahuaman overlooking the city. Both Juan Pizarro and his brother Gonzalo participated in the attack. Juan was hit in the head by a stone and died the night of 16 May. Gonzalo was able to hold the high ground across the open field from the fortress, and on the following day the Spaniards, with Hernando Pizarro leading and footmen using ladders to scale the walls, were able to breach the fortress. Here the native defenders retreated into the buildings—they were later torn down and used to construct Spanish houses in the city below—to defend themselves. Hand-to-hand combat continued for several days until the Spanish captured the towers where the last defenders held out. The Andeans counterattacked, but they ultimately proved ineffective. Sac- sahuaman's fall did not mean an end to the siege of Cuzco; fighting continued for three months. But with the approach of August's planting season, farmers began to return to their fields. Manco Inca's rebellion under his captains fared better in the Lima-to-Jauja sector, and they were able to attack Lima itself. But by November 1536 the Spanish on the coast received enough reinforcements from Panama to mount a campaign which continued into 1537.

The siege of Cuzco was formally lifted on 18 April 1537. The liberation was not completely welcomed by the Pizarro brothers, for success was secured with Almagro's return from the Chilean campaign. Manco escaped to the forests of the upper Amazon. Just over a year later the Pizarrists defeated Almagro at the Battle of Las Salinas (26 April 1538). It is uncertain if the Cabanas of Cristóbal Pérez took an active part in the conflicts from August 1535 to May 1537. His direct control over the encomienda was exceedingly short. After the rebellion began, it was impossible for any Spaniards to leave their Cuzco stronghold. We are uncertain of the whereabouts of the kurakas Ampire and Yanquinicho during these months. Surely any Andeans who supported Manco's revolt recognized that victory would result in restitution of power of the Cuzco elite through- out the region. Had the Collagua and Cabana actively aided Manco's cause, we would expect it to have been mentioned by the European chroniclers. But we find evidence of neither attacks on nor support for Pérez and his son in the accounts of the rebellion. Might some have assisted as spies and suppliers of foodstuffs? The record is silent.[15]

The encomendero Cristóbal Pérez claims he played an important role in the critical defense of Cuzco. His son, Juan de Arbes, may have learned of the up- rising after reaching Hispaniola. By the time Arbes returned to Peru, the siege of Cuzco was over. Cristóbal Pérez and his wife, Mari Sánchez la Millana, were reunited, and the family began to enjoy the profits of their Colca Valley enco- mienda. Unfortunately peace was brief, for the conflict between the Pizarro and Almagro factions exploded.[16] Almagro's expedition to Chile failed dismally. Many died during the arduous journey from the high puna of Charcas through the glaciated mountain passes leading into Chile. The Amerindians they encountered were fierce warriors and killed many of the invaders. Worse, Almagro's men found no significant deposits of gold, silver, or precious stones.[17] As the weakened remnants of Almagro's reconnaissance plodded back to Cuzco in March 1537, they took the coastal route, passing just west of the volcanic cone of Misti, past Chachani, the place where Arequipa would be founded four years later. Such a route would have taken them across the Colca River. No record remains of the crossing, but it is probable that it was in the upper valley, perhaps above present Tuti and Sibayo. If so, the members of the expedition still failed to glimpse the rich agricultural terraces of the middle valley. The fact that it took three more years before the upper valley came under the domination of a Spanish encomendero indicates this to be the likely scenario. One of the Chilean explorers marching past, Francisco Noguerol de Ulloa, still in his twenties, became one of the founders of Arequipa, and eventually one of the wealthiest encomenderos in the Colca Valley.[18]

When the Almagro expedition reached Cuzco, they found Hernando and Gonzalo Pizarro just beginning the city's reconstruction. Pizarro's forces refused to relinquish authority to Almagro, so the Chilean men took the city by force in April 1537. Francisco Pizarro meanwhile sent reinforcements from the coast to assist his brothers, and the troops of the Almagrists and Pizarrists locked in battle at Abancay in July 1537. Here Almagro was victorious, but failed to destroy his enemies. This gave the Pizarrists a chance to strengthen their position, and in the ensuing Battle at Las Salinas in April 1538 Almagro was decisively beaten, captured, and later executed on Cuzco's main plaza. Cristóbal Pérez was killed in the battle, bringing to a quick close the history of the first encomendero in the Colca Valley. He had received the Cabanas on 1 August 1535, and died on the field of Las Salinas in April 1538. The administration of the Cabana tributaries was transferred easily from father to son, Juan de Arbes.[19]

Soon other Colca Valley ethnic groups fell under Spanish colonialism. The defeat of Manco Inca, followed by Francisco Pizarro's consolidation of authority after the Battle of Salinas, left the Europeans in a powerful position. Only then could Pizarro make the first general division, the *repartimiento general*, of Indians to his followers. This comprehensive allotment in early 1538 included chieftains and their Indians who had not been previously distributed to Spaniards. In the lower Colca Valley near the coast, another group of Cabanas were distributed to Juan Ramírez. About 300 were included in the grant; they were coastal *yungas*, whose tribute included corn and coca.[20] Another set of Cabanas were given to Lope de Idiáquez. Pizarro also called for a general inspection and a tax assessment, but it appears that his orders were only sporadically enforced. The Cabana polity covered a vast terrain, and the still small number of Europeans possessed only a superficial knowledge of the territories. The Cabana tributary grant to Juan Ramírez, which left unanswered its exact relation to the Cabana encomienda of Juan de Arbes, ended in prolonged legal confrontations and led to general confusion among the distributed Cabana population. The problem lies in the Spanish misunderstanding of the nature of the Andean *señorío*. In Europe it was an administrative unit under a señor or lord, with full jurisdiction and control over territory and people. In the Andes the kuraka controlled people, not territory. There could be several kurakas in the same geographical region, in charge of different sets of people. This fundamental misconception often led to lengthy disputes in the colonial courts.[21]

Francisco Pizarro distributed other Colca Valley Indians. One group went to Alonso Rodríguez Picado, an early settler from Spain's Ciudad Rodrigo. Picado gained recognition in the conquest and pacification of Peru, fighting during the 1537 native uprising. Juan Bautistiano testified that when Lima was encircled by more than 70,000 Indians, "Alonso Rodríguez Picado in the occasion of the siege was one of those who most distinguished himself, for he killed general Tisu Yupangui," which helped break Indian resistance. He then traveled with Pizarro to assist in Cuzco's defense in 1537. His encomienda of Lari urinsaya held 600 Indians, and he had a smaller grant of 50 in the Arequipa Valley. The tributaries produced llamas, wool, and corn at the time of the original grant.[22] There is debate as to who received Lari anansaya. Some documents indicate a like number of Indians in the same so-called señorío were given to Juan Flores, 600 in the highlands, and 50 in the valley of Arequipa. But elsewhere it seems that Marcos Retamoso, from Talavera de la Reina, received the encomienda from Francisco Pizarro in Cuzco on 22 January 1540. Juan Flores had gained fame in an early encounter in the conquest of Peru, when he and Pedro del Barco, Mancio Sierra de Leguízamo, and Francisco de Villafuerte, dressed as Amerindians, made a surprise night attack with the help of Paucar Inca against an Inca ridgetop stronghold.[23]

The speed and thoroughness of Spanish attempts to exploit the Colca Valley depended on the creation and growth of European settlements nearby. Cuzco was not fully under Spanish control until after Manco's siege was lifted. Even then, because of the conflict between Almagro and Pizarro it was not until the Battle of Salinas that Colca Valley peoples began to be integrated systematically into the colonial system. The foreigners knew that they were too few in number to dominate the countryside. Andeans were remarkably effective in eliminating encomenderos who were scattered outside Cuzco during Manco Inca's revolt. Cuzco lies several hundred kilometers north of the Cabana domain in the lower Colca, too distant for encomenderos to exercise control over their tributaries. The central coastal city of Lima was ideally located for penetration of the central highlands, but was far distant from the densely populated provinces around Lake Titicaca and Charcas. Another city south of Lima, more accessible to human and mineral resources of the altiplano, needed to be established. The ideal location first seemed the Villa Hermosa de San Miguel de Camaná, founded in 1539 near where the Colca-Majes River enters the Pacific. Fresh drinking water is always important in selecting a city site, and the river provided it abundantly. Camaná founders expected it to become a major administrative center for the south coast, but the settlement failed to prosper. With heavy insect infestations, disease erupted. And the route into the rich hinterlands was more challenging than expected. Settlers did not realize when they founded Camaná that a direct trip upriver was impossible because of the deep gorge. There were easier routes into the southern highlands.[24]

Several potential city sites were surveyed; the choice fell to the Arequipa Valley on the western skirt of the Andean cordillera, far enough from the coast, at a high enough elevation to provide a healthy climate, yet near enough to permit secure sea communications. Further, the native population in contrast to other areas was not dense, and the valley provided a comfortable route to the vast altiplano via the Chili River. In 1540 outlines of Spanish Arequipa were traced and construction began. An almost perfect building material was readily available: the light, crystal-white volcanic stone, *sillar*. With seeming ease the "white city" rose from the valley floor, according to colonial accounts of its foundation. Construction of the city was a massive project, directed by Spanish settlers but carried out by Andeans, especially the Cabana and Collagua of the Colca, who both provided a substantial labor force. They were joined by others from nearby provinces: Condesuyos, Ubinas, Majes, and Moquegua. The cathedral, the city hall (*cabildo*), private residences, monasteries and convents, hospitals and a jail were all constructed. European settlers who composed the Arequipa elite were predominantly those who had laid out the city of Camaná just months earlier. Arequipa was located 100 kilometers inland, at a temperate elevation of 2,700 meters. Simultaneously, the seaport of Islay was developed. It also served as a fishing village and was primarily active during the weeks when ships from Lima, and later Chile, came and went.[25]

The Collaguas of the upper valley were finally brought under the encomienda regime as Francisco Pizarro, in Cuzco on 22 January 1540, made the largest Colca grant to his brother Gonzalo Pizarro. Gonzalo received "2,200

Indians in all said houses, in compliance with the inspection Gómez de León made." He was given *"estancias* of sheep herders and colonists . . . and miti-maes." The names and many of the place-names are spelled erroneously, as we note in the list of hamlets distributed: Ynaqui, Soro, Tuti, Tula, Condori, Chiuaia, Malco, Capa, Canacoto, Chapica, Coymo, Ynmasca, Uchuma, Cupas, and Cuparque. There were 1,400 to 1,500 tributaries, plus 40 in the Arequipa valley and 400 in Tacana. The Collaguas encomienda was only one of several that Gonzalo ultimately possessed. The same day, Francisco Pizarro distributed Indians of the central Colca Valley to loyal followers. He extended the anansaya half of Lari Collaguas to Marcos Retamoso. Pizarro gave the urinsaya half to his associate Alonso Rodríguez Picado.[26] Thus, in early 1540 Gonzalo Pizarro held the upper valley, and Marcos Retamoso and Picado shared the middle sector, while the lower portion was divided between Juan de Arbes and Juan Ramírez, then Lope de Idiáquez.[27]

The pachacuti that began in 1532 ended by 1540. The upheaval was com-plete. Inca domination of the valley was replaced by European. The brief return to local rule by the señoríos of the valley, approximately 1533–35 to 1538–40, ended as the full encomienda system, with all its damaging demands on the val-ley's peoples, was implanted (see table 1 for a summary of distribution). Surely several Cabana and Collagua were killed during these years as they fought on one side or the other in the conflict. Some Cabana may have directly served Cristóbal Pérez and his son, fighting in Cuzco during Manco Inca's rebellion. Normal agricultural activities in the Colca Valley were disrupted, and a second epidemic, this time measles in 1531–33, swept away many Amerindians. There is no evidence that Cristóbal Pérez fulfilled his obligation to Christianize his charges; nor given the chaotic situation is it even likely that he could have. Fur-ther, it is unclear if other encomenderos named between 1538 and 1540 began the arduous task of conversion. The first sustained efforts to indoctrinate began between 1541 and 1545, but the process was shaken by civil wars between the conquerors, and it took almost a decade before the presence of the church in the Andean countryside was visible.

Civil Wars of the Invaders

The 1540s witnessed the full economic, political, and religious impact of the encomienda system on the Cabanas and Collaguas. It was not an easy transi-tion as they adjusted to a system imposed by the newcomers with far greater demands than under the Inca. Furthermore, they were inadvertently thrown

TABLE I. Colca Valley encomendero holdings prior to the division of Pedro de la Gasca

	ca. 1538/40	ca. 1548
Los Collaguas	Gonzalo Pizarro 1,500 indios[a]	Gonzalo Pizarro (señorío) 1,500 indios Plus Tacana—400 indios Valle de Arequipa—40 indios
Lari Collaguas		
Anansaya	Juan Flores (or Marcos Retamoso?) 600 indios Llamas, wool, corn Plus Valle de Arequipa— 50 indios	Juan Flores, dead (Marcos Retamoso?) 600 indios Granted by Francisco Pizarro Plus Valle de Arequipa— 50 indios
Urinsaya	Alonso Rodríguez Picado 600 indios Llamas, wool, corn Plus Valle de Arequipa— 50 indios	Alonso Rodríguez Picado 600 indios Granted by Francisco Pizarro Plus Valle de Arequipa— 50 indios
Cabanas[b]		
Anansaya	Miguel de Vergara 600 indios	Miguel de Vergara, dead 600 indios—by Vaca de Castro
Urinsaya	Juan de Arbes 600 indios	Juan de Arbes, dead 600 indios—by Francisco Pizarro
	Juan Ramírez 300 yungas indios coca, corn	Juan Ramírez 250 indios—by Francisco Pizarro

into a conflict in which they had nothing to gain. Encomenderos drafted their own tributaries to serve as carriers, cooks, concubines, servants, and fighters in their battle for hegemony. The Europeans fought among themselves and even challenged the authority of their own ruler. The Cabana and Collagua were perishing, and their families starving as their finely tuned agricultural system that had taken generations to construct disintegrated. Moreover, a third great wave of pestilence, typhus, entered the realm.

Diego de Almagro's execution failed to end conflict among the Europeans,

TABLE 1. *Continued*

ca. 1538/40	ca. 1548

Holdings of others who became Colca Valley encomenderos after 1549

	ca. 1538/40	ca. 1548
Ubinas	Noguerol (de Ulloa) 800 indios Llamas, corn, wool	Miguel [*sic*] de Ulloa 800 indios—by Francisco Pizarro
Machaguay	Juan de la Torre 600 indios	Juan de la Torre 400 indios—by Francisco Pizarro
	Next to Alonso Buelta's ([*sic*]? Ruiz, who returns to Spain) 600 indios Hernando de Silva's 600 indios	Part of señorío with Hernando de Silva's 500 indios— by Pizarro
	Wife of Juan de la Torre 600 indios Plus 40 yungas fishermen— by Vaca de Castro	Ana Gutiérrez, wife of Juan de la Torre 450 indios—by Francisco Pizarro Plus 50 fishermen and mitimaes— by Pizarro Same unit as 450 indios of Alonso Buelta

Source: Loredo, *Los Repartos*, 194–204

[a]*Indios* refers to tributaries.

[b]The original grant of Cabana Indians in Condesuyo was made by Francisco Pizarro (Cuzco, 1 August 1535) to Cristóbal Pérez and his son Juan de Arbes.

because Almagro's disgruntled followers rallied behind his mestizo son, Diego de Almagro the Younger. The faction's chance to avenge defeat came in the absence of two Pizarro brothers: Hernando was in Spain, while Gonzalo explored the upper Amazon. On 26 June 1541 the malcontents assassinated Francisco Pizarro in Lima, killed many of his supporters, and assumed government. Many of those who joined were fighting for the spoils of conquest, the gold and silver they had been denied and the Indian grants they coveted. In the Arequipa district staunch Pizarrists feared for their persons, property, and Indians. The Cabana and Collagua of the Colca Valley had known internecine warfare in Inca and pre-Inca times, and if they were aware of Pizarro's assassination, they may have hoped for an improvement in their own status. Spaniards engaged in killing each other was not lamented by the valley's peoples.[28]

Even before Pizarro's assassination the Spanish Crown was concerned with chaos in Peru, and sent a royal governor, Cristóbal Vaca de Castro, to intervene and restore order. Vaca de Castro viewed Almagro the Younger and his followers as rebels against royal authority. They had killed the king's official representative, replacing him with one of their own. The inevitable battle took place at Chupas on 16 September 1542; Vaca de Castro secured a clear victory. For the third time in a decade, Colca Valley villagers watched outsiders battle each other. Eight days later several armed residents of Arequipa wrote a letter of support to Vaca de Castro from San Juan de la Frontera. Colca Valley encomenderos who signed the missive included Juan de Arbes and Alonso Rodríguez Picado. Another, Lope de Idiáquez, a Basque and close friend of Almagro, served as messenger between the royal official and rebel forces. Before joining the Peruvian *entrada* (early expedition), Lope de Idiáquez had been an official at Santa Marta on Colombia's Caribbean coast. Aware of the friendship of Idiáquez with the young Almagro, Governor Vaca de Castro employed him as messenger. It was a risky task; at one point Idiáquez reached the headquarters of Almagro the Younger at Vilcas and learned that the previous royal messenger had been executed.[29] Following his defeat at Chupas, the rebel, as his father before, was executed on Cuzco's principal square. At this juncture, the Cabanas encomendero Lope de Idiáquez seems to have tired of the turmoil and decided to return to Spain. In a most unusual fashion, he managed to arrange a transfer of his encomienda to another Basque and business associate, Miguel de Vergara. This strictly illegal transfer was authorized by Vaca de Castro, perhaps because of the indispensable assistance Idiáquez provided in negotiations.

Juan de Arbes immediately challenged Vaca de Castro's action, arguing that tributaries given Vergara were actually those granted to his father by Francisco Pizarro and they were his by inheritance. Miguel de Vergara countered that Juan de Arbes had no right to his father's encomienda, because he already had a grant, and the king had authorized a future grant to Vergara, following a general tribute assessment of all encomiendas. Vergara claimed that after Cristóbal Pérez died, Lope de Idiáquez exercised control over the Cabanas and that during that time Arbes had not challenged his possession. After Idiáquez relinquished the repartimiento, the Indians were confirmed by Vaca de Castro. The arguments being mustered on both sides could have led to a complicated suit in the Council of the Indies, profiting lawyers and judges more than litigants. Fearing the worst the two men agreed to share control over the Cabanas.

Vaca de Castro wisely confirmed that settlement for five years. In Cuzco on 6 November 1543, Vaca de Castro decreed: "To the two I entrust all the caciques and principales [the principal is the chief of a lesser division or unit, such as an ayllu] in the following form: the cacique principal of all the repartimiento of Cabana, Ichucaguana, is entrusted to Miguel de Vergara; and the cacique Tulmaque, who is second in the entire repartimiento, is given to Juan de Arbes." These were not the same Cabana kurakas granted in August 1535.[30]

With the revolt of Diego de Almagro the Younger defeated and the leaders punished, it seemed that royal authority was firmly reestablished in the Andes. But in 1542 the Council of the Indies issued "New Laws" for administration of the Indies, including articles designed specifically to protect the Indians. One effectively ended the encomienda system by limiting inheritance of the grants. Notice of this provision shocked settlers, who felt betrayed. Rather than risk outright rebellion, New Spain's astute viceroy, Don Antonio de Mendoza, suspended enforcement until review of the provisions of the laws could be conducted. Peru's first viceroy, Blasco Núñez Vela, was unwilling to compromise, insisting instead on complete obedience to the ordinances. When Peruvian encomenderos realized the viceroy's inflexibility, they rebelled. The conquerors expected to be rewarded with Indian grants and public office and wanted their descendants to inherit the grants. Each Colca encomendero chose sides, and for the fourth time the Cabana and Collagua watched invaders engage in deadly battle among themselves.

Gonzalo Pizarro was accepted as natural leader and traveled to Cuzco from his mines and estates in Charcas, where he had been exiled by Vaca de Castro. From there he challenged the new viceroy, and surrounded by supporters took Lima on 28 October 1544. Núñez Vela was captured and sent by ship to Panama. But the viceroy escaped, and from Tumbes on Peru's north coast began to amass a force to defend the royal cause. Several skirmishes occurred in 1545, and Pizarro's men succeeded in pushing Núñez Vela northward, first to Quito, then Pasto. In a battle at Añaquito, north of Quito on 18 January 1546, the viceroy lost his life, leaving Gonzalo Pizarro Peru's undisputed ruler.[31] At the same time that the rebellion was gaining momentum in the Andes, royal councillors in Spain began a series of meetings in 1545, intending to review detested provisions of the New Laws. They acknowledged that the section dealing with abolition of the encomienda was a mistake and rescinded the measure. In a mood of accommodation, the Crown appointed a new governor-general, Pedro de la Gasca, a cleric and lawyer educated at the Universities of Salamanca and Alcalá de Henares. The royal appointee departed Spain in May 1546, and reached Tumbes in June the following year. A quiet diplomat and patient negotiator, he began slowly to undermine the strength and popularity of Gonzalo Pizarro. La Gasca offered reward and recognition for those returning to the royal cause. Gonzalo's chief advisor and military commander was octogenarian Francisco de Carvajal. This inflexible leader's heavy-handed and brutal treatment of friend and foe alike, as well as the deeply ingrained respect for royal authority, gradually wore away Pizarro's popular support.[32]

In spite of negotiations aimed at ending the breach peacefully, two decisive battles were fought. La Gasca first traveled from Tumbes to Trujillo, then to Jauja in the central highlands, where he established his base. With each step he gained new adherents. Meanwhile Pizarro journeyed from Lima to Arequipa, remaining there with supporters. Pizarro, aware of the defection of many men, decided to retreat and perhaps find refuge in Chile. But the royalist army under Diego de Centeno blocked his exit. After negotiations failed Pizarro marched to effect escape, but this was impossible and on 26 October 1547 the two sides met at Huarina, on Lake Titicaca's southeastern shore. Pizarro's forces, although outnumbered roughly two to one, were victorious, thanks partly to his astute commander, Carvajal, and effective use of arquebuses. Several Colca Valley encomenderos fought on the royalist side at Huarina. Francisco Noguerol de Ulloa was severely wounded by an arquebus shot; Juan de la Torre fled the battle, leaving his weapons on the field. Juan de Arbes and Miguel de Vergara were less fortunate. Both died on the field, Vergara falling to an arquebus blast to the head. The two shared the Cabanas, and shared death on the stained field of Huarina.[33]

Pizarro's victory at Huarina, coupled with the capture of substantial booty, led the rebel leader to revise plans. He sent detachments to La Plata, Arequipa, and other cities to raise new men and supplies, then marched on Cuzco, where he was welcomed with great festivities. Here Gonzalo set up new headquarters. La Gasca and his supporters were surprised at the ease of the insurgent's victory at Huarina, but without delay the men who escaped death were reintegrated into royalist forces and La Gasca embarked on a southward march toward Cuzco. He left Jauja late in 1547, passed through Guamanga, and continued to Andaguaylas. He collected reinforcements along the way and left Andaguaylas in March 1548. Pizarro failed to block La Gasca's passage across the Apurimac River, where he could easily have been detained. By permitting the royalist march on Cuzco, Pizarro waited too long; he was forced to abandon the city and retreat to the nearby plains of Jaquijahuana. Even before the decisive battle began on 9 April 1548, many of the rebels broke ranks and crossed to the royalist side. In the ensuing clash Pizarro's forces were quickly defeated, and Gonzalo was taken prisoner. He was beheaded the following day, at the age of forty-two. With his execution, the initial period of instability in the Andean world came largely to a close. Other rebellions erupted, but none was as serious or as prolonged. Nor was there a question of the ultimate authority of the Crown.[34]

The Collagua and Cabana were much more directly impacted by the rebellion of the encomenderos than in the previous conflicts between the Europeans. Although it is possible, we are uncertain if Gonzalo Pizarro personally visited the Collaguas of the upper valley in 1540 when he first received the encomienda. Notarial records in Arequipa document that Gonzalo quickly sent a majordomo to the valley to oversee his business activities. After the conflict started, the Collaguas Indians contributed goods to supply rebel troops. Pizarro's commander, Francisco de Carvajal, wrote to his chief from Arequipa on 22 January 1547, saying that he was planning to leave Arequipa on the twenty-fourth, and would pass through the Collaguas on his way to Cuzco. Carvajal reported that he did not take the coastal route, because there were insufficient Indians to go that way, implying he was using Collaguas transporters. Diego Ramírez wrote on 22 February 1547 that he was traveling to the Collaguas en route to Charcas, planned to bring 1,000 llamas with corn, and was using revenues from the sale of cloth for Pizarro's war coffers. Ramírez described the Collaguas, saying they are "very well, and have plenty to eat," meaning that there were ample foodstuffs for the army to requisition. Only the fact that Pizarro held equally valuable encomiendas and some silver mines in the Cuzco and Charcas districts prevented him from devoting full attention to exploitation of the Collaguas grant. But as leader of the rebel army Gonzalo did visit the Colca Valley, with devastating consequences for his Collaguas tributaries.[35]

Economic resources of the valley's peoples were expropriated to support Pizarro's cause. Provisions and large numbers of native carriers were conscripted for the rebel army. The troops also needed metal. Copper was plentiful in the valley, and had been mined and processed long before the arrival of the Europeans. Friar Luis Jerónimo de Oré, taking testimony four decades later, reported that the Collaguas had "constructed a large house made of copper for the residence" of the Inca, Mayta Capac, and his Collagua wife. Gonzalo, in dire need of any metal for horseshoes as a substitute for iron, ordered walls of the Inca palace stripped. The copper supplied part of the needs of his army, but it was not enough. According to Oré's informants, Pizarro threatened to burn one of his Collagua kurakas for refusing to reveal the metal's source. Death by burning was, in the words of Cieza de León, "a dreadful death. And for them [the Andeans] even more so because," he observed, "they believe that if the bodies are consumed by fire, so are the souls."[36] Andean people embalmed their dead, protected them as huacas, and brought them out as part of the community of the living on festive occasions. Pizarro burned the heroic kuraka who refused to accede to his demands. Other Collaguas, fearing a similar fate, provided him with all the copper his horsemen required. The kuraka's immolation left a lasting imprint on the valley residents, and the conqueror Gonzalo Pizarro was both feared and hated. His execution following the Battle of Jaquijahuana brought to an end the power of the Pizarro family in the Colca Valley.[37]

Destruction of the Huacas

Destruction of the Inca palace was an element of the pachacuti, the upheaval, and it symbolized the collapse of Inca power in the Colca Valley. But for the Collagua and Cabana, that was less catastrophic than the destruction of their huacas, especially the ancestor bundles, their venerated living dead founders of local lineages. The living communicated regularly with their ancestors, whom they visited, touched, fed, gave chicha and coca. They carried them from place to place as members of the living ayllus. Full indoctrination and conversion of the Cabañas and Collaguas was a lengthy process. There were far too many Indians and too few religious to reach and convert all inhabitants. In the first stage, groups—even entire ethnic entities—were superficially converted en masse as they were subjugated. The Christian God had proven his power in the valley, just as a century before the state cult of the Inca had demonstrated its superiority. The difficulty of thorough conversion was compounded by the dispersion of the Andeans over a vast territory, in kin-related clusters that were small and separated. While Pizarro was still camped at Cajamarca, the invaders decided that for conversion it was expedient to compel the Indians to congregate in European-style towns, where they could be more easily indoctrinated and controlled. Neither Francisco Pizarro nor his immediate successors accomplished much in this regard, and it took half a century before a policy of town foundations was systematically implemented.

Conversion of the Collaguas of the upper Colca Valley was entrusted to the friars of the Order of Saint Francis, and followed a pattern found in similar Franciscan missions in the New World. Franciscans were not as careful in keeping records as were some of the other orders; their oath of poverty, largely observed, dissuaded some, especially children of the educated elite, from entering their order. It was not until late in the sixteenth century that the Franciscans in their principal monastery in Lima began to collect evidence for a history of their order in the Andes. Most of the original friars to enter Peru were by then dead. Nevertheless some of the older friars remembered the early members of the order. The interviews are typical of all oral history; there is some fancy, much fuzziness with the passage of time, and frequent repetition of what was increasingly the common stock of the oral tradition of the order in Peru. Furthermore, they are partly hagiographies; their purpose was to identify friars deserving to be remembered, as potential saints. There is hence much exaggeration, and uncritical inclusion of the "miraculous" as historical truth. Extraction of the real past from the mythohistory of the early Franciscans in Peru is difficult, though not impossible.[38]

The first Franciscan to reach the Colca Valley was probably Juan de Monzón, one of the original group coming from Central America under Friar Marcos de Niza. Perhaps invited by an encomendero, Friar Monzón entered the valley between 1540 and 1545, having set out from either the Lima convent or the Franciscan house in Cuzco, founded in 1534, and reestablished in 1538 after Manco Inca's rebellion.[39] Franciscans, as they began to record the history of their Andean undertaking a half century later, remembered Monzón as "a holy vagabond, who wandered from province to province, instructing the Indians as occasion permitted, usually in the tambos and often at night."[40] When writing the history of his order in Peru, the seventeenth-century Franciscan chronicler Diego de Córdoba y Salinas related that Friar Juan de Monzón traveled extensively through Peru on foot, always displaying great religious fervor in his efforts to convert. He was successful in converting "innumerable" Indians, and according to the chronicler zealously burned and destroyed many huacas in the process. He traveled in great poverty, without concern for personal safety. Monzón continued his endeavors in Africa, where he later was killed.[41] It is probable that Monzón was accompanied during his initial work among the Collaguas by Friar Juan de Chaves. Juan de Chaves continued in his labors until death at an advanced age. Fellow Franciscans reported that "he made long journeys on foot, because he was extremely poor; and if anyone gave him anything, he would divide it among the poor. He baptized with his own hands in the provinces of Los Pacaxes, Collaguas, and Cajamarca more than 90,000 souls."[42]

The most compelling account of the Franciscan entrance into the Colca Valley is found in their 1585 report: "The friars of St. Francis entered the province of Los Collaguas about forty years ago. They have baptized all the Indians . . . and erected in all the villages churches and convents, and with their salary and alms they have helped to furnish the sacristies with many church vestments and ornaments."[43] The author of the account detailed at great length the initial encounter in the valley:

Those Indians had many huacas and idols which were worshiped, and taken as gods. The fathers, Friar Juan de Monzón and Friar Juan de Chaves, who were the first in that province, discovered a great number of these huacas and idols and burned them and threw the ashes into a river. On Sunday, going about in search of the principal idols, they were in the plaza together to indoctrinate them and there were more than two thousand souls. The two friars were in great fear that the Indians might kill them because they were very unhappy that the idols had been taken away from them, and they understood that our Savior miraculously delivered them from this great danger, because the Indians did not harm them at all. In a pueblo called Lari, Friar Juan de Chaves had them carry the huacas that they had collected in order to burn them, and fifty or sixty Indians were loaded with them.

The implanting of Christianity required the destruction of all vestiges of the prior religious beliefs of the valley's inhabitants.

The responses of the peoples of the Colca Valley who were the subjects of the religious conquest are clouded, because there is no direct remaining account that allows us to reconstruct their memory. Life in the valley probably changed slowly at first. The valley was relatively isolated, and close contact with the Spaniards was blunted by distance and the difficulty of travel. It took time before European conquest and replacement of the Inca bureaucracy with its own had an impact on isolated districts. Lands set aside for the Inca and official cult were quickly taken over for cultivation by valley ayllus. For a brief period social and political life in the region may have seemed to be reverting to the structures prior to Inca expansion into the valley. But with the distribution of the Cabanas and the entrance of encomenderos and their representatives into the lower valley, there was a growing awareness that the foreigners planned to remain and demand even more from the local people than Inca rulers had. By the middle to late 1540s, in spite of four brief periods when the Europeans were so involved in internecine strife that their hold was tenuous at best, the full weight of European control was felt. Natives were distributed to conquerors and were expected to pay tribute, to serve in Spanish economic enterprises, to build the churches of the Colca Valley, and to assist in the construction of nearby Arequipa. Quickly these demands became excessive, far surpassing the labor requirements of the Incas. Furthermore, following the civil wars the outsiders were in even firmer control of the Andean world, and, with peace, the Europeans were able to devote closer attention to exploitation of the true source of wealth and power: the labor of the Collaguas and Cabanas.

Arriving with the conquerors were the priests and friars, who in their attempts to convince the Indians of the errors of their pagan beliefs ruthlessly destroyed anything deemed idolatrous. How did these men dare to enter the valley, with no weapons, and demand the dismantling of the religious shrines? Monzón, for example, could have been easily stopped as he set out to destroy the huacas. It is difficult to ascertain what restrained the natives; was it the audacity of the friars, or perhaps fear of the new god who appeared to favor his followers? The initial contact, and first weeks and months, must have been a time of testing as the people of alien worlds discovered each other. The challenge to local political and religious autonomy was evident to all the valley's people by 1547. By then Gonzalo Pizarro had burned alive one of the valley's principal lords. About the same time the Franciscan friars had collected and immolated the mummy bundles of the progenitors of local ayllus, scattering their ashes into the waters of the Colca River.

The disastrous pachacuti, or great turning of the earth, had come to the people of the Colca Valley. The ease with which the Spanish conquered the Inca demonstrated the strength of the new Christian God and the power of his followers. But it soon became apparent that no Spaniard was a bearded deity; nor was any European the deity's emissary. The Collagua and Cabana could acquiesce in the overthrow of the cult of the sun, a faith that represented Inca domination, a belief that had never taken a significant hold on the native peoples of the valley. Christian destruction of the local huacas was another matter, potentially dangerous for the existence of future generations. The minor huacas were easily destroyed by the first missionaries. The mummy bundles of the founders of the ayllus were searched out and thrown on the pyres. The *apachitas* were torn down, the stones scattered. Conopas were crushed. But the outsiders were not ubiquitous. A solitary traveler could carry a small burden, leaving behind the germ of a new apachita. In the solitude of the windswept puna, a herdsman could carve new conopas. In hidden niches in inaccessible canyon walls, undiscovered ancestor huacas could be given sustenance of chicha and coca leaves by respectful members of their ayllus, confident that their old powers continued. And the greatest huacas, the volcanic cone of Collaguata, and the massive peak of Hualca Hualca, true progenitors of the Collagua and the Cabana, loomed proudly, untouched by the foreigners. The forces of the mountain peaks, symbolic of the lost world, also promised to provide for future generations the precious water melting from the glaciers on their highest slopes, so long as they continued to be venerated and propitiated.

CHAPTER THREE

CRISIS OF THE NEW ORDER

Of the infinite multitude of mortals that filled those lands most are already gone; how many more can they treat worse and finish off if they [encomenderos] have titles as proof of having purchased them?
—Domingo de Santo Tomás and Bartolomé de las Casas to Philip II, in the name of the Peruvian kurakas and Indians, 1558, Archivo Nacional, Madrid.

Encomenderos: The Search for Stability

The pachacuti that destroyed the old order of the Collaguas and Cabanas of the Colca Valley had its mirror image in what happened to the encomenderos. Cristóbal Pérez was killed in the contest between the Pizarrists and Almagrists at the Battle of Salinas in 1538. Cabanas anansaya and urinsaya were vacated by the deaths of Juan de Arbes and Miguel de Vergara at the Battle of Huarina in October 1547. Fuentes was likely killed in the same battle. And just under six months after his stunning victory at Huarina, Gonzalo Pizarro was defeated at Jaquijahuana and the next day executed. His head was cut off and taken to Lima, where it was placed in an iron cage with a cautionary plaque: "This is the head of the traitor Gonzalo Pizarro, who rose up in Peru against His Majesty and gave battle against the royal standard in the Valley of Jaquijahuana." Pizarro's goods were confiscated, his houses in Cuzco were demolished, and the lots covered with salt. Los Collaguas was stripped from him and future members of his family. The world of the first colonizers was also being overturned.[1]

Gonzalo Pizarro's rebellion—followed by Pedro de la Gasca's subsequent distribution of encomiendas, general inspection, and tribute assessment—provides a watershed for both native ethnic groups and Spanish encomenderos here, as elsewhere. Men joining La Gasca to support the Crown at the opportune moment were rewarded royally, and the deaths of four Colca Valley encomenderos gave La Gasca a formidable opportunity to recompense his followers. Many receiving new grants already had close ties to Arequipa. Juan de la Torre, who had participated in the Peruvian venture from the beginning, claimed fame as one of the "thirteen of Gallo Island," men who had remained stranded with Francisco Pizarro in 1528. Although starving, they refused to return to Panama. The group was eventually reinforced and supplied, and finally reached the edges of the Inca empire. De la Torre's role in the expedition secured him the high status as an "old conquistador." Pizarro granted him (Cuzco, 22 January 1540) an encomienda in the jurisdiction of newly founded Arequipa. The grant included Indians in Machaguay hamlets in Condesuyos province, to be shared with two other encomenderos. Rapidly his 800 tributaries, many living near the coast, began to die, and within four years he complained that few remained. To prove his contention he secured testimony from a local cleric, Rodrigo Bravo, who concurred: "Each day, because of the uprising of the Inca and the altercations among the Christians, they are approaching total diminution."[2] The encomendero lamented that he could no longer sustain himself in the style befitting a hidalgo and requested a larger grant, enumerating his merits as well as his tribulations in royal service.[3] President La Gasca acknowledged his long service and entrusted him the Cabanas previously held by Juan de Arbes, along with mitimaes in the Camaná Valley. The grant was made to De la Torre and his wife, Ana Gutiérrez, on 23 February 1549. The encomendero took formal possession of Cabanas urinsaya on 26 April, as he brought before Arequipa's alcalde, Martín López, a kuraka named Cachacaguana, successor to Ayanquicha.[4] The Council of the Indies later confirmed Juan de la Torre and his wife's claims. Simultaneously, he relinquished the Machaguay encomienda.[5]

Almost immediately Mari Sánchez la Millana, the widow of Cristóbal Pérez and mother of Juan de Arbes, challenged De la Torre's possession of Cabana urinsaya. Now married to Pedro Calderón, she and her new husband filed suit against De la Torre. Testimony was taken in Arequipa in late February to early March 1550, and a subsequent Lima hearing was held on 2 April. Papers had already been sent to Spain, and were filed before the Court of the Council of the Indies in May 1550; a hearing took place in Madrid that December. Juan de la Torre mounted a strong offense, challenging Mari Sánchez la Millana's loyalty to the Crown during Gonzalo Pizarro's uprising. Mari Sánchez countered that she frequently aided the Crown, and detailed her services. She insisted she had advised her son, Juan de Arbes, not to serve Pizarro. Mari Sánchez claimed that she had hidden royalists with her Indians in the Colca Valley, thus saving their lives. Yet De la Torre produced several witnesses questioning her loyalty. One, Hernando Alvarez de Carmona, insisted he had attended a dinner party at Mari Sánchez's residence, where Gonzalo Pizarro was a guest. When Hernando and Juan left, Mari and Gonzalo remained alone. Hernando Alvarez stated bluntly that Mari "was a woman of these things of Gonzalo Pizarro and his associates." Sometime after the 1550 hearings, Mari Sánchez la Millana's pretensions to the Cabana repartimiento were set aside and Juan de la Torre began to collect tribute. The Cabanas must have known of the dispute over the grant, though to them it hardly mattered who collected their tribute.[6]

Many expected that with La Gasca firmly in control, and with the new tribute assessment and inspection of the realm completed, stability would be restored. But lingering discontent flared again into rebellion. New outbreaks of violence, especially the revolts led by Sebastián de Castilla in Charcas and Francisco Hernández Girón in Cuzco, again forced Arequipa encomenderos to chose sides.[7] Hernández Girón's uprising placed new demands on Colca Valley natives for food and transport of goods and military supplies. Arequipa encomenderos were deeply enmeshed in this conflict; and the Collagua and Cabana, unwillingly drawn into the strife, suffered needlessly. Juan de la Torre's older son and namesake was fully involved in the Hernández Girón rebellion, and with the defeat at Pucará in October 1554, Juan de la Torre "el Mozo," and other "delinquents" were imprisoned. Although the elder De la Torre could have used his influence to protect his son, he chose not to and acquiesced in his trial and subsequent execution.[8]

Even with the encomienda and land, Juan de la Torre was heavily indebted. Part of his liabilities stemmed from the expectation that encomenderos were to provide and equip fighting men during conflict and to hold public office without salary. De la Torre regularly supported two to three horsemen and during times of combat supplied up to twelve. The style befitting an hidalgo required generosity and hospitality. The encomendero held several posts in the Arequipa cabildo, and served nine years as the Crown's fiscal without stipend. The encomenderos' tribute revenues often determined their solvency; whenever tributes fell, encomenderos borrowed. Juan de la Torre was luckier than most of his contemporaries because he was exempt from imprisonment for debt, as one of the "Loyal Thirteen" conquistadores. He used this legal technicality to amass an enormous debt, an obligation which heirs found impossible to retire.

Caring for offspring was also an expensive proposition. Three years after the Cabanas grant to Juan de la Torre, his wife died. Quickly the fifty-year-old widower married Beatriz de Castilla and in 1553 fathered a son, Hernando de la Torre. Five years later De la Torre and his wife signed an agreement to marry their young son to Catalina de Contreras, daughter of Licentiate Alonso Martínez de Rivera and Doña Ysabel de Contreras, promising 4,000 pesos in *arras*, the groom's gift to his bride.[9]

Juan de la Torre traveled frequently to Lima. He met Viceroy Cañete there in 1556, and in 1565 returned to meet the new royal governor Lope García de Castro. He requested additional favors, a new encomienda with adequate revenues to support a person of his "qualities." The governor reviewed earlier grants to the elderly conquistador and simply confirmed Juan's current holdings. It was not García de Castro's policy to weaken royal authority; on the contrary, he traveled to Peru to undertake reforms that would sharply diminish the power of the encomendero elite. In August 1565 Juan de la Torre took a new public oath as encomendero. Governor García de Castro charged him to provide faithful service to his majesty — with counsel, arms, and horse — and to travel wherever needed. Although the governor informed Juan that a second oath of possession was unnecessary, the encomendero returned to Arequipa and in October presented Don Juan Llanquicha and Don Juan Tulma. "In sign of possession he took from them the cloaks they had over them, then replaced them," and repeated the ceremonial act with Camaná mitimae Alonso Fulque.[10] Later, in 1569, Juan de la Torre transferred control over some Indians in the Camaná Valley to his son-in-law Baltasar de Alcazár, who had married the encomendero's daughter, Doña Inés la Torre.[11]

At the same time La Gasca granted Juan de la Torre Cabanas urinsaya, he transferred Gonzalo Pizarro's encomienda of Los Collaguas to Francisco Noguerol de Ulloa. Noguerol had joined Diego de Almagro in Cuzco around 1535, and marched with him to Chile. He fought on Almagro's side at the Battle of Abancay in July 1537, but escaped the Battle of Salinas in April 1538 because he was guarding Pizarrist prisoners in Cuzco. With an uncanny knack for changing sides at opportune moments Noguerol de Ulloa joined the Pizarrists, which saved Noguerol's life. Francisco Pizarro found Noguerol's support useful; in 1540 he granted him the Los Ubinas encomienda. Noguerol even appears as a witness to Pizarro's will. The assassination of Francisco Pizarro in July 1541 placed Noguerol in a difficult position; to escape the wrath of the Almagrists he fled to the Audiencia of Panama, where he presented himself as a steadfast royal supporter and penned a report on conditions in Peru, requesting rewards for his services. The monarch's new agent in Peru, Governor Cristóbal Vaca de Castro, gave Noguerol scant notice.[12]

Noguerol de Ulloa and other new settlers in Arequipa debated at length the New Laws of 1542, which limited the power of the encomendero elite, and many joined Gonzalo Pizarro's rebellion. Noguerol as many others first supported the revolt, but then decided to turn coat, persuaded by Pedro de la Gasca's overtures and reassurances. He was severely wounded fighting for the king at Huarina, and after recovering joined La Gasca for the final Battle of Jaquijahuana. As recompense La Gasca rewarded the thirty-eight-year-old the rich repartimiento of the executed Gonzalo Pizarro, Los Collaguas.[13] Los Ubinas was incorporated into the Crown.[14] Noguerol de Ulloa, similar to Juan de la Torre, served in several Arequipa public offices: mayor, councilman, standard-bearer, *procurador* (solicitor), even majordomo of the city hospital.

Most of the Arequipa elite hoped that with Hernández Girón's defeat at Pucará in October 1554, the two-decade-long strife had ended at last and that stability would be assured. Colca Valley encomenderos could begin to establish dynasties, if authorities permitted the grants to be inherited. Others might return to their homeland as Alonso Ruiz had done in late 1541. Noguerol de Ulloa exercised direct authority over the Collaguas for six years, from 1549 until he left Arequipa for Lima in 1555 and eventually for Spain the following year. He had personal reasons for returning to Castile: his mother was aging, and the family needed him. But before Noguerol departed, he needed authorization from Lima's Royal Audiencia. Encomenderos, with defined responsibilities, could not leave the jurisdiction of their Indian grant without permission. The *audiencia*'s initial consent provided for a four-year absence. One reason for the audiencia's authorization was that Noguerol was chosen as a Peruvian commissioner to defend the position of the encomendero elite on the question of perpetuity of the grants. He left in his place a majordomo with legal authority to collect tribute from the Collaguas. Noguerol employed several such agents during his absence, who remitted cash to him in Spain through normal channels provided by merchant families. The encomendero's absence from Arequipa did not benefit his tributaries; indeed his majordomos frequently made excessive demands on them. Many majordomos were more interested in immediate profit than long-term survival; and when allied with kurakas, their administration was harmful to native villagers.[15]

Although a man enriched by conquest and investments in the Arequipa district, Noguerol de Ulloa's legal difficulties in Spain proved complex and protracted. He departed Peru in 1556, and as his permitted time in Spain neared its close, he was forced to ask for an extension of his absence from his encomienda, which he did receive. But a new viceroy, the first Marqués de Cañete, expropriated the Collaguas. The viceroy acted in accordance with a royal decree of Valladolid, 6 December 1558, that vacated repartimientos worth over 12,000 pesos in annual rent were to be placed in the Crown's patrimony. The tribute revenues were to be deposited in Seville's Casa de Contratación (House of Trade) to help defray costs of administration of the Indies. In November 1559 Viceroy Cañete took possession of Noguerol's repartimiento, which he proclaimed "vacated because the time has expired that was granted in license and prorogation for him to absent himself from the said realms."[16] Regular payment coming from Collaguas tribute revenues to various officials began immediately. Noguerol complained vehemently that the action was illegal, and demanded a further extension to remain in Spain to defend himself before the Council of the Indies. Although Noguerol ultimately lost the repartimiento, he finally entered into an agreement with the Crown to be reimbursed via a royal pension. Full incorporation of the Collaguas into the Crown's hands as a royal repartimiento took place in the 1570s.[17]

Cabanas anansaya must have been perplexed by the upheaval following the death of Miguel de Vergara at Huarina in October 1547. Several months after his death La Gasca transferred the grant to Miguel's relative, Captain Juan Pérez de Vergara (Cuzco, 31 August 1548). Captain Pérez de Vergara also served the Crown during the uprising of Gonzalo Pizarro, and was wounded and captured at the Battle of Añaquito. Gonzalo Pizarro then tried to persuade him to join the rebels, offering cash and an encomienda, but the captain was not to be suborned. He managed to escape and with seven or eight companions fled northward to Bogotá. The royalist contingent then descended the Santa Marta River through unsecured Indian territories in an odyssey leading them to the Caribbean coast.[18] Pérez de Vergara intended to sail for Spain to report on events in Peru. But learning that the monarch had already sent Pedro de la Gasca to pacify the land, he instead trekked along the coast to Panama, where he joined the new official.

Captain Pérez de Vergara's reward after Gonzalo's defeat was the Cabanas encomienda, with the stipulation that the Indians were exempt from tribute the first year because of the impact of the wars and population decline.[19] Given their exemption from the first year's payment, Vergara did not rush to settle in Arequipa. By April 1549 he was there, a bachelor with a valuable grant and an attractive match. Colonial officials, concerned with setting a good Christian example, preferred married encomenderos; eventually Charles V ordered all encomenderos to marry or forfeit their grant. When Captain Pérez de Vergara fell seriously ill, matchmakers became frantic. Vergara's debts were substantial, and creditors feared that his estate, without revenues of the rich encomienda, would be inadequate to repay them if he died. Captain Vergara's doctor, Licentiate Gamboa, pronounced the soldier very ill, with only three or four days to live. Pressure for an immediate marriage mounted, even though at this extremity

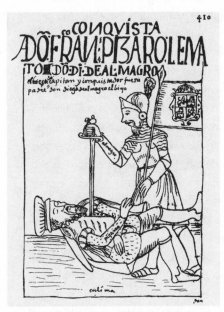

Francisco Pizarro assassinated by Almagrists
(410 [412])

Peru's first viceroy and the revolt of Gonzalo
Pizarro (414 [416])

Charles V sends Pedro de la Gasca to reestablish
royal authority (417 [419])

Battle of Chuquinga during uprising of Francisco
Hernández Girón (430 [432])

the ill encomendero was not easily forced into a union. Finally Friar Domingo de Loyola was summoned. He counseled the dying captain to place his house in order and marry the "doncella" Juana de Mercado, thus "serving God, and not leaving Indians vacated." Further, he would provide income for the young woman. Juan Pérez replied, "Well, if it has come to this, do as you think best." The friar left, and quickly returned with several witnesses, including the vicar Alonso Martínez who conducted the ceremony.

Doña Juana de Mercado was the niece of Diego de Mercado, a factor and licentiate, and had arrived in Peru from Santo Domingo one year after the Battle of Jaquijahuana. She too was pressured into the marriage. Juan de la Torre was intimately involved in working out the details; he and his wife acted as the couple's compadres. Neither of the principals was enthusiastic about the marriage; the groom confided to his friend Juan de San Juan that he "would not want to live with Doña Juana after the marriage." Doña Juana was forced to swear that she would honor the dying captain's debts, that none of his property belonged to her except the encomienda, and most important that she would marry his nephew Juan de Vergara to keep the grant in the family. One witness reported that on his deathbed the captain asked Juana to marry his nephew, "a servant of Pedro de la Gasca and a good knight," adding "it would be an honor for her to marry such a man." Crying, she promised she "would do as he ordered."

The marriage likely occurred 17 October 1549, the day the captain's will was prepared. Within three days he was dead, and Doña Juana took possession of his Indians. The prospective groom, Juan de Vergara, was in Potosí when his uncle died, and it took him several weeks to reach Arequipa. Two months after Captain Juan Pérez de Vergara died, Pedro de la Gasca noted that the captain's nephew had traveled with him to Peru, served faithfully, fought at Jaquijahuana, and was at Huaynarima where details of the general distribution of repartimientos were finalized. Since Juan de Vergara decided to remain in Peru, the victorious Gasca gave him (Lima, 21 December) the Cabanas. There was an unusual stipulation: he could not take possession until he had "married according to law and benediction under the rule of the Holy Mother Church of Rome, Juana de Mercado, wife that was of the said captain." Juan de Vergara's credentials, impressive as they were, were nonetheless inadequate to merit a grant of this magnitude. Why then, did La Gasca extend it to him? By December it became clear that Juana de Mercado had changed her mind and no longer planned to marry Juan de Vergara. La Gasca was convinced she had married the old captain hoping to acquire the repartimiento, thus making the marriage fraudulent. The stipulation in La Gasca's *merced* (grant) was designed to provide justice for the Vergaras.

Juan de Vergara returned to Arequipa and pressed unsuccessfully for the marriage. By 15 January 1550, he appeared before the city's *corregidor*, claiming he had done all in his power to marry Juana—sending vecinos, nuns, and clerics to convince her—but she steadfastly refused his hand. The spurned groom then demanded the grant be declared his. The corregidor acted, noting that Juana de Mercado "did not want to marry him" and declared the Cabanas vacated. He incorporated them into the Crown and assigned an agent to collect tribute. Juan de Vergara quickly challenged the corregidor's action. Individual Cabanas tributaries may have been aware of general arguments in the dispute and the positions of protagonists, and they were unsure of the outcome. Tribute payment to a Crown agent allowed a brief respite, especially from onerous demands for household service. Although the direct impact on the Cabana was limited, the case illustrates the complexities of gender, marriage, property, and inheritance in early colonial Peru. On 27 January 1550 Juana de Mercado announced that she could not marry as stipulated in the agreement. She then authorized a proxy marriage to twenty-four-year-old Diego Hernández de la Cuba, the brother of Licentiate Pedro Maldonado, a justice of the Royal Audiencia in Lima. The proxy wedding was celebrated in Lima's Cathedral on 25 February 1550.[20]

Fearing the loss of the encomienda, Juan de Vergara immediately protested. To prevent Juana's possession of the Cabana, witnesses contested the validity of the deathbed marriage to Captain Juan Pérez de Vergara. Those supporting Juana insisted that the marriage was conducted in good faith. Juan de la Torre, who helped arrange the union, vouched that he saw the couple "make married life together and sleep in the same bed." Others contradicted the claims of consummation. One witness alleged that when Captain Pérez de Vergara married, he declared, "He would not copulate with Juana, that he would leave her a virgin." Friar Domingo de Loyola remembered that when the marriage took place he warned the old captain "not to have carnal consummation with her," and he responded, "I'm no longer up to that."[21]

Juan de Vergara's protestations were futile. By 4 March 1550, Doña Juana, now married to Diego Hernández de la Cuba, secured from Lima's Royal Audiencia a *cédula* (order) for the Arequipa cabildo to relinquish the Cabanas to her. Armed with the cédula, she convinced the corregidor to officiate the formal act of possession. As customary, several important Arequipa vecinos witnessed the ceremony. Doña Juana produced the kuraka Alacalache. The corregidor took the kuraka's hand and returned him to Doña Juana, saying that he gave him and the other kurakas of the grant in possession as law required, and that the official was ready to defend the rights of the new *encomendera*.[22] In spite of the assumption that only men could be encomenderos, there are numerous examples in which females had the role, if only briefly. In the minority of a legitimate male heir, the mother often acted as guardian, taking full responsibility for administration until the heir reached majority. In the case of no heirs, a widow could administer the encomienda until she remarried and the grant was formally extended to her new husband.[23]

Diego Hernández de la Cuba Maldonado, Doña Juana's new husband, was from Fontiveros in Spain. He claimed *hidalguía* before Lima's Royal Audiencia, and defended his right to an encomienda on the basis of services of his parents and ancestors, and those of his wife's relatives and parents. Diego also argued that his brother, Licentiate Pedro Maldonado, had served admirably as a justice in Lima's Royal Audiencia. Doña Juana's rejected groom Juan de Vergara, attempting to retain Cabana anansaya for himself, charged that Hernández de la Cuba had entered Peru illegally when new immigration was prohibited. Nevertheless, Viceroy Antonio de Mendoza granted the encomienda to Hernández de la Cuba on 4 November 1551. Juan de Vergara protested that there was a suit pending and the viceroy had no authority to issue it to Hernández de la Cuba. But Juana's husband took possession of the Cabana tributaries on 2 January 1552. Vergara again protested, demanding the dispute be decided in Spain.

The case wound its slow path through the legal maze in the Council of the Indies. The king's fiscal Licentiate Martín Ruiz de Agreda, charged that the Cabana should be incorporated into the Crown because La Gasca's grant to Juan de Vergara was invalid. The merced required him to marry a relative within the first degree. More important, Juana de Mercado's marriage to Juan Pérez de Vergara was invalid because it was done with the intent of defrauding the king. The sentence issued on 14 April 1554 absolved Juana de Mercado and Diego Hernández de la Cuba of the charges lodged against them by Juan de Vergara and gave the couple control over the encomienda. Juan de Vergara's loss was not entirely due to lack of merit of his case. Successful litigation required capital and connections, and his resources were stretched thin. In March 1552 he petitioned the court to cancel various court fees, alleging extreme poverty. Borrow as he might, the combined resources of Diego Hernández de la Cuba and his wife were much greater, and Juan de Vergara did not possess adequate means to make the system work in his behalf.[24] Over the years, Colca Valley encomiendas were won and lost in the courts and the bedroom as well as on the battlefield. Rich tributes and the prestige of being an encomendero led Spaniards to fight, even die, to secure a grant. The Peruvian civil wars were fought precisely over encomiendas, over the nature of the institution and its perquisites.

The political and social role of Diego Hernández de la Cuba in Arequipa was similar to that of other Colca encomenderos. In September 1552 he was named one of three commissioners to evaluate the establishment of an Indian hospital in the city. In 1552 and 1556 he was entrusted oversight of assets of the deceased. He became inspector of weights and measures, was elected *regidor* (town councilman), and served several terms as alcalde. In July 1558 he was made temporary majordomo of the bridge over the Chili River, linking Yanahuara and other settlements to the west and north to Arequipa. His financial dealings and periodic purchases of agricultural land in the valley were significant.[25] The cabildo had sold parcels on the edge of the Vítor River in 1557, expecting them to be exploited by new settlers. But most buyers soon sold to others. Diego purchased ten agricultural plots, which he soon transferred to a Francisco Madueño, who in the 1560s established a vineyard. Diego's position in city administration, plus his economic backing, permitted him to make land investments, and he was among the first to promote wine production in Arequipa.[26]

But Diego Hernández de la Cuba felt insecure in his possession of the Cabanas and often returned to the viceregal court to gain title in his own right, rather than as successor by marriage. The mid-1550s rebellions of Castilla and Hernández Girón presented him with an opportunity to do just that. He expended 10,000 pesos for soldiers and arms, transferring them to General Alonso de Alvarado, leader of the royal forces. Similar to other loyal encomenderos, he fought against the insurgents on the battlefield. Following the Crown victory, Diego asked Viceroy Cañete for a fresh encomienda grant for "two lives" (i.e., throughout his life and the life of his heir). By royal authority the viceroy issued the document in Lima on 20 October 1557. On 26 January 1558 Diego appeared before the Arequipa alcalde, Francisco de Grado, and requested formal possession of Cabanas anansaya. He brought Don Luis, the *kuraka principal*, "who in his language is named Alacanavache." The encomienda, peacefully transferred without anyone's protest, was now considered a new grant, one that could pass to the legitimate children and grandchildren of the encomendero.

A new threat came during a 1561 investigation into corrupt practices in the Audiencia of Lima. Investigators discovered that Diego Hernández de la Cuba was one of several settlers giving substantial sums to Crown officials. Diego and his wife were charged with sending silver tableware worth 1,000 pesos to Doña Juana's uncle, Licentiate Mercado. The couple argued that it was a personal gift, done "out of love." Diego admitted that there was a suit pending before the court involving the Cabanas and Indians of the tambo of Siguas, over tambo service, but insisted that the silver sent to Mercado was a simple gift. More incriminating was the encomendero's request that Juan de Sandoval and his wife's uncle act on his behalf before Viceroy Cañete to recompense him for services against Hernández Girón, and to grant him the Cabana that he secured by marriage to Doña Juana. After only a few days the viceroy issued the cédula of encomienda. Further, Diego gave 500 pesos to the audiencia secretary Pedro de Avendaño, along with 45 pesos for solicitor Hernán Gómez de Herrera.[27] Diego returned to Lima for a new authorization in 1566. Because of the revelation that he may have bribed audiencia officials and because Viceroy Cañete's encomienda grants were so scandalous that the king revoked the viceroy's authority to bestow them, Diego's right to the Cabanas was again questionable.[28] All titles the viceroy had issued came under review. In order to protect himself, the encomendero asked the king directly for confirmation; included in his petition was an extensive service report. The request was reviewed by the Council of the Indies, and in June 1570 it ruled that all was in order and "there was no need to do what he asked." The Crown was satisfied that Diego's title was valid and that the earlier cédula was legitimate.[29]

Francisco Pizarro granted (Cuzco, 22 January 1540) Lari anansaya to Marcos Retamoso. Retamoso also appears frequently in Arequipa records, serving the city in various capacities, including majordomo and procurador. In April 1549 he made an excellent match, marrying Francisca de Vergara, widow of Gómez de León, a founder of Arequipa and encomendero of Camaná y los Majes, who was killed at the Battle of Huarina. In July 1549 Marcos requested permission from the city council to cut wood, important for house construction, and in late August was given land in Ocoña. He was elected alcalde in 1550, and again in 1559. Retamoso was named to a commission to inspect the district's tambos, and was elected regidor three times. He frequently expanded his urban and agricultural holdings. In 1552 Retamoso purchased land in nearby Chiguata, and the following year made new acquisitions in the city itself. He also asked the cabildo to authorize a site to construct a tile factory.[30] In January 1552, the economic interests of Marcos Retamoso and other encomenderos were threatened as Viceroy Mendoza prohibited Spaniards from using Indians to transport goods, even if they were willing and received adequate compensation. In October 1552 Retamoso and other valley encomenderos agreed to petition Lima authorities to revoke the viceroy's order, and to pursue their suit in Spain if necessary. During the uprising of Hernández Girón, royalists in Arequipa organized, and whereas Marcos Retamoso supported the local concerns of encomenderos and was named "Captain of the Men of the Cabildo," he as well as other Colca Valley encomenderos ultimately fought for the Crown.[31] In 1561 the forty-year-old encomendero testified in the inquiry into corruption in previous administrations. He too had made questionable payments to Lima's royal officials. He admitted that he paid the Secretary Pedro de Avendaño 200 pesos for "expediting" President La Gasca's cédula of encomienda. Three years later, on 6 March 1563, Marcos met his notary and prepared a will.[32]

Marcos Retamoso and his wife, Doña Francisca de Vergara, on 21 August 1563 finalized an agreement near the end of the encomendero's life that was at least in the minds of the executors designed to improve the lot of his Indian charges. The couple, "hoping to do good for the Indians of the said repartimiento, donate livestock from Castile, in order that the poor of the said repartimiento might have wool to dress themselves and to provide sustenance." Retamoso and his wife donated 800 ewes and 260 rams with the sole requirement that the kurakas and tributaries provide good pasture, and that the kurakas ensure that the natives guard the livestock. Further, no sheep could be sold until the number of females reached 4,000. At that point, a Spaniard was to be appointed to oversee the livestock, and he was to be paid a moderate salary. Each year the Indians were to shear for the "poor orphans and widows, and people in need of all the villages of the said repartimiento, so that they can have something to dress themselves in . . . , and not go about nude." The kuraka was authorized to remove from the herd males to sell in order to assist the poor and the sick, and provide support for the clerics in charge of the doctrina. The protector of the Indians, Pedro de Mendia, was present when the agreement was signed, as well as the kurakas of Lari—Felipe Visara, Carlos Ala, and Juan Arqui—who jointly accepted the donation on behalf of the Indians of the repartimiento.[33]

We are unsure of the motives of the encomendero and his wife. At the outset it seems they may have been moved by Christian charity, wishing to aid the less fortunate Indians of their grant. Retamoso could have been also prompted by guilt. As he approached the end of his temporal existence, he may have wanted to atone for past transgressions, sins even, against his charges in Lari anansaya. Good works of this nature might lessen his time in purgatory. He was not the only Peruvian encomendero to provide for some form of restitution to native Americans in a will. Or it may have been simply an astute business arrangement designed to shift woolen production from the native llama and alpaca herds to Old World sheep. His heirs would benefit, if the experiment proved a success. He left five or six legitimate children. His eldest son, Captain Francisco Hernández Retamoso, inherited the encomienda. But the large family, with costly multiple obligations expected of the encomendero elite, coupled with declining revenues from tributes, faced mounting economic difficulties.

Francisco Pizarro granted Lari urinsaya to Alonso Rodríguez Picado, an early settler from Spain's Ciudad Rodrigo. When Arequipa was founded Alonso was among those placing a stone cross next to the church on 15 August 1540, "the day of Our Lady." Throughout the turbulent civil wars Picado remained loyal to the Crown. He paid with his life, downed by five arquebus blasts at the Battle of Huarina. In spite of the seemingly clean record of royal service, there exists an incriminating letter he sent Gonzalo Pizarro from Arequipa, 29 December 1546, pledging his support to the rebels. It was a dangerous time, and like other Arequipa encomenderos he sought to protect himself.[34] When Gonzalo Pizarro's feared lieutenant Francisco de Carvajal entered Arequipa, Picado's pregnant wife, Juana Muñiz, was imprisoned and sent along with a daughter to Cuzco. Another Arequipa female prisoner, the outspoken loyalist wife of Gerónimo de Villegas, Doña María Calderón, was killed by the rebels. Picado's Arequipa household was ransacked by rebel supporters, and the repartimiento of Lari was stripped away and given to rebel Pedro de Fuentes. One witness reported that Doña Juana was pregnant at the time, and was molested by Fuentes until a 5,000-peso ransom was paid.

Alonso Rodríguez Picado the younger was born in Arequipa in 1548, about the time his father was killed at Huarina. The boy was raised first by his mother, then grandparents Alonso Méndez and Juana Muñiz. In 1556 and 1557 Alonso Méndez purchased several properties in or near Arequipa for his grandson. Following the defeat of the rebels, the younger Picado inherited the repartimiento and estate; and while still a minor took possession of Lari urinsaya. He immediately became a prized match.[35] Alonso Rodríguez Picado was about ten years old when betrothed to another child, Doña Mayor de Saravia, daughter of Doctor Bravo de Saravia, justice of the Royal Audiencia. Arriving after the defeat of Gonzalo Pizarro, the justice became one of the leading figures of the Lima court. He commanded loyalist troops against Francisco Hernández Girón at the Battle of Pucará. Not long after the battle Doctor Bravo de Saravia arranged the match between his daughter Doña Mayor and the rich child heir of Lari urinsaya. The betrothal was formalized by 1557, as the parties exchanged gifts of gold chains. Alonso entered the household of the justice, and later traveled with him to Chile, where, in his early twenties, he distinguished himself as a military commander in the Indian wars against the Araucanians. During Alonso's minority, the tribute of his encomienda was collected by a majordomo. When his grandfather Alonso Méndez died in 1562, Diego Rodríguez de Solís, perhaps the boy's uncle, assumed guardianship. The young Rodríguez Picado's links to the Colca Valley, and to Arequipa, were tenuous at best.[36]

By the 1560s it was clear to many observers that conditions were deteriorating, that not all was well in the Andean area the Europeans had entered just three decades earlier. That unease was felt by both outsiders and those subjugated. Associated with the human cost of conquest, the tribute and labor require- ments of the repartimiento-encomienda system, and the loss of Amerindians who were swept into the fighting during the civil wars of the settlers, there was an almost continuous decline in the native population. A significant element in that diminution was the introduction of Old World sicknesses. Many of the acute communicable diseases, such as measles and smallpox, which afflicted predominantly children in Europe, took a catastrophic toll on susceptible An- deans in the valley and beyond, killing adults as well as the elderly and infants. Diseases carried by insect vectors did damage as well: plague, typhus, and ma- laria arrived relatively early with the newcomers. If there were many thousands of tributaries to share the increasing burdens placed on them by colonialism, the system might have been sustained. The economic surplus that the Europeans exploited depended on surplus native labor. When the workforce disappeared, production collapsed. Settlers blamed the labor shortage largely on flight—the escape of those unwilling to continue to pay tribute—or on the supposed in- nate laziness of Amerindians, or on the excessive exploitation of the natives by more rapacious fellow colonists.

It is impossible to identify all the sixteenth-century epidemics in the Colca Valley, because the local documentary evidence is incomplete. Several epi- demics swept through the region between 1535 and the arrival of Viceroy Toledo in 1569, and they caused the deaths of substantial numbers of people. These epi- demics included smallpox, jumping ahead of the conquistadors, beginning as early as the mid-1520s. There was a deadly combination of smallpox and measles during 1530–32 that coincided with the march of the Spanish into the Inca em- pire. One or more epidemics afflicted the region in the 1540s.[37] When Francisco Pizarro granted (22 January 1540) Juan de la Torre a repartimiento in the dis- trict of Condesuyos, north of the Colca Valley, 800 tributaries were counted. Soon a new enumeration had to be conducted, "because of the Indians who died in the general epidemic." The nature of this "general epidemic" is unclear, but local loss of life must have been significant to prompt a new count. Around 1548, only 400 Indians remained in the grant.[38] Plague or typhus may have ap- peared in the Andes around 1546. The ideal European reservoir for the plague was the large black rat, absent from the New World. According to the treasury official Agustín de Zárate, rats were introduced into the Andean world in crates carried on the fleet of Gutiérrez de Carvajal, who traveled to the viceroyalty via the Straits of Magellan. They spread rapidly after their introduction into Lima. Zárate reported that the Indians called the rats *ococha*, or things that have come from the sea.[39] Whether or not the rats were the critical vectors, other native members of the rodent family, including the ubiquitous guinea pig, could act as reservoirs of infection. An epidemic of the late 1540s spared neither the Spanish nor Amerindians.[40] From about 1556 to 1560 there appear to have been a series of epidemic incursions—of influenza, measles, and smallpox—which affected the peoples of the Colca Valley. Up to half the native population of the valley may have succumbed in the first thirty years after contact.[41]

Furthermore, in the Colca Valley as well as elsewhere in the Andes the basic institution of the colonial regime, the encomienda, was failing. The fundamental purpose of the encomienda was acculturation of the conquered, while bestowing on favored settlers the fruits of native American labor, access to their agricultural surplus and precious metals that could be extracted. The Pizarro encomienda was highly exploitative; the checks against potential abuses were inadequate and encomenderos did largely what they wanted. The web of reciprocity existing under the Inca was broken; there were no rewards for the valley's people, save for a handful of collaborating kurakas. Gonzalo Pizarro's actions in the valley as he extorted men and supplies provide one of the worst examples of the violent "destructuration" (see chapters 6 and 7) caused by the unfolding explosive pachacuti. Even the religious caused consternation as they burned venerated mummy bundles. Deaths became more frequent, and the once relatively dense population of the valley began a marked decline. Without enough workers available to repair terraces and irrigation channels, the process of abandonment of fields that had taken generations to construct began. The Spanish understood that the basic colonial institution had something to do with the growing crisis and that it needed to be modified. The New Laws were designed to protect the Amerindians; in the Andes the situation worsened because encomenderos killed to maintain the order the conquerors had created. La Gasca's reforms meant the survival of the encomienda system, with minor modifications. At least with a comprehensive tribute assessment, it was possible for the Cabanas and Collaguas to know what was expected and to use colonial courts if necessary to prevent blatant abuses. Now Amerindians understood the characteristics of the encomienda and began to exercise legal options to check excesses of rapacious settlers.

The economic demands of La Gasca's modified encomienda were exorbitant. Two examples suffice to illustrate the pressures from the encomendero elite: Yanque Collaguas and Cabana anansaya. The inspection and tax assessment ordered by La Gasca clearly indicate the extent of Francisco Noguerol de Ulloa's power over Los Collaguas, and at the same time reflect what was extracted from the native populace elsewhere in Andean America at mid century. Each year the Collaguas were to give Noguerol de Ulloa 400 *fanegas* (about 1½ bushels, or 58 liters) of corn; 100 fanegas of wheat; 300 fanegas of a mixture of potatoes, dried potatoes (*chuño*), the tuber oca, and other foodstuffs, all to be delivered to the encomendero's urban property in Arequipa; 123 sheep; 27 lambs; 120 llamas and alpacas with leads and transport equipment; 30 pigs, half as prepared bacon, or if there were no pigs, then sheep at the rate of 3 pigs for 2 sheep; 150 fowl, half male, half female; 144 pairs of partridge; 72 *cargas* (measure of volume, 3 to 4 fanegas) of salt; 8 *arrobas* (measure of weight, about 25.3 pounds, or 11.5 kilograms) of candle wax; 400 pieces of the finest *cumbi* cloth; 100 pieces of the more common *abasca* wool cloth (see chapter 6 for more details on wool production); 8 arrobas of wool; and a long list of lesser items, including saddle cloth, and harnesses for horses, even 100 pairs of shoes.[42]

The labor force Noguerol controlled was a fundamental factor in subsidizing his role as a powerful member of Arequipa's elite. Some twenty-five Collaguas men and women served in Noguerol's household in the urban center. Fifteen Andeans guarded his livestock and garden plots, five of them in Arequipa and the rest in their own fields. Collaguas tributaries were required to plant, cultivate, and harvest yearly eight fanegas of corn and wheat in the encomendero's fields surrounding the city. About fifty Colca Valley natives were involved in these activities, with six serving continuously from planting until the time of harvest. In theory, the six Indians were to be given garden plots by the encomendero, where their own corn and other products could be grown. But where were the plots located, how large were they, what was the quality of the soil, and was water readily available? No encomendero was likely to have given away his best land. Additional work was required during the corn harvest of the eight fanegas of seed corn sown annually. The corn had to be shucked and the kernels bagged and deposited in the encomendero's house. The wheat was to be thrashed with the assistance of his repartimiento Indians. Beyond the immediate environs of the city, Collaguas tributaries owed other obligations to Noguerol. They were ordered to cultivate in either their fields, or in the Guaca or Lluta Valleys between Arequipa and the Colca Valley, twelve fanegas of corn and wheat and to send half the harvest to Noguerol's house in Arequipa.

Noguerol's only obligations consisted of ensuring Christian indoctrination of his charges, a fine bargain from the standpoint of the European colonizer, an unquestioned burden for the colonized forced to do the work.[43]

Cabana anansaya was inspected on 31 May 1549 by Miguel Rodríguez Cantalapiedra and Martín López. Cabana anansaya was headed by the kurakas Alacanavache and Alayaunquiche. There were mitimaes of the Cabanas grant in the valleys of the Majes, Camaná, Siguas, Vítor, and Arequipa. Each year the tributaries were mandated to contribute 80 baskets of coca, 200 pieces of cloth, with the yarn provided by the Indians, and another 100 pieces to be made from material provided by the encomendero Diego Hernández de la Cuba; there were to be 400 fanegas of corn. The *visitadores* (inspectors) ordered 30 cargas of potatoes and 4 fanegas of quinua. Fifty sheep, 25 goats, and 40 llamas were turned over as part of the tribute. Some 130 *costales* (measurement based on a large cloth sack, volume varies) of raw cotton or wool were ordered; and 30 cargas of salt. For the first year, pigs were added, 20 in all. When pigs were lacking, sheep could be substituted at a rate of 3 pigs equaling 2 sheep. In addition, 150 fowl and 90 partridges were demanded yearly. Lesser numbers of other commodities were to be paid: 9 horse blankets; 9 aprons with their halters; and 4 cargas of animal fodder. Each three months the Cabana were forced to give 1 arroba of wax for candles and 10 clews of cotton thread, at one pound each. Weekly they were to contribute 30 eggs and some fresh fish to their encomendero. Perhaps worse, from the standpoint of the time lost from community agricultural production, was the labor requirement. Similar to Los Collaguas, about 60 Cabana anansaya tributaries were to plant and harvest 15 fanegas of wheat and corn. Eighteen males and females were to provide "ordinary service," and 10 tributaries were to be available for the encomendero's personal service, including trips. Fourteen more Indians were to tend livestock. In addition, the Cabana were to pay for the local priest with the articles necessary for his sustenance, including chicha (corn beer). As in the case of Francisco Noguerol de Ulloa, the Indian grant made Diego Hernández de la Cuba and his wife rich vecinos of Arequipa, with virtually no responsibilities for the well-being of their tributaries. The reciprocity that had sustained the earlier order was shattered.[44]

The level of interaction between the people of the valley and the Europeans and the excesses that could be committed on the native population were related to the place of residency of the colonizer. At first Colca Valley encomenderos, as those elsewhere in Peru, were expected to live within the jurisdiction of their grant. We are unsure if valley encomenderos maintained regular residence within the territories of their grants, because the Spaniards quickly gravitated toward developing urban centers, where their other properties were located. In time of crisis, as during the civil wars, encomenderos frequently escaped to the relative security of the countryside, as did Mari Sánchez la Millana, who hid in the Colca Valley village of Pitay during the Gonzalo Pizarro revolt. Generally the requirement for Spanish encomenderos to reside among their charges was proving disastrous, at least from the standpoint of the well-being of the Amerindians. Many Andeans were exploited mercilessly by their encomenderos, and there was no effective way to oversee daily activities locally. In 1550, as part of a complete assessment of the encomienda system in the viceroyalty following President La Gasca's victory, Crown officials asked the Audiencia of Lima a number of questions concerning whether or not it was beneficial for encomenderos to live among their charges, and if the encomienda grant should be hereditary. The first crucial question was answered relatively quickly in the negative, and on 17 June 1555 the Spanish monarch decreed that Peruvian encomenderos could not reside within the boundaries of their grants.[45]

The issue of perpetuity was a much more complex question, not amenable to a simple solution. Briefly in the 1530s it appeared that royal authorities might allow grants to become hereditary. But the New Laws under the prodding of Friar Bartolomé de las Casas called for rapid dissolution of the system. With President La Gasca's awards to loyalists following the defeat of Gonzalo Pizarro, the issue was again raised. In 1549 a Peruvian lobby represented by Captain Gerónimo de Aliaga, one of the first settlers of Lima, and Friar Tomás de San Martín, was sent to petition Charles V to grant encomiendas in perpetuity. Arguments in favor of the hereditary grant were persuasive, and they resembled the premises of those who later defended the institution of slavery elsewhere in the Americas. Encomenderos reasoned that short-term grants led to unchecked exploitation, whereas a permanent grant forced the recipient to ensure the continued welfare of his wards. Education of the Indians, the introduction of better methods of agriculture, and full investment to develop the viceroyalty all could be expected to follow. The Indians would be protected against outsiders, and they would be nursed to health during epidemics or natural disasters. The commissioners were heard by the Council of the Indies in 1550, but opposition by Las Casas, La Gasca, and even Friar Tomás de San Martín, who had reversed his position regarding perpetuity, delayed the king's decision.[46]

A second petition was formulated at a meeting in Lima in 1554. Participants requested a hereditary grant, with the encomendero allowed criminal and civil jurisdiction and given permission to reside within the grant. The principal commissioner chosen to carry the petition to Spain was the Lima encomendero Antonio de Ribera. To the south Arequipa's cabildo reviewed the proposals, and increased the demands. Arequipeños recommended that if an encomendero were to go to Spain, he should have the right to pass the grant to male or female children for "six lives." Personal service, they argued, especially in the encomendero's household was valuable for indoctrination and Europeanization. Petitioners suggested that it was better for Indians to work in the encomendero's urban house than live in their villages in the countryside. If the king did not authorize perpetual personal service, then he should allow service for a term of six years. They argued that the king did not know the true situation in Peru and should not issue laws without *first* sending his viceroy to review local conditions. The administration of Peru in the absence of a viceroy had been disastrous; they recommended that if a viceroy died, the eldest justice in Lima's Royal Audiencia should act as viceroy until a replacement was appointed. Vacated encomiendas should be granted to distinguished servants of the Crown who had served in Peru, not to newcomers. Clergymen sent from Spain should remain in the Indies for life. One encomienda in each city should be assigned to support Spanish orphans. Encomenderos should have the power to appoint clerics of their choice. Repartimientos should be carefully assessed, with a report on local conditions, because each grant's resources were different. If the encomendero disagreed with the assessment, he should be able to demand a new one. Petitioners argued that officials should not be swayed by the account given by kurakas and Indians; they could not be trusted to tell the truth. Encomenderos who had risked so much to secure their status wanted nothing less than a hereditary grant. They expected to be rewarded with the powers of Spain's landed aristocracy, with control over both people and land. In spite of all the evidence that the Crown and the Council of the Indies opposed the creation of a landed American nobility, the encomendero elite almost succeeded.

Antonio de Ribera's final proposal on behalf of the encomenderos was presented to Emperor Charles V at Brussels toward the end of 1555, with the offer of a princely cash grant of 7.6 million pesos for the Crown if the package were accepted. But early in 1556, before a decision was reached, Charles V abdicated. Philip II, who inherited a bankrupt realm, was so pressed for funds that he rashly decided to accept the offer of the encomenderos. The new monarch informed the Council of the Indies in September that a hereditary Peruvian aristocracy, with coats of arms and complete local jurisdiction, could be authorized. But the members of the Council of the Indies, more concerned about the long-term relationship between the monarchy and the colonizers rather than a short-term infusion of funds into the royal treasury, responded with a concerted counterattack; the final ruling was delayed.[47]

Meanwhile in Peru, opposition to the proposal of the encomenderos was growing. A widely based group of kurakas and their agents met in Lima, and in 1559 commissioned friars Bartolomé de las Casas and Domingo de Santo Tomás to present their own case to royal authorities. The kurakas offered to outbid the encomenderos by 100,000 ducats. Their proposal, presented to Philip II in 1560, called for repartimientos to revert to the Crown at the time of the encomendero's death. Further, the kurakas proposed that no new grants be made. They argued that the amount of tribute should be related to the capacity to contribute, not just to population size, and they demanded that encomenderos never enter the territory of their grants. The kurakas asked for special privileges, and they proposed that the tribute of Crown repartimientos be reduced by half. They also called for the establishment of representative assemblies to make recommendations on important local problems. The native elite had learned much in the quarter century following Lima's foundation in 1535. Their children had been educated in special schools, often in the Spanish cities. They had seen how the Europeans conducted their affairs, both on the battlefield and in the court system. They were quick learners and entered the legal fray, often with success, sometimes with failure. And they had powerful allies among the Spanish, especially in the circle of Bartolomé de las Casas.[48]

In response to petitions coming to the Council of the Indies, Philip II sent a three-member commission to Peru in about 1560. The commissioners took testimony on the question of perpetuity, and for the next several years debates on the issue were frequent and heated. Opposition to making the encomienda hereditary came from several sources: ordinary colonists, who had not received grants before, had little hope of one in the future, and who wanted a "free" labor pool; the clergy, who defended the Amerindians on humanitarian grounds and on the need to prevent the creation of an hereditary New World nobility; those kurakas who did not wish to see their own power eroded by encroachments of the encomenderos; and Indian commoners, who hoped they would be better treated if they were direct wards of the royal government. Several of the most articulate clergymen and colonial bureaucrats contributed to the Peruvian debate: Domingo de Santo Tomás, Hernando de Santillán, Juan de Matienzo, and Polo Ondegardo all wrote and spoke extensively on the issue.[49]

Virtually all the Arequipa and Colca Valley kurakas became involved in the deliberations centering on the question of the nature of the encomienda system. A large contingent of native leaders (see table 2) met before public notary Gaspar Hernández on 13 November 1562, and granted legal power to a group of seven Spanish men to represent their interests. This select body was composed of the Lima archbishop Gerónimo de Loaysa, the Dominican friar Domingo de Santo Tomás, the Franciscan friar Francisco Morales, the bishop of Chiapas Bartolomé de las Casas, the audiencia justice Doctor Bravo de Saravia, Gil Ramírez Dávalos, and Alonso Manuel de Anaya. The purpose of the meeting was to send representatives to Lima to defend the interests of the kurakas before the special commission that was studying the question of the perpetuity of the encomienda. The kurakas demanded that all repartimientos be integrated into the hands of the Crown and that regarding legal jurisdiction, alcaldes, judges, regidores, and other local officials should be chosen, as was the practice among the Spanish. They also agreed to make whatever payment necessary to bring to fruition their proposals.[50]

The final report of the commission was a compromise. One-third of the repartimientos were to be placed for sale to "good" encomenderos. These grants would be hereditary, and the encomendero would have jurisdiction in the second instance. Another third would return to the Crown at the end of the "two-life" possession, if the kurakas paid as they had offered. The remainder would return to the Crown, to be assigned for "one life" to a colonist. Commissioners suggested that Indians be resettled in large villages, with their own municipal government, similar to the Spanish, with regidores and alcaldes, and appropriate laws. But the commission's report was discredited and disregarded. The three officials sent from Spain to conduct the review were accused of illegal activities, and they were arrested on Seville's docks when they returned. As their separate but related cases unfolded, a major financial scandal was uncovered. It was alleged that in Peru they and other high officials had amassed fortunes by selling justice and public office, and the king's lands, as well as vacated repartimientos. The viceroy, the Conde de Nieva, was deeply involved, and Philip II sent Licentiate Lope García de Castro to Peru to arrest him and bring him to Spain for trial. Not only was the viceroy charged with graft; a series of sexual escapades scandalized Lima society. The viceroy conveniently died several months before García de Castro reached Lima in October 1564.[51]

The debate on perpetuity continued for several decades. At one point Cuzco cabildo officers offered the king a substantial sum to make 150 repartimientos hereditary. The cabildo was aware of the chaotic state of royal finances and hoped to secure their long-sought aim by bribery. A staunch advocate of royal authority, Viceroy Toledo suggested that a few titles be sold to the most deserving settlers. In 1573 and again in 1574, the Spanish Cortes recommended sale of the right of perpetuity, using a price formula based on a repartimiento's tribute income. But the king ordered yet another commission be established to examine the problem. The 1579 Junta de la Contaduría Mayor reached a conclusion similar to that of the disgraced 1562 one. But the prudent and dilatory Philip II

TABLE 2. Colca Valley kurakas in 1562 legal action

Encomienda	Cacique principal	Principales
Los Collaguas (of His Majesty)	Don Diego Ala	Don Martín Guaguaxuri, Don García Chuquihanco, Don Bartolomé Guaguaxuri, Don Diego Achacha, Don Martín Vilcacama, Don Pablo Carisuyco, Don Francisco Guarqui, Don Phelipe Mamany
Lari Collagua (Alonso Picado)	Don Hernando Pacotinta	Don Cristóbal Xaquilpa, Don Pedro Condori, Don Diego Yamqui, Don Joan Mamanura, Phelipe Quinco, Sant Juan Myrma
Lari Collagua (Marcos Retamoso)	Don Phelippe Ala	[a]Don Diego Cari, Don Carlos Ala, Don Juan Arqui, Alonso Millque, Don Diego Hancocaba, Don Pedro Condor
Cabana (Diego Hernández de la Cuba)	Don Luis Ala Canauache	Don Cristóval Vilca Yamque, Don Pedro Taco Poma, Don García Tapaya
Cabana (Juan de la Torre)	Don García Antiala	[b]Don Carlos Llamquicha, Don Francisco Ala, Don Miguel Llamquicha, Don Francisco Capiraymi, Don Pedro Guaco

Sources: Archivo Histórico Provincial de Arequipa, Gaspar Hernández 1561–62; Eduardo Ugarte y Ugarte, "Los caciques de Chucuito y Arequipa contra la perpetuidad de la encomienda"; Puente Brunke, *Encomienda y encomenderos en el Perú*, 78–82; Efraín Trelles Arestegui, *Lucas Martínez Vegazo*, 120

[a]These six principales are identified as caciques of the province of Condesuyo.

[b]These five men are identified as principales of the Cabana repartimiento and of Pitay.

delayed a final ruling. In 1584, another proposal was made, and two years later a new viceroy recommended that all repartimientos become hereditary. One modern observer writes, "Philip II, exasperated by so much contradictory advice, suspended all further discussion of perpetuity in 1592."[52]

The Native Response

By the end of a generation, roughly three decades after the Spanish captured Atahualpa at Cajamarca, major changes had taken place. A pachacuti had occurred. It was evident wherever one looked. The number of Amerindians in the Colca Valley and elsewhere had declined sharply since the Europeans arrived. The Cabanas and Collaguas witnessed massive dying and the abandonment of many agricultural terraces. Some ayllus were approaching extinction. In spite of a dwindling population, pressures on Indian labor were increasing. In the 1560s, to the north of the Collaguas, concentrated in the provinces of Lucanas and Soras in Guamanga, the Taki Onqoy movement erupted. In keeping with basic Andean concepts of historical cycles of creation and destruction, its followers believed the ancient gods would reappear to lead a victorious battle against the God of the foreigners. With the defeat of the Europeans, abundance would return. Sickness, transported to the Andean world by the invaders, would disappear. Return to autochthonous native practices is a form of resistance no less important than armed insurrection. The resurgence of the cults of ancestors can be very effective, because they are often difficult to discover and eradicate. The Taki Onqoy movement that exploded in the 1560s in the central Andes was just one of several nativist movements of regeneration in the Americas. Its adherents preached that the people had forsaken their traditional deities, and that only by a return to the veneration of the ancient huacas could the people be delivered.[53]

Cristóbal de Albornoz, the cleric who discovered the heresy, was the first to describe the beliefs of the followers of this "dancing sickness," or Taki Onqoy. He reported that the natives became convinced that the spiritual forces of Pachacamac and Titicaca would join to expel the foreigners. The Spaniards too would be plagued by disease and death, just as the Amerindians had been. Both Luis de Olvera, curate of the Cathedral of Cuzco, and Cristóbal Ximénez, of Cuzco's Indian parish of Nuestra Señora de Belén, testified that Albornoz found that the natives believed that "the Spaniards of this land would come quickly to an end, because the huacas commanded diseases to descend and kill them all. They [the huacas] were angered with the Indians who became Christians, and if the Indians wanted sickness and death not to befall them, rather to have full health and an increase in their possessions, they should renounce the Christianity they had received, stop using Christian names, and neither eat nor dress in Castilian things."[54] The Andeans, by returning to their ancient huacas, would use the force of disease to turn the tables on their conquerors. Tawantinsuyu would be reconquered by disease!

The priests who discovered the movement were alarmed by the dedication and fervor of its adherents. Along with the secular officials, the clergy began a campaign to search out and destroy the foundations of the movement before the whole Andean world was infected. Ecclesiastical officials in the 1560s directed special attention to native practices in a concentrated effort to eradicate them. The Second Church Council of 1567–68 issued injunctions against head binding; certain hairstyles; the use of large earplugs; burial of the dead with food and clothing, even within the churches; drunken festivities, especially associated with planting and harvest; and thousands of "superstitious customs," such as the bringing of offerings of food and drink into the church on All Souls' Day. Although the Taki Onqoy movement failed to generate a strong following in the Collaguas province, it did have an impact on the mind of the encomenderos and the friars and clerics who worked in the valley, who would follow the dictates of conscience and church councils in order to continue destroying the remnants of Andean belief.[55]

Europeanization of the Andean residents of the Colca Valley, and especially their Christianization, was far from complete at the end of the first generation. Old habits lingered, and in some areas they remained strong. Customs changed slowly. Concubinage continued, disguised, but it persisted nonetheless. Although under pressure, the basic societal units of the ayllu and the saya were only modified slightly. Reverence for the traditional huacas continued as deeply rooted as at the time of contact. The discovery of the millenarian movement of Taki Onqoy in the central Andes in the 1560s shook to the foundation European confidence. It appeared for a moment that the encomendero elite was losing control of the world they had taken by conquest three decades before.

PART II. THE "REPÚBLICA DE LOS INDIOS"

CHAPTER FOUR

CONSTRUCTING AN "ANDEAN UTOPIA"

The principal reason for the *visita general* is to provide order and structure so the Indians may have competent *doctrina* and be better instructed in the elements of our Holy Catholic Faith and we will be able
to administer them the sacraments with greater facility and advantage
and they may be maintained in justice and live politically as reasoning
people as the other vassals of His Majesty. In order to achieve this end
it is convenient for the Indians who live dispersed and spread about to
be reduced into villages with design and order, in healthy places and
of good disposition.
—Viceroy Toledo's instructions for the realm's inspectors, Lima, 1569–
70, Guillermo Lohmann Villena, *Francisco de Toledo*, 1:33.

García de Castro's Reforms

A contingent of Spanish jurists, political thinkers, and theologians in Europe
and the Americas faced the challenges that confronted the colonial regime in
the 1560s. Although positions varied, there was general consensus that reforms
were necessary. The encomienda and the local elite in the Colca Valley as elsewhere needed to be placed under more direct control of royal authorities. The
native population required better protection against abuses. Effective conversion of Amerindian peoples called for immediate improvement. Somehow the
population collapse had to be checked. And the colonial authorities had to find
ways to increase royal revenues to cover the costs of administration. Many arguments had been articulated by La Gasca and justices of the Royal Audiencias.
Hernando de Santillán, Juan de Matienzo, and Polo Ondegardo played an important role in the formulation of the policies. They all wrote extensive and

perceptive treatises on how the Andean countryside was governed under the Incas and what needed to be done to consolidate royal authority. Even Andean kurakas played a part in the process. But ultimately it would be two colonial administrators who implemented the changes and hence received most of the credit or blame for the consequences. Governor Lope García de Castro was sent by Philip II to bring Viceroy Conde de Nieva to justice and to institute permanent reforms in the administration of native peoples in the Andean region. It was he who introduced the *corregimiento* system, which shifted the balance of authority from the local encomendero elite to royal governors of newly created Indian provinces. His successor, Viceroy Francisco de Toledo, completed the restructuring of colonial administration of the Andes.[1]

President La Gasca had urged reform in the previous decade. In a letter to Charles V, 17 October 1554, he delineated recommendations to improve the viceroyalty's administration. He pressed for the introduction of *corregidores* for Spanish colonial towns, cautioning that the officials should not have access to land. La Gasca warned that Peruvian "landowners are so greedy that they do not keep the rules regarding tributes and kind treatment of the Indians."[2] Licentiate García de Castro traveled to Peru with the authority to implement change. He was well versed in the law and questions of administration, having been a professor at the University of Salamanca, a justice of the Royal Audiencia of Valladolid, then a member of the Council of the Indies. He was appointed governor of Peru in 1563, and reached Lima's port of Callao in October 1564.[3] In the interval the conflictive Viceroy Conde de Nieva had died, allowing the governor to devote his immediate attention to improving local administration. García de Castro's model was peninsular. In Spain the Crown assigned corregidores to take charge of local government and to administer justice. The Catholic monarchs had used corregidores effectively to weaken the power of the nobility, thus increasing royal authority and simultaneously reducing political instability. These agents served at the will of the Crown, usually for a short and specified number of years. They were paid an adequate though modest salary.

Early in 1565 Governor García de Castro introduced the system into the Andean world. He consolidated several encomiendas in a district into a larger administrative unit, the *corregimiento de indios*, or Indian province. Many corregimientos followed earlier Inca or pre-Inca "ethnic" groupings. The number of encomiendas composing a corregimiento varied; in the case of the Collaguas, there were five.[4] The duties of the corregidor included collection of tribute, guarding against illegal actions of the encomenderos, supervision of the villages, administration of justice, and oversight of labor. The encomendero under the new system received a portion of the tribute in products or the equivalent, and some labor. The corregidor controlled all venturing into his administrative unit: Indians, as well as priests and encomenderos. Indeed, he was the new "supreme local authority." He lived in the Indian villages, in contrast to encomenderos who were forced to reside in the nearest Spanish city. His loyalty to the Crown, in contrast to the encomendero, was unquestioned. He collected tribute, and disbursed funds to kurakas, the clergy, public Indian defenders, and the encomenderos. The substitution of an appointed Crown official with the power to administer justice strengthened the authority of the central government and converted once powerful encomenderos into pensioned soldiers.

The corregidor in theory acted as a buffer between native Americans and Europeans, and was charged with the "protection" of the Indians. Yet like the encomendero he was a Spaniard, with a European worldview. The Crown realized the potential for abuse in the new system, and safeguards were established to secure justice. The new official's tour of duty was short. The Crown shifted corregidores from one district to another. He could not conduct business within his jurisdiction. He could not be related to any local encomendero. Other precautions were taken to ensure there was no collusion between the corregidor and encomenderos that might defraud the Crown. A lesser official, called a "protector of the Indians," with legal training, supposedly prevented corruption. The fatal flaw in the new system was the corregidor's modest salary. The privileges of the office fostered bribery, as the corregidor supplemented his stipend in the numerous avenues open to him. In order to prevent or limit corruption, the Crown required each corregidor to undergo a *residencia*, or review of his governance, at the end of his term. But the fact that the administrative inquiry was conducted by the man who replaced him neutralized part of the benefits of the residencia. Nevertheless if charges against the corregidor were proven, he could be fined, prevented from holding new office, and even exiled or jailed.[5]

Governor Lope García de Castro created in the Colca Valley and the surrounding puna the colonial province of Los Collaguas on 3 June 1565. The newly constituted administrative unit was bordered on the east by the new corregimiento of Canas y Canchis, in the northwest by Condesuyos, in the west by Camaná, in the south by Arequipa, in the southeast by Lampa, and in the northeast by Chumbivilcas. The boundaries were imprecise; no thorough land survey was made at the time. The vague lines separating the units ran along mountain peaks, in streambeds, or in relatively unpopulated stretches of the puna. The governor remained silent as to why the corregimiento was not named after its two principal ethnic entities (the province of the Collaguas and Cabanas, for example). The reason might have been that he had already set up the nearby corregimiento of Cabanas in the jurisdiction of Cuzco and that the use of the same name could cause confusion. García de Castro appointed Juan de la Hoz the first corregidor of Los Collaguas in 1566, and designated Yanque as the capital.[6] The corregimiento system shifted control over Colca Valley natives away from the encomenderos. The question of perpetuity ceased to be the issue that it had been, once the powerful encomenderos became pensioners. Crown authorities now fully controlled local administration in the Andes. Governor García de Castro continued in office until 1569. He set into operation the official Lima Mint in 1566. He also attempted to initiate a general population count and tribute assessment in 1565. It was never completed, although we do have his 1567 results for the rich Crown repartimiento of Chucuito. He was an active supporter of the Second Lima Church Council of 1567–68, and saw the arrival of the first Jesuits in March 1568. He tightened defenses against the Chiriguano Indians on the viceroyalty's southeastern frontier. García de Castro founded the Indian town of El Cercado on Lima's edge. In 1567 the Audiencia of Chile was established, and the operation of the Royal Audiencia of Quito was completed under his administration. García de Castro's reforms, including those in the Colca Valley, set the stage for Viceroy Toledo's more sweeping changes.[7]

Creation of the "Indian Republic"

Nowhere do we discern a better picture of the type of society that the Spanish hoped to create in the New World than in the set of rules governing the Indian communities issued by Viceroy Francisco de Toledo. This was social engineering on a scale previously unthinkable, the reorganization of the peoples of a vast empire. The year that Sir Thomas More's *Utopia* was published, 1516, Bartolomé de las Casas penned the "Memorial Concerning Remedies for the Indies." In it he suggested that the indigenous population of America be congregated in towns of 1,000 people and be placed under the supervision of Spanish administrators. These villages, clustered around a "Spanish city" would establish a New World community, one where Indians would be free vassals of the Crown and would intermarry with the outsiders. The encomienda would no longer exist, but Spanish supervisors would direct paid Indian workers in agriculture and mining.[8] Viceroy Francisco de Toledo's view of the New World "utopia" was very different.

Even with the hindsight of four centuries, it is difficult if not impossible to decipher the enigmatic viceroy. Francisco de Toledo introduced the Inquisition into the Andes. He ordered the capture, then authorized the execution, of the

Inca leader Tupac Amaru I. He created the *mita* system that provided forced Indian labor for the dangerous mercury mine of Huancavelica and the silver mountain of Potosí, as well as other mining centers and major public works projects. Toledo forced Andeans to tear down ancestral homes and congregate in newly founded European-style towns, which they had to build. The viceroy ordered a census of the realm. There is no question that Francisco de Toledo had a substantial and lasting impact on the administration of the Viceroyalty of Peru during his decade-plus tenure. The disruption caused by his policies was devastating in many respects. Yet Toledo was motivated less by hope of personal profit than by conscientious service to Crown and Church. He was determined to end instability and strove to assure that the royal revenues which fueled Spain's "world mission" were enhanced. He envisioned full Christianization of Andean native peoples and Europeans of suspect faith as well. Francisco de Toledo was the ideal bureaucrat for Philip II, with the caveat that he supported "regicide," by executing Tupac Amaru on Cuzco's public square, an act that led to his disgrace.

Shortly after he realized that he was to be appointed viceroy, Toledo began to search out information about the territories under his future jurisdiction. His concerns emerge in a series of letters to the monarch before he set sail from the port of Sanlúcar de Barrameda. He was interested in the perennial problem of the encomienda system, including the number of tributaries and their value, and the new viceroy gauged the king's position regarding perpetuity. Toledo pondered how proper indoctrination could be assured and wondered whether *doctrineros* understood and preached in the native languages; he contemplated language instruction for the religious. Toledo discussed the proper role of the secular and regular clergy in the doctrinas. His search for answers led to earlier correspondence between the king and Council of the Indies, and to the records in Seville's House of Trade. The new viceroy perused the formal reports of Peruvian bureaucrats, such as Polo Ondegardo and Juan de Matienzo, who had prepared detailed analyses of the administration of the viceroyalty and had made a series of important recommendations for the improvement of royal government. Toledo realized that even this knowledge was insufficient, and became convinced that he personally needed to inspect as much of the vast region as he could, collecting additional information on site.[9]

Francisco de Toledo disembarked in Tierra Firme in June 1569, and crossed the Isthmus of Panama before sailing for Peru. He briefly landed at Puerto Viejo and Guayaquil, then continued southward to coastal Paita. From there he traveled southward overland. The new viceroy was not the first traveler to take the coastal desert route rather than braving the slow tack southward under sail, hampered by contrary winds and a strong northward-flowing Pacific current. Further, Toledo wanted to survey Peru's north coast; to learn about its cities, inhabitants, natural resources; and to "find out the difference between government of the Yungas Indians of the coastal plains and the highlanders." In Piura he collected a list of encomenderos which provided information on whether an encomienda was held in the first or second life, and the type and amount of tribute. In Trujillo, Toledo requested a similar report. He finally reached Lima in November.[10] During subsequent months the viceroy continued collecting information he deemed necessary for efficient administration. He concluded a thorough survey of the land was needed; he wrote the king, "The knowledge that will result for Your Majesty by understanding the people of the realm, by knowing their talents and inclinations, by verifying at the personal level the facts of the case" is critical "in order to better succeed in governing the kingdom and to better serve God and Your Majesty."[11] Over time the survey evolved from a modest inquest that provided information similar to La Gasca's inspection and tribute assessment, to a complete geographical report similar to those commissioned by the monarch for other regions of the Americas. His letter to the king from Cuzco in March 1572 demonstrates that the viceroy was not solely interested in the present Andean situation; he also wished to know about conditions earlier, at the moment of the Spaniards' arrival, under the Inca, and even before. The results of this part of Toledo's probe provided the foundation for Pedro Sarmiento de Gamboa's *Historia Indica*. As the viceroy was inspecting the realm and collecting information for the new tribute assessment, and inquiring about the past, he was also issuing ordinances dealing with all aspects of colonial administration. Some decrees paralleled recommendations of Polo Ondegardo and Juan de Matienzo; others were new.[12]

The Cabanas and Collaguas of the Colca Valley were immediately affected by the viceroy's ordinances promulgated in Arequipa on 2 November 1575. Collectively the regulations provide a vision of Toledo's Andean utopia, his concept of the ideal Indian community. The ordinances outlined the institutional foundation, the form of administration, the laws and regulations of the new Indian towns established in the Colca Valley and elsewhere. The structure was complete; the construct was European. The hegemonic state left nothing to chance, from the election of village officials to the care of community livestock, to the preparation and consumption of chicha, and even the naming of children. Amerindian society was to be ordered and stable. The new structure was necessarily Christian; the intent was to silence all elements of autochthonous religion. Toledo's experiment was utopian; the consequences were not.[13]

The political organization of the Indian towns parallels that of Spanish colonial cities. There were to be two *alcaldes* (chief executive officers, similar in function to magistrates), four *regidores* (town councilmen), one *alguacil* (constable), and one *quipucamayo* (notary, or scribe). The position of quipucamayo was permanent, and the person had to be qualified for the post. We know the names of some of these officials in the valley. Don Diego Coro Inga, from the village of Coporaque, was the first scribe; he read and wrote and could also manipulate numerical quantities on the native quipu. Well into the colonial period, the counts of people and tribute goods and services were most easily kept on the quipus. Other town officials were elected, and similar to Spanish towns the annual elections were to take place on the first of January. All village elections were to be held in a similar fashion. First, the parish priest conducted Mass in the community church in the presence of town officials; then the electors went to the municipal building and elected two alcaldes, four regidores, one procurador, an alguacil mayor, and one majordomo for the pueblo and another for the hospital. Indian town government mandated in the Toledo ordinances was remarkably similar to what kurakas had advocated in their petition to Spain in the early 1560s.[14] After the elections, the new officials were assembled and an inauguration was conducted. The new officials swore an oath to fulfill well their offices. Then the *varas* (staffs) representing political authority were transferred to the new alcaldes, and the officials who had completed their term departed. The alguacil mayor was told to present two alguaciles to serve under him, for the anansaya and urinsaya. A jailor, town crier, and enforcer were named by the cabildo. These officials had to be married and be acceptable to the two alcaldes.[15]

The kurakas and principales of the valley were not to involve themselves in the elections. Specifically they were prohibited from soliciting votes for a particular candidate. If they did interfere in the process, they could be suspended from the kurakazgo for one year. Similarly, alcaldes and regidores had no authority to name kurakas or principales. It was unacceptable to elect two principales as alcaldes, although one of the alcaldes could be a principal. Father and son could not serve simultaneously, nor could two brothers or in-laws. Further, the alcaldes and regidores should not be from the same saya or ayllu. If two men were elected from the same ayllu, then the eldest was recognized, and a second was elected from a different societal unit. Non-Christians were excluded from municipal service. Nor could anyone hold public office who had been punished by priests or justices as idolaters, practitioners of witchcraft, confessors, spell casters, or supporters of the huacas. The day following the election, the town crier was to announce the residencia of the previous year's officials.

For a period of thirty days, complaints could be lodged before the notary. If charges appeared valid, the corregidor was to be notified within thirty days for appropriate action.

Indian alcaldes had jurisdiction in civil suits of less than thirty pesos in value. But they could not rule in cases involving the kuraka. Nor could the alcalde act in cases regarding the question of the kurakazgo or in land disputes between communities. Nor could an alcalde decide to what ayllu or encomendero an Indian belonged; these fell to the corregidor. But the alcaldes could rule on land disputes if the land lay within their own territory. Alcaldes had to serve as justices two to three times weekly, sitting in the village plaza at least two hours daily. On Saturdays the alcalde inspected the jail and issued decisions involving the incarcerated. He was to make certain that those jailed received food, and if they were poor, the costs were to be paid using community funds. The alcalde's decision could be appealed to the corregidor in cases over ten pesos, if the appeal were filed within one month. The fines levied by the alcalde were not to exceed one peso. Public whipping was a frequent punishment ordered by the alcalde, especially if the person was poor. If the crime committed against an Indian was by a non-Indian, then the person charged was to be turned over to the corregidor for judgment and punishment. Cases involving death, bloodshed, or mutilation, as well as witchcraft or idolatry, were judged by the corregidor.[16] The alcalde, jointly with the regidor, was in charge of safeguarding community resources and morals. He was instructed to be vigilant, making certain that no young women were herding livestock in the puna, where they might "commit evil." The alcalde was a protector of community values, on the basis of the outsider's value system. The alcalde was instructed to make certain that any blacks who might pass through the province without a travel permit would be seized and delivered to the corregidor.

Collaguas alcaldes were required to make annual inspections of *tambos* within their jurisdiction, and verify there were enough supplies and people to serve travelers. The tambos should be well maintained, and be located conveniently, especially in desolate areas of the puna. Local natives were to provide pack animals and assistants to travel with the alcaldes. Payment for transport was carefully regulated, with the alcalde and the corregidor cooperating to prevent disputes. All were admonished to bar women from the tambos, "who were examples of bad living, who ill used their bodies with the travelers." Indians had, Toledo found, discovered that prostitution in the tambos conveniently provided income that could be used to pay tribute. The viceroy ordered alcaldes, corregidores, and priests to cooperate to prevent the practice. The alcaldes were likewise to make certain that bridges and roads in the district were passable, and that in each village there was a store with "acceptable" prices.

One of the duties of the alcalde was to ensure that the minor officials performed their duties as mandated in the ordinances. Lesser officials were unpaid, but they enjoyed status and certain privileges. They were exempt from various types of manual service in the tambos, in transportation, and in bridge and road repair. Toledo prohibited alcaldes and alguaciles from carrying varas, symbols of their office, outside their jurisdictions. The only exceptions were when alguaciles were exercising their functions, such as searching for criminals in other villages. If the official took the symbol of authority outside the community, he would be imprisoned for fifteen days. During the course of many arguments, the vara became more than a mere symbol of authority; it became the actual embodiment of power. For that reason the varas were to be solid enough so as not to be easily broken.[17] A primary responsibility of the alguaciles was to make the nightly rounds. They were admonished not to enter houses unless they were searching for someone. They were to detain anyone found in the streets or plaza two hours following nightfall, and jail them until morning. In order to give advance notice of the hours of reckoning, village church bells were to be rung a quarter of an hour before the curfew. Alguaciles were warned not to enter houses of women without the alcalde's explicit permission. If any illicit relationships developed, the alguacil was to be punished severely and the corregidor notified so a replacement could be named. Further, the alguacil had to inspect the jail mornings and afternoons, and to verify that the needs of the prisoners were met.[18]

The town notary, Don Diego Coro Inga, fulfilled important duties. He was expected to reside in the town where he lived, Coporaque. He was mandated to witness all transactions. The local priest also held the power of notary. Don Diego regularly prepared wills, inventories, and reports. Anything relating to the common good of the pueblo was to be recorded, and the economic data in the quipus was to be transferred to paper, making the information "permanent." A yearly report of his work was required, with the record filed. Nothing was left to chance. Toledo even ordered that a chest with a lock should be purchased, using community funds, in order to ensure safekeeping of documents. A table should be bought, and the community was to outfit a small writing office on the building lot assigned for the notary's house. The roof was to be tiled because of the danger of fire. The room was to have its own lock and key. The notary was to honor and treat well the office (in both senses), as it provided an obvious benefit for the community. Henceforth, the quipu record would be

Cabildo acting to protect native woman (654 [668])

Regidor with his staff and quipu account record (800 [814])

The cabildo's scribe and town notary (814 [828])

A majordomo keeping watch over the community chest (806 [820])

permanent and tribute assessments would be archived to prevent future misunderstandings. The notary was called on to be faithful to his calling "to record nothing but the truth of that which passed before him, and just, without fail, in spirit of interest, love, fear, or by order of anyone."[19] Community records and official account books were kept elsewhere. A large wooden safety chest with three locks was to be purchased using community money. One key to the lock went to the corregidor, another to the oldest alcalde, and the third to the kuraka. If one of the key keepers were ill or incapacitated, the key was temporarily held by one of the other two. A smaller chest was to be purchased for safekeeping royal decrees and other important community papers, and also for a record of when the priest left his parish. If the priest traveled out of the area, he had to report in the book where he had gone and the number of days he was absent. The daily stipend of the cleric would then be reduced by the time he was away from his doctrina.

There were several other minor officials. The procurador was to foster the well-being of the "republic"; he was especially charged with guarding the village and its lands. He was authorized to present ideas or recommendations for cabildo discussion. The jailor, another important local official, was to be given a place to live. He was expected to keep the jail clean, and his prisoners carefully locked up, and he was not allowed to leave the village without permission of the alcalde or alguacil. The *pregonero* (town crier) not only made public announcements; he also collected fines that were levied locally. He and the alguacil received an extra agricultural plot for personal use.[20] Toledo expected the regulations to be honored in practice. In residencias of corregidores there are extensive records of fines that were assessed and paid. In 1585, for example, the corregidor of Los Collaguas collected 8 pesos and 6 *tomines* for infractions of the ordinances (there were 8 tomines per peso at the time of the Toledo assessment).[21]

Royal patronage linked church and state in the Spanish world, and Toledo's ordinances also touched on issues of the work of clerics in the Colca Valley. The viceroy's legislation was generally in keeping with the decisions of Lima Church Councils, especially the most recent, Second Council, and it covers all aspects of life in the doctrinas. Three days weekly the Indians were to unite prior to leaving for the morning's work to pray and hear the Doctrina. When they congregated for special ceremonies, such as the shearing of llamas, local doctrineros were expected to lead in recitation of the Creed. Children were to be indoctrinated daily. Some alguaciles apparently had ordered young women to attend doctrine too frequently; Viceroy Toledo suspected base interests and mandated that girls over nine should be indoctrinated only with their parents.

Boys were not a concern. During the visita general inspectors discovered that many Indians had fled to the puna, escaping baptism and catechism there. The viceroy ordered that all Indians were to descend to the villages until full indoctrination was completed. He charged local priests with searching out unbelievers, and the community was required to feed neophytes undergoing religious instruction. In the future, only fully Christianized Indians would be allowed to travel to the puna to tend the livestock.

The visita's commissioners also uncovered evidence that some native priests were still secretly conducting ancient religious rites. Toledo believed that such rituals harmed the spiritual welfare of the Andeans, and he demanded that the kurakas take exceptional care to root out and punish provocative religious leaders. Once discovered they were to be resettled in houses next to the Christian priest's, where their activities could be monitored easily. Toledo ordered Indians to end their ancient rites, their adoration of the sun, moon, stones, huacas, and other objects. He mandated elimination of the old sacrifices, and charged priests and friars with the task of diligently destroying all vestiges of pre-Christian beliefs. He admonished the doctrineros to learn to speak the "general language of the Inca."[22] Indians who did not speak Quechua, or Aymara, were expected to ultimately learn either Quechua or Spanish. Ironically the Spanish administrators did as much as the Incas to extend the use of Quechua throughout the Andean world.

Care was taken to assure that the native leadership provided the proper example of "Christian" living. Toledo established severe penalties for native officials who were overly indulgent in consumption of alcohol. Immediate suspension from office for a year was the mandatory punishment for an alcalde or regidor. A kuraka or principal was exiled for a year and had to serve in a monastery or hospital in the nearest Spanish city. The corregidor was authorized to find a temporary replacement, and in the case of a second transgression the offender suffered a mandatory three-year exile. A third offense resulted in permanent disbarment from office. Head officials suffered corporal punishments: 100 lashes for the first offense and 200 for repeated offenses; any additional castigation was to be decided by the corregidor. The "ideal community" could not be created without education, and Toledo's decrees set the guidelines. There were to be two teachers in each village, one to instruct reading, writing, and speaking of Spanish, the other to train singers and musicians for the church. In theory all boys were to be taught, but especially children of community leaders. Orphans were to be trained, with their expenses covered by the community. Teachers were paid twenty pesos yearly, and they received twelve fanegas of corn plus clothing.[23]

Viceroy Toledo's actions were riddled by dichotomies. At the very moment he was attempting to create the Indian Republic, an ideal Christian community in the native American countryside, he was brutally breaking the last resistance of the neo-Inca state under Tupac Amaru. The ordinances for the good governance of Andean villages came at the time that Toledo was establishing the mita system for mining labor, a system that had major destructive consequences on native American communities throughout the Andean world.[24] Europeans were attempting to establish their concept of utopian community forcibly, and they demanded full compliance. Toledo condoned coercion; he was convinced that a settlement of the native population into Christian villages was not only beneficial for earthly reasons of more efficient control of the workforce, but also for spiritual reasons. It was natural for Toledo to hope to witness successful conversion of all the Indians, and the vestiges of native "idolatries" eradicated. Theologians had argued the legal and moral implications of conquest at mid century. Toledo firmly believed in the rightness of Spain's presence in the Americas, and in the mid-1570s, still a man of action, he hoped to complete the formation of the colonial state.

The Colca Valley "Reducciones"

A key weakness in the early colonial system from the viewpoint of the peninsular bureaucrats was the indigenous settlement pattern. When the Europeans first reached the Colca Valley, native Americans were scattered as they were in much of the rest of the southern Andes, in small clusters spread across the landscape. The Franciscan 1585 report informs: "In olden times there were a great number of pueblos of fifty to one hundred Indians because at that time they were not reduced as they are now."[25] Dozens of hamlets dotted the landscape of the Colca Valley. Most of these were small, some with only a handful of families, or the members of a single ayllu. The idea of forcing the Indians to leave the countryside and settle in larger communities, where they could be more easily watched and indoctrinated, was discussed early in Peru's conquest, by Francisco Pizarro, Friar Vicente de Valverde, then others. Not long after Hernando Pizarro returned from Pachacamac, Francisco Pizarro began a settlement policy. In March 1534 Almagro wrote the king that "With the villages and communications with the Spaniards, the caciques and Indians will come more truly to the knowledge of our Holy Catholic Faith."[26] Viceroy the Marqués de Cañete in Lima on 23 October 1559 settled some Indians into towns. His successor, the Conde de Nieva wrote (26 December 1562), "I am also intending to bring together the Indians into large pueblos, because they are now scattered through the sierra without having a fixed house, and in this fashion they will have, and can have a public order and be indoctrinated, all this for the service of God and Your Majesty."[27] The viceroy notified the monarch that Licentiate Muñatones advocated the same settlement process. The members of the Second Church Council meeting in Lima in 1567–68 recommended that the Indians be reduced into villages as ordered by the king. They advised that the doctrina should not be larger than 400 married couples. If there were more than this number, then the bishop should found a second parish and assign a priest, who was to be paid by the encomendero. But the Spanish were unable to concentrate the population into larger units until they were in a position of strength to enforce such a policy.[28]

The Spanish official and jurist Juan de Matienzo outlined his vision of a settlement policy in his 1567 treatise, *Gobierno del Perú*. Matienzo traced in careful detail the formulation of the new pueblos de indios. He mapped the typical town layout that was to be applied wherever possible, with its central plaza, the church on one side and a series of houses for Spaniards and travelers directly opposite. On one of the side blocks there was to be the house of the corregidor, the jail, and the residence of the *tocuirico*, the local governing official in the time of the Inca, the equivalent of colonial kuraka. On another block to the side of the plaza the hospital was to be constructed, as well as the cabildo building and a corral for animals and storage. Matienzo believed the ideal size of the new town was 500 tributaries. If there were 600 or 700 then two towns should be founded, with the population equally divided. Each town block should have four household plots, and the streets were to be wide and straight. Whenever possible the houses of the Spanish, the church, and government buildings were to be tiled rather than roofed with ichu thatch in the traditional fashion, for tiled roofs proved much safer in case of fires. Kurakas were to receive two lots; commoners one, unless the family were large, then two. Structures should have two or three rooms so that parents and children would not have to sleep together, which Matienzo believed led to sin. They should sleep on mats rather than directly on the floor.[29]

Viceroy Toledo adopted most of the recommendations of Matienzo and the Second Lima Church Council for concentrating native Americans into European-style villages. The settlement upheaval occurred concurrently with the viceroy's general inspection and census of the realm. In the Colca Valley the *reducciones* were directed by the corregidor, Lope de Suazo, between 1571 and 1574. The official in all "reduced" 33,000 valley residents into twenty-four Indian towns. The province contained roughly a third of the native population of the entire district under the jurisdiction of Arequipa. Unfortunately, we lack documents describing the daily activities of the corregidor during these critical years in the valley's history. We do not know the reasons why one site for the foundation of a town was chosen, rather than another. Nor do we know why particular ayllus were congregated, or how they were integrated into the dual system.[30]

In a 1570 letter Toledo wrote the monarch explaining why he established the reducciones. Each new village in the Colca Valley would facilitate more successful indoctrination and better collection of tribute, something the king could appreciate. Idolatries and drunken fiestas could be more carefully controlled. Toledo's ideal community size was 400 tributaries, about the same as recommended by the Second Church Council. Toledo informed the king that the reducciones had been undertaken in Cajamarca, but he needed to do it again there, creating larger and fewer villages. He complained of the difficulties; the corregidor and officials there had been "lazy," and there was an explosion of legal proceedings involving the Indians.[31] Three years later, with considerable experience in congregating the Indians behind him, Toledo issued more specific regulations for his appointees who conducted the settlement process. He notified Captain Loyola, in charge of the reducción of the Indians of Quilcaquilca in La Plata, that he should consult with kurakas and lesser Indian officials, as well as the priest. He warned Loyola not to be swayed by requests of kurakas and encomenderos. He should conduct a careful survey of each village site, to ensure there was adequate water, firewood, and pasture and that the site was a healthy one. Toledo cautioned the captain not to let Indians build where their ancestors were buried, and to be aware that they would resist the move no matter what steps he took. Toledo instructed Loyola to admonish the kurakas that they could forfeit their positions if they failed to cooperate. He further told his appointee that he should not allow anyone to file legal suits regarding the move.[32]

The process was difficult for native Americans; they were uprooted from their homes and huacas and forced to build new communities and houses, adding more burdens to the tribute obligations. Colca Valley kurakas largely obeyed the orders and collaborated in the concentration of commoners into the villages in order to maintain power. The few Andean kurakas who refused to lend their support and revolted lost their administrative positions; some were exiled from their communities.[33] Coporaque, a principal pre-Spanish village in the valley, was expanded by the inclusion of seventeen communities and ayllus scattered in the nearby valley. No record, other than the names of the hamlets, has been found that provides a rationale for the incorporation of specific ayllus into the new residential pattern, or the reason for the placement in an anansaya or urinsaya. The new community of Chivay was created by the congregation of Indians from Canocota, Huacallihua, La Calera (thermal baths), Huyrapucco, Uscallacta, and Cumuranc.[34]

Native Americans up and down the Colca Valley, ayllu by ayllu, hamlet after hamlet, were concentrated into the new villages by Lope de Suazo during his three-year tenure as visitador and corregidor. By the time the process was completed, about 1574, there were only a handful of Indian towns, instead of dozens of settlements in the preconquest era. The Indians living in the puna above the valley floor were forced to descend, to become villagers, during at least part of the year. Twenty-four pueblos in the province of Los Collaguas were constructed by the valley's peoples during the settlement years. In keeping with the approximate distribution of the population in the corregimiento's encomiendas, 8 towns were established in the lower valley, under Cabanaconde; 6 in the middle sector, under Lari; and 10 in the upper valley, under Yanque. The names given to the villages at the time of the visita general often combined a Spanish and autochthonous term, for example, Oropesa de Tisco. It appears the choice was influenced by places the corregidor, or perhaps the local clergyman or encomendero, had ties to. Oropesa, for example, was the birthplace of Viceroy Toledo. Cabanaconde at the time of the visita was "Hontiveros," the homeland of the encomendero Diego Hernández de la Cuba. The name Hontiveros soon disappears from the record, and we know Cabana only by its original name, Cabana or Cabanaconde. In fact, all Spanish village names are erased in the valley, and quickly, save for the singular case of Madrigal, perhaps named after the birthplace of Queen Isabel the Catholic (see tables 3 and 4).

In spite of its importance as capital of the recently created corregimiento of Los Collaguas, we are unsure of the names of the hamlets from which Yanque was constituted in the early 1570s. The forced creation of the Toledo towns left a lasting imprint on those who experienced the upheaval, for this was part of the pachacuti. Such an upheaval, although relatively undocumented in the written record, was remembered and discussed by generations of valley residents, and became part of a common mythic past. Even after four centuries, in Yanque an oral tradition persists that the original settlement's name was La Brota and that the principal family was the Choque, or Choquehuanca. That family had friends, the Checas—"perhaps they were even godparents"—on the other side of the valley in a village whose ruins are today called Yanque Viejo (Ullo Ullo). The present community was created as the Choquehuancas invited the Checa family to live with them in La Brota. The Checas acquiesced and crossed the valley to live with the Choquehuancas, taking along with them their reli-

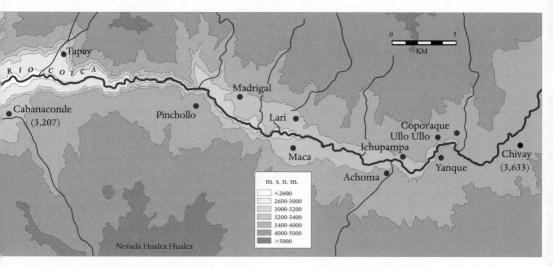

Map 2. Villages of the Colca Valley
(m.s.n.m. = "meters above sea level")

gious image with its miraculous powers. The image was carried on foot to the canyon floor, taken across the river then up the south wall to the new village, and ceremoniously placed in the church of La Brota. But the spiritual forces of the original home exercised their powers. "The next day they went to see the image, and it was no longer there; it had disappeared, the image had returned there (Yanque Viejo), where it had been." According to the legend, they carried the image from Yanque Viejo to La Brota three times, and three times it returned by night. They locked the church doors and posted guards, to no avail. Villagers maintain that the last time they crossed the river, where there is the small *calvarito*, the image had blood sprinkled on it. The last time the image disappeared forever, "they say to Cuzco." One informant relates:

> The body remained, but the body was its *pati*, as a photograph. The image had gone in the direction of Cuzco, carrying all its plants. There it formed its valley. It left depriving this pueblo. From that day on, this pueblo of Yanque has been completely deprived. It has taken the water; the water (now) comes from afar and with great sacrifice. Here, in this corner, in that hill, it has left a little spring. The water it left is only enough for small birds, that is all. . . . The image exists, they say, by Yanaoca in the department of Cuzco. This is what they have told me.[35]

This contemporary oral version of the formulation of Yanque may have some foundation in historical reality. The Choquehuancas and Checas appear

TABLE 3. Pueblos established by Toledo in the Colca Valley

Repartimientos	Pueblos
Cabana	Hontiveros, Las Broças, Oviedo, La Puente del Arzobispo, Pampamico, Guanca, Lluta, Yura
Lari	Talavera de Lari, Las Broças, Paradines, Madrigal, El Puerto de Arrebatacapas, Miraflores
Yanque	Corral de Almoguer de Yanque, Villacastín de Coporaque, Achoma, Martín Muñoz de Chivay, Villanueva de Alcaudete de Coymo, Espinar de Tute, Alcantara de Callalli, Utrera de Cibayo, Oropesa de Tisco, Caylloma

Source: AGI, Lima 464

frequently in seventeenth-century parish registers of Yanque. The Choque-huancas were probably the foremost family in Yanque anansaya, site of the ham-let of La Brota that constituted the core of the new Toledo settlement, while the Checas were the leading family of Yanque urinsaya. Still, in the twenty-first century, most of Yanque urinsaya agricultural lands are located on the Cuzco side of the river. Daily, as from the time of the Toledo congregation of the 1570s, agriculturalists of Yanque urinsaya set out early in the morning for the roughly hour-long trek down the canyon, then cross the river and climb the other bank to the agricultural fields of Yanque Viejo. On the Arequipa side, in new Yanque, agriculturalists also complain of the lack of water. Prior to the Toledo foun-dation, there was enough water for the inhabitants of both sides of the valley. The new settlement pattern required a greater volume of water on the south side of this sector of the valley because of the increased population density. The amount of water was inadequate for the demand.[36]

The contemporary visitor, who ascends the north side of the valley, and enters the remains of the village of Yanque Viejo, or Ullo Ullo, cannot but be struck by the size of the site, as well as by the large, well-constructed buildings. House after house, from one level or terrace upward to the next, punctuates the slope. The preconquest town was well laid out in order to capture the maxi-mum sunlight, with an excellent and commanding view of the south side of the canyon. The people of Ullo Ullo were uprooted by Lope de Suazo, and forced to relocate to the south side of the river and to build new homes. In so doing, the colonial state was attempting to erase the memory of the villagers

TABLE 4. "Hamlets" settled into Toledo's Coporaque, Lope de Suazo, 1574

Name in 1574	Modern name	Number of "house" sites
Tunsa	Tunsa	6–7 houses
Llanca	Llanca	More than 20 houses
Qcuita	Kitaplaza	More than 12 houses
Jamallaya	Hamallaya	No remaining houses
Suripampa	Suripampa	1–2 houses
Chiptapampa	Ch'ilkapampa	No remaining houses
Ccanaque	Qanaque	No remaining houses
Mosocchacra	Mosokhakra	No remaining houses
Muraypata	Munaypata	5–10 houses
Chucpallo	Chokpayo	3–5 houses
Marquisahui	Markishawi	6–10 houses
Machingaya	Machingaya	6–10 houses
Huaynalama	Waynalama	3–4 houses
Coporama	Wichoqata	No remaining houses
Cantupampa	Qantupampa	No remaining houses
Umañusu	Umañosu	No remaining houses
Ccayra	Qayra	No remaining houses

Source: Treacy, Las Chacras de Coporaque, 136

and forge a new social and political construct on the colonized. The temptation to remain in their native village was strong. Some may have tried to return, perhaps making the attempt three times, as related in the oral narrative. But the corregidor and kurakas made certain the return was unsuccessful. Their old houses, if necessary, were partly torn down. The officials of the new regime ultimately prevailed, and Ullo Ullo was forever abandoned. Yet the descendants of the forced Toledo migration continue to plant, cultivate, and harvest their crops in what were the living compounds of their ancestors. And the memory of the forced move was not silenced, but rather continues strong long after the fall of the Spanish empire. What is erased from the cultural memory of the Cabana and Collagua is the name of the organizer, Viceroy Toledo, and his subordinate Lope de Suazo, who carried out his policies in the valley.

Ullo Ullo, Yanque across the canyon (photo by N. D. Cook)

Ullo Ullo structure (photo by A. P. Cook)

Casa of corregidor at Yanque (photo by N. D. Cook)

Yanque parish archive, 1974 (photo by A. P. Cook)

Juan de Matienzo, Francisco de Toledo, and others were conducting a New World experiment of Renaissance-town planning on a massive scale. Dozens of new cities were being created, on the one hand, by and for European settlers and administrators, cities such as Lima and Arequipa. But, on the other hand, here in the Colca Valley as well as elsewhere in the Andean countryside, the colonizers were "constructing" hundreds of European towns in the land of peoples considered not yet civilized. In the colonizers' mind, these new towns symbolized order rather than the chaos of the barbarian world. The structure of the new Renaissance *pueblo de indios* — with its grid-iron pattern of streets intersecting at right angles, with a public plaza in the center, with the inevitable church and municipal buildings at the core — represented order, civilization, Christianity. The corregidor could feel at home, secure at the center, surrounded in an alien world by familiar structures, demonstrating the power of Imperial Spain.

The new towns were built by the Andeans, under orders of the colonial bureaucrats. They were constructed during hours, days, and weeks stolen from the normal agricultural cycle. The location of the new villages forced many residents of the Colca Valley to spend extra time commuting to their fields, week after week, year after year. The new structure meant supervision under the inquiring scrutiny of the clergyman and corregidor. The housing compounds were open to the streets; the passing colonizers could monitor and control events inside. Concubinage, possible in the small isolated hamlet, became difficult to hide from the prying eyes of priests. The rites and ceremonies of the pre-Christian era that could be supported in the distant countryside were much more difficult to maintain in the towns. But the towns turned out to be dirty; the problem of potable water was compounded by the larger population. And diseases seemed to spread more rapidly through the towns than in the fields and puna. The Europeans' utopian Indian community became just another instrument in hegemonic control over native Americans. In many areas of the Andes, the natives simply fled or returned to the countryside or puna as quickly as the town founders departed. But in the Colca Valley the towns took hold and, looking very similar to the way they did when established in the 1570s, persist.

Toledo's General Inspection and Tribute Assessment

The third element in Viceroy Francisco de Toledo's attempt to establish an Andean utopia, in addition to the ordinances for Indian towns and the reducciones, was a general inspection of the realm to set an equitable tribute assessment. La Gasca's 1549 assessment was unworkable. Too large a variety of goods were required; many of them had little value for sustaining the administrative superstructure and were of use only for the encomendero's household. Further, the La Gasca assessments failed to provide the type of detailed population information Toledo believed was necessary for operation of the system. Philip II's 1568 instructions for Toledo were vague with respect to an inspection of the viceroyalty. It seems that the monarch would have been satisfied with a list of encomenderos with their tribute assessments, and information regarding whether the tributes had increased or decreased from the era of the Incas. The results of the inspection would be most useful for Royal Treasury agents.[37] But Toledo, as he journeyed from Paita toward Lima, decided that a full inspection was needed. Resistance to the idea by the local elite reinforced his resolve; he suspected their reluctance was motivated by greed. He was convinced that the inspectors should be above reproach; otherwise, results would be of questionable value.[38] The inspectors he chose included some of the foremost figures in the colonial bureaucracy; many had extensive experience dealing with the complex issues involving the Amerindians. The most notable was Licentiate Juan de Matienzo, inspector for the district of La Plata, and author of a treatise on government. Captain Juan Maldonado Buendía and Captain Lope de Suazo inspected Arequipa. For Cuzco the viceroy chose the cleric and chronicler Cristóbal de Molina as well as Captain Martín García de Loyola, a relative of the founder of the Jesuit Order, married to the Inca ñusta Doña Beatriz Coya. In all, the viceroy selected more than sixty-three visitadores from the secular and religious arms of colonial administration to conduct the inspection and tribute assessment.[39]

The "Instructions for the Visitadores" included questions that the inspectors were to ask. If the questions had been administered carefully, the answers would have provided a global panorama of the viceroyalty of Peru in the time of Toledo. A cluster of questions centered on statistical issues; they were to determine the number of ayllus and saya and the number of kurakas in each encomienda, and to provide a list of inhabitants by several categories. The list was to include married tributaries, with legitimate and illegitimate offspring; elderly men and widowers with children; male children of all ages; the blind; and those in any other way incapable of paying tribute. There was to be a similar listing of women, including the elderly and the unmarried. Absent males were to be enumerated, and the duration of their absence noted, as well as their place of new residence. Later instructions dealt with tribute issues: the quality, type, frequency, and place of payment. After completing the first stage, inspectors were to examine local parish registers of baptisms, marriages, and deaths to ensure there was no fraud.[40] The full Toledo inspection of the Colca Valley is lost, but we have subsequent ones that are based on his format.

The summary copy of the visita general for the repartimientos of the Colca Valley provides a clear picture of the state of the system at the time of implementation in the early 1570s:

> The repartimiento of Los Collaguas that were of the encomienda of Noguerol de Ulloa are placed in the hands of the Crown and Royal Patrimony of His Majesty. In it were found during the visita general of this kingdom that was done by order of Viceroy Don Francisco de Toledo 4,026 Indians of tributary age, capable of paying the tax, the 2,499 of the parcialidad of Anansaya, and 1,527 of that of Urinsaya. There are also 641 elderly males of more than fifty years of age, including the sick or incapacitated, incapable of paying tribute, and 3,966 boys and young men seventeen years or younger, and 8,915 women of all ages and condition. Added together, there are 17,548 people.

Following this census information, the detailed list of tribute, item by item, with cash equivalencies if not paid in kind, by ayllu, was provided. In the case of Los Collaguas the annual requirement for Anansaya, after removing eighteen tax-exempt kurakas from its list, was 4,962 silver pesos, 2,000 pieces of common woolen cloth (*ropa de abasca*), half for men, half for women at a value of 2½ pesos each, or a total of 5,000 pesos. Also they were to tribute 481 head of livestock (*ganado de la tierra*—llamas and alpacas), also at 2½ pesos each, for a total of 1,202.5 pesos. The tributaries of the urinsaya, subtracting twelve tax-exempt kurakas, were to contribute 3,030 pesos of silver; 1,220 pieces of cloth, as per the Anansaya requirement, worth 3,050 pesos; and 295 llamas and alpacas worth 737.5 pesos. The princely sum of the annual Collaguas tribute reached 17,982 pesos. Note the sharp variation between this tribute list and that set by Pedro de la Gasca a scant twenty years before (see chapter 3). The Toledo assessment included the annual expenses (*gastos*) authorized as well, and it is informative to briefly examine these. "First, 3,450 pesos of silver for the sustenance and vestiary of eight priests, religious of the Order of Saint Francis, who indoctrinate all the Indians of this repartimiento." Plus there were 2,515 pesos set aside for the salaries of justices and defenders of the Indians; 600 pesos for the supply of the Indian hospitals of the repartimiento; and 880 pesos' salary for the kurakas of the repartimiento. Thus the annual expenses for the repartimiento totaled 7,445 pesos, and all but 880 pesos of this sum went largely to Spaniards. Coming into the Royal Treasury were 7,992 pesos in silver, and 9,990 pesos in goods. If the goods could be sold at auction in Arequipa for more than the assessment equivalent, then the annual value of the tribute income after expenses from the repartimiento of Los Collaguas for the royal coffers was approximately 10,000 pesos.

An additional 141 Collaguas tributaries were settled in the village of Yanahuara, also called La Chimba, on the north bank of the Chili River, just across from Arequipa. They had also been held by Noguerol de Ulloa and were now in the hands of the Crown. Furthermore, 14 elderly and infirm males, 122 boys under tribute age, and 288 women also lived in Yanahuara. Thus, there were a total of 565 Indians from the Collaguas repartimiento in La Chimba. They paid in tribute 640 pesos, 2 tomines in silver; 70 fanegas of corn at 1 peso per unit; 34 fanegas of wheat at 1 ½ pesos each; and 144 hens at 1 tomín each. The total value of the tribute paid by the 141 men was 779 pesos, 2 tomines. The expenditures amounted to 113 pesos for the doctrina, 100 pesos for the justices and Indian defenders, and 55 pesos salary for two kurakas. Other groups from the Colca Valley were settled in Yanahuara too: those of Laricollagua of Francisco Hernández de Retamoso (159 tributaries), and those of Alonso Rodríguez Picado (181 tributaries, including some in the village of Tiabaya). And there were other Indians living in the settlement.[41]

Viceroy Francisco de Toledo put the finishing touches on the administrative superstructure of the Spanish empire in the Andes. During his administration, the layout of the Indian towns—their governmental structure as well as the whole apparatus of the forced labor system for mining and for the *mita de plaza* (forced paid labor on projects of "public interest" in or near the Spanish city) of Arequipa and other urban centers—was set in place. The economic impact of the tribute assessments, which would begin institutionalization of a cash system alongside normal Andean systems of exchange of labor and goods, and of the substitution of European agricultural products for native ones, left a lasting imprint. The elimination of most of the discontent previously felt by encomenderos—as they finally accepted restricted authority and privileges, with the compensation of advancement by bureaucratic service—as well as the elimination of the threat of Amerindian rebellion were guided by Toledo's direct hand during his roughly twelve-year tenure as viceroy of Peru. As one today surveys the villages of the Colca Valley from the puna above, the vestiges of the "Andean utopia" that Toledo and his followers attempted to implant on American soil can still be discerned, particularly in the layout and social organization of each village. Yet in the end Toledo failed to create a utopian community in the Andes. The failure lies in the basic cleavage between the Andean and the European worldviews. The Spanish system was designed for regimentation and social control. The Spanish were attempting to create communities of docile citizens that could be relied on to contribute labor and tribute to an imperial regime, at whatever levels the central authorities mandated. It was utopian from the standpoint of the conquerors, not the conquered. The Collagua and the Cabana did not share the view of the outsiders. For them the true Andean utopia meant a return to the pre-Inca past, when local ayllus and ethnic units were autonomous.

CHAPTER FIVE

"REPÚBLICA DE LOS INDIOS":
SOCIAL AND POLITICAL STRUCTURE

It is said that the Lares and Yanquis, brothers who have issued from
the mountain Collaguata, established two principal villages; the one
named Yanque is where the most important lords reside and the other,
Lare, is where the lords who follow stay. They are as uncles and
nephews.
— Testimony of valley residents, 20 January 1586, Ulloa Mogollón, "Relación de la provincia de los Collaguas," 1:329.

Saya and Ayllu

The basic unit of social organization in the southern Andes at the level between
the kin-based ayllu and the ethnic unit or province was the saya, a division into
two parts, or halves. The Spaniards borrowed this non-European method of
organizing society with little modification as they formulated the "República
de los Indios," especially in the middle and southern highlands, where the saya
form of social organization persists. Our knowledge of the saya, in spite of the
importance of the institution, is incomplete because many ethnohistorians have
given greater attention to the ayllus and ethnic lords, and have failed to recognize the reasons for the importance of the dual structure in the Andean world.[1]
Duality is an effective form of organization, embedded in the structure of many
societies. Male and female, left and right, upper and lower, this world and the
other, are pairs of likes, yet are unlike images of each other.[2] Sixteenth-century
Spanish political theorists, lexicographers, and chroniclers who described the
Inca system were puzzled by the saya, and they made numerous and often con-

fused efforts to describe the institution and explain its purpose. Garcilaso de la Vega aptly pointed out the lack of economic differentiation in the halves: "The distinction did not imply that the inhabitants of one half should excel those of the other in privileges and exemptions. All were equal like brothers, the children of one father and one mother."[3] Bernabé Cobo described most succinctly the rationale for Inca use of the saya as an organizing concept: it divided the will of the subjects; stimulated competition to improve productivity; allowed for evaluation of local support for the regime. With integration into the whole of the Inca empire, it permitted a better relationship of the rulers to the local community. Further, the assigned positions associated with the saya diminished local disputes over order and precedence.[4]

Each of the Colca Valley villages established by Viceroy Toledo in the 1570s was divided into an anansaya and urinsaya. The line of demarcation between *anan* and *urin* was precise, with people settled in either saya, by ayllu clusters. The boundary was ideally a straight line, crossing the village's central plaza. In Yanque the division cut through the middle part of the church, supposedly a unifying force. Priests and friars explained that all Christians were equal. In the village of Yanque, residents of the urinsaya entered by the door at the western end of the structure, while the members of the anansaya filed in by the large side door nearest the center of the plaza. During Mass they stood in separate parts of the church. Even the parish records were kept separately by saya until the end of the colonial era. The members of saya had their opposing religious brotherhoods, or *cofradías*. Each half celebrated its own special festive days in the Christian religious cycle. Burials within the church were also by saya. Even as late as the eighteenth century, small children who died were interred in different places in the temple: those of the anansaya were buried on the right side of Yanque's church, by the Chapel of Santo Cristo, whereas those of the urinsaya were buried on the left of the transept, at the Chapel of Jesús Nazareno.

There was a parallel division of the upper part of the Colca Valley into halves, with the village of Yanque the seat of one, and Lari the other. According to the Ulloa Mogollón report, "It is said that the Lares and Yanquis, brothers who have issued from the mountain Collaguata, established two principal villages; the one named Yanque is where the most important lords reside and the other, Lare, is where the lords who follow stay. They are as uncles and nephews." Garcilaso de la Vega provided a likely elucidation by way of analogy with Cuzco: "There should be only one difference and acknowledgment of superiority among them, that those of upper Cuzco be considered and respected as firstborn and elder brothers, and those of lower Cuzco be as younger children. In short they were to be as the right side and the left in any question of precedence of place and office." Jesuit Blas Valera observed that "all the inhabitants of each village should eat together two or three times a month in the presence of their kurakas, and practice military or popular games so as to work off their rivalries and remain in perpetual peace, and in order that the herdsmen and field workers might rest and rejoice." Duality was central, and it filled a function beyond the simply administrative. Saya gave meaning to life; it helped to explain basic social relationships in the community.[5] Duality was embedded at various levels within the Colca Valley, in the repartimiento, and in the village as well. There were parallel political structures in the villages — with kurakas, principales, and alcaldes for each of the halves. At the lowest personal level, even males and females were paired in a similar dual pattern.

In the Colca Valley repartimientos were divided into halves. In Cabanaconde, for example, the tributaries of Diego Hernández de la Cuba Maldonado lived in the anansaya; those of Juan de la Torre resided in the urinsaya. Although there was always only one encomendero in the largest repartimiento in the valley, Yanque Collaguas, saya existed there also. Agricultural systems were likewise separated, a strategy that fostered group survival during periods of environmental crisis. One of the clearest examples of separation of irrigation systems can be found in the village of Yanque, with the residents of the urinsaya cultivating land on the north side of the canyon, across the Colca River, and the inhabitants of the anansaya cultivating plots on the south bank, on the same side of the river where they have their homes. Urinsaya natives, with control over lands in the area surrounding Ullo Ullo, or Yanque Viejo, maintained their own irrigation system, their independent sources of water on the north side of the Colca canyon. Anansaya villagers used a totally different source of water and irrigation system for fields on the south side of the Colca River. Yet within the village of Yanque itself, the community water system was single, with a channel entering at the east, on the anansaya or higher side of the community, and exiting on the western lower part. A fountain in the village center was shared. At first glance it seems a highly inefficient way to organize the agricultural system. Indeed, urinsaya farmers expend substantial time and energy daily walking down the steep road from Yanque, crossing the canyon, then trekking up the north side of the valley to cultivate their terraced fields. In spite of separate systems, both Yanque urinsaya and anansaya farmers continue to complain about the scarcity of water that is so necessary for community survival.[6]

The outsiders, the Spaniards, the mestizos, and the blacks who settled illegally in the Indian communities all entered an alien world. They discovered a spatial universe that had to be learned and manipulated. Amerindian *foraste-ros*, or outsiders, who came to reside for longer periods in Yanque or in other communities in the valley, were a separate case. All outsiders entering the valley experienced firsthand the dual organization. Residences of the outsiders tended to concentrate on the central plaza, in whatever plot that happened to be available to rent or much more rarely purchase. If not on the plaza, newcomers settled within the first block or two from it, usually clustering along the lines of communication connecting the village with the outside world. These residence patterns were in keeping with the local economic function of the majority of the outsiders: exchange of goods coming from the world beyond the valley. The clergy lived within church compounds and were outside the saya structure. Outsiders were foreigners to the political function of the saya. If they did participate in decision making, it was more by voice and indirect pressure than by vote at the community level. The outsiders were classified as residents in the anansaya or urinsaya, if need for classification existed, but it would be a residential classification, not a social one. If the outsider married a villager, the marriage and any subsequent baptisms were recorded in the parish register of the half where the couple resided.[7]

The ayllu, the basic element of the organization of pre-Spanish Andean society, rapidly disintegrated after conquest, especially after the Europeans entered the valley. The ayllu existed in its pristine state at the hamlet level until only the mid-1530s, when the first European grants of Indians were distributed in the lower valley. It came under severe pressure from then until the early 1570s. The major blow to the old order came when Viceroy Toledo ordered people from widely scattered ayllus to be brought together and concentrated into villages. In the process, small ayllus became integrated into larger ones (see table 5 for ayllus during this transitional period, from the end of the sixteenth century and the beginning of the seventeenth). The ayllus could function only when there were ample people to create viable societal units; when the population level became too low, the ayllus disintegrated and disappeared. There was another type of ayllu, which was purely occupational, similar to European guilds. In Coporaque urinsaya in 1604, we discover an ayllu of potters. But this ayllu was part of a larger ayllu unit, Cayao Pataca, subject to the kuraka Don Diego Chacha. In the ayllu of potters there were only six married tributaries, and four widows or unmarried women. Two members were classified as "viejos": one of them was aged fifty-six; the other was an ill twenty-year-old male. There were also eight boys and six girls in the ayllu. In Yanque anansaya there was an ayllu of weavers of the fine cumbi cloth (*cumbicamayos*), as well as an ayllu of *yana-conas* (under the Inca, servants). In the urinsaya there were separate ayllus of

TABLE 5. The ayllu in the Colca Valley

"Idealized ayllu," based on Zuidema's analysis of Ulloa Mogollón, 1586		"Census ayllu," in Coporaque visitas of 1591, 1604, 1615/16	
		URINSAYA — 1604	ANANSAYA — 1615/16
Collana	Collana (100[a])	Collana	Collana Malco
	Payan (100)	Pahana Collana	Icatunga Mallco
	Cayao (100)	Olleros Pahana Collana	Checa Mallco
		Pahana Collana	Yumasca
Payan	Collana (100)	Pahana Taypi	Calloca
	Payan (100)	Pahana Cayao	Aipi
	Cayao (100)	Cayao	Cupi
Cayao	Collana (100)	Collana Cayao de Guaraoma	Oficiales Olleros
	Payan (100)	Pahana Taypi de Guaraoma	
	Cayao (100)		

Sources: Ulloa Mogollón, "Relación de la provincia de los Collaguas (1586)," 1:330; Zuidema, *The Ceque System of Cuzco*, 116–17; 1591 from Pease, *Collaguas I*; 1604, and 1615/16 from Benavides, "Dualidad social e ideológica en la provincia de Collaguas, 1570–1731," 153–54

[a]Number of tributaries

weavers, potters, and silversmiths. In Cabana there were occupational ayllus of pastoralists and carpenters.[8]

The ayllu disintegrated principally because of catastrophic population loss. A devastating and unintended side effect of Toledo's reducciones was the acceleration of the spread of disease. Epidemic disease passes from person to person slowly in rural areas with low population density. By concentrating people into large villages, Toledo provided ideal conditions for the spread of a new round of foreign pathogens in the Andean world. An epidemic series extended through the Andes in the 1570s, concurrent with the settlement process, but it was the 1589–91 pandemic, with its mortality level of 30 percent and more, that finally eliminated many of the weakened ayllus. By the end of the sixteenth century, decimation of the population was great enough to make it impossible for the ayllu system to function as it had before the arrival of the Europeans. Nevertheless, the ayllu classificatory terminology in the parish registers of many of the valley churches continued until the early eighteenth century, indicating the importance of the traditional system. A new wave of severe epidemics of the early 1720s brought to an end the effective use of ayllu terminology in Yanque and in many other communities of the Colca Valley.[9]

Marriage and Family

Family formation varied sharply between native Andean practice and sixteenth-century Christian norms. Traditional marriage patterns quickly came under the scrutiny of the doctrinero. Yet in spite of three decades of efforts, the Church was unable to end concubinage in the Andes by the mid-1560s. The rulings of Lima's First Church Council in 1551 present a vivid picture of what many clergy believed faced them when they began indoctrination. Experience led them to worry that they might convert many who took as wives their daughters, mothers, granddaughters, wives of their fathers, or wives of their sons. The First Council ordered that in such cases the couple be baptized anyway, but then separated because it was "against natural law and was an offense to God." However, the council stated—and one must congratulate the priests for their pragmatism in accommodating to the customs of the local elite—"if they are married to sisters we will permit such until the Holy Father can be consulted to issue a final decision."[10] The council participants formally and in conformity with a papal bull of Paul III dispensed with the requirement not to marry within the third and fourth degree of consanguinity and affinity. A bull of Gregory XIII conceded the right to marry in any degree not prohibited by "Divine Right." This bull was extended by Gregory XIV and was still in force in 1611. Church fathers continued to face difficulties in implanting the ideal model of the Christian family in the Andes. The Second Church Council (1567–68) concluded that doctrineros should make special efforts to teach Amerindians that they could only be baptized and marry once, not several times as frequently occurred.[11]

The Second Church Council also examined the continuing issue of polygamy. It ruled that "when the infidel has many wives, the one with whom marriage was first contracted should be baptized and married. If the first wife is not known, then he can choose whichever he wants. . . . If he was not married in conformance to his legitimate custom to any of them then he can freely marry whomever he pleases."[12] Most marriages of commoners in the Inca period were monogamous. But kurakas and principales frequently had multiple wives. Secondary wives provided prestige and were a major asset to the family's labor force.[13] Viceroy Toledo's policies were less flexible than those of early church leaders. He was shocked by what seemed to be incest and attempted to end it in his vision for the Indian Republic. "If an Indian had carnal access to his mother or daughter, or his sister or his father's wife, or his brother's wife, or his aunt, or cousin, or with mother and daughter, or with two sisters, or ascending kin, the alcaldes must notify the corregidor so that he can punish them."[14] Punishment was substantial: 100 lashes, head shaving of the guilty, and hospital service for two years.

Before the Spanish conquest, ayllu endogamy was preferred.[15] The Second Church Council of Lima examined the subject and ruled that "Indians have liberty to marry outside their ayllu if they wish, but they are exhorted by the priests to conform in this to the customs of their land."[16] Although ayllu endogamy may have been the practice before the arrival of the Europeans in the Colca Valley, it could not have continued long. The rapid depopulation made it increasingly difficult to marry within one's ayllu, and the problem was exacerbated by successful implementation of those Christian inhibitions that involved marriage partners. Further, Toledo's reducciones concentrated people from previously separated ayllus more compactly together, leading to increased intermarriage. More important, the sharp division between the anansaya and urinsaya in the Toledo settlements of the valley ultimately resulted in saya endogamy, which replaced earlier ayllu endogamy.[17]

Efforts to modify native practices of family formation proved largely ineffective during the first four decades of Spanish control. During Viceroy Toledo's visita general it was clear to observers that couples did not enter matrimony until they had cohabited for a substantial period, united in all respects except legally. Trial marriage in the Andes was common, and it appears that trial marriages led to substantial marital stability.[18] For Toledo trial marriage was a diabolical concept, an affront to the sacrament of marriage. He ordered priests, corregidores, kurakas, and alcaldes to end what colonial authorities considered a pernicious custom. Examples were to be made of young men and women who persisted. Punishments were increased, depending on the number of violations. If a married or unmarried Indian took a concubine, he would be subjected to 50 lashes in public for the first offense, 100 for the second. If he continued for a third time, he was to be exiled from his village for six months. The woman was given 50 lashes and was condemned to serve six months in the village hospital. No married woman was to allow her husband's concubine to live in the household, a generally accepted practice. If a Christianized native had relations with an infidel or lived openly in concubinage, the first time he was caught he was condemned to 100 lashes and his hair was shaved. If he persisted, he was relinquished to the corregidor for further punishment. Women received similar penalties.[19]

Toledo and the visitadores noted it was customary when the husband of a woman from another ayllu or repartimiento died, leaving children, that the kurakas and principales of the woman's original home would come and take the widow and her children back with them. The viceroy modified the practice, ordering the widow to remain a resident of the ayllu of her deceased husband, since her children belonged to that unit and would someday be tributaries there. If the woman's kurakas and principales demanded her return then she ultimately could go back, but not before the youngest of her children reached eight. The Europeans were attempting to establish a pattern of patrilineal descent in the Andean world which would allow them to keep better track of tributaries, of key interest given their reliance on Amerindian tribute revenues. For the same reasons Spaniards attempted to enforce repartimiento endogamy. Saya endogamy was also stimulated by the colonial system. Colonial authorities discouraged the prevailing native custom of matrilineal descent, where widows and children would have received protection by returning to the woman's ayllu. Much of that support was lost in the colonial era.[20] Viceroy Toledo also prohibited any Indian woman whose husband or other relative had died to cut her hair or go to the puna lands with her husband's relatives, or to conduct any other customary ceremonies. The penalty for disobeying this injunction was 100 lashes and service in the hospital for the poor of the parish for a period of two years. In addition, under similar penalties, the viceroy prohibited women or widows under fifty years of age from serving their brother, brother-in-law, uncle, or first cousin, because in the past, "there have been great abuses."[21]

Indian alcaldes were to ensure that orphans were protected. The parish priest was to take care of their religious indoctrination. If someone volunteered, the orphan would be clothed and fed by that individual. If the child were old enough, he or she would enter the guardian's service. If the child were young and had no one to act as foster parent, then upkeep would be paid from community funds. Children of concubines were partially protected, as well as their mothers, by one of Toledo's ordinances. Children were to remain with their mothers for the first three years of life, and the father was required to support them during this period. Then the father could take the child into his own household after making provisions for the mother. The reality of the postconquest situation was quite different, and numerous unwanted wives and children were abandoned as a result of the European drive to implant monogamy in the Andes.[22]

The position of women was, as in many societies, ambiguous. On the one hand multiple wives provided status for the male in the preconquest era, while the reverse, polyandry, was taboo, indicating female subordination. On the other hand, there was substantial equality at the basic level of society, which continued into the colonial era. The economy was predominantly agrarian, and the gender role difference in the agricultural cycle was slight. Women and men had access to land and livestock. There are dozens of examples of women with equal access to agricultural resources in the sixteenth century censuses of the Colca Valley. In one case, a seventy-three-year-old widow in the Olleros (potters) ayllu in Coporaque in 1604 held extensive parcels of land. Females were active in field agriculture and in pastoral pursuits, and the labor division between male and female was less pronounced than in many societies. The Andean concept of *yanantin* reinforced the relationship of male and female: they were viewed as corresponding elements of a whole. Neither was dominant; rather, the couple is another manifestation of Andean duality. The introduction of the hierarchical and paternalistic Roman Catholic faith, which required female subservience and rejection of the woman's role as religious functionary, contradicted Andean practice. Female subservience, a legacy of European domination, has been passively and actively resisted from the time of its introduction into the Andean world.[23]

Social Engineering

Viceroy Toledo introduced numerous laws designed to establish societal values or mores that were by very nature European, Spanish, Christian. Amerindians should change their appearance to look more like the outsiders. They were prohibited from painting their faces or bodies. In order to guarantee the ideal republic, local officials were authorized to enter the homes of villagers to enforce the social legislation. Alcaldes and regidores were to inspect houses monthly to assure they were clean and the rules were respected. The ostensible purpose was to reduce the illness and deaths which resulted from lack of cleanliness. Andean people traditionally slept on the floor; Toledo ordered houses to have bed racks above the ground. Other regulations were designed to promote European habits. On Christian feast days, on Sundays, and for confession, the Andeans were required to wash their hands, face, and feet and to trim their fingernails. Toledo even attempted by decree to modify the way mothers carried their infants.

There was one traditional custom Toledo deemed worthy of retention: public dining. The kurakas, principales, alcaldes, and regidores were admonished to eat together in the plaza so the poor could join them. But the Indians and their leaders were forbidden from having the massive drunken fiestas so frequent in pre-Spanish times. Toledo and suspicious clerics feared dancing because it could lead couples to slip away to engage in illicit sex. If there were dances, they were to be in public and should be given only with license of the corregidor and priest. One Spanish practice which was strictly forbidden was the playing of dice and cards. Toledo and the inspectors noted the damage caused by gambling, for the natives quickly learned the rules of the games and became skillful and adept enthusiasts. The Spanish believed gambling led to laziness, refusal to work, and neglect by men of their wives and children. Punishments were dependent on socioeconomic status. Kurakas suffered more than commoners: a fine of twenty pesos paid to the hospital for the first offense and thirty pesos and six months' exile for the second, compared to a head shave for the commoner's first offense and 100 lashes for the second. The Spaniard, mestizo, and mulatto received for the first offense a thirty-peso fine; and for the second, fifty pesos plus ten years of exile from the village where the games occurred. Blacks were to receive 100 lashes for the first offense, 200 for the second, and 300 plus ten years' exile for the third.[24]

Indians were forbidden to purchase articles from Spain deemed by authorities as unsuitable, such as wine and fine cloth or any item valued at more than eight pesos. Anyone selling goods to Indians illegally was fined 100 pesos; the punishment increased with subsequent offences. The Spanish refused to allow Indians to possess Spanish weapons. Matienzo in 1567 had pointed out that some native artisans had become skilled at manufacture of gunpowder. Toledo's ordinances forbid arquebuses, pistols, poniards, daggers, or crossbows. If weapons were found, they were to be confiscated and sold, with the proceeds destined for the community hospital. Toledo's attempt at social and economic control came at a time in the sixteenth century when prices in the Indies, especially in Peru, were comparatively high. One aspect of the restrictions was to prevent native Americans from buying the same products as their European overlords, always a great temptation for kurakas who strove to emulate the Spanish. This regulation was supplanted by one of a far different nature in the eighteenth century, when authorities actually required tributaries to purchase foreign goods (the *repartimiento de efectos*), a measure designed to increase government revenues.[25]

In the utopian Indian Republic, the consumption of chicha was carefully controlled. Even though the alcoholic content in chicha is low, the colonizers believed the beverage led to drunken festivals during which a myriad of abuses were committed. Indeed, Spanish authorities probably preferred chicha's outright prohibition, but forced abstinence was simply unfeasible. The solution was state control of distribution of the drink. A house was to be assigned in each

Andenes and valley (photo by Greg Cook)

Yanque (photo by A. P. Cook)

village of the valley for storage of all locally produced chicha. The intent was to end bartering for the brew, which frequently ended in unnecessary and often explosive arguments. Alguaciles were to ensure the house was well guarded and anyone who refused to bring to the establishment all their chicha was to lose it. Worse, their large clay storage containers were to be broken. Local officials were authorized to find a person to record the amount of chicha delivered and the value of the containers. If a person refused to turn over the chicha the alguacil was authorized to confiscate it, with the official receiving half the proceeds and the village the other half. The chicha was to be closely guarded, and each person was able to draw out one *azumbre* (roughly half a gallon) daily. An individual could also purchase the corn beer, while the penniless poor could exchange corn for chicha, "by the ancient rule of a cup of chicha for a cup of maize." The kurakas, who always entertained guests, were allowed to have a pitcher (*cántaro*) at lunch and another at supper, but they had to pay as the rest of the villagers. Chicha was to be measured out to guests who were counted, with each receiving one azumbre. The alguacil and the chicha keeper were required to settle accounts each eight days, and to pay those who brewed the corn beer. Those responsible for collecting, storing, and dispensing the chicha were to receive one-eighth of the proceeds. That eighth was to be divided into three equal parts, with one going to the poor, one to the alguacil, and the final third to the accountant. Toledo suggested that in the future, it might be advantageous to set aside a lot in the village where the chicha for the entire community could be brewed. But presently, he noted, "it seems that with this decree we may remedy the damage that occurs with chicha. Although it is still made, the fact that it is in a depository makes its use less harmful, since the principal evil is in drinking it in their festivals without limit."[26]

Head binding continued among the Collagua and Cabana into the 1570s, in spite of regulations designed to end it. Toledo complained that children continued to die in the district as their heads were bound in conformity with traditional practices; he instructed priests, alcaldes, and kurakas to make special efforts to ensure the natives ended the custom. It was further noted that the Indians continued to give their children names in accordance with "their ancient rites and laws." The names commonly used included the moon, birds, animals, stones, serpents, and rivers. Now natives were to name their children after their father, mother, and grandparents (or ancestors). Both the kuraka and the priest were charged with ensuring this ordinance was obeyed.[27] Upon examination of kuraka names in the valley, one notes the persistence of native naming practices until after the civil wars of the conquerors, into the 1550s. It is only then, after twenty years of contact between Spaniards and the villagers of the Colca Valley, that first names begin to be those of Christian saints. Success of the clergy in this respect was slow, suggesting effective indoctrination in the valley did not occur until the early 1560s. Social control over native Americans in Toledo's ideal republic extended to children, who were taught to respect their elders. If children disobeyed their parents, then they might not show proper deference to village or imperial authorities. During the visita general the inspectors discovered instances in which children abused their fathers and mothers, and he heard that some slapped their parents and ill-treated them in other ways. Toledo vowed to eliminate such insolence, fearing that it threatened the social order. Any child who exhibited signs of such brazen disdain for parents was to be punished with 100 lashes, and the head was to be shaved.[28]

Several sections of Toledo's ordinances dealt with the issue of inheritance and were based on Spanish practice. The viceroy had been informed that in some cases when an Indian died, those who happened to be nearby took whatever they could lay their hands on, something that often left children without means of support. The viceroy therefore ordered alcaldes to ensure that if anyone fell ill, someone, if possible the parish priest or a colonial official, should be sent to prepare a will. A notary was to copy the will and compile an inventory of the estate. As in Spanish law minor children were assigned a tutor, or guardian. In Spain the male did not reach majority until the age of twenty-five, but in Andean America, in keeping with the age exigencies of the tribute system, the male upon reaching the age of eighteen was to inherit a share of the estate. Indian daughters received their portion of the estate at marriage. Indians who acted as guardians were to be individuals without direct interest; that is, not kurakas, principales, or notaries. The guardian could receive half of the tenth of the increase of the estate, including wool sheared from the livestock. Written or quipu accounts were to be carefully kept by the guardian. As in Spain legitimate children, with or without a will, would inherit the estate of their parents. If there were no children, the estate could go to other heirs named in the will, usually the nearest relatives. In theory at least, the poorest relatives were to receive the largest portion. A quarter of the estate was to be used to benefit the deceased's soul, in Masses or pious causes. To ensure compliance, Toledo provided a master form of the suitable testament. The village scribe needed only to fill in the blank spaces and witness it properly in order to complete the binding document.[29]

Traditional Andean forms of access to resources were recognized and protected in the system. Colonial censuses of the valley reveal that children, whether of the elite or commoners, had access to land and resources. For example, in the ayllu Calo of Maca on 25 January 1605, twelve-year-old Juan Tonco, son of Martín Checa, had "in Guaytoroca a half topo [see chapter 6 for details on this unit of land] of corn that borders with that of Don Cristóbal Chuqui Amque, in spite of the fact that it is listed with that of Don Francisco Condo, kuraka of this ayllu, because it belongs to this minor." Additionally the boy held "in Pallca, a half topo of corn. In Puncullo a quarter of corn, both fields were of the said his father. A house in this pueblo." Two orphaned brothers of the same ayllu, Juan Hapulla, age thirteen, and Juan Mayualla, age six, sons of Juan Hucha Cavana, had lands "in Cahavire, a half topo of corn, bordered with Don Cristóbal Chuqui Amque, and in Callcha, one topo of corn. Both fields belonged to their father." There was one orphan girl in the ayllu, "María Amancalla, daughter of Diego Yamque, aged eight, with a quarter of corn in Canllalli that was of her father." In spite of attempts to instill European marital norms, traditional Andean forms persisted for decades. In a list of the orphans of the Ayllu Curaca Collana of Caylloma, compiled on 13 and 14 October 1604, we discover "bastard brothers Marcos Guancallo, age seventeen, and Juan Chuqui Anque, eight, sons of Don Marcos Guancallo; they jointly hold eight head of camelids, five are for Marcos, and three for his younger brother." There were three orphans sharing land use. Another orphan was listed in the ayllu, eight-year-old Miguel Gualpa, grandson of Cristóbal Condori, who had four camelids.[30] In the examples of both ayllus, enough resources were allocated to the orphans to support them until they could become productive adults.

There was little debate among the Spanish on the need to "educate" newly conquered Amerindian peoples. While local settlers or colonial bureaucrats and miners might complain about the supposed inferiority of the colonial labor force, the Crown and Council of the Indies accepted the essential "humanity" of the subjected peoples and the imperative to teach them the basic fundamentals of Christian belief. Several early decrees promoted the education of Andean subjects. Charles V on 8 December 1535 commanded Peruvian encomenderos to ensure the education of sons of the native elite. Later the encomenderos were mandated to hire someone, preferably a clergyman, to undertake the task. In 1550 the Crown demanded that the religious orders active in the Andes fulfill royal decrees for education of the Amerindians. Community schools were established in the Colca Valley. Although some existed prior to Toledo's general inspection, the viceroy's decrees issued at Acos on 27 November 1570 set the format for the establishment of schools for young Indian males. Specifically referring to mission schools of the Franciscan Order, the viceroy stipulated that there be two teachers in each school. One of the educators was to ensure that the native boys learned to speak, read, and write Spanish. The other was to teach Indians to sing and play musical instruments, such as the flute. They were to educate children of all social groups, but especially those of the kurakas and of the more wealthy, who were expected to become community leaders. Orphans were to be instructed as well, using community funds for support. On Saturday and festivals, there were to be singing and music in the churches. Singers were exempted from personal service and the mita in 1570, and their tribute was to come from community funds. Their salary was twenty silver pesos, and they received one piece of *ropa de abasca* (common-quality alpaca textile), one *manta* (blanket), a *camiseta* (shirt), and twelve fanegas of maize. Their qualifications and stipends in the Arequipa district were modified: a ladino Indian (Hispanicized, one adept in both languages)—and "there are plenty of them in all parts"—was to be schoolmaster; the local cleric chose him. The salary was two abasca cloth *vestidos* (garments), six fanegas of maize or chuño, and twelve sheep per year, paid from community funds.[31]

As early as 1563 the Franciscan friars Hernando de Barrionuevo and Juan de Vega reported that there were schools for male Indian youth in their doctrinas. There young men were taught the "doctrine, to be assistants for the Mass and singers of the vespers, and players of musical instruments, the result of which," they noted, "is that the divine offices are more successful and the natives attend them with much pleasure, for they are great lovers of music." The Franciscans perhaps more than other orders in Peru regularly employed music and songs in conversion and indoctrination. And because there were insufficient Franciscans in the countryside, they elected to train and engage the Amerindians as much as possible, using *indios ladinos*, as sacristans and singers. Toledo allowed for these alternatives and exempted the specialists from tribute and mita service. In January 1593 Archbishop Toribio Mogrovejo wrote to the king requesting confirmation of the exemption that seemed essential for successful indoctrination.[32] A key to the success of the effort was the spread of Spanish, as a ladino Indian was the preferred instructor. In Toledo's republic young men were not expected to remain in school beyond the age of thirteen unless they were the sons of kurakas. Children of the poor did not attend school as long, but in all cases boys were to join their parents working in their family's agricultural plots after the day's classes. Girls were not schooled at all.[33]

Some schools in the Colca Valley fulfilled their initial role, especially in educating male youth of the local elite, and by 1585 six of ten kurakas were able to write. There are rare glimpses of how the school functioned on a daily basis in the villages on the river's edge. In 1604, Juan Colque, thirty-four, was exempt from paying tribute because he was a teacher in Coporaque. He was married to Clara Colla, twenty-four, and they lived in the urinsaya along with two sons, the seven-year-old illegitimate Juan Colque, and the four-year-old legitimate

Sebastián Colque. Yet efforts to maintain community schools in the villages of the valley were in the long term frustrated. In April 1635 Arequipa bishop Pedro de Villagómez offered to open his residences "for a school for the young boys of the caciques in order that they be nurtured with public order and good manners . . . , thus ending the barbarous customs of their elders."[34]

Indian hospitals in the provinces were directly influenced by the evolution of hospital care in the nearest Spanish urban center, Arequipa in this case. In late September 1552 Arequipa's cabildo concluded that they needed to found a hospital for "natives" and poor Spaniards. They entrusted three people, including the Collaguas encomenderos Juan de la Torre and Diego Hernández de la Cuba, to conduct a survey of potential building sites for a hospital. Fewer than five months later, in February 1553, Licentiate Marco Antonio, a "married and good man," was appointed the hospital's physician. The council authorized purchase of land from Juan de San Juan, and in August paid 1,500 pesos for structures that would be used for the first hospital. In January 1558 Arequipa's corregidor informed the monarch that the hospital for poor Spaniards and Indians had been endowed with rents from eleven properties, houses, and stores, located on the main plaza. Having established the hospital, cabildo members expressed frequent doubts about qualifications of the city's surgeons, barbers, pharmacists, and doctors. At its session of 26 January 1560, the cabildo ordered medical practitioners to present copies of their degree certificates within three days. The ruling was not continuously enforced, for three decades later, in December 1590, after a complaint from Miguel Morillo that "many people" were practicing in the city without examination, the cabildo issued a similar order.[35]

Construction of the Colca Valley hospitals was ordered at the time of Viceroy Toledo's reducciones. Normal financing for operation of the Indian hospital was provided by a special annual one tomín assessment per tributary. Village alcaldes were in charge of collecting money and depositing it in the hospital's treasury, where the majordomo could oversee the disbursement of funds on a daily basis. Other hospital revenues were generated from fines assessed for infractions of Toledo's Indian ordinances. Village alcaldes and regidores were required to regularly inspect the hospitals in the repartimiento and to guarantee their staffs were adequate. If any medications were missing from the inventories, they were to be replaced using community funds. The parish priest was also charged with ensuring the proper operation of the local hospital and the administration of the sacraments to the ill. Further, each settlement was to send two or three boys to apprentice with a barber in Arequipa. They were to be taught techniques for the correct setting of broken bones, and for bleeding, a common general remedy of the colonial era.[36]

Several hospitals were built and operated in the valley during the sixteenth century. During an epidemic in 1577, the kurakas of Yanque petitioned the viceroy for two surgeons or barbers. Hernán Pérez Moreno was named and was examined to ensure proper qualifications; he served in Yanque, Chivay, Coporaque, and Achoma. Martín Ortiz was assigned to the puna towns of Callalli, Tuti, Tisco, and Sibayo in the upper stretches of the valley. Each barber was to receive a stipend of 300 pesos, paid semiannually. Manuel de Carvajal was a valley surgeon in the early 1580s. Pérez Moreno may have practiced twenty years in the valley, because in September 1597 he asked the corregidor, Diego de Peralta Cabeza de Vaca, to increase his salary. He noted that the previous corregidor, Lucas de Cadabal, paid surgeon Fernando Cornejo a 400-peso stipend, and complained the land was "rugged and expensive." The corregidor replied that the stipend stipulated in the tribute assessment was 300 pesos. If the payment were to be modified, it could be done only with viceregal authorization.[37] Thermal springs in the middle Colca Valley were important for the cure of certain complaints in Inca times. Baths at Coporaque had been used by the Inca. The water was very hot according to contemporaries, and quite "healthful." The waters were reputedly beneficial for the treatment of ulcers and sores. In the 1580s Spaniards reported that people from all the province, and "even beyond," came to effect cures in the Coporaque thermal baths. The fame of the healing qualities of the waters continued. Friar Diego de Ocaña, who traveled through the Collaguas in 1603, wrote that "a very large river passes through this valley, and on its banks are some admirable baths. The water descends from the top of a mountain, and when it mixes with the river water, it becomes warm. It is very comforting to bathe there; the baths are very healthful, and there are always in these baths ill Indians who take the cure. A house was built there, on the riverbank, and all is very well kept."[38]

Europeans attempted to modify the social order of the Collaguas and the Cabanas. They imposed foreign customs and values on Andeans and taught them the Christian doctrine. According to the corregidor, Ulloa Mogollón, by 1586 the people of the valley learned easily and were generally compliant: "Their understanding is, for Indians, good, because in their doings they demonstrate reason and in what they learn they are successful, and for that reason there are good scribes and singers and musicians of flutes and oboes, and if they trained them in other more profound things they have the ability for it." The influence of the Franciscan friars and their efforts in educating the populace through music are evident in this assessment. Yet the corregidor's comments regarding the "inclinations" of the Colca Valley dwellers reflect the typical European stereotype of the native American: "They are commonly disposed to fiestas and banquets and amusements; in their own way they are affable and not especially greedy, and because of this, they are noted as lazy, timid people and of little use."[39]

Kurakas and Political Authority

The kuraka acted as a link between local inhabitants and the outside world, and following conquest the native elite played a key role in the process of the integration of the Indians of the Colca Valley into colonial Hispanic society (see table 6). Before European domination the kuraka — whose allegiance to the Inca was unconditional — was responsible for collecting products that were due the Cuzco elite, for organizing and directing the labor force for the construction of local tambos, terraces, irrigation systems, roads, bridges, storage facilities, palaces, and temples. He was expected to maintain local people loyal to the Inca overlords. Kurakas were also responsible for selection of warriors when necessary, and as Ulloa Mogollón reported, Colca Valley fighters served as far away as Quito and Charcas. In return for their support, the Inca bestowed special rights and privileges on the local elite. Kurakas were distinguished from the commoners by their rich clothing, multiple wives, use of personal retainers, access to silver and gold, and cumbi cloth. Houses of valley kurakas were larger than those of average families, with roofs of thicker ichu thatching. Sons of kurakas were sent to Cuzco for special training, and they were expected to participate later in broader imperial administration. Yet kurakas remained integrated into their communities; they were expected to share generously and to provide hospitality. They distributed llamas, coca, and other products to community members. They officiated over local festivities, and they administered justice.[40]

The privileges and the duties of the kurakas were sweeping, and it is likely that their authority was even more extensive under Spanish colonialism than in the Inca period. Kurakas and principales were major enforcers of social legislation. The kuraka was expected to provide an example for other members of the community to follow. He was to live as a good Christian, and his children were to be educated by the priest until the age of fifteen. Kurakas were to advise the doctrinero of all important events in the life of community members so he could baptize, confess, and ensure that the local ill entered the hospital. During the 1570s and 1580s much stress was placed on the proper education of the sons of kurakas as a means of Hispanicizing native Americans, and ultimately making them better Christians. Again the Spanish followed an Inca custom,

TABLE 6. Sixteenth-century kurakas of the Colca Valley

Year	Repartimiento	Kuraka	Encomendero
1535	Cabana	Ampire	Cristóbal Pérez
1535	Cabana	Yanquinicho	Cristóbal Pérez
1543	Cabana anansaya	Ichucaguana	Miguel de Vergara
1543	Cabana urinsaya	Tumalque	Juan de Arbes
1549	Cabana urinsaya	Cachacaguana (successor to Ayanquicha)	Juan de la Torre
1549	Cabana anansaya	Alacanabache and Alayaunquiche	Juana de Mercado
1558	Cabana anansaya	Luis Alacanauache	Diego Hernández
1562	Cabana anansaya	Luis Ala Canauache	Diego Hernández
1562	Cabana urinsaya	García Antiala	Juan de la Torre
1562	Lari urinsaya	Hernando Pacotinta (d.)	Rodríguez Picado
1562	Lari anansaya	Phelippe Ala	Marcos Retamoso
1562	Yanque Collaguas	Diego Ala	Crown
1563	Lari anansaya	Felipe Visara, Carlos Ala, Juan Arqui	Marcos Retamoso
1565	Cabana urinsaya	Juan Llanquicha and Juan Tulma	Juan de la Torre
1586	Cabana urinsaya	Francisco Anti Ala, Juan Ala, Pedro Ancas Cabana	Hernando de la Torre
1586	Cabana anansaya	Luis Ala, Miguel Canauache, Diego Ala	Diego Hernández de la Cuba
1586	Lari urinsaya	Cristóbal Cusi, Marcos Guancallo, Diego Vaanqui	Alonso Rodríguez Picado
1586	Lari anansaya	Juan Caquia, Felipe Alpaca, Juan Arqui	Francisco Hernández Retamoso
1586	Collaguas urinsaya	García Checa, Francisco Chacha, Francisco Ingapacta	Crown
1586	Collaguas anansaya	Juan Halanoca, Miguel Nina Taipe	Crown

Source: From various chapters and notes within this book

sending the sons of kurakas to special schools, which were established in major provincial cities. There was an important school for kuraka children in Lima in the district of El Cercado under the control of the Jesuits, the most effective educators of the colonial era. There was another in Cuzco, also with Jesuit teachers.

Yet high expectations of educators in the 1570s led to frustration a half century later. The Cuzco bishop Fernando de Vera wrote the king in February 1635, lamenting that native villages were being destroyed because of bad kurakas. He complained that the sons of kurakas did not learn the Christian doctrine supposedly taught by the Jesuits but instead "evils, sins, and all," he added, "leave as ladinos." According to the bishop, they returned to their communities following their years of study acting as "demons." The young future leaders dressed in fine silks as rich Spaniards, they refused to work, they took from commoners what they had, and they were closely allied with corregidores and clerics. Bishop Vera concluded that the best solution would be to close the schools and "use the money for something more useful."[41]

The schools did succeed in acculturating the sons of kurakas, although not as intended. Andean villagers entered Indians, and exited as "ladinos," Hispanicized. To the chagrin of Bishop Vera, the Spaniards the native elite emulated were not of high moral character. The sons of kurakas became culturally Spanish, losing many of their ties to their communities. Under the Inca, sons of kurakas returned to their homes, remaining culturally Collaguas and Cabanas. The Inca often made sure they married daughters of the Cuzco or provincial elite elsewhere, thus cementing a bond between Inca and local ethnic units. But in the colonial Spanish regime there was a major difference; the sons rarely married daughters of the conquistadores. They returned instead as sycophants of colonial bureaucrats. A gradual shift was under way that ultimately placed many kurakas in the camp of the foreign overlords, separating them from their village relatives. This process continued until the native base of the kurakas' power was eroded to the point where they were no longer respected by their subjects. At this juncture they faced the choice of whether to continue as Spaniards or return to their native roots. The culmination of the process was reached in the eighteenth century, and it resulted in rebellion.

The kurakas' dilemma in the Colca Valley and elsewhere lies in their role of being the ones largely responsible for the collection of tribute for their Spanish overlords. Under the new regime implanted on Andean peoples, as finalized by Toledo, almost all males between the ages of eighteen and fifty paid tribute and provided some kind of service during the course of the year. Viceroy Toledo ordered that if a male were not married at the age of eighteen, the age when he reached tributary status, he had to pay one-half until the age of twenty, at which time he paid the full quota, even if unmarried. If anyone was omitted in a population census, the corregidor was to be notified and the person making the denunciation was to receive the personal service of the uncounted individual for life. If the person were so sick that it was impossible to pay tribute, then the money was to be paid from the community chest. If men occasionally worked as free wage-laborers, they still were required to contribute, and they were not exempt from personal service. Under the Inca regime, tribute assessment was by ayllu and saya. In the new system, the tax was to be based on the actual number of Indians. Corregidores supposedly made adjustments when necessary to ensure that the tribute was roughly related to the local natural resource base. If there were substantial inequities in the land available for certain tributaries, then the corregidores were authorized to redistribute land to achieve a new balance.[42]

Tribute was of key importance to the Spaniards, and the kuraka was charged with gathering it from repartimiento Indians, then transferring it to colonial officials on mandated payment dates. The kuraka collected both cash and commodities and made certain cash was deposited in the community treasury. Toledo noted that there were many relatives and sons of kurakas who did not contribute, yet they were usually the most wealthy in the community and could easily afford to pay. Several Collaguas kurakas held land in the towns on the edge of Arequipa, and at least one had holdings in the parish of Santa Marta within the city. Several Colca Valley kurakas maintained extensive commercial contacts with Arequipa merchants. Toledo ordered inspectors to ascertain which local chiefs might be superfluous. The sons of kurakas and their legitimate brothers were freed from personal service in the tambos and plazas, and from construction of roads and bridges, but they were required to pay tribute. Only the oldest son of the kuraka, designated to succeed his father, was exempt.[43]

Toledo prohibited kurakas from collecting anything directly from women, a sign of frequent abuses. Women were prohibited from spinning wool or providing personal service for the kuraka's household. Nor could women who married outside their ayllu be charged for tribute by their native ayllu, since the male's residence was the key element in tribute. If a kuraka attempted to collect tribute from local women or from old or infirm men, he could lose his office for four years. Despite having the power to collect tribute, the kuraka was unable to unilaterally make distributions under the pretext of paying tribute. If it were necessary to make some form of division for the good of the community, it was to be done by the village council, and the alcalde and regidores were required to agree to the proposal. Alcaldes and kurakas had limited authority to choose Indians to work on public projects, such as roads, churches, and tambos, or to plant and cultivate village fields or guard community livestock. The distribution of workers for these activities was to be made on an equal basis, by saya and ayllu.[44]

The kuraka shared power in overseeing tambos within his jurisdiction. He was to prohibit boys from serving in tambos unless they were at least seventeen, for inspectors discovered that younger boys were often hurt or became ill during tambo service. Further, the kuraka had to certify that the Indians who worked in the inns were trustworthy. The legislation suggests that in the past many were trying to improve their economic position by theft. Native pack drivers, for example, who were stationed in the tambos reportedly took goods of travelers, leaving them stranded on the road. Kurakas had many other responsibilities. They were to make sure the Indians worked hard, and they could assist in organization of cooperative labor projects. But they could not enter into contracts with individual Spaniards without the corregidor's approval, because of possible harm to commoners. Kurakas were to force the yanaconas to pay full tribute and assist in service. They were held responsible for tracing Indians who had moved to other doctrinas. Neither the kuraka nor other Indians were allowed to have black slaves, because "of the harm they did to the natives." Kurakas could not assist in building new monasteries without viceregal authorization. Toledo stated that if friars ordered kurakas to help supply a labor force, the kurakas should take special care not to assist. In some districts, early doctrineros had access to a substantial unauthorized Indian labor force.[45]

During the visita general, the viceroy discovered that it was customary in many parts of the Andean world for kurakas and principales to provide banquets and give presents to Spaniards. The cost of such extravagance was high, and kurakas often confiscated community goods to help pay for the festivities. Toledo ordered tributaries excused from defraying the costs of such gifts and fiestas, and he required the corregidor and priest to ensure the ordinances were enforced. It was also noted that in some locales, sons replaced their elder fathers as kuraka and principal, and at times sons failed to care for their parents. Toledo therefore ordered kurakas to retain half their estate and not transfer it to their children while they were still alive.[46] Several Toledo ordinances limited the display of the kuraka's prestige. The kuraka was forbidden to travel by litter, unless he were ill; nor could he travel on horseback without special permission of the viceroy. When kurakas made trips, they were ordered not to journey with more service Indians than necessary to carry out their business. They were admonished not to bring along "suspicious women." If the kuraka traveled to a Spanish city to pursue a lawsuit, he could only be accompanied by two Indians. The kuraka was to provide a stipend for his assistants if the suit involved him alone. But if the legal question were a community matter, expenses were to be paid from the village fund. If kurakas used Indians as messengers, they too were to be paid for their services.[47]

Toledo especially wanted to limit some of the traditional sexual prerogatives that he believed kurakas commanded. They were ordered not to impede the marriage of widows and young unmarried women, because many had in the past enjoyed "the services of females for their own lewdness." Further, it was expressly forbidden for kurakas and principales to round up young women and lock them up for their own pleasure. Young women were admonished to remain in their own homes. If the local elite persisted, the penalty was severe. An official who broke the regulations three times lost his position. Yanaconas, or other Indians who assisted the kuraka in abuse of women, were fined 50 lashes for the first offense. Repetition resulted in 100 lashes, and the head was to be shaved and the guilty party exiled for a year.[48]

Much energy, that sometimes led to arguments and fights, was spent on the issue of succession to the kurakazgo. Preconquest succession varied; in some places, the first son became the new kuraka. Elsewhere it was the most able son. In others, when the father died the first son became kuraka, then the second, third, and so forth until all the brothers had taken a turn. Then succession fell to the first child of the first son, continuing in that fashion. The Spanish were confused by mixed rules of inheritance and attempted to institute European primogeniture as rapidly as possible. In so doing they hoped to avoid lawsuits between contenders for the kurakazgo, a subject that too quickly plagued colonial courts. Natives who profited most in an arrangement of direct succession from father to eldest son immediately supported the European tradition. One manifestation of the shift was the adoption of the Spanish naming system by the kurakas, who alone of the native peoples of the Colca Valley consistently used the family name. Indeed, they adopted the Spanish custom at the end of the first generation after the Europeans arrived. The European tradition of naming did not extend to the principales. For example, in the inspection of the ayllu Pahana Taypi Pataca of Coporaque urinsaya in October 1604, the principal Don Mateo de Aguila had three sons: Francisco Guayua Pidco, who was then ten; Pedro Condor Caquia, five; and his illegitimate fifteen-year-old with the same name as the second legitimate son, Pedro Condor Caquia.[49]

There were challenges against the establishment of primogeniture in the Collaguas area, just as elsewhere in the Andes under the new order. Ulloa Mogollón reported that among the Collagua prior to the Spanish, it was customary for the kurakazgo to pass from the current kuraka to his legitimate brother, even if a legitimate son were available. Viceroy Toledo in the 1570s noted that in the Inca system, "when one of the kurakas died, the Inca, who had been the person who had given the kurakazgo, and invested the kurakazgos, did not give them to the eldest sons of kurakas, but to the most capable person, or to other Indians chosen from among his relatives or others of ability and sufficiency." Toledo, dedicated to fostering rapid conversion, made certain that only the most able and Christian sons of the kuraka could receive the kurakazgo, "if of sufficient age, and if not . . . the brothers and relatives and other Indians." If this strategy were used, Toledo believed that kurakas would train their children to be examples of Christian virtue. If kurakas failed to search out idolatries and witchcraft and eradicate them, they could lose their positions. During the visita general Toledo ordered commissioners to determine who the kurakas had been in each district under the Incas, and who their children were, and if they were good Christians and likely candidates for future service.[50]

When the question of succession was tested as it was in the Colca Valley, Viceroy Toledo modified his position, permitting local custom to prevail:

In the visita general ordered by me for the province of Los Collaguas . . . , the cacique principal who was named for the Indians of Yanque Collaguas . . . , was Don Diego Guana Ala, who, I am now informed by corregidor Jusepe de Villalobos, is dead, and he left an illegitimate son and also a brother, both of whom now claim to be kuraka. . . . The said corregidor has sent me certain information made at the request of Don Francisco Ala, the illegitimate son, and with it a request that I name one of the two, the one which seems most qualified to be cacique principal . . . , that he can govern, and the suits and differences among the Indians will come to an end. Keeping in mind the factors of ability and sufficiency of Juan Alanoca, brother of the . . . [kuraka, and who] at the present governs . . . , that he is such a person and that during the time that he has used the said position and post he has done it with great rectitude, diligence, and care. . . . From here onward he continues in the post and in accordance I name him cacique principal of the said pueblo of Yanque Collagua . . . , as was the said Don Diego Guana Ala, deceased brother, and other caciques, his predecessors, and as such I give him the investiture of the said kurakazgo principal in order that he and no other Indian can use it, from the date of this my provision onwards, for all the days of his life.[51]

In this instance Viceroy Toledo respected the Inca custom in the Colca Valley of appointing the brother of the dead kuraka. But he may have done this because of the illegitimacy of Diego Guana Ala's son and claimant to the kurakazgo. In 1604, in Coporaque urinsaya, ayllu Pahana Cayao Pataca, we find another example in which it seems that an illegitimate son faced difficulties in becoming a principal. Here Don Pedro Nina, the natural son of Don Felipe Cavan Supo, aged twenty-eight, was listed as a principal. He was married with two children. But Don Martin Nina, aged forty, was the acting *mandón* of the ayllu.[52]

Viceroy Toledo stipulated that the position should in no way be construed as hereditary, that neither the kuraka's children nor heirs had any claim on the position. After the appointee's death, Crown officials reserved the right to appoint a successor, choosing the most able and Christian of the candidates. Toledo wanted to ensure only the highest power could appoint kurakas and that encomenderos and ecclesiastical officials had no legal authority to name them. At the time of a kuraka's death a list of his sons was to be made, with a description of the qualities of each. The names and qualifications of anyone else in the province capable and inclined to be kuraka was to be provided. The sealed list was to be sent to the viceroy, with the alcalde exercising the position temporarily until the viceroy's choice was made public. Toledo made his decision regarding the issue of succession in the Collaguas while still in Lima (23 June 1580), shortly before initiating his return voyage to Spain.[53]

By 1591 Juan Alanoca was dead, and Francisco Ala, the illegitimate son of Diego Guana Ala, was again attempting to be installed as kuraka of Yanque Collaguas anansaya. Francisco Ala was supported in his quest by most of the other leaders in the valley. Agustín Cassa, Pedro Caquia, Alonso Arochura, Miguel Horuro, Pedro Ancha, Bartolomé Cassa, Miguel de Sotomayor, and "many other principales of this province" presented a petition to authorities requesting that Francisco Ala be named. It was endorsed by "the *segundas personas* [secondary leaders] and principales of the pachacas of this pueblo of Yanque of the Royal Crown, and the other villages subject to it." They all attested to Francisco Ala's strong and Christian character and pledged him their support. On 1 December 1591, the corregidor, Gaspar de Colmenares, agreed to name Francisco Ala kuraka with the condition that he secure viceregal confirmation within a year. The same day "at the doors of the house of his residence" and in the presence of the kurakas and segundas personas, and many others, the oath of office was administered. Francisco Ala publicly promised to diligently collect the tribute, guard the ordinances, see to the propagation of Christianity, end idolatries and the drunken festivals of old, and be a "good example" of Christian living for the other members of the community.[54] In Yanque's lower half, the urinsaya, in 1591 the real authority was exercised by an uncle of a child kuraka: Don Francisco Ingapacta acted for the nine-year-old kuraka principal, Jusepe

Ingapacta. Don Francisco maintained his power for several years. In the inspection of Yanque urinsaya in 1617, then sixty-two-year-old Francisco Ingapacta continued acting as chief of the lower half of Yanque Collaguas.[55] Disputes over succession in the Colca Valley continued because the rewards of office were substantial, and kurakas found it difficult to establish and maintain a line of succession, in part because of a continually shrinking population base. Later, Don Francisco Bautista Ala succeeded in the kurakazgo of Cabanaconde urinsaya "by having married Doña María Churumama, daughter of the said cacique, and there did not remain [after that] another male heir of the said Don Francisco Ala."[56]

CHAPTER SIX

TRIBUTE AND THE DOMESTIC ECONOMY

> House. Martín Anco, 27 years old
> María Carua, his wife, 24 years old
> Bernaue Achira, his son of seven
> Pedro Ancotani, 2 years old
> in Vilchocata a quarter topo of maize
> in Cocatire a quarter topo of maize
> in Apopampa a quarter topo of quinua
> in Cayra a half topo of maize next to
>   the royal road
> in Chapichapi a quarter topo of quinua
> in Compoyo a quarter topo of quinua
> in Catuavi another quarter topo of quinua
> in Tanapata a quarter topo
> one *oveja de la tierra* [llama or alpaca]
> —Census of Coporaque urinsaya, Collana
> ayllu, 13 August 1591, Pease, *Collaguas I*, 347.

Tribute and Tributaries

Native American tribute and labor were the foundation stones that supported the colonial empire the Spanish established in the Andean world. Of course precious metals were exploited. The conquistadors discovered and stole enormous caches of gold and silver in Cajamarca, Jauja, and Cuzco. But most of the initial treasure, including Atahualpa's ransom, was quickly exported to Europe. The tedious and dangerous mining work then had to be organized and implemented. Mineral production was volatile, expanding and collapsing with the richness of the ores and the technological level of exploitation. Unlike mining production, for which output was limited, tribute could be increased by raising assessments, even when the population was falling.[1] In the Andes the tribute system evolved rapidly in the first years, with one formulation at the time of the first Pizarro grants, a restricted system under the New Laws, a modified institution following the La Gasca reforms, and finally the structure implanted by Francisco de Toledo. The mature "República de los Indios" of Toledo curtailed further evolution of the tribute system in the Andes for several decades, and it remained much as it was in the 1570s well into the next century.

A remarkable shift—from a long list of tribute goods mandated under the La Gasca regime—to a very limited one (see table 7), began even before Viceroy Toledo's arrival. Comparison of various assessment lists for the repartimiento of Yanque Collaguas illustrates the magnitude of this development. The encomendero of the 1540s and '50s was a virtual lord; his tributaries provided a myriad of goods and services, and what the encomendero did not sell, he consumed. They brought him numerous tribute items, from candle wax to game birds for his dining table in Arequipa. Tributaries tilled his fields, guarded his livestock, and transported his goods, and Indian women turned his bedcovers. The encomendero often rented services of his Indians to other Europeans. The native workers were required to produce, in addition to the American agricultural products, European ones, such as pigs, sheep, or wheat. These foreign products were just one element of a broader process of ecological change precipitated in the Andes following arrival of the Europeans.

The Toledo tribute regime was based on existing structures, but the viceroy did modify it as he had modified the corregimiento system. Already, in 1559, the Marqués de Cañete had authorized commutation, a cash replacement for tribute goods, of many of the articles for the nearby repartimientos of Ubinas and Majes. That assessment was not far different from the one Toledo used just over a decade later in the Colca Valley and elsewhere in the viceroyalty. García de Castro's corregimiento system had eliminated any vestiges of political control the encomenderos exercised over the natives, and had transferred them to short-tenured bureaucrats. The Toledo tributary assessment stripped economic control from the encomendero class. The corregidor, with the assistance of kurakas, collected tribute; they paid doctrineros and even the encomendero. And in Yanque Collaguas, instead of the dozens of items on the La Gasca assessment, there were only three: silver, cloth, and indigenous livestock (llamas and alpacas).[2]

During the first decades under Spanish domination the Cabana and Collagua tributary was roughly equivalent to the Inca runa: the adult, male, married

TABLE 7. La Gasca, Toledo, and Esquilache tribute assessments for Yanque Collaguas

La Gasca (1549)	Toledo (1572)		Esquilache (1618)	
ANANSAYA AND URINSAYA	ANANSAYA		ANANSAYA AND URINSAYA	
400 pieces of cumbi cloth	Silver:	4,962 pesos	Silver:	4,741 pesos,
100 pieces of abasca cloth	2,000 pieces			5 granos
400 fanegas of corn	of abasca		2,380 pieces	
100 fanegas of wheat	cloth:	5,000 pesos	of abasca	
300 fanegas of potatoes,	481 llamas:	1,202.5 pesos	cloth:	5,950 pesos
chuño, oca			561 llamas:	1,427.5 pesos
123 sheep				
27 lambs	URINSAYA			
120 llamas and alpacas,				
for transport	Silver:	3,030 pesos		
30 pigs (or 20 sheep)	1,220 pieces			
150 fowl	of abasca			
144 pairs of partridge	cloth:	3,050 pesos		
72 cargas of salt	295 llamas:	737.5 pesos		
8 arrobas of candle wax				
100 pairs of shoes; various	*Toledo total:*	*17,982 pesos*	*Esquilache*	*12,118 pesos,*
mixed items, including			*total:*	*4 tomines,*
harnesses, saddle cloth				*5 granos*

Labor:
25 men and women for
household service
15 to serve guarding livestock
8 fanegas of wheat and corn
to be planted and har-
vested in encomendero's
urban fields
12 fanegas of wheat and
corn to be planted and
harvested in native fields
in Guaca or Lluta Valleys

Source: RAH, no. 9-4664; AGI, Contaduría 1786, 1822; Justicia 448; BNL, B 115

head of household, living within the ayllu. Toledo simplified the system, basing it on contributions of the male population, using a chronological age group of eighteen to fifty. As in Inca times, kurakas, principales, and elder males as well as the infirm were exempt. It is difficult to judge the exact number withdrawn from tribute by illness or infirmity. In the ayllu of Coporaque urinsaya Pahana Taypi Pataca in 1604, there was a 40-year-old exempt because he was crippled, a 38-year-old with a broken leg, a 30-year-old with a heart problem. There were thirty-seven in the ayllu of tribute age. The principal was exempt, as was the native schoolteacher; both were listed in the census in the "tributary" section. The three "infirm" within the same age category were on the list of "viejos and impedidos." But the same census inspector included the ill with the tributaries in the next ayllu. A hospital levy was part of the tribute load. It was one tomín per tributary, a uniform assessment throughout the Andean world, in contrast to the tribute rate, which could vary from one repartimiento to another, based on the assumed capacity to contribute.[3]

Of the five administrative units in the valley, the repartimiento Yanque Collaguas provided the highest revenues for the Crown, with a direct silver payment of almost 8,000 pesos, plus goods. The goods paid in tribute included over 3,000 pieces of abasca cloth, a major product in the colonial economy, marketable in Lima and the mining centers and exportable to Chile and beyond. There were two types of woolens: cumbi and abasca. Cumbi was tightly woven from the finest wool, with elaborate designs, and was highly prized. The abasca was common cloth, and provided the normal worker's garb. Although designs and colors might vary, the cloth normally "consisted of straight panels that when shorter and narrower were turned into breechclouts and sleeveless shirts for men, and when longer and wider were wrapped around the body and pinned for women." Adding almost 800 llamas, the value of the annual tribute totaled 17,982 pesos, and after deducting administrative costs the Royal Treasury received 10,537 pesos.[4] Kurakas collected tribute and turned it over to the corregidor biannually: Christmas (Navidad) and the day of St. John the Baptist, 24 June. Local treasury books are filled with entries such as the following: "Item. We have taken charge of 970 assayed pesos in reales of 12½ reales per peso that were received from the Collaguas of Your Majesty on 7 August 1583, for the 388 llamas and alpacas for six months beginning on Saint John's Day of 1583 at a rate of 2 pesos 4 tomines for each animal, in conformity with the assessment found on page 141."[5]

The ecological unity of Yanque and the two Lari Collaguas repartimientos of the middle valley can be seen in the tribute quotas set by Toledo. Tribute for Lari was in silver, abasca cloth, and llamas and alpacas. In the lower valley, with its warmer climate, the tributaries of Cabana contributed cotton cloth, corn and wheat, and chickens. Juan de la Torre's tributaries must have had some access to puna resources as well, for a small number of llamas were demanded. No camelids were paid by the Cabana half that was controlled by Hernández De la Cuba; those tributaries supplied cotton cloth and chickens. The tributaries of De la Torre did not; again the tribute suggests access to low-elevation fields in De la Cuba's grant. Both Cabana encomenderos received part of their tribute in gold, which was not true for the repartimientos of Lari and Yanque in the middle and upper valleys. Among the Collaguas Indians reduced in La Chimba of Arequipa, a silver payment was demanded but no highland products. Similar to the repartimientos of Retamoso and Picado, tributaries planted, cultivated, and harvested a field of corn and wheat. In the singular example of the Cabana Indians of De la Torre settled in the valley of Camaná, we note the coastal environment: tribute was furnished only in cotton cloth and dried sea fish, plus some silver.[6]

In 1559 the Viceroy Marqués de Cañete ordered the Arequipa corregidor, Alonso Manuel de Anaya, to allow commutation of tribute. He argued that some of the lesser items of the tribute assessments of La Gasca and the Royal Audiencia required much work to produce and that it would be better to "take gold and silver from the mines many have." With the commutation agreement, the Indians were to assume the costs of doctrina directly. In theory no tithes (diezmos) were required from tributaries; the kurakas were ordered to donate directly to the church monthly two fanegas of maize, two fanegas of wheat, and one ewe. Every four months, tributaries were to give one pig and one carga of salt and firewood to the local church. In addition, they were to deliver eight sheep weekly (divided equally, males and females), and each religious holiday a dozen eggs and some fish. They were to refrain from giving chicha. Stipends of doctrineros were paid directly from the local office of the Royal Treasury.[7] The goods that the Cabanas and Collaguas were required to contribute were assessed at a monetary figure that frequently had little relationship to true market values. When market prices rose above assessed figures, astute villagers often attempted to sell the goods themselves and substitute a monetary payment. In June 1584 tributaries gave 970 silver pesos instead of llamas, "because they did not bring in the articles as customary for the said period, day, month, and year." Valley tributaries were quick to learn the European-imposed system and were adept at using it to their advantage whenever they could, just as they manipulated the colonial legal system to protect their rights.[8]

Colonial bureaucrats were often reluctant to accept commutation, because they faced loss of substantial supplementary income. For example abasca cloth assessed at 2½ pesos was sold by treasury officials to Juan de Salazar, for the six-month payment period ending Christmas 1583, for 3 pesos, 7 tomines. In the June 1584 payment, the cloth was purchased by Antonio de la Cuba at 3 pesos, 4 tomines per piece. The following Christmas payment, the Collaguas cloth was sold to Antonio de Oviedo for 3 pesos. The June 1585 payment was acquired by Antonio Hernández at 3 pesos, 3 tomines. The same figure applied for the following Christmas payment. The June 1586 sale went to Francisco de Almonte at 3 pesos, 7 tomines. In 1591, the sale price was about 3 pesos, 1 tomín per piece. The "wholesale" price of abasca cloth constantly fluctuated, but at levels substantially higher than the set tribute assessment of 2½ pesos. The "retail" price was even higher than the wholesale. The cloth was often transported to mining centers and sold at inflated prices. Market conditions varied but given the profits to be made, both Crown officials and private merchants preferred payments in kind rather than cash commutation.[9]

Tribute payment in cash rather than in goods was strongly resisted by those who stood to profit most by the system. The passion of their arguments is highlighted in a memorial to the viceroy composed by Luis de Peralta, Arequipa's general solicitor, in the name of the city council. He complained bitterly that "because of the commutation to silver instead of contributing in kind, much hunger has resulted, and there is a lack of common necessities of the realm, particularly in the city of Arequipa, because by freeing the Indians from paying their tax in kind, they do not plant or grow, or work more than only enough to earn the tribute money. . . . From this are born idolatries, drunkenness and incest, which are so carnal that neither mothers nor sisters are spared, and the Republic suffers." Viceroy Luis de Velasco was persuaded by this petition, and he issued an order in May 1597 for the Indians to pay as fixed in the assessment. If the corregidor allowed commutation, he had to provide a full explanation.[10]

The precious metals gold and silver, so frequently included in tribute assessments, have puzzled many because the source for the monetary payment is unspecified. Clearly some tributaries worked for wages; others sold products in the market to secure cash to cover the assessment. In the case of the Colca Valley, local deposits of silver ore and gold nuggets or dust were regularly exploited at the household level. Treasury records of the 1580s provide evidence that valley tributaries diligently searched for silver deposits as well as concentrations of gold. In 1586 Gabriel Ala of Yanque Collaguas delivered worked silver weighing 3 marks, 3 ounces to be assayed (the mark was 230 grams). The monetary value was 7,593 *maravedíes* (the peso at the time was worth 450 maravedíes), minus assay costs. Juan Ala deposited 1 mark, 100 ounces, worth 3,656 maravedíes. In February 1586 Felipe Yaure tendered 5 marks, 2 ounces, which converted to 11,812 maravedíes. Don Diego Chacha and Juan Poma deposited 10 marks, 6 ounces. Diego Chapi converted 7 marks, 5 ounces, and in April 1586, Pedro Chicha gave 9 marks, 2 ounces. Don Francisco Ingapacta presented 7 marks; Don Diego Chuquianco 5 marks. One of the largest assays from Yanque Collaguas was made by Don Juan Alanoca on 27 April 1586: 20 marks, 2 ounces, which converted to 45,562 maravedíes. In all cases the marking fee was 1 percent (456 maravedíes in this case), then the diezmo was subtracted from the remainder (it would equal 4,510 maravedíes in this example). Colca Valley women also brought in precious metals to be assayed and marked. Ynés Vilca presented 2 marks, 3 ounces. According to Royal Treasury data, at times substantial amounts of precious metals were tendered by Cabana tributaries lower in the valley. In 1586 the Cabana kuraka Don Francisco Antiala gave 57 marks, 7 ounces of worked silver worth 129,818 maravedíes, and 198 pesos of gold, the latter of which was converted to 111,375 maravedíes.[11]

The tribute system proved profitable for those willing to exploit native American contributors. Juan de Ulloa Mogollón, the Los Collaguas corregidor for five to six years, was charged with illegally extracting 30,000 pesos. Several of his critics denounced him during his residencia, detailing how at one time he had suggested to the kurakas that they collect directly from tributaries the livestock required in tribute. He pointed out that they could then sell the animals in the Arequipa market for 5½ pesos per head, sometimes even 6 or 7. Many in the valley collaborated in this scheme. The mestizo Gonzalo de Buitrón, who had been in the Colca Valley from about 1574, and Hernando Alonso de Badajoz, who lived in the corregidor's house, participated in the venture. In one of the most notorious cases, the kuraka Francisco Maqui took Indian herders and llamas to distant Potosí and sold the animals. Other witnesses detailed how Ulloa Mogollón illegally sold 400 fanegas of corn from native community lands to his friend Hernando Alonso de Badajoz. He then transported the corn to Carabaya, a rich gold-mining area on the eastern slopes of the Andes, where he sold it for 5 pesos per fanega. In another instance, with the complicity of the corregidor, Ulloa Mogollón, Hernando de Badajoz used Collaguas Indians to transport wine from coastal vineyards to the Canas province, and even as far away as Cuzco.[12]

Colonial officials profited handsomely during the sale of tribute goods, and their methods were mostly illegal. The Arequipa Royal Treasury agent Sebastián de Mosquera, who served in the 1590s, faced several accusations at his residencia. Finding ample cause, the Royal Audiencia appointed Doctor Chacón to investigate the case, and the judgments were issued in Lima in 1598. During his term Mosquera sold at public auction Collaguas cloth to the merchant Pedro de Vera, and allowed the merchant to pay at a future date, rather than paying in cash. It was revealed that another merchant, Hernando de Argomedo, would have immediately paid the Crown cash for the cloth. Mosquera sold the goods to Pedro de Vera and for this favor received a kickback of one tomín for each piece of cloth.[13]

In spite of the onerous character of the tribute regime, native Americans resisted in a thousand small ways. They delayed payment of tribute, they fled, and they subverted the system by providing inferior tribute goods. They might obey the precepts but provide a minimal product. *Mitayo* (one who does mita service) labor, in spite of the clamor of settlers for workers, was notoriously inefficient. Forced work never generates maximum productivity. It is no wonder the Spanish characterized the Indians as "lazy," just as slave owners in the antebellum South of the United States described their plantation laborers. Tributaries in the adjoining repartimientos of the Majes and Ubinas provinces provide several examples of resistance. Pedro de Puerta, a tribute collector of the repartimiento of Ubinas from July 1566 to June 1570, complained of the quality of tribute goods: "The said cloth is of the meanest kind, and is of lesser price and value than any other of Arequipa. In effect it is and has been because the Indians make them with vicuña wool, rough and coarse. That of cotton is also coarse and poorly made, and the *lliquillas* [small square cloth for carrying goods, or infants, on one's back; see figure 40] of both are small, 3/4 of a vara in length, as half lliquillas." Today, vicuña is considered as providing some of the world's finest wool. Yet oddly, this sixteenth-century Spaniard complained about its coarseness! Pedro de Puerta lamented that the wheat Ubinas tributaries paid is "sierra wheat, small and dark, and not as good as the rest of the wheat that there is in . . . Arequipa." Chili peppers were likewise of poor quality, charged the frustrated corregidor. Especially revealing are his comments about hens: "They are small and skinny birds taken down from the sierra, and the Indians are accustomed to giving the worst that they have." The complaints about the Majes are similar: "The Indians generally are accustomed to giving the worst they can find, some are old and skinny, others small hens and cocks, and those of the sierra have little value." Coca leaves from the Majes repartimientos, charged Pedro de Puerta, were "coquilla of a small and yellow leaf, similar to the valleys of Lima and the others of the yunga [coastal lowlands], . . . nothing like those of Cuzco, . . . and the *cestos* (baskets) are so mean and bad that they give in tribute, they. . . . are small, light, and have little coca." Later, in 1573, Puerta complained that he was trying to force nearby Ubinas tributaries to pay him "quickly" the 160 pesos they owed. Delayed tribute payment, or contribution of inferior goods, was effectively used by Ubinas, Collaguas, and Cabanas tributaries to subvert the colonial system.[14]

Control over and access to labor and goods of the Colca Valley during Inca rule were tempered, and functioned within the Andean framework of reciprocity. The outflow was minimal, and there was compensation in the form of access to power within the Inca bureaucratic structure. In the Spanish colonial system, in contrast, the outflow of labor and goods was incessant, and the quantities demanded were far in excess of what had been required under the Incas. The storehouses, or q'olqas, were emptied to help fill the insatiable demands of both individual Europeans and of state policy that was more concerned with foreign affairs than with the welfare of the native American. Passive resistance to the foreign masters was effective and ultimately less costly than outright rebellion, which usually carried disastrous consequences for the Andeans. Furthermore, in the Colca Valley as elsewhere Andean people quickly learned to use the colonial administrative and judicial system to their advantage, which afforded some protection against the most burdensome abuses.[15]

Farming and Land

There was a vast difference between the views of native Americans and Europeans regarding access to and control of land resources. Spaniards, first along the coast, then in the highlands, attempted to amass estates, putting together *chacras* (small fields) into minor *ranchos* then into large haciendas with clearly defined boundaries. The concentration of European-controlled land in Peru has been studied by several scholars. From the Andean perspective land was a resource for community crop production, and variety was a key to the Amerindian's subsistence strategy, where a single large farm of solely quinua would have been unthinkable. Small plots of various types of agricultural products scattered in different ecological zones were the ideal.[16] Andean land measurements during the sixteenth century were imprecise. The visitadores who inspected the region and compiled complete reports on resources speak of "*topos, patas, andenes,* and even *un pedacillo* (small piece) of land. The pata, according to González Holguín, refers to an *andén*, or terrace, and the size is variable; whereas the *tupu* (topo) is a measure of land. John Murra argues that the topo referred most appropriately to cultivable land capable of providing the minimal needs of a couple. In the Colca Valley the topo is a plot of land, associated with a defined terraced and usually irrigated surface. Each topo was unique. Each had its name or "address"; its own particular characteristics of soil, humidity, and sun exposure that were intimately known by the people who worked it as well as by the other members of the community. The average modern topo in the valley has a surface of 3,496 square meters, or slightly more than one-third hectare.[17]

Spaniards initially believed that vast tracts of land in the Andes were vacant. But much of this uncultivated soil was in reality resting, lying fallow, according to an Andean concept that Felipe Guaman Poma de Ayala referred to as *manay*. It is still common practice in the Peruvian Andes to plant corn in the same field for seven to ten years, then to leave the plot fallow for the same period. Potatoes follow a four-year cycle, with potatoes planted the first year; early potatoes the second year; ocas and *mashuas* (Andean tuber, highly nutritious) the third; and wheat the fourth, followed by a fallow period of six to seven years. Fallow land could be used for grazing, and each family had plots in all stages of rotation. Colonial descriptions of extensive unused land on the slopes of the Andes must be understood and evaluated on the basis of the principles of crop rotation and fallowing.[18] Ulloa Mogollón noted a variety of crops were grown in the valley in the late sixteenth century. He mentioned maize, quinua (*Chenopodium quinoa*), potatoes, and ocas. From agricultural censuses of Coporaque, one finds also *kañiwa* (the seeds, high in protein, can be toasted and ground into flour, which is then prepared in a variety of ways; *Chenopodium pallidicaule*). It is likely that *tarwi* (a highly nutritious Andean legume; *Lupinus mutabilis*), *añu* (tuber, similar to mashua), and *olluco* (*Ullucus tuberosus*) were also grown. Corn was one of the prized products of the valley, and Coporaque was near the uppermost limit for its cultivation. Using llama dung as fertilizer helped bring high yields on the warmer, well-watered terraces. Significant amounts of quinua were grown, and its altitudinal adaptability was wide. Its nutritional value is high; it contains 14 percent protein, and its fresh leaves are even richer than spinach. It also has a high content of vitamins, especially vitamin E. Potatoes were grown, but not as intensively as in other parts of the Andes. The dry months near harvest as well as the danger of frost or freezing temperatures meant that potatoes were often imported into the valley, as today. There is substantial variation in the distribution of crops within each section of the valley as a consequence of differing ecological conditions. Lower in the valley, in the village of Tapay, a number of tributaries grew *lúcuma* and *pacay* trees. Sixty-year-old Zezilia Cani of the ayllu of Taype Pataca farmed in Pallaharana two andenes of lucri corn, and had in the same place two lúcuma (*Lucuma obovata*) and two pacae (*Inga feuillei*) trees. In each place the distribution of crops from one year to another tended to remain relatively constant. In Coporaque urinsaya's three agricultural censuses — 1591,

1604, and 1616—topos dedicated to maize ranged only from 51.4 to 58.3 percent; while the range for quinua was 38.4 to 43.7 percent, and potatoes from 0.5 to 1.0 percent.[19]

The Andean system of land use was complex, and its nature challenged European understanding. Inspectors recording the land detailed to them by local informants must have been struck by the variety of crops available to most community members. Variety was greatest for the native elite. The kuraka principal, Don Jusepe Guaasuri, of Yanque urinsaya in 1591 was only nine, but as the legitimate son of Don Pedro Auca he had one topo of maize in Ullo Ullo, a topo of quinua in Chillapama, a topo of quinua in Ullo Ullo, another of quinua in Harasaya, a topo of maize next to the pueblo of Capistaca in Arequipa, a topo of maize in Achapru, another topo of maize in Guaypata in Arequipa. In Colca he had another topo of maize, in Guanca the same, in Urasara a topo of quinua, in Uroyca a half topo of maize, and in Chaquipalla a quarter topo of corn. There are other examples as well. Acting "gobernador" of the urinsaya, Don Francisco Ingapacta, had claim to over seventeen plots of land, planted in maize and quinua scattered within a 100-kilometer radius from Yanque. Yet no single plot was large by European standards.[20]

The agricultural landscape in the Colca Valley is dominated by small terraces and plots, from the edge of the escarpment above the river's bank, upward toward the sharp slopes of the surrounding mountains. Fields were kept green largely by irrigation. Although historically there have been wet periods, when rainfall supported agriculture, there have been longer dry periods, when irrigation canals and the construction of terraces were the only means of maintaining or increasing productivity. Terracing requires an enormous expenditure of labor, and good organization and planning. Archaeological evidence suggests that terrace farming and canals existed in the valley from the early Wari period (AD 600) and probably earlier. The question of sequence is open: which came first, canals or andenes? One contemporary resident of Coporaque perhaps provided the answer when he said, "You do not buy the plates before the pots." That is, contemporaries for whom water is so critical believe that there must be water or canals before there can be successful agriculture. And great effort continues to be expended to make certain there is water. Today the relatively small village of Coporaque maintains over fifty canals![21]

Today distribution of water from the canals traditionally takes place as part of the *mita global*. Following the agricultural calendar, workers go to their fields on the morning of their irrigation assignment. The first comes in September, before the rains, when it is time to prepare the soil for the cycle's planting. The length of the canals varies. In Coporaque one of the channels, called the Inca

Canal, starts at the Sawara River at an elevation of 3,670 meters, and runs for 5 kilometers, descending 110 meters during its course. The Qachulle Canal runs for 6 kilometers. Most Coporaque canals are fed by river waters, but a handful have springs as their sources. Just west, Yanque urinsaya has its own distinct set of canals for irrigation of its fields. The same holds true for Yanque anansaya on the south side of the Colca River. Here the primary source of water comes from streams created by the melting snow and ice on the peaks above, and some springs. Neither Yanque nor Coporaque secure irrigation water from the Colca River, which is far below in the canyon bed. Even in the twenty-first century, pumping water upward several hundred meters would be ineffective.[22]

The andenes require intensive labor to construct, and regular care must be expended to maintain them in good condition. Indian alcaldes and kurakas were required to make certain that water channels and fountains functioned properly, and they directed their cleaning and repair. The stone walls of the terraces were vulnerable during floods and earthquakes, as well as experiencing normal erosion, and the tillers of the plots were responsible for their upkeep. The Indian alcalde was to inspect the andenes, and if they were not in good condition, he could order repairs at the owner's cost and levy a six-peso fine that was applied to maintaining the Indian hospital.[23] Although it is possible to construct new andenes anytime during the year, it seems that the rainy season is the preferred time, for the moist soil is much more compact and less likely to shift. A supply of small- to medium-sized stones is readily available throughout the zone. A terrace wall 60 meters long by 2 high and 2 wide requires about 200 square meters of stone to construct. Traditionally, basalt stone shovels with wooden handles were used for excavation. Pointed digging sticks were also important in the work. Men and women work together in today's efforts, with children participating by carrying smaller stones, a work pattern that has been passed down. Terraces were started from a lower level, moving up the slope. To secure the base of the wall, it is best to excavate the soil to reach solid stone. The key to a stable base is not the size of the stone that is placed on the foundation, rather its shape, how firmly it fits in its place, and then how the other stones that are its neighbors "lock" into each other. The base might consist of several stones in width, then gradually narrow as one moves up. Terraces may consist of stones of hundreds of different sizes, giving a "rough," textured look. A smooth surface does not matter for this type of work; what is critical is stability. Topsoil is moved away during the process, then replaced, compacted, and finally leveled. Key in the leveling process is to make certain that there is enough slope to permit the natural flow of irrigation water from one side of the andén to the other, and toward the lower part, where the excess flows to water the terrace below. The leveling process can take several tries before it is acceptable. The length of most andenes in Coporaque ranges from 30 to 60 meters; the width is less than 10 meters. In Coporaque it was rare to have a terrace with a wall over 3 meters high. The terraces in the Colca Valley were not built by simply constructing a wall and letting "erosion" do the job; rather they were built by hard work and careful planning.[24]

Most daily activities were associated with subsistence, and in the case of the Cabana and the Collagua that meant midvalley farming and high-elevation herding of llamas and alpacas. Ethnological data on the community of Coporaque help illuminate the sequence of activities connected with the agricultural cycle. With the exception of some European crops now grown, the sixteenth-century agricultural calendar would have been little different from that of today (see table 8). The annual cycle began between July and mid-August, when on especially well-situated andenes an early planting (called *michca* or *mishka*) could be done. According to González Holguín, *michca* refers to "early corn that ripens quickly, and the first *chocllos* [ears of corn] that mature, and all early fruit or the first to ripen quickest." The early corn, potatoes, or beans (*habas* or lima beans, a contemporary valley favorite) can be harvested from February to March. Only a few of the Coporaque andenes are located in a zone whose microclimate permits a successful early crop. One place, Chokpayo, in a small depression, is at a good angle and elevation to maximize absorption of solar radiation. It is protected from winds and can support two crops a year: habas in the *michca*, and barley, planted in December and harvested in May. The major planting (*siembra grande*) takes place around the middle of August. In most cases the soil, which is dry from about May, is quite hard; and the process begins with a flooding of the terrace in order to supply the moisture critical for a later planting, and to soften the soil so that it is easier to work. The flooding of each terrace takes four to five hours. The soil is then broken, or turned; in the traditional system, it was done with the digging stick. In modern times cattle cultivate larger fields, pulling iron farm implements. Planting should be done within five days of irrigation to ensure sufficient moisture for proper germination. Irrigation continues until the annual rains, which begin in December and run through March. Traditionally, dried camelid dung provides fertilizer, and it was carried in large sacks from the "deposits" to the andenes. Corn requires the heaviest applications of fertilizer, potatoes less. Ash from hearths in the cooking compounds, as well as from the burning of annual plant residues left in the fields, is also spread on the ground to improve output.[25]

Agricultural rituals are linked to the calendar and are unlikely to have changed much in sequence since Europeans came, but there have been prob-

Planting the fields in August (1153 [1163])

Irrigating the terraces in November (1161 [1171])

Harvesting the corn in April (1141 [1151])

Collecting the potatoes in June (1147 [1157])

TABLE 8. Annual agricultural calendar, Coporaque, circa 1985

Month	Tasks
July	*Michca*, early planting, irrigation with turning of soil; preparation of soil for planting (August–October) of corn and habas
August	Michca continues to midmonth; preparation of fields for corn and habas; some fields irrigated; cleaning of the canals; irrigation of alfalfa
September	Irrigation and planting of habas, white corn, and wheat
October	Irrigation and planting of corn, potatoes, and barley; hilling up of michca crops
November	Irrigation and planting of potatoes, barley, and alfalfa (mixed with barley); first hilling up of habas and quinua
December	Irrigation and late planting of barley and alfalfa; hilling up of corn and potatoes; application of fertilizer; general irrigation
January	Second hilling up of corn and potatoes
February	Continuation of hilling; harvest of michca habas
March	Harvest of michca corn; collection of corn of the *siembra grande*
April	Cutting of the habas, corn, and quinua; potato harvest; drying of the corn; quinua thrashing
May	Harvesting and thrashing of barley, harvesting of habas
June	Last cutting and thrashing of barley

Source: Treacy, *Las Chacras de Coporaque*, 196

ably some variations in specific timing, ritual phrases employed, and practices from one community to another. In contemporary Coporaque the agricultural rituals begin in October with the family's *hayliy*, associated with planting corn, the major crop linked to rituals. According to González Holguín, *hayllini* means "to sing in the chacras, or celebrate in dance with triumphal or victorious songs." The invocations of hayliy call for successful germination, ample water, and ideal growing conditions for a good harvest. The family appears in the field in midmorning, along with a small group of neighbors linked by the reciprocal work relationship of *ayni*. The head of the household provides seed corn, *aguardiente* (brandy), and plenty of chicha. A stone object, as in the pre-Columbian times, is often placed near the field's center as a focal point for the ritual; sometimes the bag of seed corn is placed atop it. First aguardiente is shared in a small cup passed from person to person, and is followed by large *keros* (Inca-style drinking vessel) of sweet chicha, prepared by the female household head. As the process gets under way, to appease Pachamama, chicha is poured into the seed bag or on the earth that is to be planted. There are shouts of "Hayliy" and responses of "Hayliaway, hayliaway" as well as words of praise and invocations of Santiago, Coporaque's patron saint; San Isidro Labrador, patron saint of agriculture; and Mother Earth, Pachamama. There is a festive and anticipatory mood with talking and joking. The mixture of Christian and preconquest religious ideas associated with agriculture—the most important human activity in the valley—persists in indigenous rituals, in spite of efforts by colonial officials to extirpate such practices. Survival of preconquest rituals attests to the strength and adaptability of the valley's peoples.[26]

The procedure of community land distribution was codified in Toledo's ordinances and was based on what the colonizers believed autochthonous practice was, as modified by the viceroy's concept of the ideal republic. During the resettlement program of the 1570s, entire ayllus and parcialidades were moved from one location to another. New land was distributed in their new residences. Much of this land belonged to the original inhabitants; the consequence was a flood of lawsuits that plagued colonial officials. In theory the Indians were to receive land of equal quality to that they left behind, but in places where several groups were settled in close proximity the goal was difficult, perhaps impossible, to achieve. Original inhabitants were especially unhappy with the new order. Toledo ordered visitadores to carefully mark out the land and distribute it in order that families receive plots both near and far, so all would be equal. The practice of land distribution in the Colca Valley seems to have followed the pattern. There are glimpses of the process in the 1591 census of Yanque. In one case, the census lists "Pedro Arosquipa of 24 years, brother and son of the said Francisco Vira his brother of nine years, Pedro Cayllaua his son of four years." The visitadores noted, "They have to distribute to them more chacras and hand out those inspected," indicating the procedure followed.[27] Although women had access to land, on average their plots were smaller than those of males, with some notable exceptions. In Yanque in 1591, thirty-year-old Doña María Caruacarua—one of fourteen widows in her ayllu and the only single woman with land—had plots scattered in the valley, in the puna, and in distant Arequipa: "in Yautaraure a topo of maize, in Chano a half topo of maize, a house lot in

Arequipa, in Challuanca a half topo, in Chuca a topo of maize, in Tacahua two patas, in Collota a quarter; in Patarana another quarter, in Copo another quarter, in Chacape two patas, in Culpa another quarter, in another Copo four patas of maize, in Challuanca another quarter, in another Challuanca another quarter, in Challuanca a pata, in Ota Ota Vilcauyo a pata, in Huaynauyo another pata, and in another quarter in Challuanca." María is the only woman classified as "doña" in this ayllu, and her agricultural holdings are more extensive than those of most families.[28]

Spanish settlers opened a Pandora's box in the Andes with the introduction of Eurasian crops and animals. Andenes were small plots. Pigs were among the worst offenders, doing extensive damage to the structures as they rooted along the edges of the terraces in search of food. The Spanish requirement of pigs as tribute was a formula for disaster. Colonial authorities soon recognized this, and as early as 27 May 1552 Arequipa's city councilors ordered that no one was to raise pigs within the city's jurisdiction. Kurakas and alcaldes were to be vigilant to ensure livestock did not enter cultivated fields. But one day of damage took weeks of hard labor to repair. Toledo and others intended to introduce European agriculture into the Andes. The encomendero Marcos Retamoso, of Lari anansaya, fostered introduction of Old World livestock in his will of the early 1560s. Sheep damaged the native ecology, especially in the puna where they cropped the grasses much shorter than would llamas and alpacas.[29] Wheat was the staple of the Europeans. Newcomers to Tawantinsuyu at first found maize less palatable, and they included wheat in the tribute assessments in order to stimulate production. But as much as they wanted wheat, production lagged. In 1590 the cabildo of Arequipa issued an ordinance that directed natives who planted wheat to turn over to the city's public granary one fanega of wheat yearly. They lamented that Spanish production in the Arequipa Valley reached a mere 2,000 fanegas, while Indians in the valley produced 100,000 fanegas of corn. Of that, officials complained, 60,000 fanegas were used for chicha with disastrous consequences for "public order." The cabildo ordered that any Indian with chacras within six leagues of the center had to plant one part in wheat, and give one fanega to the *alhóndiga* (public granary). But such an action of the cabildo required the viceroy's authorization, and there is no indication that was forthcoming.[30]

Viceroy Toledo, intending to assist the native agriculturalists, ordered that where land was flat enough the corregidor was to introduce oxen and European plows, to be purchased with community funds. The ostensible purpose was to ease the burdensome labor of the native Americans. Community members were expected to share in using the plows and oxen, and the corregidor was to make certain that there were no abuses. Each community was to chose two sixteen- to eighteen-year-old men, and send them to the nearest city where they could learn the art of blacksmithing. The knowledge was indispensable for making and repairing plows, and various iron tools and objects could be made for local use. Yet introduction of oxen and plows into the Colca Valley would benefit only the local elite, the kurakas who controlled the slightly larger flat plots of land. Further, oxen consume large amounts of fodder and can disrupt irrigation channels. In the Andes where terrace systems predominate, traditional digging sticks are more friendly to the environment than European plows powered by large draft animals.[31]

Although haciendas soon came to dominate the landscape around Spanish Arequipa, and from there down the valley toward the coast, they failed to develop in the Colca Valley during the colonial period. The desire of communities to control their lands through traditional mechanisms of distribution was one factor preventing growth of the estates. Another reason is ecological; the small terraced plots, with their different crops and soils, were difficult to piece together into larger units that could be profitably exploited. Spanish legislation regarding inheritance also influenced local custom. Only entailed estates, created by special decree, were inalienable at the owner's death. The normal Spanish practice was for assets to be roughly equally divided when the owner died, with female children receiving their fair share. Only the *mayorazgo* (entailed estate) or lands held by the Church were not broken up and sold to individuals. For example, in 1662 the Spaniard Juan de Mendoza bought a small parcel of land called Llatica, near the Tapay annex of Paclla, from the Madrigal and Tapay priest Estevan del Corral y Besoz. Contemporaries observed that by the late eighteenth century, the estate had been broken up into so many small pieces by mestizo heirs that most of the remaining owners were hardly distinguishable from Indian commoners.[32]

Pastoralists

The herding of llamas and alpacas in the puna is highly productive, something the Spanish—finding it difficult to adjust to life at high elevations—initially failed to recognize. Much of the good puna pasture, some 14,000 square kilometers in the Collaguas province, lies between 4,000 and 4,500 meters' elevation. Spaniards viewed the extensive punas of Ranran and Coito, and others, as too desolate. Further, the pastoralists lived in a dispersed pattern, in rudimentary cottages next to stone corrals, where the herds were kept at night.

Conversion efforts in the puna were a challenge to the religious. There were too few Indians, too scattered to make doctrinas feasible. In the puna there were far more llamas and alpacas than people. A report of 1585–86 documents more than 25,000 head of livestock in Callalli and Tisco alone. An estimate of the camelid population in the entire district in 1981 is 70,000 llamas and 180,000 alpacas. Not only did the Toledo tribute regime require finished cloth products from the Collaguas; it required livestock too: some 481 from Yanque anansaya each year, 295 from the urinsaya, 265 from Lari anansaya, 242 from the urinsaya, and even 36 from Cabana urinsaya. Colonial church and secular officials unsuccessfully strove to concentrate puna pastoralists into villages, where they would be easier to watch and indoctrinate. The settlement of the llama and alpaca herders into villages would disrupt the traditional pattern of resource utilization, and it was resisted. Almost immediately, pastoralists left the settlements and returned to the puna to tend livestock as they had for generations. The Toledo ordinances accepted the reality; pastoralists were permitted to go to the puna so long as they frequently returned to their doctrinas for Mass and baptisms.[33]

Domestication of llamas and alpacas took place at least by 1000 BC; their smaller relatives, the guanaco and vicuña, remain wild. The llama is the larger of the two, at 1.0 meters in height (the average measurement of the back; the head and ears reach taller than the height of a man) and approximately 110 kilos in weight. The alpaca is slightly smaller at 0.9 meters height, and 100 kilos weight. The two can interbreed, and the variations carry several names. Colors vary from pure blacks and whites to brown, or there can be any variation of patterns of mixed color. Andean pastoralists have special names for the color schemes. Wild guanacos were hunted for meat, and vicuñas captured for their fine wool. The llama has multiple uses. It is a pack animal. Its skin and wool, although not as good as the alpaca's, can be used for all types of products. Its strips of sun-dried meat (*charqui*) can be consumed. Its dried excrement makes an acceptable combustible in a place where firewood is scarce, and it makes an excellent fertilizer. Their bones can be used for implements and musical instruments. The alpaca is too small to act as a beast of burden, but its wool is prized and it generally can be utilized in ways similar to the llama. The natural highland range extends from central Peru into northern Argentina, at elevations of about 3,000 to 5,200 meters, depending on latitude, types of soil, topography, and humidity. The puna grasslands to the north and south of the Colca Valley, at 3,800–4,300 meters, are ideal for camelid pasturage. In spite of the adaptation of the camelids to their environment, mortality is high, especially for recently born animals. Between 25 and 40 percent of the young in a flock die the first year. There is generally only one birth per mother each year, which puts pressure on pastoralists to preserve and augment their herds. That extends to close supervision of reproduction. Males, larger than the females, indiscriminately take several mates. The first intercourse for the female is in the second year. It is a rough affair, often resulting in severe abrasions for the female and frequent abortions. For this reason, careful pastoralists separate males and females, select proper mates, and supervise the process. Given the challenges of herding, ritual was important in fostering the prosperity of the flocks.[34]

Puna pastoralism did not fit easily into the ideal of Toledo's utopian Indian Republic, which was based on town life. Hence many ordinances dealt with pastoralists and their economy. Various rules were designed to thwart pagan rites. Pastoralists could not be absent in the puna longer than six months; then they had to descend to their villages for indoctrination. Kurakas were charged with keeping track of tributaries so that no one lived permanently in the puna. Priests were to maintain a list of pastoralists so that they would know where everyone was. Sundays, as many pastoralists as possible were required to descend from the punas to attend Mass with other villagers. If it were impossible for all to descend, then "half" were to return each Sunday. To protect the herds' integrity, Toledo ruled that on one Sunday the household head should come and the following Sunday, his wife and children. During the return to the villages, clerics were to make certain all were indoctrinated, and that newly born infants were baptized.[35]

In order to prevent loss of livestock, Toledo ordered — his regulations similar to those regarding the sheep herders' organization (*mesta*) in Spain — that Indians carefully guard the animals. Each herder was responsible for keeping close track of the number of livestock in order to deter theft. Indians found to be stealing livestock were punished by public flogging; repeat offenders were whipped and their heads shaven. The pastoralist was admonished not to integrate someone else's livestock into his own herd. If there were loose animals grazing nearby, he was required to descend to the nearest village and notify the owner. The animal's owner was expected to pay for its recovery in fleece at the time of shearing; the amount was to be assessed by the alcaldes. When the animals were sheared, the kuraka, priest, and corregidor were to divide the wool and distribute a share to the poor. The Indians were authorized to take the animals to the areas of best pasture in the summer, and in the winter to the highest and driest parts. Toledo provided special instructions for the tending of sheep, recently introduced into the Andean environment. When the herd in an area reached 2,000 ewes, the excess should be sold. If cattle were introduced, the excess of 50 bulls should be disposed of yearly, and when the number of cows reached 300 (of calving age), then the increase beyond this figure should be sold at market. Conservation of the wild herds of the vicuñas and guanacos also concerned the viceroy. "Henceforth without my license no one may make the general hunts of vicuñas and guanacos. Because of past hunts the number of these livestock has greatly diminished and they are of little value for the production of wool or dried meat."[36]

In Yanque anansaya, Toledo's visitadores concentrated an ayllu of yanacona pastoralists. In contrast to the other tributaries in 1591, almost all in this group lacked access to valley farmland. They did have herds of livestock; of the eleven married tributary yanaconas, Matheo Mamani had 10 head of livestock; Miguel Cala, 20; Francisco Loa, 50; Philipe Cacha, 30; Alonso Coa, 50; Andrés Caquia, 50; Phelipe Caillaua, 80; Pedro Guanaco, 50; Francisco Caquia, 40; Bartolomé Caquia, 20; and Juan Vicsa, 30. Three unmarried tributaries held livestock, with 10, 10, 20 respectively; four unmarried tributaries had no livestock.[37] Only two Yanque anansaya pastoralist yanaconas had access to land; these were located at Tiabaya in the valley of Arequipa. Andrés Caquia with wife and son held in Tiabaya a topo of chacra, and 50 head of cattle. Phelipe Caillaua, 18 years old; his wife, Ysavel Horchama; and their 2-year-old son had in Tiabaya a topo of chacra and 80 head of cattle. By any standards for sixteenth century rural Andean society, these two families were well off, living primarily by livestock herding.[38]

In the higher elevations of the Colca Valley, some families combined livestock herding with farming activities. In Tisco (4,242 meters) in 1591 the principal of the ayllu of Collana Malco, Don Gabriel Cama, aged forty-eight, was married to Lucía Paylli of the same age. The principal's household included three legitimate children aged 9 to 25, along with five illegitimate children aged 1 to 15. The oldest legitimate son, Thomas Callipampa, was married and lived in the house with his wife and one-year-old son. Don Gabriel's possessions are impressive:

in Coymo a topo of maize, in Ancuri a quarter of quinua, in Casacalla a quarter of quinua, in Otaycane another topo of quinua, in Pampa another topo of quinua, in Cassosina a quarter of quinua, in Cotauiri another quarter of quinua, in Noqueuiri a half topo of quinua, in Chilla Cauca another half topo of quinua, in another [place called] Cotauiri another quarter of quinua, in Arequipa in El Palomar two and a half topos that stretch to Arequipa, in Totoca a topo of potatoes, in Larcarana another topo of potatoes, in Parar Parara another topo of potatoes, in Chuniparme a topo of potatoes, in Sique Sique another topo of potatoes, and one hundred head of llamas and alpacas.[39]

Needed products were acquired via family and ayllu access to various types of resources at distinct ecological levels, and by barter. Barter exchanges were not based on assigned monetary values. Nor were transfers recorded, because the colonial state failed to level taxes from barter of goods or labor. The process is best understood through modern ethnography. Juvenal Casaverde R. studied exchange (*trueque*) in the Colca district in the early 1970s, immediately preceding the destructive impact of the Majes irrigation project. Barter existed between the coastal valleys, the Colca proper, and territories as far away as Cuzco. In the lower valleys of Camaná and Sihuas, trueque provided chili peppers, fruit, corn, and wheat. Charqui—as well as fresh meat, wool, textiles, and skins—were exchanged. Caylloma pastoralists obtained fresh and dried potatoes from the Cuzco district. Contemporary pastoralists confirm that for many generations, trips with llama packs were undertaken in order to secure the foodstuffs they could not produce. Exchange did not take place in an open market in a village square; rather it was done with "relatives" or "known ones," perhaps of the same ayllu. The transfer took place in their household compounds, with recipients providing a place for the outsiders to stay and fodder for llamas. In the early 1970s some women in Cabanaconde would await incoming pastoralists at the town's edge to encourage new contacts. Normally, outsiders visited the same compounds each year. The introductory gift was a leg of llama, at which point the head of the household would bring out the items they had agreed to barter for during the previous visit. Potatoes and chuño are two key products in this reciprocal system. Excess products were available for exchange with other people who were "known" by household members. There is no direct monetary equivalent for the articles changing hands. Maintenance of social relationships, stability, and continued access to basic subsistence commodities are the salient features of this relationship. One key factor in these exchanges is the attempt to avoid gyrating price fluctuations in the local market. In 1957 an arroba of chuño was pegged at 20 soles; in 1967 it was 120. Gifts of local products were presented to the visiting herders, reinforcing reciprocity. Both parties knew that differences in the "cash value" of the products might be large, yet both sides maintained the traditional relationship because it was critical for group survival.[40]

Agriculturalists of the Colca Valley in the latter part of the sixteenth century had ample access to resources, to the irrigated terraces and the puna grasslands. Nevertheless, the burden of tribute was heavy. Although tribute assessments were based on counts of individuals, the entire community was responsible for making payment to colonial officials. In some instances such a system could benefit the individual, who might be ill or absent. By permitting the community to meet the demands of the metropolis, there was some flexibility in instances of individual emergency. Ulloa Mogollón reported in 1586 that "those who have food give it to those who do not, by means of exchange *trueco* (exchange or barter) of livestock, wool and other such things." What was lacking in one province was exchanged with goods of another. "And in this manner each one is provided for as with people of reason."[41] As long as there were enough tributaries to cover the total assessment, the system worked; but when the number of people fell sharply, it became a serious burden. New tribute assessments were periodically conducted but not frequently enough to prevent hardship in years immediately preceding new counts. Even with rapid depopulation, the community was required to pay the fixed assessment until a new census was taken to readjust the relationship between the tribute assessment and the number of people. By the end of the sixteenth century and the beginning of the next, many interest groups in the Spanish colonial system collaborated to delay new tributary counts for as long as possible, which caused increased exploitation and dislocation.

The economic foundations of the Collagua and the Cabana were shaken in the first three generations after arrival of the outsiders. Inca hegemony had existed within a framework of Andean reciprocity. Cuzco exactions did not have a negative impact on population size or economic output for local subsistence. Labor demands were seasonal and did not disrupt the agricultural economy. If anything, state projects such as road and bridge construction improved movement of people and commodities. There were restrictions preventing the free flow of people from beyond their ethnic enclaves or "provinces." But given the vertical economy, the ayllu-based networks for the transfer of subsistence products, and the lack of a "market economy," free spatial mobility of peoples was not a priority. However one characterizes the nature of the Inca "polity," subsistence needs of the people were met. Spanish conquest and settlement changed radically the relationship between local peoples and central authority. The human base began a precipitous century-plus decline. Since all economic activities in agricultural societies are related to population size and quality of the labor force, the decline resulted in a decrease in production. Under the encomienda regime, local goods stipulated as tribute were removed from the indigenous community and funneled into colonial administrative centers. The goods or cash equivalents flowed to Arequipa, Lima, and ultimately the European metropolis. The labor requirements of the colonial system funneled Cabana and

Collagua tributaries to Arequipa. Their seasonal removal from the Colca Valley did not respect the traditional Andean agricultural calendar. Tribute quotas remained at constant levels until a new population count lowered the assessment, reflecting the downward population trend. A profound disintegration, or "destructuration" as Nathan Watchel terms it, shook the Andean world in the first generations after Old World contact.[42] It culminated in abandonment of terraces and canals that had been used for centuries. In spite of the deterioration, valley people retained the basics of farming and pastoralism. Some European crops and animals were introduced, and various native species disappeared. But not all was lost: the Cabanas and Collaguas have survived, and in spite of continuing pressures for cultural transformation, old ways of guaranteeing subsistence in a hostile environment have prevailed.

CHAPTER SEVEN

EXTRACTIVE ECONOMY

[There is] too much to tell Your Majesty about, other than for us to certify that many have fled and absented themselves, leaving behind their villages and roots. They will continue to flee daily because they say that if they have to return from the mita and service in the city of Arequipa to rest in their homeland, and here are compelled to serve in the obraje without giving time to rest with wives and children and attend to their fields, that more will want to leave for faraway lands than remain in their own, and the damage will be felt more each day.
—Kurakas of Los Collaguas to the king, 1614, Archivo General de Indias, Lima 144.

The Collaguas Mita

The mita was a pre-Spanish Andean institution that was adopted by the Europeans to solve the shortage of voluntary wage labor. The Inca regime mita was a labor draft for major construction projects: the building of q'olcas, tambos, roads and bridges, and regional administrative centers. In theory the mita was carefully planned and monitored to avoid disrupting the normal agricultural cycle of conscripted workers. During the 1530s and 1540s the Spaniards had little occasion to need the mita. These were years of exploration, conquest, and exploitation of available precious metals, as well as native uprisings and civil warfare between the Europeans. If an encomendero needed laborers to transport goods or construct his residence, he conscripted a group of his charges. If non-encomenderos required workers, they might hire laborers, or convince an encomendero to "rent out" some of his tributaries. By the time Spaniards began to settle and build cities, haciendas, and churches, the labor shortage was acute, for the native population was collapsing.[1]

The founding in 1540 and construction of Arequipa was a key factor in the evolution of labor in southern Peru. The initial decade was a trying period for the colonizers, who faced the difficulties of establishing town government, laying out streets, and building houses. Chaos resulting from Gonzalo Pizarro's rebellion did not contribute to stable growth. Miguel Rodríguez de Cantalapiedra initiated the local labor draft when he requested permission to use encomienda Indians to construct his house in Arequipa. The Crown responded to his request, authorizing him and other Arequipa settlers to secure Collagua and other native workers: "There are some vecinos in Arequipa who have been unable to build their houses because of the altercations. We authorize all vecinos of the city of Arequipa to make Indians work to erect their houses with the Indians . . . in encomienda, paying them for their work in accordance with what Indians doing similar work in the city are paid. . . . The Indians should do it only if they are willing. There should be no force involved, and they should be given and paid daily for their work one tomín and one cuartillo of maíz." Collaguas workers also helped construct Arequipa's Franciscan convent, completed in 1569.[2]

Colca Valley migrants were often mistreated in the Spanish urban center. Arequipa's municipal council (22 October 1550), attempting to protect Indians during their journey to the city, levied a 200-peso fine for settlers who abused the mitayos. During the inspection of Captain Juan Maldonado de Buendía in the 1570s, fines were levied and collected from several arequipeños for ill-treatment. Juan de Mora was fined twenty-five pesos for "malos tratamientos" of an undefined nature; several others received ten-peso fines for similar offenses.[3] The residencia of the Arequipa corregidor, Pedro Sánchez de Coz, conducted in the mid-1630s, contains several examples of abuse. The corregidor was accused of using Indians from nearby corregimientos to plant his own fields and not distributing them for the city's mita de plaza. Other colonizers were fined: the tailor Gabriel de la Peña was fined "for bad treatment of an Indian"; the alguacil Julián de Yebra was fined by the local protector de los indios for mistreating natives. Another set of charges involved the Spaniard Gaspar Falcón, who during an altercation with Domingo Cacha seriously wounded him, causing him to lose an eye. Charges were lodged against Doña Isabel Cayantes "for keeping Indians locked up." In another case Pedro, Pablo, Plaudo, and Francisco Pacheco were fined "for having entered the house of Don Melchor Maldonado with unsheathed swords and taken out an Indian woman." Indians were not always the innocent ones. Pedro Gómez brought suit against an Indian woman named Andrea "for burning his rancho." And Juan Bautista de Espinosa charged an Indian tailor named Juan and others, for tying up his black male slave and abusing him.[4]

The Collaguas who transported goods or people were exploited by the religious as well. During a secret inspection of nearby Chucuito province in the 1570s, it was revealed that several Dominicans abused the Amerindians. The inspectors Friar Pedro Gutiérrez Flores and Juan Ramírez Segarra discovered that the Collagua kuraka Pedro Alanoca had been so severely whipped by Friar Domingo de Mesa that he was confined to bed for two months. An angry Friar Martín de Sandis, they charged, laid on the kuraka more than fifty lashes because "he did not bring Indians rapidly enough to help transport a friar who was traveling to the coast of Arequipa." Mistreatment of the Amerindians by Dominicans in their Chucuito doctrinas was so deeply rooted and so contrary to his concept of the "Ideal Republic," Viceroy Toledo felt compelled to divest the Order of their control of the rich province; he replaced them with Jesuits.[5]

The economic crisis of the 1560s in the viceroyalty was the consequence of several factors. One was the shrinkage of manpower, the key element in production. Another was that silver output at the rich deposit of Potosí, discovered in 1545 by the yanacona Diego Gualpa, began to fall rapidly as the best ores were processed and the veins were depleted. The native process of extracting silver from ore by using *huayras* (ichu-grass-fueled air furnaces), worked only with higher grades of ore. The mercury amalgamation process requiring less heat had been developed earlier; but mercury was needed both in the Iberian Peninsula and New Spain, and its transport was costly. It was the Portuguese miner Enrique Garcés who realized the value of mercury deposits discovered in the central Andes in 1559. Nearby, four years later, natives showed Amador de Cabrera an even richer source. These deposits were the foundation of the mercury-mining center of Huancavelica. Potosí miners first resisted the new amalgamation method, but Fernández de Velasco's successful demonstration in 1571 convinced Viceroy Toledo and the miners that the process could be profitably employed at Potosí. Further, the method could be used to extract silver from the waste heaps of two decades of mining at Potosí, and was economically viable even with ore deposits that contained only a small percentage of silver. Virtually the entire mountain of Potosí was now commercially exploitable. But for this to happen the labor force had to be increased because it was necessary to produce and transport the mercury, mine the low-grade silver ore, grind and mix it with mercury for amalgamation, and finally extract the silver.[6]

Native Americans were generally unwilling to work in the mines for the stipend most operators intended to pay, and they tended to reject the regimen-

TABLE 9. Toledo's mitayo assignment for Potosí, 1578

Repartimiento	Tributaries	To Potosí	Active mita
Yanque Collaguas	4,085	408	136
Lari of Picado	1,218	121	40
Lari of Retamoso	1,333	133	44
Cabana of De la Cuba	778	77	26
Cabana of De la Torre	567	56	19

Source: Lohmann Villena, *Francisco de Toledo*, 2:359–98

tation of even a free wage-labor system. Consequently, in the 1560s there was a series of debates between Spanish reformers, clergymen, encomenderos, and miners over how best to organize labor to meet the Crown's thirst for American bullion. Many of the same people who debated the question of perpetuity of the encomiendas argued this issue too. The solution was the perverse adoption of the Andean mita. One-seventh of the tributary population of a given repartimiento was granted out to serve on the mita draft each year. Those Indians falling under the jurisdiction of major mining mitas such as Huancavelica and Potosí probably suffered most, because of the problems of transportation and the dangers involved in the mine labor and the amalgamation process itself. There was no legal escape from forced labor except incapacitation or death. The mita was justified by claims that labor was needed for vital public works projects such as the building of churches, roads, and bridges, and also for the bullion to defend the political and religious policies of Imperial Spain.[7]

The Collaguas first appear in Potosí's general mitayo allotment issued by Viceroy Toledo in Lima in August 1578 (see table 9). The number of mine workers was allocated according to a sliding percentage of the tributary population, with those closest to the mines bearing the highest burden. For Charcas the requirement was 17 percent, for La Paz 16 percent, for Collao and Canas 15 percent, and for the Canas nearer Cuzco 14 percent. For the Collaguas it was set at 10 percent, for although the corregimiento was far from the mines, the explanation was that "there are many Indians in the said province." The phrasing of the requirement is instructive: "Yanquicollagua of the King, with 4,085 tributary Indians is obligated to have in the said Villa [Potosí] 408 Indians; they have to contribute 136 for mita service." The Collaguas were not in Toledo's original Potosí mita allocation, because he ordered that "regarding who has to govern the Collaguas and the Cabanas," someone would be entrusted, but for the present it should be the same person who is in charge of the mitayos from Canas y Canchis. Mitayos from the Colca Valley were listed in Toledo's distribution to Spaniards resident in Potosí in 1578. They fall into the group designated to serve in the grinding mills, difficult labor at best but not within the mines themselves. The mill operator Luis Capoche received nineteen Cabana mitayos of Juan de la Torre's encomienda. No other specific allotments of Colca Valley mitayos to individuals in the mining center were recorded.[8]

Collaguas mitayo service in Potosí was brief because of vocal and persistent demands for them by the Arequipa elite. As early as the 1582 earthquake, Collaguas mitayos were shifted away from the Potosí operation. Viceroy Toledo ordered Collaguas mitayos to work in the fields and haciendas of Camaná, Siguas, Vítor, and Arequipa and to assist in transporting wine to places as far distant as Cuzco and Potosí. They were required to work in Arequipa on bridges, roads, a public granary, the house of the governor and corregidor, the cabildo building, a jail, a school, and the construction of churches and monasteries. Other Collaguas mitayos were assigned to private individuals for various types of service. In August 1590 the city council received a request for mitayos to ship wine to Potosí from the area of Chucuito. In December 1590, the master lime maker Alonso Ochoa requested the cabildo fulfill its promise to grant him mitayos for lime production. In April 1591 Ochoa was allocated ten Indians from the mita "chica" and double that number from the mita "grande." In August 1601 Viceroy Luis de Velasco ordered the Arequipa corregidor to ensure that each tambo had at its service six mitayos. They were to be paid one-half real (34 maravedíes) daily for their travel and assistance in providing livestock fodder, as well as other "duties." To protect their health, the viceroy ordered that no mitayos change residence from one elevation to another substantially different one. Mitayos were to be chosen from villages nearest the tambo. In October 1600 Viceroy Velasco ordered Arequipa's corregidor to distribute to Beatrís Volante, widow of Juan Mexía, four mita Indians to guard her forty or fifty mules contracted to transport supplies to the city. In May 1620 Juan Ruiz de Monjares presented a viceregal cédula to the cabildo granting him six mitayos to plant his crops in the Arequipa region. Local authorities granted six to eight mitayos from the Collaguas, of the "mita ordinaria."[9]

Abuse of Colca Valley mitayos who were transporting goods was notorious. There were complaints that Collagua and Cabana mitayos were exploited while carrying wine from the Vítor Valley to Potosí. One reason was that those using Indians to ship wine regularly sent other goods as well. Viceroy García Hurtado de Mendoza issued an order in January 1592 forbidding the practice; there was only temporary compliance. Economic interests of the Arequipa elite, especially those involved in wine production, took increasing precedence over good treatment of the natives. Shortly before May 1597, Luis de Peralta sent the viceroy a report about the wine-producing valleys of nearby Siguas and Vítor. Part of that report centered on use of mitayos in transportation "to Siguas, which is the valley with the lowest production, where Indians from the corregimiento of Los Collaguas and Cabanaconde are sent. And to Vítor, which has the largest harvest . . . , they only give the Indians of Collasuyo and Chimba for . . . transportation, but the Collaguas and the Cabanas are much more numerous than those of Collasuyo and Chimba." Peralta pointed out: "It is only just that the work should be divided equally in conformity with the harvests"; he suggested that special commissioners or clerics should be authorized to make a just and equitable distribution of the Arequipa native labor force. Peralta, a staunch supporter of the system, believed that mitayos would not have time on their hands to do mischief and participate in drunken fiestas. He argued that in spite of the time it took to travel from Cabanaconde to Arequipa, which according to his calculations required eight to ten days along a route without villages, the Indians were still accorded ample time for planting their own crops. Viceroy Luis de Velasco was swayed by the request of the Arequipa petitioners, and in May 1597 he ordered Collaguas and Cabanaconde mitayos to assist in wine transportation from the Vítor Valley.[10]

Within a year, use of Collaguas mitayos for wine transportation led to fresh complaints, this time from the kurakas of Yanque and Lari, who lamented to the viceroy that mitayos from their repartimientos were residing in the pueblos of Guanca and Lluta, but were included in the censuses in highland population centers. These Indians were required to pay tribute in Yanque and Lari, and they were included in the census on which the one-seventh mita requirement was based. Informants charged that "these two villages of Lluta and Guanca are situated in the high sectors of the Pitay valley and they take them without count or right to the said valley, and to other warm lands [tierras calientes] where they die and have greatly diminished in number." Viceroy Velasco studied the petition; in October 1598, he ordered that Indians from Yanque and Lari who lived in Lluta and Guanca could not be forced to serve in wine transportation in the lower valleys.[11] At the same time the viceroy attempted to end the disorder caused by uncontrolled exploitation of Colca Valley natives who served as muleteers in Arequipa's mita de plaza. The kurakas of Alonso Picado and Francisco Retamoso complained to the viceroy that each mitayo was allocated an unwieldy number of mules and horses to guard day and night, from 30 to 40, and at times as many as 50. Under the circumstances, with inadequate fodder or pasture available, mules wandered into surrounding cultivated fields, inflicting extensive damage. Farmers obviously demanded that the mule drivers pay for losses, and the muleteers in turn went to the Indians. The kurakas Agustín Casa, Felipe Ala, and Marcos Guancallo petitioned the viceroy to prohibit nighttime use of mitayos for guarding the mules. After reviewing the evidence, the viceroy ruled that the number of mitayos was part of the "mita de plaza" and could not be increased. The Indians could only work during the day: "at night they are, and have to remain free." Further, he mandated that any damages done by mules and horses could not be charged to the Indians.[12]

Priests were sometimes assigned mitayos, causing frequent complaints. In June 1604 Viceroy Luis de Velasco granted the cleric Don Martín Abad de Usonsolo use of six mitayos each Monday for his house and service. The priest forced the mitayos to cultivate his corn and wheat fields in the Arequipa Valley. Don Martín originally requested access to mitayos living in La Chimba, or Yanahuara, probably from the Collaguas, because these were settled close to his fields. In November 1604 the priest filed a complaint against Arequipa's corregidor, because he had not delivered the mitayos as the viceroy ordered. The Crown official countered that the mitayos had not been allocated to the churchman, because the priest was absent in Cuzco, having been ordered there by the bishop.[13] Religious organizations also received mitayos. Jesuits in Arequipa managed to gain access to thirteen Collaguas mitayos, which they retained for many years. During the administration of Viceroy Príncipe de Esquilache, Jesuit Alonso Huertas de Herrera requested thirteen Indians to assist in constructing the Jesuit residence. The Marqués de Guadalcázar issued the order. But the initial grant of Collaguas workers was insufficient to complete the task, and in November 1625 the Jesuits asked for a continuation of the Collaguas mita privilege because "at the current rate of building, it will take six years" to finish. The corregidor authorized use of Collaguas mitayos but for only four years. Near the end of that period the Jesuits asked for another extension, this time for six to eight years. They lamented that their slaves died in construction and they needed more laborers. This time the viceroy authorized six years. In August 1635 the Protector de los Indios accepted use of Collaguas mitayos by the Jesuits, and in December 1635, Viceroy Conde de Chinchón ordered a prolongation for another six-year term. Other extensions were granted in subsequent decades, as the Jesuits successfully developed a technique to retain continuous access to Indian workers outside the encomienda system.[14]

Labor in the mines was the most dangerous form of mita work, and the Collaguas attempted to avoid it. Colca Valley natives were fortunate because they lived far distant from the most deadly mining mitas of Potosí and Huancavelica, beyond the 200 leagues from the mining center of Potosí, the maximum distance allowed for mitayos to travel. Nonetheless, miners frequently pressured royal authorities for a quota as outlined in Toledo's 1578 mita provision. There were provinces that came under the draft that were even farther away than the Collaguas, but the fact that the vecinos of Arequipa needed Collaguas workers meant that each time Potosí mining interests pressured for new mitayos, the Arequipa cabildo vigorously protested in the viceregal capital, with positive results. In April 1597 Viceroy Luis de Velasco once again confirmed the exemption of the Collaguas from the Potosí mita.[15] Nearer mining centers also pressed for Collaguas mitayos. In 1591, some 500 Collaguas Indians were initially assigned to the silver mines of Choclococha, along with equal numbers from the provinces of Parinacochas and Aymaraes, and 300 each from Andaguaylas, Lucanas, Soras, and Andamarcas. But because of the distance, and more important the pressure of arequipeños, jealous of their prerogatives, it is unlikely that Collaguas mitayos served at Choclococha.[16]

The discovery in 1626 of silver at Caylloma, within the jurisdiction of the Collaguas, resulted in immediate demands for Indian labor that could only be satiated by a mita draft. The first Caylloma draft was issued in April 1639 by Viceroy Pedro de Toledo y Leiva, Marqués de Mancera. He granted 800 mitayos from surrounding corregimientos. The Collaguas contingent amounted to 324 mitayos in keeping with its proximity and other requirements in neighboring provinces. Viceroy Mancera's quota at first ignored the question of the already-assigned mitayos, the 249, for example, that Philip II had authorized for Arequipa's mita de plaza. The city's general solicitor, Pedro de Irusubieta, immediately appealed to the viceroy that the city's prerogatives were being ignored, because the acting Collaguas corregidor, Felipe de Albornoz, refused to send mitayos to Arequipa as required by earlier decrees. The solicitor demanded that the viceroy order the Collaguas corregidor to fulfill his responsibilities, and recommended that the viceroy reach a decision as quickly as possible, given the gravity of the situation and local needs. The answer was the reduction of Arequipa's mita de plaza to 230, with the stipulation that they were "reserved" but not "excluded" from the mining mita of Caylloma. In late September to early October 1642, the local official was authorized to compel delivery of mitayos to Arequipa. Two years later, in March 1644, Collaguas lieutenant governor Pedro González de Huelva was notified. He curtly responded that he would speak to the "governor of the Collaguas" about the matter. A continuous debate raged between mining interests in Caylloma and the Arequipa elite over use of Colca Valley mitayos. In October 1697 the cabildo still demanded that decrees authorizing mitayos for the mita de plaza of the urban complex be enforced.

They complained to the monarch that enforcement of the provisions was entirely dependant on the "will of the corregidores of the Collaguas province, and only by the powerful hand of Your Majesty can this disobedience be altered." The Crown's reply in June 1700 suggests the declining power of the Arequipa elite, for the *fiscal* stated that there was absolutely no justification for Arequipa to have the mitayo concession. "They can cultivate the fields with voluntary Indians or blacks," he argued and pointedly observed that the mitas were an "odious" offense to good government.[17]

The Maca Obraje

The colonizers' *obrajes*, or textile factories, were detested by Andean natives. Local manufacturing of cloth had been traditionally a family affair, from preparation of the yarn to the completion of the final product. Work in hastily constructed large stone buildings, where dozens of obraje workers could be locked in from dawn to dusk by Spanish overseers, was alien and unhealthy for the native laborers. Spaniards were aware of the advantages of premodern mass production and attempted to introduce it, as Nicholas Cushner has documented in his study of Jesuit obrajes elsewhere in the viceroyalty. The extensive puna above the Colca Valley provided ideal conditions for vast herds of livestock, llamas, alpacas, and wild vicuñas for wool. The Spanish quickly noted the potential of Collaguas cloth production and included it as a major component of tribute. Some of the best of the woven cloth equaled the quality of that produced in Spain. Friar Diego de Ocaña, who traveled extensively through America in the early seventeenth century, spent three weeks in Yanque on his way from Arequipa to Cuzco. While there, Doña Ana de Peralta, the wife of the corregidor, Gonzalo Rodríguez de Herrera, gave him a bedcover made by the Indians. Because it was "of such fine wool and exquisite colors," Ocaña took it back with him to Castile so that he could show people there the quality of the work. In contrast to other parts of the Andean world, the attempt to set up obrajes in the viceroyalty moved slowly and was delayed until the early seventeenth century; the effort ultimately floundered.[18]

The attempt to establish obrajes in the Colca Valley was flawed from the start. Viceroy Mendoza y Luna, the Marqués de Montesclaros—contrary to long-established rules prohibiting the granting of favors to relatives and members of his retinue—provided revenues from the Collaguas province to Doña Elvira de Vargas, wife of his nephew Rodrigo de Mendoza. The pension was for 6,000 pesos, to be paid from tributes of the repartimiento of Lari Collaguas of Francisco Retamoso, who had died. At the same time the viceroy issued a license to construct an obraje "of *paños* [cloth] and *sayales* [coarse cloth]." It was to be constructed by the Crown's Indians and those of Alonso Picado. This was a serious challenge to Arequipa officials as well as to natives of the Colca Valley. The viceroy's relation to the king required that any charges had to be carefully and tactfully presented and substantiated.[19] On 5 March 1614 Yanque Collaguas kurakas along with those of Lari of Alonso Picado congregated before the notary in Arequipa, and granted a power to the king's fiscal in the Council of the Indies to represent them and all the Indians of the Collaguas, especially "regarding the grievances that they receive from the new obraje of Don Rodrigo de Mendoza."[20] Three days later Pedro Ybáñez de Yruegas, Arequipa's protector of the Indians wrote the monarch explaining in detail both the plight of the Indians and the deleterious consequences of a textile factory for the vecinos of Arequipa. Rodrigo de Mendoza and his wife were building an obraje where Indians "serve as slaves, making sackcloths most inconveniently, because it consumes the Indians, takes them from their service to the surrounding communities, causing them to cease to transport the production of the silver mines, and results in many other damages." The protector knew he was approaching potentially dangerous ground, and intoned, "as it concerns a relative of the viceroy, nobody is pressuring." He circumspectly explained his own actions: "The defense of their cause concerns me as their protector, by title of the viceroy. . . . There has not been a solution nor will there be one if Your Majesty does not act. . . . I supplicate . . . that you remedy these most miserable evils . . . and order demolition of the obraje." Alonso Picado in a letter to the king the following week (15 March 1614) likewise phrased his text carefully, explaining that since the viceroy was "out of sight of Your Majesty, we have lost all hope here that his relationships might be remedied; I supplicate Your Majesty with all the humility that I can, that it would be of service to order a review."[21]

The long report that the Cabanas and Collaguas kurakas directed to the monarch outlines in vivid detail the nature and impact of developments taking place in the valley. It also provides insight into the kind of response the kurakas hoped their petition would elicit:

> We say that in addition to the innumerable labors that the Indians of the said province give now, another has been added, no less than all the rest. An obraje for cloth manufacture and other things is being established in the repartimiento and encomienda of Don Rodrigo de Mendoza, next to an Indian village of your Royal Crown, named Maca, by license that his uncle the Marqués de Montesclaros has given. He has ordered us to

give perpetually 150 Indians daily, with tributaries and young men divided among the Indians and villages that are placed in your Royal Crown, and of the encomiendas of Alonso Picado and Don Rodrigo de Mendoza. They are founding and constructing the said obraje on our lands and with the water mill that we have.

The water mill, on the edge of Maca, was controlled jointly by the Indians of Lari anansaya and urinsaya and had been in operation for several years.

When work began we spoke out against it and presented petitions and appeals, although they did not admit us before, because it was a case that concerned the viceroy's nephew. We were threatened to not give testimony. Hence we asked the corregidor of the province Captain Martín de Gartelú and notary Francisco de Cocar, but all attended to the pleasure of the said viceroy in order that the obraje might be constructed, and we were frustrated of all hope of assistance. Rodrigo de Mendoza named as his majordomo and super-intendant of the obraje none other than notary Francisco de Cocar, and the corregidor made him the lieutenant general of the whole corregimiento. With that authority he was able to begin the obraje with such speed and molestations of Indians that we could not act."[22]

The Colca Valley kurakas made several charges against Rodrigo de Mendoza and his wife. They complained the land was taken for the site of the obraje without compensation and another lot was set aside to make the machinery for the cloth factory. This was prejudicial because they were already short of land. The kurakas accused Mendoza and the others of taking building stones and other materials from Maca, without requesting them from their true owners or paying for them. They charged that the notary Francisco de Cocar sent a Spaniard to Alonso Picado's village of Tapay with authorization to cut timber. Using force and contrary to the wishes of the true owners, Mendoza removed the wood and transported it to Maca on the shoulders of the Indians "by one of the most difficult and dangerous routes in the realm." This was particularly prejudicial because Tapay was the principal source of lumber for the construction of churches and houses in the province. Armed with the authority given him, Mendoza paid two pesos for beams worth four. Villagers complained that two large houses of previous kurakas were taken and dismantled for building material for the obraje, without authorization of the heirs or a payment. Again all lumber removed from the houses was transported by the Indians to the building site. Kurakas accused Francisco de Cocar of forcing the Indians to work in

TABLE 10. Obrajes within sixty leagues of the Collaguas, circa 1614

Location	Owner	Distance in leagues
Guaro	Juan Alvarez Maldonado	40
Arequipa	Gómez de Tapia	18
Yucay	Augustinian friars	40
Urubamba	Doña Beatriz Coya	40
Paruro	Pedro de Vargas	35
Santiago de Arapa	Miguel de Berrio	45
Quispicanche	Rodrigo de Esquibel	38

Source: AGI, Lima 144

the construction of the obraje. He loaded them with stones, limestone, and bricks, and continually mistreated them in so many ways that there was

> too much to tell Your Majesty about, other than for us to certify that many have fled and absented themselves, leaving behind their villages and roots. They will continue to flee daily because they say that if they have to return from the mita and service in the city of Arequipa to rest in their homeland, and here are compelled to serve in the obraje without giving time to rest with wives and children and attend to their fields, that more will want to leave for faraway lands than remain in their own, and the damage will be felt more each day.

Further, kurakas charged that they were ordered to give 150 Indians from the three repartimientos, to be divided between tributaries and boys under eighteen. They stressed damage inflicted on the health of child workers. The kurakas argued that what was being done actually constituted the grant of another encomienda, making Mendoza their perpetual lord, contrary to all legislation. Lastly, the kurakas declared that there were already seven obrajes within a radius of sixty leagues and that more would be illegal (see table 10).[23]

Collaguas kurakas then detailed the service required of Colca Valley tributaries in the early seventeenth century. In the ordinary mita de plaza of Arequipa, kurakas were to distribute 250 Indians weekly to vecinos and residents. Another 175 Indians were given, an allotment continuing into the second decade of the century, to rebuild the city after the 1604 earthquake. In addition they sent 35 mitayos to monasteries and to individuals who received special allotments. The total reached 460 Indians. Beyond this number, Collaguas mitayos daily had to deliver to Arequipa residents 250 cargas of firewood, carrying it on their shoulders from two leagues up the slope of the volcano, "something that no other city of the kingdom is accustomed to." The kurakas complained: "When we commit some error in this service in the plaza . . . we are whipped and shaved, and out of fear of this we rent Indians from other places and pay them eight pesos monthly out of our own money." The Collaguas province was required to supply another 500 mitayos yearly for transport of wine, raisins, figs, and other foodstuffs taken from the warm valleys. These goods were loaded and carried to Potosí, "to Cavana Colla and those in the direction of Cuzco to Hatun Cana. From the valley to the highlands there are forty leagues of unpopulated lands." The kurakas denounced mita service in the obraje as an unjust burden, and lamented they could not "meet the requirements" and that they would "fall into debt." They added that there were no longer enough Indians to do all demanded of them. And they reminded authorities that they worked in two tambos, Chivay and Caylloma, "where we go and serve carrying from our villages supplies of firewood, fodder, maize, kettles and pitchers and the other things necessary for the enjoyment of the Spaniards." With all the services already required, it "would not be just" to finish the obraje and serve in it also.[24]

At the time the kurakas were protesting to the king, the Collaguas corregidor, Captain Martín de Gartelú, died. In an odd and ominous twist, none other than Francisco de Cocar was named corregidor. This appointment was a clear case of conflict of interest, since he was the overseer of the construction of the obraje and was in the employ of Mendoza. The new corregidor vigorously increased the labor force, and with "new and doubled annoyance," according to the charges of the kurakas, attempted to complete the obraje's construction before the king could send an order for its demolition. Cocar was unable to finish construction of the building to house the equipment, but he did attempt to convince royal authorities that the obraje in Maca was already in production. As part of that effort he sent to Arequipa for two looms, which he assembled in the village inn, and ordered the Indians to commence weaving. He hoped that in this way he could certify that the obraje had been completed and was operating. The kurakas countered that the mill was not functioning and that Cocar only constructed some houses that were in the process of being roofed; "there is neither the gear machinery, nor the looms, nor the wheels or any of the other things necessary for the obraje."[25]

In the end, opponents of the obraje won; a royal cédula arrived ordering demolition of the structures. But in spite of the monarch's orders Mendoza and his wife continued operating the mill for another six months, at which point kurakas realized that more action was needed. They again filed a complaint explaining their plight, pointing out that Indians were now fleeing the province. They warned that it seemed that the draft would become perpetual and pressed ahead: "We humbly supplicate Your Majesty not to permit the said obraje."[26] Finally, on 30 January 1615 the king wrote Viceroy Montesclaros and reminded him of the cédulas and instructions issued by previous monarchs, as well as his own instructions of appointment and regulations prohibiting new obrajes without prior consultation and specific license from the king and Council of the Indies. The ruler again ordered demolition of the cloth factory and asked the Royal Audiencia in Lima to keep him informed on the status of the execution of the order.

The illegal obraje was not the only issue involving the viceroy's nephew. The king informed the viceroy in early June 1612 that he had learned that Rodrigo de Mendoza was granted a spacious open parcel between the Rimac River and the royal government houses in Lima, where the fairs and public market generally took place. The enterprising nephew began to construct a house; the cabildo immediately complained that the plaza was public property and that the viceroy had no right to grant it to anyone. The monarch questioned the justices of Lima's Royal Audiencia and the viceroy whether the charges were true or false,[27] and the fiscal in Lima, Licentiate Cristóval Cacho de Santillán, was instructed to investigate alleged corruption in the court. Evidence that the nephew's brother-in-law Nicolás de Mendoza Carvajal operated an obraje in Cajamarca was soon uncovered. He too was charged with abusing Indian laborers, forcing them to come from distant areas. They were not paid on time, their workload was heavy, all contrary to royal ordinances protecting obraje workers. The fiscal also examined general working conditions in the obrajes and reported to Spain that cloth factories constituted one of the worst abuses for natives in the viceroyalty. Defenders of the obrajes countered that labor in textile mills was better than any other because the work was done inside, not in the open air, where cold and the rain were endured in full force. Licentiate Cacho de Santillán countered that the workers were "forced and oppressed with ill treatment" and that obrajes were little more than prisons. In some obrajes children were forced to work, receiving miserable compensation. Collaguas kurakas had denounced that children were incorporated into the tribute regime in spite of their age. Viceroy Montesclaros, facing the threat of more detailed scrutiny by the fiscal, revoked the grants to his nephew. But Rodrigo de Mendoza complained to the Crown, arguing that his rewards were just, considering his services as well as those of his wife's family. The fiscal noted that the charges and countercharges stemming from the investigation had led to delaying execution of the order for the dismantling of the Collaguas obraje.[28] Continued pressure of allegations by kurakas, encomenderos, the protector of the Indians, the cabildos of Arequipa and Lima, and the deepening investigation of the king's attorney led to the removal of Viceroy Montesclaros. The king in February 1614 named the Príncipe de Esquilache as his replacement, and Montesclaros was told to leave Peru early in 1615. At about the same time, the corregidor of the Collaguas was replaced by Jerónimo de Pámanes. Most important for Colca Valley natives, the fiscal reported (11 May 1615) that the offending Maca obraje had been demolished.[29]

The frustrated attempt to establish an obraje in the Colca Valley by a viceroy's relative tells much about the operation of the Spanish empire at the local level. Maca was one of the smaller villages in the valley, yet it became the seat of a controversy that led to the royal court. The village was important because it had a working water mill, used for the grinding of the valley's grain; and there was sufficient water to power another mill for a cloth factory, as well as Indians nearby to provide a labor force. Viceroy Montesclaros, an individual closely tied to the monarchy, took to the Indies a large retinue of friends and relatives. His nephew was an eligible match for the local elite and was able to marry into one of the richer Creole families. The viceroy rewarded the couple by a grant of income from a recently vacated Collaguas repartimiento, followed by a license to build a textile factory in the valley. Arequipa's elite saw a clear threat to their continued access to native workers and immediately lodged complaints. One member of the Arequipa elite, the encomendero Alonso Picado, directly faced the threat. Colca valley kurakas joined in the suit, as did the protector of the Indians. Complaints about the viceroy's conduct went from the valley's villages to Spain, where the Council of the Indies ruled for the plaintiffs. Viceroy Montesclaros was removed from office and returned to Spain. In blocking operation of an obraje, the Collaguas won because the Arequipa elite and the Creole faction in Lima wanted to check the viceroy. They, along with the Indian protector, valley kurakas, and some doctrineros joined forces to prevent tampering with the system. Ordinary Indian workers did not savor the triumph for long. Just a decade later a rich lode of silver ore was discovered at Caylloma.

The settlement of Caylloma was the most distant village from the floor of the Colca Valley and Arequipa. Situated near the northern edge of the corregimiento, at an inhospitable site and a high elevation, it initially served as a center for the local herding of llamas and alpacas and as a stopping place on the road between Cuzco and Arequipa. Few Spaniards found it likeable when they chanced to rest for a night. The Caylloma cleric Bartolomé de Vega, who administered to the spiritual needs of the 600 Indians of the repartimientos of Alonso Picado and Retamoso, complained in 1596 that he needed every one of the 600 pesos' yearly stipend he received in order to survive. He lamented that there was much work and little reward, that the food was terrible, and that Caylloma was in the middle of nowhere.[30] In 1586 the inspectors of Los Collaguas reported that "no mines of gold or silver have been discovered in this province, but it is reputed that they are there." In 1626 speculation became reality. The discovery that took place on the northern fringes of the province came to have disastrous consequences for both natives of the Colca Valley and for those in surrounding districts. The rich silver deposits were located near Cucho, a small hamlet not far from Caylloma but annexed to Lari and under the religious charge of the Franciscans. The silver ore was discovered by two brothers of the Gamero family, miners from the village of Pampacolca in nearby Condesuyos province.[31]

As the mining center grew, two parishes were established: one for Spaniards, the other for Indians. The Franciscan church, dedicated to St. Francis of Assisi, was built using tribute designated for church construction and maintenance. An Indian hospital was also constructed at Caylloma. Provisions for the settlement were frequently in short supply. Miners at Caylloma often found it preferable to purchase highland wheat, rather than buying it from Arequipa and transporting it to the mining center.[32] Several of the mines were located about two leagues from the town's center. The mills were powered by water from a stream that began several kilometers away; and nearby Lake Vilafro, roughly a league in circumference, was used to store water for the mills during the dry season, generally August through October. During years of peak production, the annual output reached 100,000 marks of silver. During its heyday twenty-four mills ground the ore in preparation for the extraction of silver by the amalgamation process. Small deposits of gold, tin, lead, copper, and sulphur existed in the district as well, but they were not mined because of the high cost of extraction.[33]

Viceroy Conde de Chinchón wrote to Philip IV in April 1631, describing the mines and reporting that he had sent the lieutenant Don Francisco Sigoñez y Luján to inspect the site. Luján's report was enthusiastic: the mines yielded excellent ore, and there promised to be an ample quantity of silver. A Royal Treasury office was established and functioned for 150 years, 1631 to 1781. The viceroy had recommended, given high production costs, that instead of paying the fifth (*quinto*) of mine production at Caylloma to the Royal Treasury, that a tenth be paid instead. The king refused but did authorize 7.5 percent for the first four years of production, to be followed by the normal quinto. Miners who flocked to the new center quickly requested a mitayo distribution, but the viceroy told the king that he had not yet reached a decision on that issue. Philip IV in March 1633 requested a full report and review by the Council of the Indies regarding the question of mitayos for the mine operators. He thanked the viceroy for his prudent and zealous service, and confirmed the establishment of the treasury office. Regarding mitayos, the king wrote, "I leave it up to your good judgment. You are there and know the problems in the district and the demands already made on the Indians." He noted he was well informed that many Collaguas tributaries were already serving in the Arequipa mita and exhorted the Conde de Chinchón to investigate if it might be possible to "exempt them from this requirement, or moderate it." If the viceroy did issue a grant of mitayos for the miners, he was told to establish the proper wages.[34] The geographical setting of the site created immediate supply problems for miners who wanted mitayos. There was heated competition between various mining centers for mitayo workers. The Huancavelica mita draft extended to the edge of the province of Los Collaguas, and at various times Potosí miners demanded a supply of Collaguas mitayos. Mine operators at a third mining center, Castrovirreina, located relatively close to Caylloma, also coveted a mitayo draft. The proximity of Arequipa was critical. The city's vecinos wanted to retain their supply of mitayos, just as they had when threatened by the Maca obraje draft, and they acted as a buffer against pressures from Caylloma miners for more workers. Yet there was no question that some Collaguas mitayos would be assigned. They lived, after all, in the province where the mines were discovered.

Even at its best Caylloma never approached the importance of the great mining centers of Potosí or Huancavelica, or even Castrovirreina. Production at the various mines of Caylloma rose and fell during the century and a half of the existence of its treasury office. Some initially rich mines were quickly depleted, and operators were forced to turn their attention elsewhere. In 1647 Alonso Amado Lobato, who owned and worked the mill of Chipacha for sixteen years, reported he was exploiting the rich mine of Tintamarca, eight leagues from

Caylloma. Two leagues beyond, in the same mountain range, he was working the mine of Misagunca y Chinchón. In contrast to Caylloma there was ample firewood and pasturage and a river providing water year-round. He petitioned to leave Caylloma to establish a new mill in Tintamarca, just across the border in the Condesuyos corregimiento. Lobato had been authorized to use sixty-two Caylloma mitayos, and requested permission to shift forty-five of them to the new location. His request was granted, with the support of the corregidor of Condesuyos, largely because the mitayos would not have to leave the corregimiento.[35] In January 1648 Don Pedro Sagrado Manrique began an inspection of Caylloma's Royal Treasury. His inquiry failed to uncover substantial fraud or abuse, but the visitador was shocked by the run-down state of the treasury office. He reported that "the wall is somewhat dangerous" and the roof leaking severely. He warned, "Because we are presently in the time of the rains, the wall and the roof could collapse," and he ordered the immediate transfer of all records and stocks in the office to the principal hall in the local treasury official's home. The Indians bore the brunt of the removal, transporting materials from the unsafe building to the temporary quarters.[36]

Working conditions at Caylloma were excruciatingly difficult, as in other major mining centers in the Andes. Labor was dangerous, with constant threat of cave-ins and illnesses associated with the noxious metallic dust emitted by the continuous work with the picks. To ease suffering natives turned to their traditional palliative, coca leaves. Coca use was ubiquitous in Andean America; it dulls sensations of pain and hunger. The church also promised a release from pain, as the immediate anxieties and complaints of the more convinced recent converts were channeled into religious rituals. In the colonial Andes miraculous events were not uncommon, and Caylloma yielded its own. At the beginning of the third decade of the seventeenth century, an astonished Indian miner unearthed what seemed to be a set of three crosses of the Calvary in the mine of Diego Bravo de Saravia. On the eve of the Invention of the Holy Cross, in May 1631, as the Indian pickers were following a silver vein fifty *estados* (measurement, approximately the height of a man) beneath the surface, they found in a concavity in the vein a "strange calvary formed by three crosses." In the words of a seventeenth-century cleric, "Inside such a mass of metal, it could only have been created by the omnipotent hand of God." The largest of the three crosses was in the center. The Indian laborer inadvertently broke the cross on the left; the two remaining ones were chiseled out of the stone together. The material was "no less admirable than the shape of the crosses." It was not silver, but a cloudy crystal, "still of undeterminable type." The crosses were perfectly wrought, albeit rough, similar to the wood "of the true cross." News of the discovery spread immediately, and as it was brought to the surface, 200 Spaniards and 500 Indians were on the scene to witness the event. The largest cross was placed in the sanctuary of the parish church of Caylloma, where "it is seen and venerated by the Franciscans." The mine owner took one cross for himself, and the third broken one remained in the mine along with the pick of the Indian who discovered them.

The symbolism was lost on no one, especially clerics. The sign was marveled at by all, "in proof of the truth of the passion, death, and redemption of the human species by the true son of God, Jesus Christ, on the mysterious tree of the cross." According to one cleric the miracle came at a time when there were "defamations, obstinacies, Hebrewisms, in the new regions." The sign became a valuable tool for Caylloma's clergy as they moved against presumed enemies of the Church. And the cross in the mine was a symbol, a new spiritual force, a new huaca, for the Andeans who toiled to extract the precious ores for the Spaniards. The corregidor, Diego Bravo de Saravia, immediately began construction of a church for the Spaniards. The new church, named Santa Cruz (some called it the Church of the Hospital), was used until 1777 when a fire ignited by flames of candles left unattended by a woman parishioner burned the wooden main altar, then spread and destroyed much of the structure.[37]

Mita Service in Public Works

The Andean economy was geared to local self-sufficiency, yet a remarkable infrastructure of roads, bridges, and tambos useful for wider economic and political integration had been developed long before the Europeans arrived. There was a brief period of decay during the conquest period, and some sections of the existing Andean road network were inappropriate for horses and wheeled vehicles. Following the end of the civil wars in the 1550s, Europeans made efforts to maintain the infrastructure as a necessary foundation for the colonial economy, both internal and external. The public inns, tambos that so impressed Europeans when they first entered Tawantinsuyu, were just as important for colonial officials to maintain as they had been for the Inca. And preservation of a road network paralleling the Inca one was critical. Governor Cristóbal Vaca de Castro in 1543 noted that from Cuzco to Arequipa there were long stretches of puna land with little to sustain travelers. From Hatun Cana, located one day's journey from the village of Yanaoca, to Arequipa, the traveler was required to trek five to six days over frigid highlands where there existed little fuel or food. Vaca de Castro considered it improper for Indians to travel this route, especially those burdened with heavy loads, and ordered the people of Canas to use the Collaguas route. Six years later La Gasca wrote the king to report that silver mined from the recently discovered Potosí mines was transported from the highlands to Lima via the Cabana road to Arequipa's coastal port. In 1586 Ulloa Mogollón reported that the royal road through the province of the Collaguas was "reasonably" good and that the other route, through Velille, was more winding and rugged.[38]

The tambo of Siguas was one of the most important tambos in southern Peru. Humiliating exploitation of local native laborers, especially women, was common in tambo service. For the public good of the colonizers, not the colonized, La Gasca ordered the Cabanas of Diego Hernández de la Cuba to serve in the tambo of Siguas. In 1550 the cabildo of Arequipa mandated, in detailed fashion, that tributaries from surrounding repartimientos serve in the Siguas tambo in rotation. Tributaries of a minor son of Gómez de León were to be posted from December through March; then those of Juan de la Torre from April through July; and finally the tributaries of Diego Hernández de la Cuba for the remainder of the year. In 1557 the obligations of those who were engaged in Siguas tambo service became so aggravating that Don Pedro, kuraka of Siguas under Antonio Gómez de Buitrón, complained bitterly to authorities. The frustrated kuraka charged that the Indians of Lucura (perhaps Lluta?) and Cabana that were tributaries of Diego Hernández de la Cuba had absented themselves from service for a period of seven months. The kuraka's own Indians were unable to work their fields in the countryside. Further, there were too few Indians appearing for duty in the tambo. He demanded that officials order the Cabanas to return to tend the tambo. The Arequipa cabildo concurred, and mandated that Juan de la Torre and Diego Hernández de la Cuba's Indians return to serve in the Siguas tambo.[39]

Around 1556 the Siguas tambo was sold, an unthinkable act in the traditional Andean system, but characteristic of the evolving colonial economy based on Old World notions of property. Juanes Navarro purchased the tambo, acting at the time as guardian for Antonio Gómez de Buitrón, who was a minor. Two years later, in January 1558, Francisco de Torres, protector of the Indians in Arequipa, spoke in defense of the Cabanas kurakas. He contended that the kurakas of Siguas, perhaps at the instigation of Antonio Gómez de Buitrón, had demanded that the Cabanas tributaries serve in the Siguas tambo. According to Torres, the service posed a significant health threat. He noted the Cabanas were highlanders and that service in the yungas near the coast frequently led to illnesses and too often death. He contended that the tambo was now in private hands, not held by the entire community as before, and therefore Cabana tributaries should not have to work for a private master. Cabanas kurakas testified that under the Inca they were not required to tend the Siguas tambo and served only in the tambo in Cabana, as they still did. If at any time they served in Siguas, it was against their will and under orders of captains and others during "the period of altercations" at the time of La Gasca.[40]

The testimony of the cleric Juan de Córdoba is especially informative regarding risks to the indigenous population associated with tambo service. He had been a clergyman in Cabana for five to six years, arriving at the end of the Gonzalo Pizarro revolt. He testified:

> The Indians from Cabana who descend to serve in Siguas become ill and die, and the people who travel through take them [the Cabana tambo mitayos] as far as Camaná, and bring them even to this city [Arequipa]. Some of those who go to Camaná, as it is so far from their own land, remain and fail to return to their homes. I know this because I have been entrusted with the doctrina of the Indians of Cabana and I know by memory and book, and by inspection and taking count of them. I have found that many Indians, and children and women, and chinas (a Hispanicized Indian female) are missing because they have descended to serve in Siguas. The remainder have said that those missing are dead and lost, and I have seen many ill Indians return and I have cured them.

Juan de Córdoba's testimony supports the position taken by Cabanas encomenderos who were losing manpower. They often complained about the ill effects of migration of highlanders to the coastal region.[41]

Don Juan, kuraka of Andagua in the next major valley system north of the Colca Valley, an area known as the "valley of the volcanoes," also testified. He said that he knew that "the Indians of Cabana greatly feared the descent to Siguas, because they became ill there." He understood their feelings well, because he was also a highlander, who "feared" Siguas and similar "tierra caliente." Don Juan added, "In the time of the Inca the Indians of Cabana did not serve in Siguas, but on the contrary, in Pampacolca," which is in the highlands. The Mercedarian friar Juan de Heredia, resident in Cabana about three years, concurred that migration to the lowlands was a cause of illness and death. He testified, "The Indians of Cabana keep a record by the quipu of those who have died, and many have, both in Siguas and in other parts of the yungas."[42] Having resided in Cabana two years, the Mercedarian friar Gregorio Palacios concurred. At the conclusion of the investigation, the Arequipa corregidor,

Alonso Martínez de Rivera, ordered the Cabanas freed from mita service in the Siguas tambo. He also commanded local Indians under control of Antonio Gómez de Buitrón to continue to provide workers for the tambo.[43]

During the conflict between the royalists and encomenderos, both factions moved goods and weapons along the route through the Colca Valley. Francisco de Carvajal wrote in 1547 that he preferred the route because there were insufficient transport Indians along the coast. In 1569 Philip II prohibited the use of the Cabanas of Hernández de la Cuba as cargo transporters. The monarch had been informed that they had been forced to carry large packs of goods from one location to another and that it was especially dangerous for the natives to transport commodities from the sierra, where the Cabanas resided, to coastal sites. Cabanas tributaries had, for example, been sent to the port of Chule and to other warm sectors of the coast. They had even been forced to work in the tambo to make *mullos* (beads from reed shells for the *chaquiras*, necklaces) and *cestos* (baskets); as a result, many fell ill and died. Further, the Indians of Cabana had been used to transport articles in the highlands as far away to the southeast as the province of Collao, and northward to Cuzco. The Cabanas carried goods on their backs or acted as pack drivers. Philip II ordered cessation of the abusive practice.[44]

It is not surprising that some of Viceroy Toledo's Ordinances for the Indian Republic involved regulation of the tambos. The basic rate for overnight stays was set at one-half real; the rate remained in force until 1621, when it was increased to one and one-half reales for tambo service, and two for guarding and feeding pack animals. Travelers were forbidden to remain in the same tambo for more than three days. Local tributaries, as in Inca times, were required to maintain the inns. They served in various capacities at the inns, except their administration. They cleaned the establishments, they loaded and unloaded the pack animals and provided fodder for them, and they prepared the food for travelers; and in spite of prohibitions, native women often engaged in prostitution.

Bridge construction in the Colca Valley was especially important for communications and commerce. The river cut a deep canyon, and passage at many locales was difficult, even at low water during the dry season. In most places crossing the river on a regular basis was mandatory for survival, as in the case of Yanque urinsaya agriculturalists whose plots were on the other side of the river. The primary problem in bridge construction was economic, payment for workers and materials. The nearest Spanish-style stone bridge was on the northern edge of Arequipa, where settlers using the local native labor force, including many from the Colca Valley, constructed a bridge across the Chili River connecting the urban center with Yanahuara and nearby communities. With this bridge they were able to link the predominantly Indian villages of Yanahuara and Cayma to Arequipa, and to the Collaguas province and Cuzco beyond. In a cabildo session in June 1560, some 3,000 pesos were authorized to cover stipends of Indians engaged in the construction of the bridge. The bridge was destroyed in the 1582 earthquake; reconstruction took several years. Arequipa's cabildo in August 1590 requested permission from the viceroy to levy a 1 percent tax on all merchandise entering the city for a four-year period, in order to rebuild the bridge. But in the countryside in the Colca Valley, Indians, following native practice, were responsible for the construction and maintenance of bridges.[45]

Several bridges were built across the Colca River during the colonial era. Because of both the width and depth of the canyon, virtually all of the early bridges were suspension, made of rope cords with a woven floor that at times included wooden planks. Native suspension bridges were much better adapted to the Andean environment than the stone-arched bridge construction of the Europeans. The collapse of the stone bridge across the Chili River in Arequipa in the 1582 earthquake provided a reminder that native technology was usually best. The first stone bridge across the Colca canyon, linking the village of Yanque to the fields of Ullo Ullo and the communities of Coporaque and Ichupampa, was not erected until the early eighteenth century. In 1703 it was pointed out that a new church at Yanque was nearing completion, and the local labor force could be transferred to construct a stone bridge across the canyon. Officials at Caylloma and Yanque agreed such a bridge would aid commerce both within the valley, and with the Caylloma silver-mining center to the north. A bridge would also benefit friars making their rounds to administer the sacraments. In February 1704, a total of thirty-one mitayos from Chivay and Yanque were authorized for two years for bridge construction across the valley just below Yanque. But Arequipa's cabildo complained that local hacendados would be hurt by the labor shortage that would result from use of mitayos originally assigned to the city's mita de plaza. Cabildo members also queried why a stone structure was necessary when for centuries a suspension bridge had been adequate. This time interests in the valley prevailed, and the mitayos built the bridge. The present structure, completed in 1801, links Yanque and the north side of the canyon. It is fine for people and pack animals, but is of little use for wheeled vehicles because of the steepness of the access road and the narrowness of the bridge.[46]

Short- and long-distance migration has always been a characteristic of the Andean world, in spite of attempts to limit it by both the Inca and the Spanish. The very nature of the ayllu, designed to guarantee the securing of all necessities from a variety of ecological niches, stimulated the movement of people. Migration to the coastal waters to obtain dried fish, or short-term travel to secure salt for the ayllu's annual needs, were common. Pastoralism in the puna lands fostered longer-distance movement of people, as they tended flocks of llamas and alpacas. And there was "mandatory" migration for major labor projects under the Inca, and for war and defense. Forced movement of people intensified under the Spanish colonial system, with long-distance mita service in the mines, and shorter-distance mita requirements in the nearest center of Spanish authority. The distance from the Colca Valley to the city of Arequipa was substantial, and there was relatively close contact during the colonial period. Indeed, communications were likely to have been more continuous in the colonial than in the modern era, when the traditional transportation network broke down. Close ties between valley residents and Arequipa were partly the consequence of the ethnic enclaves in and around the city that were reinforced by the encomienda system. All Colca Valley encomenderos had tributaries settled in or near Arequipa, as illustrated by Viceroy Toledo's tribute assessment (see table 11). Collaguas and Lari tributaries were settled in La Chimba of Arequipa. Some from Cabanaconde were concentrated in Tiabaya, an agricultural community in the Arequipa Valley, while others were downriver from Cabanaconde in coastal Camaná.[47]

The community of La Chimba, or Yanahuara, existed before the Spanish foundation of Arequipa. Between 1536 and 1539 a group of religious headed by Friar Pedro de Ulloa began conversion efforts in the Chili Valley. Ulloa founded a small church, which he dedicated to Saint John the Baptist; from that time the settlement of Yanahuara was also known as the "Villa de San Juan Bautista de la Chimba." Viceroy Toledo reorganized the town as a reducción in October 1576. Because of its proximity to Arequipa, La Chimba grew rapidly, soon becoming the principal native residence for those who migrated from the north to work in the city. It was essentially an Indian village during the colonial period. Nearby fields were cultivated with a variety of crops that were sold in the urban market of Arequipa: corn, wheat, potatoes, fruits, and vegetables. The population of La Chimba was 8,139 at the time of Toledo's census. In a 1792 count, only 1,466 residents of the village remained.[48]

TABLE 11. Colca Valley enclaves settled in Arequipa's Yanahuara,
or elsewhere under Toledo

Enclave	Tributaries	Boys	Old and ill males	Women	Total
Los Collaguas	141	122	14	288	565
Lari (Francisco Hernández Retamoso)	169	159	9	312	649
Lari (Alonso Rodríguez Picado)	181	192	11	421	805
Cabanaconde (Diego Hernández de la Cuba) (in Tiabaya)	11	—	—	—	—
Cabanaconde (Hernando de la Torre) (in Camaná)	25	—	—	—	191

Source: Cook, *Tasa de la visita general de Francisco de Toledo*, 218–27

Some Colca Valley natives migrated to the far-distant viceregal capital. A
number of the Collaguas and Cabanas, after spending time in Yanahuara or
Arequipa first, traveled to Lima and worked in the city at the beginning of the
seventeenth century. In the census taken in 1613 of the Indians living in Lima,
we discover twenty-four-year-old Diego Felipe from La Chimba who migrated
to city about 1608, and was sacristan in the parish of San Sebastián. His encomendero in Arequipa was Gerónimo de la Cuba, and the kuraka was his own
father, Juan Ascala. At the same time, we encounter in Lima an eleven-year-old
boy named Alonso, who was a servant in the house of the treasury accountant Sebastián de Mosquera, a past Collaguas corregidor and later treasury official in Arequipa. Alonso's father was named "Alonso Picado"; he was also from
La Chimba, and his father's encomendero was Captain Francisco Retamoso.
The young servant had been in Lima only a few days when the census was
taken. Also in Mosquera's house resided a twelve-year-old boy from La Chimba
named Martín. He had been born in the accountant's house in Arequipa; his
parents were listed as "unknown." Although Mosquera certified that he was a
mestizo, the census taker noted the boy "dressed as an Indian." One wonders
what the exact relationship was between the Royal Treasury accountant and
this mestizo child of "unknown" parents born in his own house.[49] Other Indians from La Chimba resided in Lima in 1613. A thirty-year-old tailor, Alonso
Conde had migrated to Lima about 1598. He was married to a sixteen-year-old
named Juana Ballacho, from coastal Ica, and they had a three-year-old daughter
named Beatriz. Then in the household of Juan de la Fuente we find a twelve-
year-old servant who worked in the house of Juan de la Serna for about two

years. His father had died in Majes, but his mother, Inés, was still alive in Arequipa. Cabanaconde was the origin of one fifteen-year-old Indian servant, who lived in the household of Alejos de Montoya. The young man had migrated to Lima three years earlier, and reported that his kuraka was Martín Antiala and his encomendero was Hernando de la Torre. Numerous other Indian migrants from in and around Arequipa lived in Lima in 1613; they were mostly servants or artisans.[50]

The Collaguas and the Cabanas were engaged simultaneously in two economic systems: domestic and extractive. The domestic was based largely on subsistence agriculture. But the tribute regime imposed by the Spanish was more purely extractive, by appropriating both locally produced goods and the labor of the Amerindians. Since wages were an insufficient incentive to capture the labor of the Collaguas and Cabanas, the colonial state resorted to forced labor, with a certain percentage of the native population required to work a specified number of days each year. The colonial state attempted to defend mita labor, for the "commonwealth." In theory there may be some justification for labor to construct churches, hospitals, roads, bridges, public granaries, and government buildings. These benefited both the Indian Republic and the Spanish, although the Europeans clearly had the best of the bargain. Other uses of forced labor are hardly justifiable: the work on the houses and fields of the encomenderos, extraction of minerals in the mines, work in the textile factories, long-distance transport of commodities, service in distant tambos. Migration, both forced and free, dislocated Andean peoples, removing them from their home provinces and funneling them into new situations. Moreover, in the extractive economy labor and value were exported to the metropolis, leaving behind increasing poverty and, with time, environmental degradation.

CHAPTER EIGHT

INDOCTRINATION AND RESISTANCE

A shaman had fooled the puna herdsmen and residents of Lari and Cabana, and many others in this province. . . . He convinced them that atop a snowcapped peak named Curiviri there was a great toad he called Ampato, and that this toad was god, and he defecated gold.
— Francisco Hernández testimony, 21 January 1584, Archivo Nacional del Perú, Residencias 5, cuad. 9.

Institutional Structure

Along with the sword of Santiago came the cross. Yet in spite of the encomenderos' obligation to see to the indoctrination of their charges, their efforts were meager and the results disappointing. The colonizers never doubted the moral imperative to convert Amerindians and the superiority of Christianity, and they intended to assist the Church in saving souls, both native Americans and their own in the process. Indigenous religion was to be swept aside, and the religious memory of Andean peoples silenced. The encomenderos were ill equipped for this daunting task, and even as they first surveyed their grants they tried to secure legitimate catechists—priests and friars—to begin the conversion efforts. Relatives of encomenderos were preferred, because they were most likely to accept the encomenderos' treatment of their charges. If no relatives were available, then perhaps clergy from the same city or region in Spain were secured by the encomendero, for similar reasons. But qualified religious were hard to find, especially at first, and making headway in the construction of an alien and complex religious system posed a challenge. There were after all upwards of 70,000 people in the valley when the Europeans arrived. The small number of religious, the language barrier, and political instability during the first years after Cajamarca resulted in a veneer of Christian concepts covering an underlying foundation of Andean beliefs. Nevertheless, as a testament to the fervor of the first religious to enter the Andean world, conversion, even if incomplete and using mass baptisms, was achieved within a generation.[1]

Unlike most other Indian provinces in the Andes, where indoctrination was undertaken by either the secular or religious clergy in order to avoid confusion and potential disputes, the task of conversion in the Colca Valley was shared. Some Indian parishes were assigned to secular priests, while friars were given others. Complicating matters in the Collaguas province, Mercedarians worked in the lower valley and Franciscans in the upper. Members of the Franciscan Order were invited to convert the Collagua by either Gonzalo Pizarro, the first encomendero of Yanque, or the Lari encomenderos Marcos Retamoso and Alonso Rodríguez Picado. The religious orders generally stressed obedience, dedication, and the value of leading an exemplary life. They also emphasized courage of Faith and the virtues of martyrdom. In their work in the doctrinas, dedicated friars tended to outdo the secular clergy in conversions, and the Spanish Crown supported their efforts. The inadequate number of secular clergy available to serve isolated Indian parishes also led the Crown to appoint mendicants to administer many doctrinas.[2] Formal founding of Franciscan doctrinas in the Andean countryside followed establishment of their principal monasteries in the major Spanish cities. The Cuzco convent was founded in 1534, then refounded in 1538; the Arequipa house dates from 1552. The monastery of the Immaculate Conception of Yanque—with its doctrinas of Coporaque, Achoma, and Chivay—was established in 1560; Callalli—with its doctrinas of Tute, Tisco, and Sibayo—was created at the same time.[3] The Franciscans were under the general commissioner of the Order, resident in Lima, and it was customary to rotate friars after a three-year residency in a doctrina, to avoid close attachment to the local population. The first of the secular clergy would have been sent by the leading religious authority in Lima, or initially from Cuzco. In the early seventeenth century, following the foundation of the diocese of Arequipa, the city's bishop assumed jurisdiction over the Collaguas doctrinas.[4]

All parties recognized that use of mendicants was a temporary expedient, that ultimately Indian parishes would be transferred to the secular clergy for administration of the sacraments. But no one at the beginning was certain how many years were needed for this process to be completed. Very quickly, in the 1560s the Franciscan commissioner, Luis Zapata, began to move in that direction, creating profound disquiet among members of his order.[5] Subsequently, in 1584 the general commissioner, Friar Jerónimo de Villacarrillo, began in earnest to withdraw the friars, believing their task was fulfilled in many doctrinas. He recalled the friars to their monasteries in the cities; required them to relinquish Indian parishes; and admonished them to return to the life of prayer, contemplation, and poverty originally called for by Saint Francis.[6]

Three sixteenth-century general church councils held in Lima set the foundations for the operation of the Peruvian Church during the colonial period, both in urban centers and in the countryside. The First Council (1551–52) met as stability in the Andes seemed at last assured. Much time was devoted to reviewing the situation in the doctrinas and to establishing guidelines to improve the speed and quality of conversion. The village of each major kuraka, it was decided, should have a church. Wherever important local idols were discovered, they were to be destroyed and replaced with a church, or at least a cross. No one above the age of eight, excepting the ill and elderly, should be baptized without first undergoing thirty days of indoctrination in the native language. Clergy were charged with recording names of those baptized. Aside from recording the assigned name at baptism, the priest was to note whether the person was legitimate, the names and origins of the parents, and the names of their kuraka and encomendero. Council participants insisted that the native name given before baptism be recorded too. The names and residences of godparents concluded the information. Priests were required to sign the entry and record the baptismal date. They were also ordered to maintain marriage registers.[7] Requirements for careful record keeping later became part of the legislation of the Council of Trent. Unfortunately the results, of substantial ethnohistorical value, have not been found. One wonders if clerics actually did keep full account of native and Christian names, given the pressures of indoctrination and inadequate resources.

The men who met in Lima for the First Council were deeply concerned with the need to curtail a variety of abuses prevalent during the early days of indoctrination. Clergy were prohibited from collecting tribute for the encomenderos and from engaging in commerce. Another common problem facing the doctrineros in the Indian communities was access to and use of religious structures. At first it was common practice to use the local tambo, often the largest edifice in a village, for religious instruction until a more fitting permanent church could be erected. Tambos had served as eating and sleeping places; both Europeans and Amerindians continued the practice even after the tambo was converted to a Christian temple, shocking church leaders. Other abandoned structures were appropriated, and priests were ordered to lock the doors and cover the windows so no livestock could enter, nor allow the buildings to be used for nonreligious purposes. Priests were to ensure that all churches had doors and

Coporaque church (photo by N. D. Cook)

Chapel of Santa Ursula, Coporaque (photo by N. D. Cook)

Yanque church, urinsaya entrance (photo by A. P. Cook)

Yanque church, anansaya entrance (photo by N. D. Cook)

locks and that they were closed when not in use. One of the more important of the mandates of the First Council was the requirement that the Pater Noster, Ave Maria, Credo, and the Lord's Commandments be taught in the native languages.[8]

Clerics who met for the Second Church Council (1567–68), in addition to reiterating many provisions of the previous council, ordered the new converts to present their newborns for baptism within eight days. Church leaders again emphasized that sections of doctrine considered essential be imparted in the native tongue.[9] Failure to teach the articles of the Faith in the predominant languages continued to concern subsequent Peruvian church councils. Viceroy Toledo also stressed the need for priests to know the language of their doctrina, recommending that no one be appointed doctrinero until he had mastered the language. Those already in rural doctrinas who did not know the language should either be removed or receive a lower salary until achieving proficiency. Toledo reported that during his visita, one Indian complained to him about the linguistic incompetency of many curates. The viceroy consequently established a chair of Indian languages at Lima's university and instructed officials not to grant the bachelor or licentiate degrees without language study. Priests should not be ordained without proficiency in an Andean tongue, and all doctrineros should be examined within a year by a language professor at the university. Yet Toledo was unwilling to permit ordination of those who possessed the greatest linguistic ability: mestizos. They "might know the language, but lack the virtue," the viceroy argued, insisting it was better to have a Spanish priest with a translator than a mestizo.[10] Language examinations were conducted, although the policy was never consistently and uniformly enforced. As late as the Sixth Lima Church Council (1772), church officials reiterated the need for clerics in the doctrinas to be able to communicate in the native languages.[11]

Second Church Council participants returned to persistent issues of rites and customs they deemed pagan, practices that demanded elimination. Head binding of children, so common in the preconquest Colca Valley, was expressly prohibited. Ritual cutting of hair or wearing it in certain styles was forbidden. Indians were ordered to stop burying their dead with food and clothing. The deceased should be interred within the church. Natives were to end the custom of bringing food and drink into the church on All Souls' Day. They were ordered to terminate the offerings and festivities at planting and harvest, and other "thousands" of ceremonies and rites. Church Fathers accepted the possible efficacy of native medicine and allowed Amerindian doctors to continue curing with local herbs and medications, as long as they stopped their chants and "superstitious ceremonies."[12] The Second Church Council was soon followed by Viceroy Toledo's ordinances, which covered all aspects of religious life in the doctrinas, and by modifications made by his successor, Viceroy Martín Enríquez.

Lima's Third Church Council, in 1583, directed by Archbishop Mogrovejo, was perhaps the most important in the colonial era, and its decisions left an impact on the valley for several generations. Council participants issued a comprehensive set of instructions for the doctrineros. The religious were to act as the primary protectors of native Americans. Limits on economic activities of churchmen were carefully set; they could not trade goods or own cattle, fields, vineyards, or workshops. Priests could neither rent out Indian laborers, nor act as agents and send them to the mines. "The doctrineros should also know that it is completely forbidden to have mills, obrajes, and to engage in any type of commercial activity. Those who have taken as their task the ministry of the teaching of the Gospel in no manner can serve God and money at the same time."[13] This rule was frequently breached, and ecclesiastical officials decided that strong punishment would have to be meted out to reduce abuses. Past fines were insufficient; henceforth, anyone breaking this rule would be excommunicated. Normal standards for priestly conduct were reiterated by the Third Council. Clerics were forbidden to keep company with women and were not allowed to employ native women or young men of school age as household servants. Priests were not to play dice or cards. They could not inherit Indian property.[14]

Council officials again debated the proper size of doctrinas, finally recommending that whenever 200 Indians lived in an area, they should be congregated and a priest be provided. If there were over 400 tributaries in the parish, a second cleric was to be attached. Village churches scattered up and down the Colca Valley are a result of this measure, and of Toledo's settlement ordinances.[15] Priests were implored to ensure that Indians ended their "barbarous and savage" customs. Their houses should have tables and beds, and they should be kept "clean." Shamans should be separated from the community because of their bad example and damage they could inflict. Further, the council stated, "because in place of books the Indians have used and continue to use as records devices of different strings that they call quipus, and with these conserve the memory of their ancient superstitions and rites and ceremonies and perverse customs. We order the bishops to diligently and fully remove from the Indians the memoriales or quipus that serve for their superstition."[16] On the one hand, Toledo was encouraging community notaries to retain the quipus for statistical record keeping; while on the other hand, the Church was ordering their destruction. In spite of the Church's efforts, some natives did retain memory of the use of quipus for more than numerical records. A 1602 Peruvian Jesuit annual letter reports that a blind Indian confessed for four days, using a quipu with various markers of stones, bones, or feathers to remind him of the sins he had committed. The Jesuits came to accept the idea that the quipu represented a real form of writing, and they made serious efforts to learn the secrets of their decipherment.[17]

Religious authorities were preoccupied with the dual questions of idolatries and the ethical conduct of doctrineros. The ethical standards established for the clergy by the Church were high, and were designed to promote the religious well-being of the native residents of the Andes. Yet it is apparent from regulations that Peruvian Church councils regularly issued that the morals of clergymen charged with indoctrination of Andean people were far from exemplary. Many priests were as prone to simony as secular authorities in charge of encomiendas. Sexual temptations were constant; not all clerics resisted. The numerous and detailed rules governing clerical behavior in the doctrinas, repeatedly issued—such as avoiding contact with women and young boys—provide evidence of frequent sexual misconduct. In addition to attempting to improve the standards of the religious, the Crown tried to guarantee that encomenderos, who initially were responsible for spiritual indoctrination of their Indians, actually did carry out their obligation of "Christianization." More than one encomendero was fined for not fulfilling his duty. At the end of Pedro de Valdés's 1574 inspection, several Arequipa encomenderos were charged for failing to indoctrinate their Indians. Some Colca Valley encomenderos among the group were punished for "lack of doctrina." Juan de la Torre was fined 160 pesos, and Diego Hernández de la Cuba was assessed 40 pesos.[18] The size of the fines did not cause economic hardship for either, but the fact that they were levied at all provided an example to other arequipeños that the Crown was serious about its commitment to successful conversion of Amerindian peoples. Furthermore, these infractions and penalties raised eyebrows among members of Arequipa's Spanish community. Much more substantial were the fines stemming from charges lodged in the late 1570s before Lima's Royal Audiencia for inadequate indoctrination. Francisco Noguerol de Ulloa was fined 3,000 pesos, and a levy of 1,173 pesos against Alonso Rodríguez Picado was pending.[19]

It was unusual for an Indian province to be ministered by both the secular and religious clergy, and there were regulations to prevent it. Restrictions existed with good reason; jealousies as well as differing approaches to indoctrination and the relation of the catechized to the Christian "fathers" could cause controversy, doing more damage than good. Nonetheless for a substantial period, seculars and religious shared in the task of indoctrination in the Colca Valley. Perhaps the reason was the original distribution of the valley's inhabitants: the Cabanas and Collaguas were separate ethnic entities. Although conflict between the secular and religious clergy in the valley is not unexpected, what is perhaps surprising are divisions within the Franciscan Order that complicated the friars' efforts. The question centers on the nature of the Order and the proper role of the friars. There was a sharp dichotomy between Saint Francis's vision of a life of monastic contemplation and prayer, and the special millenarian mission in America: conversion of the "heathen." The millenarian "call" was strong, and some Franciscans toured Iberian monasteries to secure recruits for their expanding efforts in the Indies. The Crown took the millenarian position, as did several Franciscan theologians of the period. But not all members of the order agreed; hence the internal debate within the Franciscan community. In 1569, the head of the Order in Peru withdrew the Franciscans from doctrinas in Cajamarca. The Indians who had been indoctrinated by the Franciscans resisted the effort to transfer the doctrinas to the seculars and sent a delegation to meet the recently arrived Viceroy Toledo. Concerned by the remonstrances of the Indian representatives from the Cajamarca district, Toledo visited the Franciscan monastery in Lima. There he consulted with their general commissioner, ordered a count of the number of friars in the city, and promptly mandated their return to the Cajamarca doctrinas. Toledo preferred members of the Order to staff the doctrinas as long as necessary to ensure the indoctrination and well-being of the natives. He did not favor all religious orders; nor did he always maintain good relations with the secular hierarchy.[20]

Shortly after Viceroy Toledo began his return journey to Spain in 1581 the Franciscan general commissioner in Peru, Jerónimo de Villacarrillo, transferred the Indian parishes in the Colca Valley to the jurisdiction of the bishop of Cuzco and the secular clergy. The Collaguas inhabitants sharply protested his move, as earlier Cajamarca kurakas had done, appealing first to Lima, then Spain. Pressure directed by local kurakas continued several years before bearing fruit. In January 1586 Collaguas leaders testified:

The friars of Saint Francis built the churches that exist in the whole province, and they led us in worship until about two years ago [c. 1584], when they left the doctrinas and returned to their monasteries under the orders of their Commissioner, Friar Gerónimo de Villacarrillo. This saddened the Indians so much that they daily weep for the Franciscan priests, and they are so attached to them, and they love and respect them so affectionately that they have tried with all their might to get them to return to take charge of the doctrinas. In the place of the friars have come the clerics of the Order of St. Peter [secular clergy]; these are not as welcome as the friars.[21]

The kurakas made damning charges against the priests: they traded in cloth and bags, they were engaged in transportation of wine and livestock, and they charged excessive fees for the sacraments. Pressure for reinstatement of the Franciscans to the Collaguas doctrinas continued several years. Finally in March 1590 the new viceroy, García Hurtado de Mendoza, ordered the friars back to the valley. In keeping with Franciscan tradition, twelve men were named for the Collaguas effort. Philip II confirmed the order four years later, in January 1594.[22]

The return of the Franciscans was relatively easy in most parts of the Crown grant of Yanque Collaguas, where they had their strongest roots. But seculars in some villages resisted, and violence erupted. The events allow an intimate glimpse of the often tense relationship between the secular and regular clergy in some Andean doctrinas. In December 1585 Collaguas kurakas complained to the corregidor, Juan de Ulloa Mogollón, that there were still no Franciscans in the province. In September the following year, Luis Jerónimo de Oré, solicitor of the Franciscans in the Collaguas, presented papers before Alonso Osorio, the corregidor and *justicia mayor* (chief justice) of Arequipa. Viceroy Conde del Villar had ordered the return of the Franciscans, and Friar Oré asked the corregidor to execute the order. Already the restitution had begun, but the Franciscans faced difficulties in Lari with Father Hernando Medel, who insisted that the doctrineros of Lari had to have regular appointment from the bishop. Oré countered that this had never been the case in the past and asked for the restitution order to be enforced according to the spirit and letter of the law. The corregidor agreed. Nevertheless Medel refused to leave, and Lari remained in the control of the clerics four more years.

On 10 July 1590 a group of Franciscan friars headed by Luis Jerónimo de Oré met in Lari with the Collaguas corregidor, Captain Gaspar Verdugo. Oré, acting as convent solicitor, presented Viceroy García Hurtado de Mendoza's

His favorites were the Franciscans, as is evident here (629 [643])

A Mercedarian overseeing cloth production (647 [661])

An Augustinian, enforcing the rule (643 [657])

A Dominican "directing" a native woman's cloth manufacture (645 [659])

order that gave the Franciscans control of the doctrinas. Following standard procedure, the order was read in the presence of the corregidor and the cleric, Andrés de Arana. The corregidor took the cédula, placed it on his forehead, and vowed to execute the order. Arana replied that he would obey the command but needed a copy to prepare a reply, "within the time you give," attempting to delay the order's execution. The friars demanded the immediate withdrawal of the priest from both the church and his house. Arana refused, and, flaunting an official letter of presentation for the doctrina, he insisted he had a right to remain. Soon Arana stood at the door of his house, then locked it, barring entry. While the friars were discussing the situation, the church doors were suddenly thrown open and the monks rushed in. Following an oration, they headed for the sacristy, but Father Arana blocked the door. In the meantime a group of friars poured into the sacristy by another entrance and from there were able to enter the priest's residence. They locked all the doors, rang the church bells, then opened the doors again, in an act of possession. The corregidor duly confirmed their possession according to the provision of the viceroy. Father Arana loudly protested that he held the parish by "just title" and requested that the corregidor recognize his rights.[23]

The following day the group went to the nearby pueblos of Maca and Ichupampa, its annex. Both doctrinas were administered by cleric Juan de Camargo, who also defended his right to the doctrina, arguing that he should not be expelled from it without a hearing. The corregidor responded that he was executing the king's orders. On 12 July, the group went to Tuti and read the order to the cleric Adrian de Asperamonte. He said he would obey, but would appeal to the audiencia and king. The following day the Franciscans occupied in the same symbolic fashion the church of Sibayo, an annex of Tuti.[24] The forced restoration of the Franciscans did not end conflict; there was now a clear breach between the religious order and the secular authorities of the diocese. Almost simultaneously with reinstatement of the Franciscans in the valley, the Cuzco bishop Gregorio de Montalvo filed a complaint, maintaining that the clerics should continue in their posts. The bishop argued that according to the Council of Trent a secular priest should impart the doctrine to parishioners. Montalvo inferred that clerics were better equipped than friars to administer sacraments to Andeans, who had "such deficient intelligence and such depraved nature."[25] Further, the friars used their own unauthorized works in indoctrination. That, the bishop contended, could only lead to confusion and be harmful to the Faith.

Bishop Montalvo directed his outcry to Peru's resident provincial, Friar Hernando de Trejo, then in Guamanga's Franciscan convent. Trejo received the bishop's orders that the three friars be removed to permit the clerics to return to their "rightful" posts on 13 November 1590. Provincial Trejo was assisted by the Franciscan court solicitor Friar Mateo de Recalde. His response was detailed and stressed the correctness of the order's position; the Franciscans returned at the bidding of Viceroy García Hurtado de Mendoza. The solicitor Recalde explained that he had petitioned the viceregal court to have the Franciscans removed, fearing possible damage by posting clerics and friars in a single province. For the "peace and improvement of the doctrina," he argued, it would be better to have either one or the other, not both. Recalde admitted that Villacarrillo had earlier withdrawn the Franciscans from the province; at the time they lacked enough friars proficient in the language. He noted the friars were reluctant to leave, partly because the Collaguas was a Crown repartimiento. During Viceroy Conde del Villar's administration, restoration of the doctrinas began. Recalde pointed out that the Franciscans had already left some of the best doctrinas in the realm, and had no "desires or pretensions." Moreover the king wanted friars in some doctrinas; he was after all sending them to the Indies at his own expense. Recalde declared that the Council of Trent did not prohibit Franciscan activities in Indian parishes and suggested it would be easy to transfer the three dispossessed clerics to benefices elsewhere. And costs of indoctrination by friars were half those of clerics. In the end Recalde and Trejo submitted themselves to the authority of the bishop of Cuzco. Then, "for the tranquility of the friars it would be beneficial to leave these and all the others that we have . . . , all the friars are by their rules subject to the bishops, and must obey their commands. Therefore, I ask to take leave not only of the three doctrinas cited by your grace, but also all the doctrinas of the province of Los Collaguas, and will turn over all to whoever you present." Trejo also requested that the Franciscans be removed from all the remaining doctrinas "we have in your diocese . . . , Guayllabamba in the Yucay valley, and Pocsi in the district of Arequipa."[26]

While secular and Franciscan authorities debated the issue, a new commissioner, Friar Antonio Ortiz, arrived in Peru. Already in October 1590 he had formulated a response to the king's request that provincials inform him of their position on retaining the Indian doctrinas. "In my judgment, engagement of our friars in the doctrinas is not suitable for the conscience of Your Majesty, nor that of the bishops, nor for the good of the Indians, nor for the perfection of the friars." Indians were under the complete jurisdiction of the bishops, who necessarily had full control over their flocks. There should be priests, and their tenures should be long so they would truly know their parishioners. He concluded, insisting that conditions the missionaries faced daily in the doctrinas were contrary to the precepts of the order: "I cannot ease my conscience until the friars are out of them, or I am out of this position."[27]

In mid-December 1590 the Franciscan solicitor Friar Recalde was in Lima, prodding officials for copies of all documentation regarding Franciscan activities in the Collaguas. By April 1591 Lima officials authorized the Franciscans to retain the doctrinas in the Collaguas under Crown administration, and again recognized the right of friars to dispense the sacraments. In September 1592 the Royal Chancellery sent Recalde copies of decrees referring to the Collaguas he had requested. On 25 November 1592, Justice Baltasar de la Cruz of the Council of the Indies recommended that for "the general and common good . . . of the Indians of the province of los Collaguas and Cabanaconde," all doctrinas should be restored to the Franciscans. He noted some clerics had "fortified" their positions, setting a poor example for the natives, and he urged the Franciscans to return to the Collaguas as originally ordered by Viceroy Toledo. De la Cruz concluded that "as these Collaguas, all their life, have been under the good treatment of the friars, they feel [maltreatment] more than the others, and thus the caciques have come many times to the city, expending much money in order to achieve this end." In November 1593, Philip II referred to Recalde's request and stated that the Council of the Indies had reviewed attempts of the bishop to name clerics to the Collaguas. The king ordered the friars to continue in their doctrinas. On 6 December 1593, Philip II ordered that anything given to the Franciscans in Peru for support be called alms, not a stipend, "for the good of their consciences."[28]

Philip II on 6 January 1594 confirmed the Franciscan position. His decision was based on a thorough evaluation of the charges against the seculars and the rationale for the return of the Franciscans. The monarch noted that friars had been active from the inception of conversion efforts in the valley. Furthermore, during the visita general Viceroy Toledo had confirmed the jurisdiction of the Franciscans from their centers at Lari and Yanque. After Villacarrillo ordered the removal of the friars, the secular clergy who assumed the vacancies were not as well liked by the native parishioners as the mendicants had been. Philip II referred to a pastoral inspection by Archdeacon Pedro Muñiz of the Cuzco cathedral church. During the visita he discovered that "in the year that they [seculars] were there, they did many things to harm the Indians with their dealings and agreements, and levied on them such excessive baptismal and marriage fees . . . that he [Muñiz] charged that all were simoniacs and ordered them to return to the Indians more than six thousand pesos that they had usurped during that year." Inflated fees levied by unscrupulous clerics were always fuel for reformers. Abuses may have been worse earlier, when ecclesiastical controls were weak. Charles V in June 1552 notified the bishop of Cuzco that he had received reports that some clerics were charging exorbitant baptismal and burial fees. Indians resorted to burying their dead in the fields rather than properly interring them at the very time that the church was attempting to eradicate ancient burial customs. As a result of the findings of Archdeacon Muñiz the fiscal of the Royal Audiencia proceeded against guilty priests, and they were deprived of their doctrinas and forced to return the 6,000 pesos they had extracted from the Indians.[29]

Conflict between seculars and regulars in the valley continued, especially in Lari in the middle valley. Lari kurakas in the mid-1590s were forced again to appear before the viceroy and Audiencia, presenting a royal order to Viceroy Marqués de Cañete (Madrid, 6 January 1594) to turn over both Yanque and Lari Collaguas and their annexes to the Franciscans. In July 1595 the kurakas, with support of Antonio de Torres de la Fresneda, the "protector general de los indios," appeared in Lima to request a letter of execution of the earlier royal decree. But the four clerics serving in the Lari district challenged the kurakas, arguing that their voice be heard.[30] The kurakas and their supporters contended that clerics did not hold their doctrinas by title, but were simply appointed, and that appointment could be revoked at any time. They maintained that the spiritual welfare of the villagers should be the uppermost concern. The kurakas argued that the clerics had fulfilled spiritual obligations, but "the Indians as ignorant people, knowing that they have disgusted and offended the priests, go fearfully to confession." The clerics prepared their defense in Ichupampa in November 1595. The priests stated they had peacefully entered the province when Commissioner Villacarrillo recalled the Franciscans, and they held proper letters of presentation. The clerics insisted that although the kurakas alleged Indians complained about seculars, there had been inspections and at no time were they charged with abuses. Also, the new bishop of Cuzco met the general commissioner of the Franciscans and the two came to an accord whereby the Franciscans were to retain all of Yanque, while four clerics were posted in Lari. Viceroy Luis de Velasco reviewed the arguments; in September 1596 he decreed that for the common good, the friars should return to their doctrinas and the clerics be removed as the Indians petitioned. But the dispute continued into September 1598, when Viceroy Luis de Velasco reported to the king that four Collaguas doctrinas were still being served by clerics. He wished to enforce their removal, but these parishes were under the authority of the bishop of Cuzco. The viceroy requested a new royal order to break the impasse, suggesting that whenever a doctrina was vacated only friars should be presented.[31]

Friars and clerics faced periodic inspections of their doctrinas by visitadores assigned by the nearest bishop. In the sixteenth century the Collaguas were within the diocese of Cuzco; by the second decade of the seventeenth century, the province was under the bishop of Arequipa. Bishops frequently ordered "secret" inspections that served a purpose similar to the residencia conducted to review the administration of corregidores. Inspections were intended to ensure the doctrinero was properly exercising his pastoral duties. In the late 1590s the Cuzco bishop, Antonio de Raya, appointed the curate Diego Bravo Mexía to inspect the Collaguas and Canas y Canchis. Bravo Mexía traveled to the Colca Valley and initiated the visita after conducting Mass in the church of Madrigal. The church was filled with people from the doctrina and its annexes, along with some Spaniards and priests. Notice of the inspection was loudly read to the assembled group, first in Spanish, then Quechua and Aymara. Upon completion of the Mass, the inspector removed his robes and put on a choir cloak. Singing the *"Innodeveni creator,"* with oil and chrism on his hands, he led a procession into the baptismal chapel. There the confraternities and their majordomos were present, the ceremonial candles of the cofradías were lighted, and the baptismal font and holy water were inspected. The visitador found the water pure, the baptismal font clean. The procession then filed out of the chapel and returned to the nave of the church, where the visitador led a response for the confraternity Animas de Purgatorio (see discussion in the next section), then asked the resident curate Francisco Lorido Flores to absent himself from the doctrina. Lorido walked to the village of Maca, and the secret testimony began. When it was completed, the priest was asked to return. The findings issued by Bravo Mexía in December 1598 confirmed that Lorido "used his office in the said villages with love and charity"; he had done well in indoctrinating and catechizing and deserved an appointment where he could provide even greater service to the Church.[32]

There were other inspections of Lorido's tenure at Madrigal, with similar results. In May 1607 Licentiate Pedro de Mansilla found Lorido's work "exemplary." The inspector and licentiate García Ortiz de Cervantes in June 1610 ruled his work was well done. Another secret visita was conducted by Licentiate Pedro Fernández Barrias in Madrigal in October 1612. It might appear that all inspections were perfunctory, with the results always favorable to the cleric. But in 1612 two charges were lodged against Lorido, and he was found guilty and fined on both counts. He was assessed six pesos for not having designated anyone to act in his absence from the doctrina to provide the sacraments of baptism or confession "in case of necessity," when death appeared imminent. Further, he was fined eight pesos for not "teaching to his flock the Catechism of the *Santíssimo Sacramento* composed by the Father Friar Luis de Orue" (Luis Jerónimo de Oré) as had been ordered by Bishop Antonio de Raya. He was admonished to "henceforth teach the said catechism." But overall the curate had performed well, and, according to the visitador, the Madrigal church largely through Lorido's efforts was "the richest and best served in all this province." In 1615 Lorido applied for transfer to a better post: in Lima, Cuzco, Charcas, or preferably "in the city of Arequipa." He was ultimately successful.[33]

Not only were secret inspections frequently conducted; it was the regular duty of bishops to inspect their dioceses and perform the sacrament of confirmation. In the case of a large diocese such as Cuzco, it was virtually impossible for a bishop to complete a personal inspection; these were often left to appointees. The first bishop to inspect the Collaguas was Pedro Perea, after Arequipa became an independent diocese. The diocese of Arequipa had been created by a bull of Pope Paul V on 6 July 1609, and confirmed by royal cédula in June 1612. The first two appointees died before they reached their post. It was not until 1 August 1619, that the third bishop, the Augustinian friar Pedro Perea, entered the city to assume his diocese. Bishop Perea conducted two inspections of the Collaguas, although he reminds us that it was not easy, because the "roads were very difficult." During his second visita in May 1621, he recommended the division of some doctrinas, including Lluta, and another that, he said, "the Franciscans have in the Collaguas." On another occasion Bishop Perea charged Archdeacon Pedro Alonso Bajo, who had been acting as governor of the diocese before Perea's installation, with a number of offenses. He had been favoring the Collaguas corregidor, Jerónimo de Pámanes, and assisting Francisco Lorido, then a church canon in Arequipa, to enter a cloistered monastery.[34]

Several years later Bishop Pedro de Villagómez y Vivanco conducted another Collaguas inspection. His tenure in Arequipa was brief (1635–40), followed by three decades of service as archbishop of Lima. His *visita pastoral* took him to numerous villages in the district of Camaná and Caylloma from June 1637 to February 1638. In a letter to the king in April 1636, Bishop Villagómez complained that many in the diocese entered and left the doctrinas, especially Franciscans, with only the authority of their superiors, without examination, approval, or license; he demanded that they be appointed under authority of the local bishop. The bishop had sent the Cabanaconde curate, Juan de Galdo Arellano, to inspect the eight Franciscan doctrinas in the Colca Valley. The Franciscans always objected to inspections by seculars, but the snooping of this neighboring priest was particularly offensive and they objected vigorously.[35] In 1639 Bishop Villagómez was unable to undertake his pastoral inspection due to illness and sent instead two Jesuits to the Collaguas and Conde-suyos, where they moved against idolatries. Many times the Franciscans had requested that ecclesiastical visitas of their parishes be conducted by bishops only.[36] The Franciscans charged that inspections by secular clergy were fraught with abuses.

Bishop Villagómez reported to the king on 18 April 1638 that he had searched out many huacas, ancient burials, and idols and superstitious objects and had destroyed 3,000. During his tour in Arequipa he helped finish construction of the city's cathedral, and he made efforts to improve the Convent of Santa Cata-lina. Villagómez secured fame as one of the leaders of the extirpation campaign, later publishing the *Carta pastoral de exhortación e instrucción contra las idolatrías de los indios del arçobispado de Lima* (1649). The zealous bishop made certain that the huacas discovered by visitadores were collected and destroyed and that the native shamans were castigated, and made examples of for the rest of the Indians. In the second visita, the bishop reported he had learned that many corregidores were not investing the one-tomín tax the tributaries were paying for the upkeep of the diocese's Indian hospitals. He noted there were only two functioning hospitals at the time, a "poor" one in Camaná, and another in Cay-lloma, where the corregidor had established a mita quota for its service. The bishop also emphasized that in the doctrinas administered by the friars, there was only weak subjection to ecclesiastical authority.[37]

The split in the valley between the secular and regular clergy continued. Of seventeen clergymen in the corregimiento in 1697, eight were Franciscans. The colonial church, as the state, was a multifaceted institution, with many branches and with frequently conflicting interests. The tension between the secular clergy and the orders was just one element of a broader problem. There were jealousies between dioceses, and even individual clerics. Furthermore, the religious orders enjoyed special privileges, granted earlier by either the Crown or the pope. Friars insisted on being inspected by their own commissioners, which led to more freedom than might be expected in a tightly knit hierarchi-cal structure. Some believed that at times, freedom verged on license. In 1635 the bishop of Cuzco, Fernando de Vera, wrote the king that he, and the eccle-siastical and secular cabildos, had been subjected to a sermon in the cathedral (28 February) delivered by Friar Buenaventura de Salinas, in which the Francis-can made these charges about the king: he "governs tyrannically, and mort-gages this kingdom, and gives encomiendas to flatterers that go about near the person of Your Majesty, and takes them from the sons of the conquista-dores, and other things so contrary to the truth." The outraged bishop began immediately to collect evidence in order to punish the outspoken friar.[38]

One of the principal functions of the parish priest following successful conversion to Christianity was the regular administration of the church sacraments. Baptism, the initial sacrament, was essential in the Catholic eschatology for salvation from the stain of original sin. One wonders what the Cabanas and the Collaguas thought about the concept of original sin and other complex elements of the Faith that the doctrineros were attempting to impart. However complicated the theological issues may have been, the friars and priests in the Colca Valley followed diligently and blindly their assigned task. In accordance with the dictates of church councils, they tried to baptize infants within eight days of birth. Only rarely does one discover in the remaining parish registers of the valley a child baptized later than mandated. The clerics faithfully recorded the required information: the date of baptism, the age of the infant, the status of legitimacy, the names of the parents and godparents. These rules were carefully laid out in the Second Church Council in Lima (1567–68), and they coincided with the mandates of the Council of Trent. Doctrineros also maintained a record of similar information on marriages. As an incentive, church fathers who met at the Second Council allowed *borracheras*, or drunken feasts, following a baptism, though non-Christians were excluded from the celebrations.[39]

In order to better understand the problems facing the clergy in the Andes, let us follow the traditional parish routine in the Colca Valley in the early 1590s under the Franciscan regimen. Pedro Hancocalla, the legitimate son of thirty-two-year-old Pedro Hancocalla, was born in October of 1590. He was baptized a few days later in the church of Yanque. Following the format provided in the *Manualum* of Franciscan Friar Luis Jerónimo de Oré, the infant was carried to the church in a white coverlet (chrisom), a symbol of innocence. The friar had prepared the cross, a lighted candle, the holy oil, and the chrism. The godfather held Pedro's head over his right arm — if it had been a girl, she would have been held over the left one. The duality in the gender symbolism would not have escaped the assembled kin group. At the baptismal font, the friar began the ceremony with the catechism in Aymara so that those attending would understand its meaning. The friar placed salt in the infant's mouth to free him from corruption of sin in preparation for receipt of divine wisdom. He then touched the infant's ears and nose with saliva; he anointed the infant's chest and back with holy oil and his head with chrism. As he took the holy water from the baptismal font, the friar sprinkled it over Pedro's head, reciting in Aymara "*Napi baptizama, Auquina, Yocansa, Spiritu sanctonsa Sutipana, Amen.*" The well-known phrase "I baptize you in the name . . . ," rendered in a mix of Aymara and Latin, is a brief reminder of how difficult it was to encompass important doctrinal concepts in Amerindian languages. The native words were charged with nuances that could and often did carry hidden meaning for native speakers. Line by line analysis of the early manuals and sermons, as well as of catechisms for the Andean region, can help us understand why native belief remains imbedded in Christian practice generations after conversion.

Had Pedro been in danger of death, baptism would have been immediate. Friar Oré warned in his *Manualum* that a weak infant should be baptized as the head emerged from the womb, even if the sex of the child was unascertainable. If a child was born in a place without a clergyman, in an emergency any Christian could perform the act of baptism. When the friar recorded Pedro Hancocalla's baptism, he followed the decree issued by Lima's Third Church Council regarding the surname of Indian children. But if we look at the last names of the other siblings in the family, we note that Pedro was the only boy who bore his father's surname. We would not expect those children of Pedro Hancocalla and María Mamanca who were born before 1583 to have been named after their parents, such as eleven-year-old Phelipe Vicsa or ten-year-old María Oque. But two other children, six-year-old Phelipe Caillagua and three-year-old María Carua, should have carried the last names of their father and mother respectively. There were many other cases in Yanque where the priest did not follow the rule and continued to give arbitrary last names to the children he baptized. But the same is true even in Seville parishes of the period. Surnames were assigned without thought of the admonitions of the Tridentine Council. Regarding Christian names, Friar Oré, who composed the widely used *Manualum* while in the Colca Valley, recommended, "The curate priest should counsel that the baptized receive the name of a saint so that he might imitate an excellent virtue and sanctity, and his soul might be awakened with greater fervor in the service of God. And it is hoped that the saint, whose name he receives, should be his patron to help conquer all the disturbances of his soul and body."[40]

With the arrival of the Europeans and Christianity, native practices of family formation were modified as quickly as monogamy could be enforced. Autochthonous preferences persisted, but the exterior conformed to the Catholic sacrament of holy matrimony, as modified by the Council of Trent. Lima church councils molded European tradition to fit Andean customs, as necessary. Polygamy was prevalent in the Andes; the First Council required Christian marriage to the first wife unless she did not convert, in which case the male was free to marry any of his Christian wives. In conformity with a bull of Paul III, and ratified by the Second Church Council, native Americans were exempted from the rule not to marry within the third degree of consanguinity and affinity, as long as the parties were baptized. Kurakas were permitted to marry only after they expelled from their household concubines and other "suspicious" women. But parents were to allow their children freedom of choice. In spite of a half century of Christian efforts, there were gaps between the ideal and the real. The Third Church Council still faced the problem of marriages within prohibited degrees. "Matrimony between brothers and sisters must never take place again, not even if you discover it among the pagan unconverted," clerics in the field were warned. Henceforth when adults were baptized, doctrineros were to take great care to find out the degree of kinship between couples and to separate them if necessary.[41]

All too frequently doctrineros were called on to prepare their parishioners for death. As outlined by Oré there were two formulas: The first was described as a "brief exhortation for the Indians that are very near the end of life, to be given by the priest, or someone else who was to assist them in the good death." The second was for those whose final hour was not imminent and whose soul needed thorough preparation. The brief form was often used in accidental death. There are several cases in the parish registers of Yanque of people falling to their death in the Colca canyon, or of being struck by lightning.[42] The longer form included confession, restitution, a last will, communion, extreme unction, and the final statement of Faith. The dying person was required to swear in the following form: "All the rest that our ancestors worshiped were demons, were fake and false gods; and thus I reject them, and take as a lie."[43] There were three forms for the burial service. A special one for infants was probably used most frequently, given a high rate of infant mortality.

Burial practice varied sharply from the pre-Christian era. Prior to the arrival of Europeans in the valley, the deceased were placed in a flexed, or sitting, position; wrapped into mummy bundles; and finally deposited in burial chambers, in caves, or in niches in the agricultural terraces. Once firmly in control in the Colca Valley, the doctrineros buried as they did elsewhere, under the church floor. For 300 years the dead of the communities up and down the valley were interred in the churches or when necessary in the adjoining courtyards. The deceased were duly recorded in the burial registers. In the Spanish Christian worldview, the body was temporarily housed in the most holy of locations, the church, awaiting the day of Resurrection. The practice meshed with the desire of the doctrineros to eradicate all vestiges of traditional rites and to end veneration of the huacas.[44] Social status was indicated by the place of burial in the church, as in Spain. Kurakas and their families were buried closest to the main or collateral altars, or in the baptistery. Commoners were more likely to be in-

The role of song in indoctrination (666 [680])

Listening to the "Word" (609 [623])

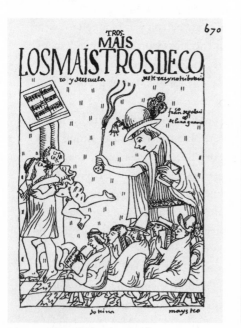

Listen carefully children (670 [684])

Confraternity of the Animas de Purgatorio (831 [845])

Baptism (613 [627])

Confession (615 [629])

Matrimony (617 [631])

Christian burial in the presence of the ayllu, saya, and confraternity (619 [633])

terred under the main vault, with those of lowest status farthest from the altar. This practice, European in origin, fostered the evolution of a class system, as the local elite increasingly adopted the customs of their Spanish rulers.

The daily routine of the doctrineros in the Colca Valley was similar to that of clergymen throughout the Indies. Mass, baptisms, marriages, confession, instruction in the Faith, and caring for the ill were all part of the normal regimen. Yet there were special days, usually associated with the rich liturgical Christian calendar—such as All Souls', Nativity, Lent, Holy Week, the Annunciation, and the Ascension—that required additional attention of the doctrineros. And there were crises that necessitated extraordinary duties, such as praying for rain, or for protection against earthquakes or floods, or against crop failure. At times doctrineros might be asked to exorcise spirits. Friar Oré provided for that contingency in his *Manualum*, but his orations tell us more of what the typical sixteenth-century European priest expected to find, rather than the nature of traditional Andean religious concepts. The churchman speaks of beasts, demons, Satan, and spirits to be exorcised. The sign of the cross, the crucifix, and the saints of the Church and the angels were called on to assist in driving out evil forces.

Doctrineros regularly used music in their efforts to convert. In addition to using voice, talented friars and priests often employed the flute and violin as they worked in the countryside. Frequently, travelers in the Andes commented on the new converts who went about their work singing hymns. The Franciscans were noteworthy in this regard, and by the early seventeenth century "miraculous" conversions in the viceroyalty attributed to Francisco Solano occurred in part because of his musical gifts. Luis Jerónimo de Oré regularly used song in both service and teaching in the Colca Valley and elsewhere. The most important work of the friars was the successful evangelization of the native peoples, and it could not be undertaken without the ability to communicate basic tenants of the Faith in their own languages. The earliest attempts of the religious to convert and baptize the Indians were difficult and fraught with misunderstandings, given the problem of translating church doctrine into an alien tongue. Almost immediately, clergymen began the arduous task of translating their message. Each order developed its own "form" of Christian doctrine, and there were often subtle and sometimes significant variations in the translations. Theologians recognized this variation could lead to doctrinal differences, something to be avoided in the era of the Catholic Reformation and Inquisition. In order to establish a uniform "Christian Doctrine" for evangelization, the Third Lima Church Council set up a commission of linguists, which was made up of Dominican, Franciscan, Augustinian, Mercedarian, and Jesuit scholars. The group finally composed a carefully worded translation of the Christian doctrine that was printed for use by all doctrineros.[45]

Religious confraternities (*cofradías*) were established in virtually all Andean doctrinas. These brotherhoods, patterned after those of Spain, provided important links between the institutional church and parishioners. The cofradía served a religious and social function. Andean ayllus had acted traditionally as a source of aid during times of distress, and the doctrineros recognized the value of the Christian cofradía in their attempt to fully convert native peoples. Members sponsored religious festivities, contributed to the general upkeep of the church, and fostered the "cult" of the community's patron saint. Cofradías also provided a form of security, assisting the family during the death of one of its members. When there was more than one cofradía in a given church, the brothers often competed to outshine each other during the festivities of their patron saint.[46] By 1586 several cofradías had already been established in the Colca Valley. In Yanque we find one of the principal devotional confraternities, Animas de Purgatorio (Souls of Purgatory), and the most popular sacramental cofradía, the Santíssimo Sacramento (Blessed Sacrament). We lack the daily operational records of the early cofradías of the Colca Valley, yet there are occasional glimpses, widely separated in time. In 1653 the bishop of Arequipa conducted a pastoral inspection of the valley. The majordomos of the cofradías in Yanque were Pedro Paco and Juan Checa, and the brotherhoods collected offerings and prepared and sold chicha to help finance the celebrations of the Day of Corpus Christi and All Saints' Day.[47]

The earliest clergy to have entered the Colca Valley would have conducted services in the open air, at first in the plazas of the small hamlets scattered throughout the valley, or occasionally in tambos. The reason for outdoor services was not only the absence of a church structure; the Franciscans were consciously attempting to re-create the experience of the early Christian Church in their New World missions. The first Franciscans to work in the valley, Juan de Monzón and Juan de Chaves, preached to and converted the natives outdoors. By the time the Franciscans were permanently established in the valley, it became necessary to erect fitting houses of worship and solid residences for the doctrineros.[48] In 1560 Friar Jerónimo de Villacarrillo, head of the Order in Peru, sent four Franciscans to work in the valley. The village of Coporaque was chosen as their headquarters in the region. The selection of a significant native settlement as the nucleus of Franciscan endeavor was a practical choice, and common Spanish practice elsewhere in the Andean world.[49] The building, in contrast to many other churches in the valley, which are laid out on an east-west line, is on a general Cuzco axis. Other important churches, at Cabanaconde and

Lari, are also on a Cuzco axis, suggesting Inca period structures were appropriated. Foundations of east-west-oriented churches were laid out during the Toledo settlements of the 1570s, a pattern prevalent in most other Colca Valley temples. The Inca period structure utilized for part of the doctrina's temple in the center of Coporaque may have been in a ruinous state by the time the Franciscans oversaw its lengthening, and reconstruction of its upper walls and roof, and the building of a principal entrance facing Coporaque's plaza. On the west side of the building was another plaza where open-air masses were conducted. A small chapel dedicated to Santa Ursula was constructed on the opposite side of the plaza, perhaps even before the erection of the church. In 1565 the church was devoted to San Sebastián; when it was consecrated in 1569, it was dedicated to Santiago. This was the seat of the Franciscans in the valley during the initial decade. The Franciscans also oversaw construction of a bell tower on the eastern side, by the entrance. Small cloister residences for the friars were hastily erected on the east of the church. An Indian school and hospital were included in the Coporaque compound and were fully functioning by 1580. Today all that remains are the church, the chapel, and the cloister's decayed remains.

Just as the Coporaque monastery was being completed, Viceroy Toledo's resettlement policy was put into effect, shifting the center of authority to the south side of the valley, to Yanque, the chief political seat of the corregimiento of Los Collaguas. Construction of a fitting church for the headquarters of the colonial province was now of paramount importance. The Yanque church was situated on the south (Arequipa) side of the plaza, one-half in the upper saya, the other in the lower section. The main altar of the church was placed at the east end of the temple, the side of the rising sun, an association surely appreciated by native parishioners. There were two doorways. One, on the side of the plaza facing north, was used principally by the anansaya; the other entrance, at the west end, was for urinsaya residents. Little information exists on the actual erection of the church at Yanque that must have been initiated in the mid-1570s. Viceroy Toledo did report that it was customary for the natives to do the actual construction of the churches and cloisters, with the Crown and encomenderos donating images, ornaments, and bells. There are records of the corregidores making payment for various aspects of building and ornamentation of the structures. Lucas de Cadabal in the early 1580s paid Lari urinsaya kuraka 128 pesos for woodwork for several churches. In Cabana anansaya numerous individuals contributed almost 300 pesos "for the ornaments bought for the churches of the repartimientos of Cabana anansaya and urinsaya." The merchant Antonio de Rivera and the tailor Pedro Gutiérrez provided "some things," and cleric Bartolomé Muñiz bought a *Santo Rey* from cleric Antonio Marcello.

Other people purchased gilded ornaments and an iron mold to bake communion wafers. Some thirteen pesos were paid by Cabana anansaya (urinsaya gave nine pesos four tomines) to carpenters building the churches of Guambo and Cabana.[50] By 1586 Yanque's first church was completed and in use. The walls were of stone, clearly taken from structures in the small hamlets the natives abandoned when forced to congregate in Yanque. Some finished stones in the walls of the present church retain traditional Andean symbols, raised relief serpents or the snail. The roof of the first church was of wood, as many others in the valley still are, and thatched with ichu grass in the traditional style. The first edifice may have varied in size from the contemporary one but not significantly. The modest Franciscan cloister on the south side of the building was erected quickly, in the same fashion as houses of commoners. In all cases church construction in the Colca Valley in the 1570s was a community effort, directed by doctrineros.[51]

Resistance and Accommodation

During the 1580s doctrineros realized that Christianization of the Collaguas and Cabanas was superficial at best. A variety of factors coalesced during the decade, causing a native reaction against the new order. First the protective Franciscans vacated the valley, and many of the seculars who replaced them lacked their commitment. Corregidores and encomenderos faced fewer checks as they exacted tribute and labor service. Second, the Toledo settlement program had run its course, and native villagers faced the reality of a long-term residential pattern that made little sense in the Andes. Population was rapidly declining. By 1580 fewer than half the number living and working in the valley prior to the arrival of the Europeans remained. The general apprehension generated a response that manifested itself in reemergence of ancestral rites. Return to autochthonous ritual and belief is a powerful form of resistance, no less compelling than armed insurrection. Resurgence of traditional cults is effective because is it difficult to discover and stamp out deeply held beliefs of the people, especially those living in isolated stretches of the high puna. The earlier emergence of the Taki Onqoy movement in the 1560s alarmed church authorities, and although it was confined to only a small territory, efforts were made to quickly stamp out the belief that ancient gods would reappear and defeat the God of the foreigners, restoring autonomy and prosperity.[52]

Ecclesiastical officials in the 1560s began to direct close attention to native practices and their eradication. Viceroy Toledo in the next decade likewise devoted attention to the problem of idolatry. Several ordinances that dealt with ecclesiastical affairs are similar to the mandates of the First and Second Church Councils. Simultaneously, Toledo succeeded in destroying the neo-Inca state at Vilcabamba. During the 1570s there were regional outbreaks of idolatry. In late November 1573 Toledo informed the king that more than sixty people had been sacrificed in a village near Lima, because the "Great Lord of Pachacamac" had incited believers. The huaca had been angered because no one sacrificed to him any more, as they had under Inca rule. Lima's bishop moved quickly against those responsible for the deaths. In 1580 Toledo reported an incident in the Conchucos province where several people were convinced a man was god, and they were following him. Authorities moved rapidly in this case also.[53]

Idolatries in the Colca Valley in the 1580s were uncovered during the residencia of the Collaguas corregidor, Lucas de Cadabal. During his self-defense he called numerous witnesses to attest to his diligent work in furthering the religious conquest of the region. The resident surgeon Manuel de Carvajal testified on 7 January 1584 that the corregidor was very active searching out idolatries and witchcraft and had discovered that some natives had reentered ancestral burial chambers, where they were conducting traditional rites. Lucas de Cadabal ordered removal of the bones of the huacas, had them burned, and castigated the idolaters. The kurakas Juan Caquina of Lari anansaya, and Cristóbal Cusi of the urinsaya testified with other community members that "Lucas de Cadabal searched out idolaters and witches with great care, and the four or five which he discovered in the pueblo of these witnesses he seized and castigated, and banished them from this province." The Caylloma cleric Sebastián Durán reported the corregidor "was especially diligent in extirpating idolatries and witchcraft while among the natives of the province. He had come to know which Indians were practitioners, and in what places, and in order to extirpate and verify it, he had gone even to the punas and other inhospitable parts, with great risk to his person." The scribe Don Diego Coro Inga confirmed that the corregidor had managed to "extirpate and destroy the idolatries, learning who had been engaged in them and in witchcraft, and in that fashion had uncovered the idolaters and shamans. He castigated them and exiled them from the province. He had burned and buried the idolatrous objects in order that never again would there be memory of them." Diego Coro Inga must have accompanied Cadabal on some of the campaigns, and he remarked that the corregidor traveled widely, facing "harsh dangers and thundering waterways and snows, at great danger to his person."

Investigators discovered that idolatry in the Colca Valley was much more serious than revealed by the discovery of ayllu-based ceremonies associated with the huacas in the burial chambers, and witchcraft. The resident Spaniard Francisco Hernández testified (21 January 1584):

> With this witness and other Spaniards he [the corregidor] traveled on the track of idolatry through many parts of this land until he had verified that a shaman had fooled the puna herdsmen and residents of Lari and Cabana, and many others in this province. . . . He convinced them that atop a snowcapped peak named Curiviri there was a great toad he called Ampato, and that this toad was god, and he defecated gold, and Lucas de Cadabal arrested this man . . . , and went with him to the said mountain which is in a very high puna with dangerous precipices. There he discovered idolatries that he extirpated, and castigated them rigorously.[54]

Ampato the toad is significant in Andean mythology and appears in many legends. Any belief that "this toad was god, and he defecated gold" challenged the religious superstructure of the outsiders in the Andean world. The toad as a huaca represented a threat to European religious and social hegemony as well as to the economic order based on Indian labor. Ampato would be able to relieve the natives of the tribute and labor burdens imposed by the foreigners, providing the Cabanas and Collaguas with a steady source of wealth. The gold, the "sweat of the sun" in the mind of the Inca, would give them power in colonial society. The cult of Ampato appears to be a purely local response to European domination. There is no direct mention of destroying the new order and returning to the old, as with the Taki Onqoy cult and its millenarian overtones of the overthrow of foreign control. Accommodation to the new order, rather than its destruction, seems inherent in the Ampato cult. The natives would have ample access to what was deemed necessary for survival and success in the new society: gold. The people of the Colca Valley had returned to their roots, the volcanic cone of Ampato, and the volcano as it issued the flowing liquid gold from its belching mouth would deliver them from oppression.

There were other vestiges of old beliefs uncovered in the province. One mid-seventeenth-century Franciscan chronicler remembered the work of Luis Jerónimo de Oré in the early 1590s, and reported that the friar went about the province "with a cross in his hands, and he did it on foot, without sandals. He discovered many huacas and idolatries, and among them a seat of bronze, which he had founded into bells for the new churches he built."[55] The symbolism of this narrative is striking. The "seat" of bronze was Inca, and associated with Inca political and religious hegemony in the Colca Valley. The recasting of the metal into bells for the church at Coporaque, or other valley churches, symbolized Christianity's replacement of the pre-Spanish state religion. Each time the bells tolled, calling parishioners for indoctrination or for another event in the daily religious calendar, the new religion was reinforced in the minds of the people. The bells represented the new church and its authority. And on a quiet day, the bells of one village could be heard in the next. The bells from the churches of Coporaque and Yanque for example, separated by the canyon and on opposite sides of the river, can be heard as they announce the time for prayers, or at times a death or an emergency. Further the Franciscans in the valley used the gold and silver found in some of the huacas, reworking it for various religious objects for the churches. The gilding of the altars came partly from this source of the precious metal. Another important religious symbol of the new order is the burial of the deceased within the church rather than outside in caves or niches. Church architecture and layout also symbolized the power and authority of the new religion. When feasible, Christian temples were built on preexisting religious foundations. The fact that the church was constructed on the main plaza, at the center of the villages, also had a significance that was not lost on parishioners.[56]

In 1601 Bishop Antonio de Raya of Cuzco sent Licentiate Loarte de Avila to inspect the Collaguas, and sections of the Condesuyos of Arequipa and coastal Carabaya. Specific villages were named in the Collaguas: Maca, Madrigal, Lluta and Guanca, Caylloma, Cabana and Pinchollo. The list indicates there may have been reason for suspicion of idolatries in or near these pueblos. But Avila's mission was cut short by a new order suspending the visita, "for just causes," and transferring Loarte de Avila to villages in Condesuyos and Pomatambo. In the 1620s, there were campaigns against idolatry in the Arequipa district; Pablo José de Arriaga had mounted similar campaigns in the Huarochirí region.[57] The Council of the Indies reviewed carefully these campaigns in Peru and wrote to the archbishop of Lima, expressing its measured conviction that the best way to eliminate idolatry was by "the example of good living of the ecclesiastics, especially three types of people — doctrineros, visitadores, and preachers. If any of these are evil doers, the Indians will not be able to distinguish the true Christian life, and truly the devil's idolatries will be confirmed."[58]

What the people of the volcano actually accepted of Christianity in the first and second generations after the arrival of the Europeans is difficult to ascertain. Certainly the externals of the Faith were adopted as the ceremonies, and especially the more important sacraments, became a focal point for the valley residents. Baptisms, marriages, and celebration of Christian feast days formed a major part of the life cycle of the people, and the church soon absorbed a significant portion of the free time of parishioners. The confraternities provided an institutional channel for religious expression that could be monitored by church officials. The rocky process of transculturation was under way.[59] Yet at the same time the early missionaries and their secular counterparts, in their headlong pursuit of attracting and retaining new converts, were often ruthless and fanatical—destroying venerated objects, searching for idols and idolatries, and terrorizing the natives into submission. Some accepted, perhaps confused and frightened, but others could not and did not. Even after more than four centuries of Christian control in the Colca Valley the apachitas exist within sight of church entrances, and in the churches offerings of fresh chicha and coca leaves can be found at the altars, indicating the full power resulting from persistence of earlier religious concepts in the Andean World. And above the villages of the Colca Valley the majestic volcanic cones continue to instill awe and respect, and continue to be venerated.

PART III. THE "REPÚBLICA DE LOS ESPAÑOLES"

CHAPTER NINE

CRISIS IN THE "REPÚBLICA DE LOS ESPAÑOLES"

The majority of the vecinos and natives within the district have come down with [the sickness] and are ill or have died. Because of it, there has been no one to look after the harvesting of the wheat that has been planted. If it is lost there will be grave consequences and great need will befall this republic. That will happen if the rains begin now, as each day they are expected to begin, for the season is so advanced.
—Cabildo of Arequipa, 26 December 1589.

The greatest calamity that has ever taken place in any republic in the world has happened to this city. For the past year and a half there has been a continuous rain of ash . . . , and [the only way to] placate the ire of God Our Father . . . , is to remove the public sins and scandals of the republic.
—Cabildo of Arequipa, 30 October 1601.

Cabana Conde, the encomienda that I was given, is of such little value there is not sufficient income to sustain oneself . . . , it was worth 5,000 pesos to Juan de la Torre, but now is valued at less than 2,000 pesos yearly.
—1 March 1611 service report of Hernando de la Torre Padilla, Archivo General de Indias, Patronato 124.

The Spanish were urban folk by choice and necessity, and the Americas provided the opportunity to create new cities in the wilderness.[1] Conquest of Andean America was coupled with the foundation of European urban centers: San Miguel de Piura in 1532; Jauja in 1533; Quito and Cuzco in 1534; Lima, Trujillo, Guayaquil, and Puerto Viejo in 1535; La Plata and Chachapoyas in 1538; Huamanga in 1539; and Arequipa in 1540. The Spanish congregated for purposes of defense, religion, family formation, festivals, and recreation; and they participated in government, in planning, and in directing their New World destinies. With the exception of Cuzco, it was possible to carefully create the new city, following a well-formulated plan, rather than settling haphazardly. To the Spanish, town planning represented authority and civilization rather than chaos and barbarism. Town sites were surveyed; inspectors checked for water availability, soil quality, proximity to building materials, temperature and rainfall, and the nearness to an Amerindian labor force. The layout of the town, with its rigidly applied gridiron pattern, also represented order and control. At its center stood a large open public space for meetings, celebrations, social activities, and the public market. The church faced the plaza, as did a city hall, often a jail, a hospital, or other important government structures. Indian towns founded under Viceroy Toledo followed a similar pattern of urban planning.

Colca Valley encomenderos, due to their income and access to Indian laborers, became immediately part of Arequipa's elite, and they were active in its municipal government. After the mid-1550s encomenderos could only reside in the cities, away from their grants, and they were required to be married. With the exception of doctrineros and corregidores based in Indian villages, virtually all the rest of the Spanish, mestizos, and blacks lived in European-style urban centers. City building lots were distributed, often the day the city was founded. The wealthiest encomenderos received lots closest to the center: the most prestigious sites were nearest the plaza, not the periphery, where Indian settlements were created. The lot was large enough to accommodate the living quarters, along with a patio, a kitchen, a garden, and housing for Indian servants, black slaves, and Spanish retainers. Most had a compound or corral for horses and equipment. A quarter of a city block, or more in exceptional cases, might be given to one of the encomendero elite. And plots of land were distributed in the Arequipa valley as well.[2]

The valley's encomenderos were an important part of Arequipa's colonial society, as they attempted to re-create the Spanish world they had left behind, transplanting to Andean soil their own concept of the European social order. In the Andes the Spanish and Amerindians lived in separate worlds. Both had their political leaders in parallel administrative systems. And just as Indian communities were divided by saya, Spanish cities were also divided but in their case along lines of economic class and caste. There was constant movement back and forth between the citizens of the "República de los Indios" and the "República de los Españoles." They lived and worked in the same geographical space and interacted with each other in the workplace. They suffered similar fates in time of natural disasters: earthquakes, volcanic eruptions, floods or droughts, crop failures, and epidemics. Both had their own internal hierarchies, but their narratives were different. One was the narrative of the outsiders, who exercised authority and constructed their own histories. The other was the narrative of the subjected, whose histories were controlled by the foreigners.

The fate of the Colca Valley encomenderos varied as they attempted to secure wealth and position and to establish American dynasties. Their story takes us from the disastrous beginnings of the earliest generation, whose lives often ended on a battlefield; to the second wave, starting at the end of the civil wars in the mid-1550s, encomenderos who after initial difficulties were able to amass fortunes and assume leading social, political, and economic roles in Arequipa. But by the mid-1580s a combination of the effects of Crown policy to weaken the encomenderos, and a series of crises, seriously undermined the old elite. The fate of the Colca Valley encomenderos is linked closely to that of their Indian tributaries. A continuously declining population base resulted in shrinking incomes. The exact chronology of the process varies from one encomienda to another, but the consequences are similar.

Lari

Both Lari encomiendas of the middle Colca Valley date from grants originally made by Francisco Pizarro in 1540. The upper section of Lari Collaguas was given to Marcos Retamoso, while the lower half went to Alonso Rodríguez Picado. Their sons ultimately inherited their fathers' encomiendas, and both families played prominent roles in the evolution of Arequipa.[3] Marcos Retamoso, as the encomendero of Lari Collaguas anansaya, frequently served in Arequipa as the city's alcalde or regidor; gradually he developed an estate by systematic purchase of agricultural lands in the valley. At the time of his death in 1563, Retamoso left five or six legitimate children. The oldest boy, Francisco Hernández Retamoso, inherited the encomienda, and his mother, Doña Francisca de Vergara, acted as guardian for the minor children. Such a large family with the multiple obligations expected of the encomendero elite, coupled with declining revenues from the encomienda, presented substantial economic challenges for Marcos's heirs in subsequent years.

Marcos's son, "Captain" Francisco Hernández Retamoso, was receiving the benefits of the encomienda at the time of Viceroy Toledo's inspection in the 1570s. Although there were a total of 1,325 tributaries, by the time salaries of

250 pesos for eight kurakas, 1,095 pesos for five Franciscan doctrineros, and 833 pesos for Indian defenders were deducted for expenditures, only a mere 472 pesos in cash and 3,975 pesos in products remained for the encomendero's family. There were also 159 Lari tributaries settled in La Chimba of Arequipa, which provided the family with greater resources: almost 750 silver pesos in cash, 50 fanegas of corn assessed at 1 peso each but worth much more, 40 fanegas of wheat at 1½ pesos, and 136 chickens valued at 17 pesos. But more important, Retamoso provided agricultural land for his tributaries, who were required to prepare, plant, cultivate, and harvest six fanegas of either seed corn or wheat grain for the encomendero's household.[4] Yet with such a large entourage to support, coupled with a declining population of tributaries, the family's economic situation was already critical by the mid-1570s. In 1575 Francisco Hernández Retamoso was sued in Arequipa for nonpayment of one of the installments on a long-term property mortgage (censo) in the valley. In 1584 the family received only 663 pesos in tribute. Similar to his father, Captain Francisco Hernández Retamoso held public office; for example, he was alcalde of Arequipa in 1593. But public service provided status, not income, which the family desperately needed.

A new tribute assessment of the encomienda was conducted in 1602; by then his tributaries had fallen from 1,333 to 978, and there was about a 30 percent reduction in the encomendero's annual income. In 1611 new suit was filed to collect debts owed by the Retamoso family, again for nonpayment of censos to both monasteries and private parties. Captain Francisco Hernández Retamoso had married Mariana de la Cuba Maldonado, and they had several offspring, including at least one son.[5] Captain Francisco Hernández Retamoso died about 1611; from then on the encomienda was administered by his brother, Pedro Retamoso de Vergara, until his death in 1626. The family's economic difficulties were exacerbated in the 1620s, and the heirs faced legal challenges. Family vineyards in the Siguas Valley were sold to raise cash, but failed to pay off the full amount of the liabilities.[6]

From 1540 Lari Collaguas urinsaya was under the control of the Arequipa founder Alonso Rodríguez Picado, a close friend of Francisco Pizarro. When Picado was killed at the Battle of Huarina, his infant son—also named Alonso Rodríguez Picado—inherited Lari urinsaya "in the second life." For the next several years, his ties to the encomienda were tenuous, and tribute was collected in his name by various majordomos. The boy was raised first by his mother, Juana Muñiz, then by his grandparents. Even as a child he was a good match, and a marriage was arranged with Doña Mayor de Saravia, the daughter of

Doctor Melchor Bravo de Saravia, a Lima Royal Audiencia justice. When the betrothal was formalized by 1557, Alonso was about ten years old. In 1561 Marcos Retamoso mused that Picado and his bride, Doña Mayor, were "both children and minors." In 1565 Doctor Bravo de Saravia was appointed first president of the newly established Audiencia of Chile, in Concepción, and the young Picado accompanied his father-in-law to his post. There the boy began military training early, fighting against the Araucanians when he was in his late teens. By the time he reached his late twenties, he was a recognized leader of colonial military forces on Chile's frontier, "a good soldier, well liked by all." In March 1575, while in Concepción, he prepared a service report requesting favors. He emphasized his extensive service, and claimed he had expended about 100,000 pesos of his estate, obviously based on tributes from Lari, without compensation from the Royal Treasury.[7]

In 1583 Alonso Rodríguez Picado was back in Arequipa, where he filed a new service report before the city's corregidor. Based on his prior military experience, in 1591 Viceroy García Hurtado de Mendoza, the second Marqués de Cañete, appointed the Lari encomendero as captain of the Company of Fifty Gentlemen and "Arquebusiers," a Peruvian equivalent of the palace guards and the second such company to be established. The post generated a yearly stipend of 800 pesos. In October Picado appeared before the viceroy and took the oath of office, to "defend the Crown and be a loyal and faithful servant." The opportunity came quickly: in 1592 Lima received notice from the governor of Brazil that five English corsairs were headed for the Straits of Magellan. Viceroy Cañete named Rodríguez Picado lieutenant and captain-general of the Royal Armada, which included three galleons equipped with artillery, munitions, army and naval personnel, and supplies. He and other arequipeños were commanded to protect Pacific shipping, and especially the treasure shipment scheduled to be sent from Upper Peru to Callao, then to Panama. Picado sailed from Callao toward the port of Arica, where he supervised loading of the gold and silver from the mines of Upper Peru and transported the bullion safely to Lima. He did so twice, in his own words providing "great service for the Royal Treasury."[8]

In late 1592 Alonso Rodríguez Picado requested that his encomienda be allocated for another life, giving him the income he claimed he needed to "continue his services." He noted that he had contributed two loans to the king. One of 2,500 pesos, half his yearly income from Lari, was made in the time of Viceroy Toledo. Another loan of 1,000 pesos was under the Marqués de Cañete, a "forced donation" that other Arequipa encomenderos made to the Crown. He insisted he had expended 120,000 pesos to serve the king: "For it I have sold all the land, houses, city lots, and censos that I owned, and in great quantity, and have taken loans on my Indian incomes, having spent splendidly in the service of His Majesty." In September 1593, Cristóval de Morales testified that Rodríguez Picado merited reward because his encomienda "is of little value compared to what he deserves." In 1595 Picado asked for the position of general of the Royal Armada with the appropriate salary. In the margin of the document one official recommended that "he be proposed for corregidor of Cuzco."[9] It is unclear if he was immediately appointed to the post. In 1603 and 1608 he served as Arequipa's alcalde. In May 1612 the Lari encomendero asked to be named governor of Chucuito or Cuzco, because the current governors were approaching the end of their terms. If these positions did not materialize, Picado asked for another post in Peru. He also requested that the repartimiento should be inherited by his wife, because they had no children who could assume the grant. In 1615 he supported the kurakas of the Colca Valley in their attempt to halt construction of an obraje. Alonso died in 1616, at the age of about sixty-eight, and was buried in the main chapel of Arequipa's Convent of Santo Domingo.

Following the childless encomendero's death, the grant did fall into the hands of his wife's relatives, the Bravo de Saravias, although in the 1630s the encomienda was still referred to as the "Collaguas de Picado." By 1633 the encomienda was held by Don Diego Bravo de Saravia, "in the second life." At that time, Don Diego's nephew, Diego de Montalvo y Saravia, still a minor, requested the encomienda be given to him when his uncle died. This future transfer was authorized by Viceroy the Conde de Chinchón in November 1633. The minor was under the tutelage of his mother, another Doña Mayor Bravo de Saravia, widow of Don Juan Jiménez de Montalvo, a justice of Lima's Audiencia.[10] In June 1641 a different Don Juan Jiménez de Montalvo, perhaps a son—a licentiate and collegiate at the University of Salamanca in Spain—was granted 800 ducats' annual income from Lari, a pension paid intermittently through 1665.[11] But the direct line of the Lari urinsaya encomienda granted in 1540 had ended in 1616 with the death of the second Alonso Rodríguez Picado. Picado's wife's family was able to secure control over the encomienda and authorization to collect tributes directly for "two generations," which continued into the mid-1630s. At that point the Crown extended pensions from the income of Lari tributaries to one or more relatives, even those living in Spain. For all practical purposes, the rich encomienda of a century earlier was now just the source of a modest government pension.

Juan de la Torre, a close friend of Francisco Pizarro and one of the thirteen who stayed with him on Gallo Island at the low point of the second expedition, was granted Cabanas urinsaya by President La Gasca in 1549.[12] Following his older son's and namesake's treason and execution after the Battle of Pucará, it would be a son by his second wife who inherited the grant several decades later.[13] The elder De la Torre was uncertain of the legality of his grant and petitioned Governor Lope García de Castro to reconfirm it. In August 1565 he swore once more to support the Crown as a loyal servant with arms and horses, and took a new act of possession in Arequipa early in October. The encomendero spent his later years primarily in Arequipa. In April 1572 he was named Arequipa's ambassador and solicitor to defend its interest before Viceroy Toledo and the Council of the Indies. He was charged especially to secure recognition of the city charter and was instructed to raise questions about the impact of the visita general on Arequipa.

When Viceroy Toledo passed through Arequipa in 1575, the aging encomendero was one of the city's principal representatives at the many public activities celebrating his visit. De la Torre must have impressed the viceroy, who suggested that he compose a narrative of his view of Peru's conquest. In October 1575, in recognition of his services he secured a decree from the viceroy that "he could not be imprisoned for debt, nor could his arms and horses be removed." The following year, when Toledo asked for a *servicio gracioso* (donation), to help pay for the war against the Turks, Juan contributed 900 pesos, and "it was well known he was not a rich man, because of his personal contributions to cover the costs of the various civil wars." A number of elite Arequipa women donated jewelry for the cause as well. Juan's wife, Doña Beatriz de Castilla, and their daughter Doña Ynez de Padilla contributed several pieces of jewelry worth 870 pesos.[14] In March 1576, Juan de la Torre donated 600 pesos more for the royal cause from Cabanas tributes. Juan's complaints of indebtedness notwithstanding, the elderly encomendero extracted enough income from his Cabanas charges and from profits from investments to lead the comfortable life of a Spanish gentleman.[15] Juan de la Torre died between 6 and 10 January 1580 and was buried in the Cathedral of Arequipa in the presence of all the city's leading vecinos.[16]

Juan de la Torre's eldest son, Hernando, married to Doña Catalina de Contreras, inherited the grant, and Viceroy Toledo in May 1580 confirmed Hernando's succession with an important stipulation: "for the days of your life and no more, because afterward they are and have to remain vacated." In December 1580 the young encomendero and his kurakas appeared before Arequipa's corregidor for an act of possession. Later that month Hernando presented his service report before Arequipa's alcalde, noting that revenues from the repartimiento were inadequate. He then requested that the grant be made perpetual, or at least for the king to grant it for two lives to his eldest son, Juan de la Torre, who was "named after his grandfather." Unfortunately the young Juan did not survive to inherit the grant. The response came the following October, when Viceroy Martín Enríquez extended to Hernando de la Torre another grant, consisting of a paltry twelve married Arequipa Yanaconas that were vacated by the death of Diego Hernández. In June 1590 Hernando was named ambassador by the cabildo to travel to the Lima court of Don García Hurtado de Mendoza, second Marqués de Cañete. He planned to go, but at the last minute a broken leg dashed his hopes of making the journey. The Arequipa cabildo selected another Colca Valley encomendero, Alonso Picado, as a substitute. Several times between 1590 and 1592 Hernando donated to the king's treasury. In July 1590 Viceroy Cañete thanked him for the money contributed as a "servicio gracioso" to be used against the English. Viceroy Cañete wrote another letter in April 1591, and a third in November 1592, thanking him for animating others in Arequipa to donate sums for the king's purse. In 1591 he contributed 2,000 pesos as a "servicio gracioso," from his Cabanas tributes, and the same year his wife, Doña Catalina, donated 100 *botijas* (clay vessels) of wine worth some 300 pesos from their vineyards.[17]

Acting on Hernando's behalf, his brother-in-law Don Juan de Olacaval y Arteaga presented a new service report for the encomendero before Lima's Royal Audiencia in November 1594. When Francis Drake and Thomas Cavendish entered the Pacific, citizens of Arequipa helped defend the nearby seaports of Chule and Quilca. Hernando de la Torre proudly claimed he had participated in Quilca's defense against the corsairs, spending heavily in the process. He took along his sons and servants, his friends, arms, and horses, and guarded the port with Arequipa's corregidor. As had his father, Hernando held several municipal posts, including *alcalde ordinario* (deputy magistrate) and *alférez mayor* (chief standard bearer). When the king ordered assignation of sales tax collection in Peru, Hernando was placed in charge of its distribution and collection in Arequipa. In spite of extensive agricultural holdings and revenues from Cabanas tribute, his debts mounted, reaching the staggering sum of 40,000 pesos. His large family proved costly: by 1594, Doña Catalina had given birth to nine or ten children; two boys and six daughters survived. Hernando requested a yearly compensation of 14,000 pesos for his service to the Crown. In the meantime, the royal reply regarding the future of the encomienda was non-committal. In 1597 the king wrote that following Hernando's death, the viceroy should not give the encomienda to anyone else until a review could be conducted.[18]

Hernando de la Torre died on 25 April 1610. The city's notary García Muñoz certified, "Today, standing in the houses of the residence of vecino Hernando de la Torre, who died naturally, we see the said Hernando de la Torre lying in a casket in a salon of his house." His oldest son, Hernando de la Torre Padilla, appeared before Arequipa's alcalde ordinario in March 1611 and requested that Cabanas urinsaya be given him freshly for his own services as well as those of his ancestors. He also claimed that his financial situation was critical and asked for the new grant to be for two lives. He lamented that he was left with numerous sisters and a mother to care for. Two of his sisters were of marriageable age, but with inadequate dowries. His father left many debts, "because Cabana Conde, the encomienda that I was given," he explained, "is of such little value there is not sufficient income to sustain oneself. . . . It was worth 5,000 pesos to Juan de la Torre, but now is valued at less than 2,000 pesos yearly." Further, powerful earthquakes and a rain of ash following a volcanic eruption had destroyed much of the family's estate. In 1614 the Council of the Indies reviewed his request, but did not issue an immediate ruling. Hernando complained that the De la Torres, similar to other encomendero families, were reduced to requesting public office. By the 1630s the Crown had appropriated the tribute of Cabana urinsaya, while the minor children of Hernando de la Torre were receiving an annual pension of 1,471 pesos from tribute receipts of La Chimba of Arequipa.[19]

Diego Hernández de la Cuba received Cabana Anansaya near the end of the civil wars, though under questionable circumstances: by marriage to the young widow Doña Juana de Mercado, who had married the elderly Captain Vergara to maintain the grant within his family. Following the captain's death, Doña Juana had reneged on her promise to marry a younger relative and had instead quickly married Diego Hernández de la Cuba (see chapter 3). Ultimately confirmed in the grant by Viceroy Antonio de Mendoza in 1551, Diego collected tributes from the Cabanas until 1579, when Viceroy Francisco de Toledo withdrew his encomienda three days after his wife's death. On 30 January 1579 the Arequipa councilman García Gutiérrez de Escobar initiated, with the Royal Treasury accountant, legal proceedings against the estate. They argued that "because Doña Juana de Mercado, wife of Diego Hernández de la Cuba, died this past Wednesday 28 January, of natural causes and on the twenty-ninth was interred in the Franciscan monastery," the Indians which she inherited "by the death of her first husband Juan Pérez de Vergara" were now vacant. They therefore must be incorporated into the Crown from the date of her death. The Cabanaconde kurakas Don Pablo Vilca Yanqui and Don Juan Vica Yanqui, as well as Don Diego Ayanso of Yura, subject to the Cabana kurakas, were called before royal officials. The meeting ended with a formal ceremony of possession by the two men "until Viceroy Francisco de Toledo can act."[20]

The following day the shocked encomendero presented himself before officials and protested the grant's abrupt removal, arguing that he had received it for two lives. He demanded its immediate return, promising to present his own legitimate cédulas of encomienda. Ranting that his wife had just died and he was still in a state of bereavement, he complained about the great injustice. The officials maintained that the Crown had a legal right to act because the grant was vacated by the death of its holder. Diego Hernández de la Cuba rushed to Lima to protest before the Royal Audiencia, and by July a legal action was in full process, with the encomendero suing for damages and court costs. The fiscal, protecting the Crown's interests before the Audiencia, claimed Hernández de la Cuba was not truly dispossessed, because he never legally held title to the encomienda; it was only his wife's. Viceroy Toledo had placed it in the Crown's hands to use the tributes "for the expenses of the galleys of this sea." Diego's claim of having a cédula of encomienda from the first Marqués de Cañete was invalid because Cañete only had power to grant vacated repartimientos, and "this one was not."[21] Toledo's action in the case of the Cabanas was precipitated by foreign pressure. In the 1570s English corsairs shook Spanish confidence by penetrating an area previously believed safe from attack by foreign interlopers. Francis Drake entered into Pacific waters from the Straits of Magellan in April of 1578 and sailed northward along South America's coast, reaching New Spain the following April. Along the route, Drake's *Golden Hind* damaged Spanish shipping in Santiago and Arica, then, on 13 February 1579, Lima's port of Callao. The Punta de Santa Elena was captured by the corsairs, with its treasure of 300,000 pesos. Toledo responded by ordering construction in Guayaquil of a new galley to patrol Pacific ports and protect shipping from Lima to Panama. Until then there was little provision for sea defense along the coast, or a means of paying for naval protection. Cabanas anansaya provided the government with a needed source of revenues, and Viceroy Toledo seized the moment to incorporate the grant into royal patrimony.[22]

Diego Hernández de la Cuba was outraged that the encomienda was expropriated, no matter that the cause was the defense of the Indies. His case moved ahead with legal arguments before the Audiencia from July through the end of November 1579. In December the justices ruled in support of his claims. But Fiscal Alonso de Carvajal rejected the decision, charging that the Audiencia lacked jurisdiction in this instance because the viceroy had placed the repartimiento in royal hands. Cabana tribute disbursements appear in the Royal Treasury account books for the year as assigned for payment of the galley's construction, "for the guard of the coast of this South Sea." In January 1580 the Audiencia allowed ninety days to prepare appeals, weakening Diego's position. His counsel replied that the Audiencia had already supported his claim, so this action was unjust.[23] By March 1580 the fiscal again attacked the authority of the Marqués de Cañete to issue encomiendas. He noted that Charles V had ordered in December 1555 that Cañete could only grant vacated ones. He pointed out that Philip II in December 1560 decreed the removal of grants that Cañete had made to several people, including his legitimate son, a nephew, and his "bastard son" Felipe de Mendoza. The fiscal also referred to an order of Viceroy Conde de Nieva in May 1560, canceling the encomiendas and extensions granted by Viceroy Cañete. But the same viceroy simultaneously requested full reports on those who had been given grants by Cañete, allowing for reward of grantees who really merited it. Late in August 1580 the Audiencia issued a ruling that confirmed its earlier decision upholding the claims of Diego Hernández de la Cuba. But Fiscal Carvajal again complained the Audiencia had no right to intervene, that this was a matter for the Royal Treasury and corregidor in Arequipa; he rejected the authority of the Audiencia to issue the letter of execution necessary to enforce the decision. With the Audiencia unable to reach a final ruling in Lima, the case was appealed to the Royal Court of the Council of the Indies. In April 1581 copies of all relevant papers were made, and Diego was authorized to sail personally or send someone to represent him before the Council to pursue justice.[24]

Diego Hernández de la Cuba departed for Spain with Viceroy Toledo's fleet in 1581 to defend his rights to the Cabanas. In Spain Diego met briefly his son Gerónimo, who had been living there since 1568 with two sisters also sent to the motherland to be raised by relatives. Twenty-five years old, Gerónimo began in 1582 the lengthy procedure to secure license to return to Peru, while his father remained in Spain for another decade, supporting himself with income from his Arequipa properties. Papers filed in order to return to the Indies provide excellent insight on how the family was managing its estate, and their economic strategies. Diego was arranging a marriage between his eldest daughter, Doña Bernaldina Maldonado, to the wealthy Cuzco encomendero Francisco de Valverde. He intended to send her on the Indies fleet along with her brother Gerónimo and younger sister Doña María de la Cuba. In addition to making plans for those three children, Diego requested permission to transport six female servants and slaves and four male servants. Their labor was needed, he said, because his daughters' quality was such that without maids, "they would be most indecent." He also requested authorization to send up to 2,000 ducats' worth of silks, clothes, and other things necessary for his daughters' household without payment of duties, and permission for Don Gerónimo's servants to travel with a full set of weapons as befitting their status and future service. The encomendero's fourth surviving child, Don Antonio de la Cuba, had remained in the Indies. From Peru, Francisco de Valverde had sent to Spain authorization to perform a proxy wedding with Bernaldina, with a provision that if she changed her mind, entered the convent, or married someone else, then he was to marry her younger sister Doña María. The proxy wedding was celebrated in the parish church of San Cebrián in Hontiveros in the diocese of Avila, on 24 January 1582. The encomendero stood alongside his daughter as the proxy vows were administered. The girls had been living in Medina del Campo, where another Collaguas encomendero, Noguerol de Ulloa, and his wife had retired. Permission to sail for Peru was granted in February 1582, with authorization to transport the servants and slaves, but the encomendero was required to pay duties on the goods.

Don Diego's right to the Cabanas was ultimately confirmed by the Council of the Indies. His cause was vindicated, but he was no longer the rich man he had been, largely because of the continual decline in the population of his grant. Hernández de la Cuba pressed on at court for other favors, and was finally awarded a six-year governorship of the rich Crown province of Chucuito. The salary was substantial, but the fringe benefits were much greater: he would control distribution of the mita labor force from 17,000 tributaries. Securing royal favor had been costly. According to his son, he wasted much of his Peruvian estate in Spain, and near the end his debts totaled 12,000 ducats.[25] After substantial effort and surely more cash, he managed to secure royal nomination (1592) to the military order of Santiago. But Don Diego Hernández de la Cuba never reached his Chucuito post; he died in Panama en route to Peru in August 1592.[26]

In spite of legal issues, Don Gerónimo de la Cuba Maldonado inherited the Cabanas. He frequently "served the king well" in the years after his return from Spain in 1582. He too helped defend Arequipa's port of Quilca against the English. He was elected Arequipa's alcalde ordinario four times, and was corregidor of nearby Camaná in 1614. Gerónimo began to gradually retire his father's debts, but at the same time he was accumulating massive liabilities of his own. He married off his younger sister Doña María to the corregidor of Arequipa, Don Diego de Treves y Brito, providing a princely dowry of 30,000 pesos.[27] In June 1597 Gerónimo married in Lima Doña Elvira Dávalos Santillán, daughter of Don Juan Dávalos de Ribera, knight of the Order of Calatrava, and grand-daughter of Captain Nicolás de Ribera, one of the thirteen faithful stranded with Pizarro on Gallo Island. She was also granddaughter of Licentiate Don Hernando de Santillán, judge of the Royal Audiencia. Licentiate Santillán died poor and, according to Gerónimo, had not provided well for his heirs.[28] In spite of family connections, tribute from the Cabanas, and properties in and around Arequipa, Gerónimo's fortunes dwindled. In 1606 he complained: "There has been a very great diminution, so much so that in the latest inspection there were 120 fewer Indians than before. And with the great ruin and calamities of ashes, earthquakes, flooding of the rivers, and losses, as is public and notorious, all my haciendas and houses are now worth 10,000 pesos of rent. I am poor and in need, with many obligations." His financial difficulties were the result of three factors: debts inherited from his father, demographic collapse, and natural dis-asters, especially earthquakes and the volcanic explosion of 1600. One witness testifying to the encomendero's worth reported that when his father went to Spain, he had taken loans on the haciendas. His income came from the rents of the Cabanas Indians, and the Lluclla vineyard in the Siguas Valley that was administered by Gerónimo's brother, Don Antonio. The Colca Valley corregi-dor, Juan de Vera, concurred that the decline in the tributary population had reduced the encomendero's income substantially. In addition to losses in the 1600 and 1605 earthquakes, there were shifts in the riverbed, causing severe crop damage. In Lluclla the family's vineyard was destroyed, along with houses and wine cellars. More than 2,500 botijas of yearly production were lost. The en-comendero's vineyards originally produced 3,000 botijas annually; his wheat lands were still unproductive in 1606. He lost a yearly income of 10,000 pesos.[29]

Gerónimo's economic difficulties were exacerbated by a large family. He complained he had "three daughters and a son, and the said Doña Elvira my wife has a disposition so that one might expect that she will have many more children." The family, as others who could, left Arequipa following the vol-canic explosion of Huaynaputina in 1600. They fled to Lima and stayed with Gerónimo's father-in-law, Don Juan Dávalos de Ribera. In 1606 Gerónimo pre-sented his service report before the Royal Audiencia hoping to receive govern-ment appointment that would allow the family to regain its foothold. The Royal Audiencia supported his request for an office, and in May 1607 the king named Gerónimo de la Cuba Maldonado corregidor of the province of Huaylas. In 1614 we find him serving as Camaná's corregidor. The encomendero became a corregidor, a salaried official in the colonial bureaucracy. Retention of a re-partimiento provided prestige but inadequate revenue to support the needs of an elite household. Cabanas anansaya was vacant in the 1630s, following Gerónimo's death. He left several children, including the principal male heir, Don Diego de la Cuba Maldonado y Dávalos, who married Doña Inés Ibáñez Dávila y Zegarra Peralta. Descendants of the family survive in Arequipa.[30]

Yanque Collaguas: Encomenderos to Corregidores

Francisco Pizarro granted the richest encomienda in the Colca Valley to his half brother Gonzalo Pizarro in 1540. After Gonzalo's execution, following his failed uprising against the Crown, Pedro de la Gasca granted Yanque Collaguas to the Arequipa founder Francisco Noguerol de Ulloa. He administered the grant until 1555, when he returned with his wife, Doña Catalina de Vergara, to Spain. Lima's Royal Audiencia authorized the encomendero to leave the Colla-guas under administration of a majordomo for up to four years, when he was required to return. But Noguerol's return to the Indies, if ever intended, was delayed, as various legal issues consumed time and money, part coming from Collaguas tributes. Royal revenues were rarely adequate to cover the burden of empire. Bankruptcy was a constant threat, and the Crown made periodic efforts to increase income. One method was to expropriate encomiendas and transfer tributes to the Royal Treasury, for deposit in Seville's House of Trade. In 1558 this became royal policy, as all vacated encomiendas with annual rent over 12,000 pesos were to be appropriated. Because Noguerol had left, his grant was declared vacant, and the new Viceroy Marqués de Cañete took control of Los Collaguas in November 1559, along with two other Arequipa encomien-das. The viceroy's action added to Noguerol's legal burdens in Spain, and he battled several years in the Council of the Indies to retain his tributaries. In the mid-1570s the Collaguas were finally incorporated into the Crown's patrimony. As compensation Noguerol received royal revenues from city sales tax of Me-dina del Campo, where he and his wife settled, and recognition of his claims to a titled estate. Noguerol was willing to compromise because he did not plan to return to Peru. Nor did he have legitimate offspring to inherit the grant. Henceforth Yanque tributaries were administered by corregidores.[31]

The corregidor was required to live in the village chosen as administrative center for the Indian province. He, with the kurakas, was responsible for trib-ute collection and its transport to the nearest Royal Treasury office. Unlike the encomendero, he administered local justice. His tenure was brief, and his in-come was a salary. Further, the corregidor administered all five encomiendas in the Colca Valley. When corregidores assumed their posts, the direct influ-ence of encomenderos over the Cabanas and Collaguas was sharply curtailed.

Encomenderos still wielded substantial economic power due to investments and especially due to their increasing control over nearby land. Yet their overall influence was declining as the corregidor became the key figure in Indian administration. But the corregidores failed to become a permanent local force, because their term was limited. Only if they managed to link themselves to the encomendero elite could they become a significant local force. The Crown recognized that possibility and attempted to prevent it by making it illegal, in theory, for the two groups to unite by marriage.

Most Crown officials, even viceroys, were subjected to residencias, official inquiries into their activities at the end of their term in office. In the case of corregidores, the replacement generally conducted the inquest. Public notice was given by town criers, and anyone could enter charges against the official. Complaints could cover a wide range of issues: absenteeism, collection of excessive tribute, engaging in illegal economic activities, failure to oversee justice or make certain that the doctrina was being administered, marriage to locals, or failure to ensure the laws were properly administered. If it was warranted, the official could be fined, imprisoned, exiled, or barred from future public service. The residencia did check blatant abuse. Many corregidores carried out their work diligently and honestly, and even fostered what they believed to be the best interests of their charges. But others tried to amass as much wealth as possible in their short stay in the Andean countryside. Lucas de Cadabal, who began his tenure as Collaguas corregidor in 1581, provides an instructive case. He was succeeded in 1584 by Juan de Ulloa Mogollón, who conducted the residencia of his predecessor. The Caylloma-based priest Sebastián Durán, Lari's doctrinero, testified that Cadabal was especially diligent in his efforts to extirpate idolatries and witchcraft. Yanque's Indian scribe Diego Coro Inga stated that Cadabal had discovered and destroyed huacas, punishing natives who persisted in pre-Christian rites. Durán reported that with steadfast effort Cadabal forced tributaries to plant and cultivate wheat, causing it to become a major valley product. Francisco Ala, Yanque's alcalde ordinario, said that before Cadabal's arrival it was necessary to "bring in the wheat and bread from the city of Arequipa and the Pitay Valley, and other places as far away as twenty leagues." But now bread was plentiful. Antonio Fernández of Yanque stated that wheat was presently cheaper than in Arequipa or Pitay. Cadabal was responsible for building a grist mill in Lari; Lari's kuraka Marcos Suyo boasted of the mill being "so good" it could "grind anything . . . necessary for the whole province." Cadabal assisted villagers to develop community fields to increase income. Francisco Hernández said that before Lucas was corregidor there were no community goods, but "now all the communities are rich and support hospitals and doctors." Cadabal also spearheaded the search for new mines and supervised the completion of tambos, cabildo offices, and bridges. The scribe Diego Coro Inga affirmed the corregidor finished the major public buildings in the province that had been started during the Toledo reducciones. The priest Durán asserted that Cadabal was just, ensuring that the Indians paid tribute equally according to the number in each ayllu and that the natives liked him better than previous corregidores. The comment "he leaves the province a poor man, taking with him only his salary" is one of the more eloquent recommendations a corregidor could receive. But the accomplishments of Lucas de Cadabal are policies that benefited the colonists and Crown as much as the valley's native residents.[32]

Daily activities of corregidores can also be gleaned from Lucas de Cadabal's residencia. Much of the official's time was spent collecting tribute and dispensing the money as allocated in the assessment. When Ulloa Mogollón began his inquiry into Cadabal's administration, he summoned Juan Alanoca and Pedro Auca, the keepers of the keys for Yanque's community treasury chest; he opened the box before several witnesses. Contents included account books and the reserves of three previous corregidores: Josepe de Villalobos; his predecessor, Juan Durán de Figueroa; and an earlier corregidor, Juan de Vergara, with tributes from the first payment of Christmas 1575. Three pay periods administered by Cadabal for June and December 1582, and for June 1583, were audited. Yanque's corregimiento expenditures included salaries for several Franciscan doctrineros, as well as a small amount paid to Father Muñoz for the purchase of a blank book to record doctrina revenues. Some 375 pesos were paid for church salaries in La Chimba of Arequipa, where many Colca Valley migrants temporarily resided. Surprisingly, 48 pesos 6 tomines had been returned to the treasuries in Lari urinsaya and Cabana urinsaya because the Indian justices had been overpaid! Another modest sum was transferred to Dr. Cosme Carrillo of the Arequipa treasury office because of an accounting error. The corregidores' salary of 1,138 pesos 5 tomines was paid from the Yanque treasury for the period 10 February 1582 to 15 December 1583. The Indian justices collected a 351-peso yearly stipend. The Indian hospitals received 567 pesos 5 tomines, a sum actually paid to Cornejo, the surgeon of the province, whose annual salary was 400 pesos. Almost 300 pesos were disbursed for hospital supplies: oil, figs, sugar, honey, physics (purges), Paris green, solimán, and other products. Kurakas and principales received 1,320 pesos in salaries.

Records for Lari anansaya are equally informative; here the corregidor Cadabal, the kuraka principal Juan Caqui, and the scribe Juan Suyo unlocked the three-keyed chest. The doctrinero's stipends were duly recorded, along with the corregidor's, and those of the legal defenders of the Indians. The kuraka Juan

Caquia received 192 pesos for "woodwork on the churches of the province." The encomendero Francisco Hernández Retamoso and his mother, Doña Francisca de Vergara, received 663 pesos for three pay periods. Cabana anansaya Indians were given 18 pesos for unspecified "grievances." The hospital's barbers, workers, and majordomos of Lari anansaya were paid; and another 134 pesos one tomín were spent to purchase "oil, honey, solimán, Paris green, oil of Aparicio, other medicines, raisins, and wine, and a gold-plated instrument case, and other middling things, and a gift for the said hospital and the poor who are cured in it."[33] Community account books of Lari urinsaya and of Cabana anansaya and urinsaya were also carefully audited.[34]

Flow of tribute revenues through the hands of corregidores provided ample opportunity for personal enrichment. Control over the mitayo labor force gave the official even greater authority. Not all corregidores resisted the temptations. In 1596 Diego Peralta Cabeza de Vaca became the new corregidor of Los Collaguas. He was encomendero of Capachica in Upper Peru, and a rich mine operator, controlling silver deposits in the province of Sica Sica near La Paz. Furthermore, Diego Peralta Cabeza de Vaca's family lived in Arequipa; he was active in commerce, with stores and land. As corregidor he illegally attempted to use Collaguas mitayos to work in his mines at Sica Sica. Almost immediately he was blocked by Arequipa's cabildo, which saw a threat to the district's own supply of mitayos.[35]

In spite of decrees to prevent abuse, personal relationships led to entanglements between officials in Lima, Arequipa, and the Collaguas. The web of intimate contacts between bureaucrats and settlers is vividly illustrated in the residencia of the Arequipa treasury official Sebastián Mosquera. In April 1593 Mosquera presented a petition to the residencia judge, Fernando Vega y Loaisa, in which he answered charges lodged against him. During the inquiry officials wanted the treasury agent to travel to the Collaguas, Condesuyos, and elsewhere to face local charges. Mosquera complained that there were no valid charges against him and that he had personal problems with Gonzalo de Vega y Loaisa, the brother of the residencia judge, and with Gonzalo de Buitrón and Alonso Osorio. Mosquera insisted that accusations against him were frivolous and he should not need to travel to the provinces to face "insignificant" charges. Mosquera further argued he should not be required to travel to the Collaguas, because of his relationship with the notary there who was an intimate friend of Alonso Picado and Gonzalo de Buitrón. He was also a friend of Mosquera's "enemy" Alonso Osorio. Mosquera's difficulties with the Buitrón family dated back to the 1580s, when he fined Antonio Gómez de Buitrón and others for "certain wounds they had given to Josepe de Villalobos," the Collaguas corregidor from 1579 to 1581. One of the most damaging charges against Mosquera was that he was receiving kickbacks on cloth sales from Collaguas tributaries to his close friend. Witnesses claimed that in the June 1591 payment, he defrauded the Crown of 900 pesos in the scheme. Mosquera was imprisoned, but was subsequently freed by the viceroy.[36]

Corregidores of the Colca Valley faced numerous economic challenges, including initial high transportation costs to Peru. Many corregidores intended to bring families to the Indies, hoping to marry their relatives into the wealthy Creole elite. The example of Diego de Treves y Brito stands out. In March 1586 Philip II named him corregidor of both Arequipa and the Collaguas, and informed Viceroy Conde del Villar of this unusual dual appointment. The corregidor's father had served the Crown over fifty years, and during his youth Treves y Brito was a page at court. The new corregidor prepared his household for the journey to Peru. He requested permission to take with him and his entourage 100 arquebuses and other equipment because, he contended, "that land is a frontier that could be infested with corsairs."[37] But he was unable to set sail until two years later, largely due to delays caused by Spain's preparations for the 1588 Armada against England. When the new corregidor's group reached Tierra Firme, several fell ill; then they were delayed during the southward voyage to Lima by "poor navigation." In the meantime the Conde del Villar had been replaced by a new viceroy, García Hurtado de Mendoza, the second Marqués de Cañete, who refused to confirm Treves y Brito's appointment to two corregimientos simultaneously, insisting it contradicted prior royal decrees. Furthermore, Viceroy Cañete reduced his salary. The corregidor was shocked by this turn of affairs, and wrote a long letter of complaint to the king. He lamented he expended more than 20,000 ducats to transport himself and family and that he was heavily indebted. He finally assumed his post in Arequipa in late 1590, but continued to lodge grievances: "The salary is so small and the land so poor." He complained that Viceroy Cañete had restored the sales tax in the district, and it was causing much hardship. With the "calamities of earthquakes, pestilence, moving the port, the lack of transport for wine," conditions in Arequipa were deplorable. Treves y Brito continued his efforts to secure the joint appointment, stressing that others in the Indies had served in dual posts. The corregidor's financial position in Arequipa only improved when he married Doña María de la Cuba Maldonado: she was the sister of the Cabana anansaya encomendero, Gerónimo de la Cuba Maldonado, who promised a hefty dowry of 30,000 pesos.[38]

By the 1620s there were notorious abuses of the system by many corregidores. In spite of the threat of the residencia to uncover graft, inadequate salaries coupled with the view that public servants ought to be rewarded for their services, resulted in wrongdoing. One official wrote the king that corregidores were actively engaged in economic pursuits and, rather than protecting the natives as mandated, they were exploiting them. Some corregidores established their own textile factories; others took native cloth goods as payment for tribute that were assessed two pesos each, then sold them for seven to eight. The residencia, designed to check abuses of public officials, was not functioning as intended. Lima's Royal Audiencia in May 1616 reported to the king that corregidores were deeply involved in the control of local branches of the Royal Treasury office; were engaged in illegal trade in cloth, wine, livestock, and other goods; and were closely confederated with other Spaniards and kurakas. During residencias Indians "tempered their complaints in order not to fall from grace of the incoming corregidor." Kurakas, to protect their own positions, chose to accommodate those in power.[39] But no matter what the level of corruption, the system was more attuned to maintaining royal authority in the Indies than the encomienda had been. Loyalty of salaried public officials in the Andean countryside was unquestioned, in contrast to that of the encomendero elite. The corregimiento system was a success for the imperial cause, but for Colca Valley natives the corregimiento, just like the encomienda, was authoritarian, exploitative, and alien.

Decline of the Colca Valley Encomenderos

Several factors led to the inability of the encomenderos to establish lasting dynasties in Arequipa. Initially there was the exceptional mortality from battle, as Spaniards fought over the spoils of conquest. The first generation of Europeans in the Colca Valley, from 1535 to 1548, had not fared well. Both repartimientos of the Cabanas, as well as that of Yanque Collaguas and half of Lari, were vacated by the deaths of their encomenderos. And the Crown's refusal to allow the perpetuity of the encomienda doomed the chances of their recipients to ever establish an economic power base similar to the Spanish landed aristocracy. The second generation, roughly spanning the years from La Gasca's assessment through the administration of Viceroy Francisco de Toledo, or 1549 to 1580, did reasonably well as a group. One option was to extract as much wealth as possible from Amerindians—and from investments in land, mines, and perhaps commerce—then return to the motherland and enter the Spanish elite. Francisco Noguerol de Ulloa, the encomendero of Yanque Collaguas, is a good example of a successful returnee. But beyond a contrary royal policy and high battle mortality, another problem existed. Some encomenderos, such as Noguerol de Ulloa and Alonso Rodríguez Picado the younger, failed to produce legitimate offspring to inherit their grants. The opposite, too many children, could also threaten the economic viability of the encomendero elite. The De la Torre and Cuba Maldonado lines, with very large surviving families, faced financial difficulties. Numerous daughters, requiring substantial dowries to secure desirable matches, could sap the liquid assets of their families. Even the dowry for a prestigious convent was formidable. Direct economic pressure from the Royal Treasury also depressed incomes of encomendero families. Frequent "gifts" extracted during financial crises were rarely repaid, and were more appropriately "donations" than loans. Encomenderos were expected to serve freely in local administration and to arm, fight, and supply others in emergencies, such as uprisings or foreign attacks. Moving slowly and systematically, the Crown was successful as it progressed from the New Laws to the establishment of the corregimiento system, limiting the power and authority of the encomendero elite, and then finally breaking them altogether.

But the most important factors in the decline of the Colca Valley encomendero elite were ecological. Natural disasters—such as floods, earthquakes, droughts, insect infestations of crops, and demographic factors—all contributed to population decline, undermining the economic base of the encomenderos. Oftentimes these ecological factors are interrelated. The aboriginal population density in valleys near the volcanic cone of Misti was never as high as in many other areas of the southern and central Andes. Violent earthquakes were frequent enough so that in spite of the richness of the soil and normally adequate rainfall, the region extracted more from human habitation than it gave. The forces within the earth were recognized and feared by the native Andeans, who attempted to propitiate those forces with regular sacrifice, especially to Solimana, Coropuna, and Ampato, the most spectacular of the volcanic cones.[40] The modern discovery of the sacrifice of a young woman on the summit of Ampato gives credence to respect shown by the natives of the Arequipa district to the great snowcapped huacas that dominate the skyline and seem to mediate between the subterranean and the celestial. Europeans did not fully recognize the forces of the earth, so feared by Andeans, and after the settlement at coastal Camaná failed, they moved to higher elevations, finally establishing themselves in Arequipa at the very base of the Misti volcano. It is a spectacular setting for a city, but the move from the coast in 1540 was an invitation to disaster, and generation after generation of residents have paid the toll. With great effort, and substantial use of the Indian labor force from the Colca Valley, the city was con-

Arequipa's destruction by volcanic explosion and rain of ash, from Guaman Poma (1053 [1061])

structed, then reconstructed over and over, using the very material produced by the volcanoes: the white, light, volcanic stone sillar.

The first major seismic event experienced by Europeans in the Arequipa district is vividly described in Viceroy Martín Enríquez's letter to Philip II. Midday on 22 January 1582 there began a "movement of the earth so great that within four credos [recitations of the Creed, the sixteenth-century method used to estimate the duration of an unusual and potentially deadly event] all the city was ruined; there was not a house remaining nor a temple that did not cave in." Thirty-six or thirty-seven died, and the viceroy admitted that had the event occurred at night, many more people would have perished.[41] More were injured than killed outright. On the coast, a tidal wave surged into Arequipa's port of Islay. The water channels supplying the town crumbled, and the streets were inundated. Vineyards in nearby valleys were destroyed, pack animals were lost, and there was "a plague of flies and rats." Days following the earthquake observers noted that many highland vicuñas, guanacos, and deer entered the city.[42] On 1 February the cabildo met and authorized commissioners to supply Indians to rebuild the city. The encomendero Hernández Retamoso was named commissioner for "Los Collaguas y Cabana," and was charged to first survey damage there and then help collect a labor force for Arequipa. On 19 February the viceroy authorized an Indian labor draft to initiate reconstruction; at the same time, he asked city authorities to consider moving the settlement to an entirely new location. Cabildo members discussed the question at length but concluded on 14 April that "there is no commodious place to move the settlers to; all are agreed that the city should be rebuilt on the present site where the city was founded."[43] The viceroy then authorized 1,300 nearby mitayos for one year for reconstruction; the privilege was extended by the Audiencia for six months. The viceroy in Lima on 20 December 1584 issued a grant of 500 mitayos to continue the task. The city solicitor complained that housing was still unavailable for merchants and other outsiders, and many commercial interests were leaving, imperiling the growth of the center. City officials asked for a three-year extension of the mita. Viceroy Conde del Villar in March 1589 provided 500 Indians for the work for another year.[44]

One of the most complete descriptions of the mita's operation at the local level stems from the Arequipa allotment of Viceroy Conde del Villar on 13 June 1589. A list was prepared for the distribution of mitayos to rebuild the city, and also for the ordinary service they provided. The officials noted 3,996 tributaries lived in the Crown repartimiento of Yanque, but of these 437 were settled in the puna village of Tisco, beyond the twenty-five leagues' maximum distance from the city of Arequipa. Thus there were 3,559 tributaries eligible for the Arequipa

TABLE 12. The 1589 mitayo allotment from the Collaguas for Arequipa

Encomendero	Tributaries	Beyond 25 leagues	Eligible for mita service	Mita quota of 1/7	Ordinary service	Reconstruction of Arequipa	Guard of livestock
Collaguas of the Crown	3,996	437	3,559	508	110	335	63
Francisco Hernández Retamoso	1,319	250	1,069	152	44	57	51
Alonso Rodríguez Picado	1,206	250	956	136	40	47	49
Diego Hernández de la Cuba	772	—	772	110	35	36	39
Hernando de la Torre	557	—	557	78	20	25	33
Total	7,850	—	6,913	984	249	500	235

Source: Barriga, Los terremotos en Arequipa, 37–39

mita draft. Of these, 110 were reserved for ordinary service, 63 for transport of goods and the guarding of livestock, and 335 for reconstruction of the city (see table 12).[45] On 20 July 1589 the cabildo met and agreed on the distribution of part of the Colca Valley mitayos to Spanish residents and institutions. Two valley encomenderos held office in the cabildo that year: the alcalde, Francisco Hernández Retamoso, and the regidor, Hernando de la Torre. The cabildo notified the Collaguas corregidor, Garcí Mendes de Moscoso, that of the 500 Indians from the Arequipa district, 98 were to come from the Collaguas. Ten of the Collaguas mitayos were allocated for the hospital, 6 were assigned to the Jesuits; most individual recipients, including Hernando de la Torre, received labor lots of 6 mitayos each.[46] Colca Valley mitayos were expected to serve three months each year in the city. Not only did they help rebuild; they also served in wine production and transport and in shipment of merchandise. A kuraka traveled with each group of mitayos, and the workers were recorded by name and ayllu. In 1589 the Collaguas mitayos had not been sent, and Arequipa merchants and meat venders had to travel to the Colca Valley to requisition them. Some arequipeños complained they expended time and effort, and had lost 100,000 pesos in wine and livestock. Cabildo officials blamed the Collaguas corregidor for failing to send the mitayos as in previous years. Once initiated, this "reconstruction" service continued whether or not initial repairs of the earthquake damage were completed; as late as 1597, another viceroy authorized continuation of the "special" mita.[47]

Before 1589 ended, Arequipa faced a new challenge: epidemic disease. Measles, smallpox, and typhus ravaged the district. On the day after Christmas 1589, the Arequipa cabildo met in an emergency session to discuss the course of action, because "the pestilence of smallpox and measles has arrived . . . , and the majority of the vecinos and the natives within the district have come down with it and are ill or have died." In the Colca Valley, Friar Luis Jerónimo de Oré kept careful "enumeration of the Indians who have died in the general epidemic of smallpox and measles" in the village of Coporaque.[48] The effects of the epidemics reached beyond disease mortality: "Because of it there has been no one to look after the harvesting of the wheat that has been planted. There will be the gravest of consequences, and a great need will befall this republic if it is lost. That will happen if the rains begin now, as each day they are expected to begin, for the season is so advanced." Facing imminent disaster, the Arequipa cabildo ordered that the work should be "assigned to all, and that each one was to go to his pueblo and fields surrounding the city, in order to harvest the wheat, and place it in balconies and safe places where it can be guarded, secure against the rainfall, and afterward it can be threshed when the epidemic has passed." Among others, two Collaguas encomenderos were charged to oversee this effort: the alcalde, Francisco Hernández Retamoso, was to direct the harvest in Paucarpata, and Hernando de la Torre in Pocsi.[49] The epidemic series that hit the environs continued into 1591. Amerindian mortality was very high; at least a third of the native population died before the epidemics ran their course.

An equally devastating natural disaster swept Arequipa a decade later. On 19 February 1600, the Huaynaputina volcano in nearby Ubinas province exploded. The sound was so great it was heard within a radius of sixty leagues. Winds carried ashes north to Panama and even to the coast of Nicaragua, and over the Andes into the tropical Amazon rain forest.[50] Father Luis de Leyba, vice-rector of the Jesuit school of Chuquiabo, traveled to Arequipa to survey the damage and assist victims. He was unable to take the normal route from Jesuit mission towns in Chucuito on the edge of Lake Titicaca toward the coast and nearest to the province of Ubinas, where damage was most severe. He remained in the highlands, continuing to Cuzco, where he initiated a backward trek toward Arequipa. In Cuzco, around Easter time, ash began to fall, obscuring the sun and covering fields. The Cuzco road passed through the Colca Valley, and from the heights above the village of Yanque, Leyba noted ashes at a depth "greater than a palm." After midday, as the winds began to intensify, he and a companion had to travel side by side in order not to become separated, because it was impossible to see. During the journey they met Indians and Spaniards fleeing the disaster, who warned him that it was "rash and foolish for anyone to go to the city now, where everywhere in the fields and streets one finds dead livestock which have starved." When Father Leyba reached Arequipa, he realized that there was little he could do to assist victims, so he returned to the Colca Valley, where he spent a month. There he learned that prices in Arequipa were rising sharply: corn prices more than tripled, with each fanega fetching thirteen to fifteen pesos. Products were transported from as far away as Cuzco to provision survivors. Settlers were selling gold and silver objects, clothing, and anything else of value, to buy food. Father Luis de Leyba reported that for a time Arequipa was called "Little Potosí, for the abundance of silver that was carried away."[51]

Natives of the Colca Valley returned home to repair family houses, irrigation canals, and agricultural terraces. Although less severe than in Arequipa, there was damage in the valley. Ash ten to twelve centimeters deep covered crops. But rainfall, coupled with careful cultivation, permitted a partial harvest of the year's planting. Conditions were more catastrophic in Arequipa, nearer the volcano, where the depth of ashes exceeded a meter. The weight of the ash was enough to crush many houses, clog water channels, destroy roads, and smother crops. Viticulture ceased for five to six years. There was no hope for the corn and wheat harvest in 1600, and the results of the next year's planting were questionable. Arequipa's vecinos found themselves in the midst of a serious crisis without an adequate labor force. They noted that Indian workers fled; the few remaining were tending their own fields. The council called on all residents to join in to help open water channels and clean the streets, in order to avoid the "sickness and pestilence that will surely happen if it is not done." They requested the viceroy to authorize 2,000 Indian workers for three years to repair the damage. The viceroy granted 1,000 from the Collaguas for six months, under the usual stipulations. As the six months were closing, Arequipa requested 500 yearly for two more years. The viceroy responded by granting 500 Indians for six months; there were further extensions.[52]

Immediately, Arequipa officials sent for mitayos who had fled to the Colca Valley. They ordered the Collaguas corregidor on 10 April to send 1,000 Collaguas workers. If the Indians had to go back to their fields to plant their own crops, it was acceptable as long as they returned afterward to Arequipa to finish the year's mita. The cabildo sent messages to Condesuyos, asking for 200 more mitayos. In the Cuzco district they petitioned the corregidores of Cabana, Urcosuyo, Canas, and Canchis to send wheat, chuño, fresh potatoes, and wax. On 16 April the cabildo received an offer of assistance of Indians and supplies from Don Melchor Dávalos de Castilla, corregidor of the Cabana province. On 30 May the Arequipa cabildo thanked him for sending 300 Indians for repair of the city.[53] Years later, in 1611, the corregidor of Los Collaguas, Gonzalo Rodríguez de Herrera, informed the king how well he had served the city of Arequipa, ensuring that each month 600 Indians from the Collaguas were engaged in cleaning the city of the debris and rebuilding its houses, and in repairing vineyards and haciendas in the valley. He claimed proudly he had "brought victuals valued more than 70,000 pesos from Cuzco and other parts, with which the said city was supported until its harvest."[54]

Colca Valley mitayos played a crucial role in Arequipa's reconstruction, though there were complaints regarding their participation. Frequently laborers from the Collaguas did not arrive as quickly as expected. To secure an adequate labor force, the cabildo commissioned the regidor Andrés de Herrera to travel to the Colca Valley to arrange for the transportation of the workers. On 30 March 1601 the cabildo received a letter from Viceroy Luis de Velasco committing 500 mitayos from the Collaguas, as in 1597. The stumbling block was the Collaguas corregidor, who insisted the city could only use the laborers for two months and that the common Indian workers would have to be paid one and one-half reales daily, and the kurakas two reales, 50 percent more than the normal rate. In May the cabildo notified the corregidor that mitayos should remain for the entire year. In August the corregidor was in Arequipa, directing the labor force, and the cabildo tried to reach agreement on their differences. But disputes between the corregidor and the Arequipa elite continued. In March 1602 the cabildo discussed the "little punctuality" of the corregidor of the Collaguas in enforcing viceregal provisions regarding mitayos for Arequipa, especially for repairs after the volcanic eruption. They complained that the Indians had fled to him, and that he extended the rest period between the mitas. Furthermore, many of the Collaguas living in La Chimba, or Yanahuara, fled after the fall of "ash and the explosion of the volcano."[55] In January 1603 the relationship between Arequipa's officials and the Collaguas corregidor, Gonzalo Rodríguez de Herrera, was strained. Kurakas of the Collaguas had presented a petition to the Arequipa solicitor Pedro de Obando regarding mitayos from Caylloma, the most distant town in the corregimiento. At issue was the twenty-five-league distance limitation. Arequipa's cabildo asked for copies of the documents regarding which Collaguas mitayos were exempt from their draft. Earlier decrees were examined, and the city's solicitor concluded there should be no exemptions. Arequipa charged that the Collaguas corregidor failed to send the stipulated one-seventh, not even the twentieth part, and that the cabildo should reject a reduction.[56] Rodríguez de Herrera is not the only example of a Collaguas corregidor who resisted demands of arequipeños for workers. Colca Valley officials, kurakas, and clerics often joined to "protect" Cabana and Collagua tributaries. They did it to nurture their own labor force as they constructed valley churches and engaged in other works.

Little did Arequipa residents realize how long their tribulation would continue when they began rebuilding following the volcanic explosion. In late October 1601 cabildo officers lamented: "To this city has occurred the greatest calamity that has ever taken place in any republic in the world. For the past year and a half there has been a continuous rain of ash on the city." None of the crops survived the disaster. Religious leaders admonished that the only solution was to "placate the ire of God Our Father . . . , to remove the public sins and scandals of the republic."[57] But all the rituals, religious processions, prayers, and ceremonies — as well as the strenuous work of reconstruction falling so heavily on the Collaguas — came to nothing. On Wednesday, 24 November 1604, between 1 and 2 PM, another major earthquake devastated the city, undoing previous repairs. The cabildo met in the plaza in a hastily constructed shelter; no suitable structure remained standing. Again the first business was the repair of water channels for the city and its fields. Similar to events in 1600, all vecinos and residents were ordered to work jointly to put the water system back in order to prevent starvation, a calamity worse than the original earthquake. The cabildo reported to the viceroy that forty people were killed in Arequipa and nearby villages, and they requested a three-year labor force of 3,000 mitayos from the Collaguas, Condesuyos, Cabana, and Cabanilla del Collao, to rebuild the city.[58] Damage occurred in the Colca Valley too. A population count that was being conducted in 1604 and 1605 was interrupted. The visitador Gerónimo Dávila was having difficulties reaching villages: "In the four leagues from here [Lluta] to the pueblo of Guanca where they are reduced, one cannot travel because the roads have collapsed and there have been landslides, with the tremor and earthquake that occurred on 24 November of last year."[59]

Earthquakes, volcanic eruptions, and heavy ash that smothered crops made life difficult for both Europeans and native residents from Arequipa to the Colca Valley. Following immediate mortality at the time of the seismic events, there was increased mortality afterward from food shortages and disease. Hydraulic systems collapsed, and clean drinking water was scarce. But so long as there were abundant native workers, the European elite could start afresh; they could rebuild their homes and begin to amass new fortunes. The key survival factor is the size and quality of the workforce, and Amerindians were more prone to die than the Europeans who continued to settle in increasing numbers in the Arequipa district. There were about 70,000 Amerindians living in the Colca River watershed when the Europeans first touched Peru's north coast. Some were killed during warfare; many succumbed to disease and exploitation in building the Arequipa settlement, or in the fields and houses of encomenderos. When Viceroy Toledo's agents conducted a census and tribute assessment in 1572–1573, they found a population of 33,900. When a new census of the Collaguas was completed in 1604, only 22,869 remained. Especially distressing is the large number of old or infirm males in 1604, unable to engage in viable economic activities. Equally alarming is the sharp drop in the number of boys under eighteen; they are practically halved in the period, a portent of worse times ahead. Rather than stemming the tide of disintegration, Toledo's Andean utopia accelerated the process. By concentrating a scattered population into dense village clusters, Toledo established an ideal environment for the spread of infectious disease.[60]

Devastation caused by Old World epidemics that entered the Andean world continued long beyond the first and second generations after contact. The first pandemic in the mid-1520s, probably smallpox, was followed by smallpox and measles between 1530 and 1532, then plague or typhus in 1546–49, and influenza and smallpox between 1558–60. Epidemics occurred in 1577–78, near the end of the Toledo resettlement process. The most lethal and well-documented epidemic series was a combination of measles, smallpox, and typhus in 1589–91. Thirty years later, in 1618, an epidemic of smallpox again swept the viceroyalty. In 1640 colonial authorities sent a report to the Council of the Indies stressing the weakened and dissipated state of the Collaguas as the number of Indians continued to fall. The nadir was probably not reached until the middle of the eighteenth century, after a devastating 1719–20 epidemic series that included smallpox, typhus, plague, and influenza. At the lowest point, there only remained about 10,000 Amerindians in the entire Colca Valley.[61] In 1586 the valley appeared to Europeans as "healthful": "and there are no illnesses in it because it is cold and dry." Two centuries later Tadeo Haenke characterized the conditions differently: "The dominant vice of the people is drunkenness, and their common illnesses are typhus and pleurisy."[62]

EPILOGUE

ANDEAN COUNTERPOINT

The dualism of Peruvian history and soul is expressed in our time as a conflict between the historical form that evolved on the coast and the indigenous spirit that survives in the sierra, deeply rooted in nature. . . . Neither the Spaniard nor the Creole could understand or conquer the Andes.
—José Carlos Mariátegui, *7 ensayos de interpretación de la realidad peruana* (1928), 134.

When he [Inkarrí] wanted to construct chacras, that is terraces, they constructed themselves; the stones formed together into walls, they formed themselves into terraces.
—Testimony of Yanque informant, 1974, Pease, "Collaguas: Una etnia del siglo XVI," 148.

The people of the volcano survive into the present, in spite of centuries of colonialism and decades of efforts to mold them into part of the national identity. More recently, they have resisted pressures to become part of a global economy. In language; agricultural practices; rituals associated with all aspects of everyday existence; human relationships at the level of family, ayllu, and saya; and reverence for the forces of nature, the people of the Colca Valley show striking similarities to their ancestors of a half millennium ago. They persist in contrast to many other Amerindian groups. They survive in spite of great pressures: environmental change, the exactions of a colonial system based on exploitation of human labor, a shift from reciprocity to an extractive economy, the efforts to make them conform to a European model of "citizenship" in the "República de los Indios," forced religious conversion, compelled migrations to Spanish urban centers, and wave after wave of Old World diseases. Their survival tells much of the human condition in general, and the nature of modern Andean society in Peru in particular.

The earth's landscape is in process of constant change. The peoples of the valley believed with good reason that the Andean soil is alive, moving. Along the central coast it was believed that when the great huaca Pachacamac shook its head, the earth trembled; if Pachacamac turned over, the earth would be destroyed. The forces of the great mountain peaks were venerated, and sacrifices were left on their summits. Ecological change is rarely noticed in a single human generation, unless precipitated by a cataclysmic event such as a volcanic eruption or a massive landslide that sweeps homes and agricultural terraces into the riverbed in the canyon below. But change does take place. The Andean cordillera is prone to movement, located so close to the meeting of two of the earth's great plates. From the summit of Hualca Hualca (6,025 meters) overlooking much of the Colca Valley to the deep trench off the Pacific coast, a horizontal distance of only 100 kilometers, the vertical distance from the bottom of the trench to the mountain peaks is twelve kilometers. Few places on the globe's surface can match such great variation in so short a distance. The cordillera still seems to be growing, rising to greater heights. The upward thrust of even one or two meters can result in changes in water flow patterns, disrupting agricultural systems. Irrigation channels that fulfilled their function in the late fourteenth century became ultimately inoperative and had to be abandoned or rebuilt. Sometimes rebuilding or moving the channels is impossible. Springs dry up and disappear. Thermal baths that flourished when the Spaniards arrived were gone by the end of the colonial era. Some hot springs that were active near the edge of the Colca River below Yanque no longer exist.

Simultaneously as the earth pushes upward, the elements tear it down. Wind and rain slowly wear away softer surfaces of the Andes. Fertile soil is created by the process, collecting on the more gentle slopes, or in human-made terraces. Yet the mighty force of the water of the river strips away layer after layer, cutting deeper and deeper gashes in the canyon. Only the hardest rock surfaces resist the process of erosion. When the river gouges deeply enough, banks above the edge become unstable, and disastrous landslides occur, sweeping away topo after topo of maize, quinua, or potatoes. These sections can only be restored with great expenditure of human effort. A large and well-directed labor force can produce significant change in the ecosystem using indigenous preconquest technology. But the size and quality of the labor force is crucial, and that element was in a state of punctuated decline following the arrival of the outsiders in the 1530s. A constantly shrinking workforce could not keep up with the challenges of the Andean environment. The loss of a few topos of cropland by landslide or a discarded canal was not critical after the demographic losses of the first generation following contact with the Europeans, as land and people declined simultaneously. In Inca times population pressure in the Colca Valley propelled collective effort to replace lost terraces and create new ones. With demographic collapse, the imperative of population pressure was gone. Hence fields fell into disuse, retaining stones or walls crumbled, and with continual erosion these pressed on still-cultivated cropland at lower levels, resulting in a cycle of reduced agricultural productivity. Aerial and satellite photographs of the valley highlight substantial stretches of terraces that are no longer in use. Approximately 20 percent of the agricultural terraces of the community of Coporaque are abandoned. After examination of the possibility of tectonic shift as well as evaluation of the impact of the introduction of European crops and animals, John Treacy concluded that the critical factor for Coporaque field abandonment was depopulation, with its concomitant decrease in need.[1] A positive aspect of this finding is that given contemporary increasing population pressures, much of the lost land can be recuperated.

Beyond the control of indigenous or even modern technology is the ultimate source of water for the crops of the Andean valleys: rain. The amount of water falling in the western side of the Andean mountain chain depends on many factors: the temperature of the surface water along the Pacific coast, and the speed of winds that push the moisture upward, as well as the land temperature. There are short- and long-term variations in rainfall. Every few years the cool Humboldt Current shifts, allowing more moisture, rising temperatures, and heavy rains, causing floods and destroying irrigation systems. But there is a rapid return to the normal pattern. Gradual, almost imperceptible changes also occur that over the long term result in centuries of drier decades, then damper ones. For the past half millennium, perhaps even from the thirteenth century, there appears to be a tendency toward a drier climate, resulting in gradually diminishing agricultural productivity.

The biological expansion of Europe involved more than the introduction of disease pathogens that ravaged the human population; it also resulted in the introduction of nonnative plants and animals. Most American grains and tubers were more productive, per surface unit of measurement, than Old World crops. Fields of quinua, maize, and potatoes yielded more fanegas per surface unit than wheat or barley. Europeans by the 1570s demanded as tribute only a small variety of products, requiring increased concentration of native productive capacity on those deemed important in the tributary regimen, which led to a loss of native Andean agricultural products and technologies. Already by the end of the sixteenth century, some native American crops were no longer cultivated in the Colca Valley. The introduction of European livestock posed a greater threat to the fragile ecosystem. Llamas and alpacas were perfectly adjusted to life in the Andes, and extensive herds grazed the puna grasses without permanently damaging the vegetation. In spite of the excellent wool these animals produced, the Europeans, insisting on sheep fiber, introduced sheep along with goats. The Spanish introduction of cattle, horses, donkeys, and pigs presented greater problems in cultivated fields. The Colca Valley suffered less than some other agricultural regions in the Andes, in part because the first sheep and goats did not prosper at more than 4,500 meters' elevation in the surrounding puna, nor did other livestock find sufficient pasture in the valley's terraces.

The Colca Valley did not become a hacienda district, as did some other parts of Peru. Two factors made it difficult to establish haciendas in the Colca Valley. One was environmental: little flat grazing land was available. The other was the strength of community. Over many generations the foundations of collective labor for local survival were strongly embedded in the mind of the Cabanas and the Collaguas. The family, the ayllu, and saya by nature stressed traditional values of maintaining what worked so well in fostering group survival. Fortunately the Spanish legal system recognized traditional systems of land tenure and protected community lands against private encroachments. As long as there was someone available with a legitimate claim to defend the community, the courts in Peru as in Spain upheld community rights over water systems, pasturelands, and woodlands, along with natural resources in general. The European hacienda did take root in the nearby Arequipa Valley, where land cultivated by Collagua and Cabana migrants living in La Chimba and other surrounding towns quickly came under the pressure of European livestock. Damage was extensive—pigs proved particularly devastating to corn and other crops as they uprooted arequipeño fields and retaining walls.

The church played a major role in the Colca Valley in the process of accommodation and survival of the Cabanas and Collaguas. The uncontested "mandate" of the religious was conversion, and the valley's people were compelled to recognize the universal omnipotent Christian deity. Mass conversions came with surprising speed; they were followed by a more tedious and contentious process of catechism. The earliest friars and priests baptized tens of thousands of Colca Valley residents, and the native Americans accommodated to this "conversion." They even allowed the destruction of the revered ancient valley huacas, often to the surprise and relief of those conducting the immolation of ancestral mummies. Catholic hegemony was tolerated because the power of the Christian God was demonstrated, just as the cult of Inti had been accepted after Inca conquest. Christianity itself was altered according to the demands of survival, and in spite of the power of colonial authorities, the Colca Church was fragile at best. The Church among the Collagua and the Cabana could not enforce immediate doctrinal orthodoxy. The natives were viewed as minors who needed to be taught the intricacies of the Faith with rewards and punishments. Children err, and the friars recognized failure not as the work of the devil, rather as the imperfect faith of recent, childlike converts. Many clergymen believed that greater orthodoxy would come with time, and might take generations.

Initially less offensive native practices were tolerated in the valley. Family formation customs such as trial marriage and the levirate were overlooked. Traditional patterns of naming of children were maintained for several generations. The ayllu persisted, as did the saya, in spite of a pre-Hispanic relationship to religion in the case of the ayllu, with its veneration of ancestors. The native ritual calendar was integrated into the Christian calendar, and Christian saints became new "huacas." In the native mind they could be propitiated, just as the old huacas had been, by offerings of coca and chicha and by burning incense. What was unacceptable to the Church was the development of rites that challenged Christianity. In the Colca Valley the Church more completely catechized than in some other parts of the Andean world. The Taki Onqoy movement of the 1560s failed to penetrate the valley in any significant fashion; neither did the idolatries that were so widespread in the Huarochirí region in the second decade of the seventeenth century. The Ampato cult was a challenge, grown out of desperation in the 1580s; it did pose a threat, and its adherents were sought out and silenced by the authority of the corregidores. The Church at first did not reject traditional native medicine in the valley, and healers continued their craft after conquest. When European "doctors" and hospitals that were established in the valley failed to save lives during epidemics, the Indians could turn to native practitioners, though their cures proved equally ineffective.

The Cabana and the Collagua accommodated to the demands of the new colonial regime. Andean kurakas were cognizant participants in this process. They strove to regain political authority that they held before it was usurped by the Incas, and to retain it, albeit under the eye of colonial bureaucrats. The Spaniards could not have administered the vastness of the Peruvian viceroyalty without the complicity of the kurakas. Kurakas observed and interacted with the European world, and their children studied in schools established in Spanish cities for the training of the native elite. Yet in spite of imitation of the newcomers—by adopting the dress, language, and religion of their colonial rulers—the kurakas could never cross the racial divide that permeated the colonial order. Furthermore, although they might "become" European, Hispanicized, their position was dependent on their ties to local ayllu and saya. In order to survive, the kuraka needed to have the respect of his ayllu and community. That respect was linked to his ability to represent the interests of common tributaries to the outside world. It was also dependent on how well he manipulated the system of reciprocity. Under the colonial regime the Cabana-Collagua kurakas were relegated to being functionaries who collected, then channeled, tribute and labor to central authorities in the provincial capital of Arequipa and the viceregal capital of Lima. Reciprocity existed in the colonial regime only at the local level where successful kurakas continued, as best as they could, to return a severely restricted amount of goods and services to community members. Continuation of reciprocity was increasingly difficult as the colonial era wore on and as pressures mounted on the resource base. As the kurakas ultimately were forced to demand payment of goods and services from the common tributaries, and as they were no longer able to exercise the reciprocal function they once had, the foundation of the system shifted from reciprocity to exploitation. And exploitation finally led to open rebellion. The Andean concept of reciprocity did not die in the colonial era, battered as it was. Reciprocity survived into the national period, functioning best at the lowest level, the family and vestigial ayllu, and the saya in communities where saya organization persisted. Community reciprocity persisted as a basic element of group survival. Thatching of houses still involves reciprocal relationships, as does annual cleaning of irrigation ditches. Exchange of goods—especially maize, coca, chuño, and wool—involves noncash, reciprocal forms and is based on social relationships. Reciprocity continues to provide the foundations of community security that the nation-state has uniformly failed to furnish in rural districts of Andean America.

The kuraka's power was checked from the time of the establishment of Toledo's "República de Indios" by the two elected alcaldes from each community's saya. The checks and balances of the Hapsburg colonial structure blocked not only the emergence of a New World European nobility; by setting up native alcaldes versus kurakas, they had a mechanism to prevent the kurakas from establishing a hereditary local lineage. In the end, the rebellion of Túpac Amaru II sealed the fate of kurakas in the minds of colonial bureaucrats. They could no longer be trusted, and the "elected" alcaldes thereafter largely replaced the kurakas at the local level. With independence the alcaldes were increasingly "appointed" by central authorities. Many republican politicians believed they were acting in the "best interests" of the native American, who continued to be stereotyped as unintelligent, childlike, and in need of "education for advancement." The more the political authorities of the nineteenth century became associated with the outside world of Arequipa and Lima, and the less linked by kin and ties of reciprocity to the Colca Valley, the more exploitative they appeared to local commoners.

The people of the Colca Valley accommodated to the regime as long as accommodation allowed survival. It was a process of transculturation. Collagua and Cabana selectively tested, adapted, and adopted elements of the culture of the foreigners. The Europeans likewise tested, adapted, and adopted Andean culture. Andean modes of organizing people were adopted by the Spanish bureaucracy. The larger groupings of saya that the Inca used to control people, though alien to the European, were maintained. The mita continued to the end of the colonial era. Periodic censuses—population and resource assessments similar to those the Inca had conducted—continued under colonial administration. Tribute items were modified, yet many of the products that long before had been stored in the Inca q'olqas were the same as those extracted by the colonial bureaucracy. Construction and maintenance of agricultural terraces and irrigation channels continued under Spanish rule, with little change in technology. The animal-powered iron plow did not replace the hoe and digging stick in the Colca Valley, except on the rare land surfaces that were both larger and level. No important technological transformations occurred among the puna pastoralists. Rituals associated with the agricultural calendar were changed only to the extent that external Christian saint's days were superimposed. The customary Andean offerings endured as chicha, guinea pigs, coca leaves, and llamas—sacrificed before the arrival of the Europeans—continued to be offered. The addition of candles and wine, aguardiente, and "holy water" did not transform the meaning of the ritual. Christian efforts at extirpation did not destroy the huacas. The apachitas; the conopas; the huacas of the ancestors; the springs, lakes, and elaborate rock formations; and the great volcanic cones all continued to be venerated. Most important, Quechua and Aymara were not replaced by the foreign tongue.

The Andean ayllu constituted a largely self-sufficient community. In the pre-Inca period ayllus linked, creating small regional states. The Inca state superimposed itself on the Andean community and made new, more extensive demands for cloth, maize, metals, labor, women, warriors, and even colonists. Some of the commodities and people were for the support of the political elite, and some of the goods were consumed in ceremonial offerings that characterized the Inca political-religious system. Submission to the Inca state was mandated, but the relationship between the community and the state was not based on a one-directional flow of goods and services. In emergencies, state storehouses—the q'olqas that warehoused goods—were opened to transfer goods to where they were needed. The Inca state had a redistributive function, although more was

Yanque woman and child (photo by N. D. Cook)

removed from the local economy than was returned. Nonetheless, the position of the Inca state was not challenged by the Collagua and the Cabana. Association was fostered between the local Colca Valley leadership and the Inca elite. Marriage took place, cementing the relationship. Children of the kurakas were trained in the capital.

The arrival of the Spanish interrupted the evolution of the Inca state, and it destroyed aboriginal ties of reciprocity at the state level. The Spanish colonial system, tested elsewhere in the New World before it was introduced into Peru, differed from the Andean tradition. It is true that the Europeans allowed for the retention of some local prerogatives: the kurakas were perhaps more powerful under Spanish rule than under the Inca. The communities established in the Andean world by Viceroy Toledo allowed for local Indian self-government with annual election of town officials. But tribute and labor service dominated in the colonial regime. Tribute at first supported the encomendero elite; then, with the corregimiento system, tribute provided the cash to support the bureaucracy. When tributes dwindled, there was still enough to pay a good portion of the salary of the colonial bureaucracy. Unlike under Inca rule, in times of crisis the colonial "state" did not aid; rather it demanded more for itself, as in the example of arequipeños' demanding mitayos following natural disasters. The labor force demanded by the European colonial system helped build the public offices, hospitals, and churches in the viceroyalty. The Amerindian workforce also tilled the fields of private encomenderos, built their houses, transported the goods of merchants, and mined the gold and silver that provided the wealth of the Indies. In the case of the rich Collaguas province, there was excess cash, which was extracted and flowed to maintain the Lima bureaucracy and assist in paying for the Pacific coastal defense of Spain's South American empire. From Peru the excess was funneled toward the center of power, the Iberian peninsula, to uphold state imperial policies on the continent.

The independence of Peru in the early nineteenth century did not alter the image of the state as an exploitative mechanism operating in the Andean countryside. Indeed, under the young republic, the situation may have worsened. The Spanish state, in spite of its role in the extractive economy, did attempt to limit excesses of the colonial elite. The New Laws of the 1540s were designed to protect the native Americans. The colonial response to the legislation was the violent eruption of the Gonzalo Pizarro revolt, a revolt that almost lost Peru for the Crown. A modus vivendi was reached after the rebellion that allowed the colonial order to continue into the mid-eighteenth century. It was at this time that the Bourbon monarchs began to modify the old system, to make adjustments, to experiment, and to reform. The reforms came to be seen as a threat to the old order in Peru: the Creole agrarian elite, merchant and banking families, miners, and kurakas as well. The new intendancy system that replaced the corregimientos was designed to provide greater centralized control. Peninsular officials weakened local prerogatives. The forced sale of goods instituted in 1750 placed new exploitative demands on native commoners. The attempt to collect a higher sales tax at the local level increased pressures further. In response came a wave of revolts that broke out in the 1780s and threatened Spain's colonial empire in the Andes.

Laws regarding the indigenous community in Peru in the nineteenth century were haphazard, partly the result of nine constitutions (1823, 1826, 1828, 1834, 1839, 1856, 1860, 1867, 1879). With independence there was agreement for the immediate abolition of the onerous burden of tribute, but it came back in 1826, only to be ended by Ramón Castilla in 1854, then reintroduced by Mariano Ignacio Prado in the next decade, in 1866. The Republican requirement was disguised by a new label: the native "contribution" (*contribución indigena*). Laws on Indian voting rights, on political authority in native communities, and on the question of the sale of land were also chaotic, often confusing even to the educated elite.[2] The new Republican state in 1828 provided a threat to the local community as great as any of the colonial era, with a new land law that authorized the sale of native community lands to outsiders. New officials probably acted out of goodwill, in the tradition of nineteenth-century Liberals who saw a link between economic growth and widespread private landholding. The Liberals believed that sale of corporate lands, in the southern Andes represented primarily by the Indian community, would help create in the Andean world an independent yeoman farming class. But this concept was inconsistent with the mode of land access based on centuries of Andean tradition. By the 1840s, Santiago Lira was able to point out the weaknesses of the evolving Republican agrarian system in the Colca Valley, with a rapid change in the distribution of land taking place. The land law of 1828 was reconfirmed by an 1876 decree under Manuel Pardo, and reinforced, because it prohibited the Indian community from blocking sales by legal actions. The new Republican state was no better able to provide basic services to the valley than had the hegemonic colonial regime. Schools, bridges, and hospitals were beyond the capabilities of the Peruvian Republic of the mid–nineteenth century. The new republic collected "contributions" and extracted soldiers, but could not meet the demands of Andean reciprocity. The interests of the central state were contrary to the interests of the Andean community; the dysfunctional relationship plagued the body politic throughout the twentieth century.[3]

The basic political and social structures of the Andean world have been remarkably constant over the past half millennium. The concept of duality is one of these constants, and it operates at several levels: male–female; upper–lower halves or saya; upper–lower worlds in the cosmological scale; Indian Peru–European Peru. Duality is the Andean counterpoint. The dichotomy of outsider versus native was created and accentuated by the colonial creation and evolution of the "República de los Indios" and the "República de los Españoles." Duality has provided social stability, even at historical points when conditions were explosive. The term *duality* is multilayered. On the one hand, the dual world that continues in the contemporary Andes persists as the world of the Indian in opposition to that of the non-Indian. Others argue the concept of duality is best delineated as the world of the coast versus the sierra. Some suggest duality is seen in the confrontation of the center versus the periphery, Lima versus the provinces, in an argument similar to the Argentine dynamic of the port versus the pampas. On the other hand, some suggest that duality that characterizes the Andean world is that of saya, so pervasive in the southern highlands. At the local level that interpretation can be seen in the villages of the Colca Valley, still divided into halves, into anansaya and urinsaya. Here the traditional relationships and ceremonies are retained, permitting survival in time of crisis.

The complex varieties of Andean duality have often been overlooked by historians who specialize in the northern and central highlands of Peru, in part because in these areas many elements of the Andean system were swept away in the first generations after conquest. This seems to be the case for Huarochirí and Ayacucho districts.[4] Andean ethnohistorians, trained in heavy use of colonial documentation, have largely ignored the role of the saya, while modern anthropologists have examined its function, indeed quite extensively because of its pervasiveness in the Andes.[5] Any discourse on dualism and its relation to Andean reality is influenced by the compelling ideas of José Carlos Mariátegui, the leading Peruvian intellect of the twentieth century. Mariátegui set the boundaries of debate: "The dualism of Peruvian history and soul is expressed in our time as a conflict between the historical form that evolved on the coast and the indigenous spirit that survives in the sierra, deeply rooted in nature." Yet Mariátegui, a brilliant and incisive thinker, was a member of the Lima intelligentsia and represented the coastal Creole viewpoint; he was strongly influenced by readings in the political economy of nineteenth-century Europe. He dissected Andean reality from an academic-based, textual perspective.[6] By contrast José María Arguedas, raised in the highlands and speaking the language of its peoples, reached a much clearer understanding of the Amerindian. The anthropologist Arguedas—in spite of a solidly researched and now classic work on Indian communities, *Las comunidades de España y del Perú*, and his *indigenista* novels, which have received widespread literary analysis—is often ignored by contemporary interpreters of Peruvian reality.[7] The same is true of novelist Ciro Alegría, whose 1941 *El mundo es ancho y ajeno* (*Broad and Alien is the World*) remains a starting point for anyone wishing to understand the indigenous masses of the Peruvian sierra.[8]

The duality of the Colca Valley peoples is deeply ingrained and continues to exert a profound influence. In contemporary Yanque, duality extends into cemetery space, where the dead are buried as they were for centuries in the church, by saya. In the early nineteenth century church burials were forbidden, for health reasons. The cemetery, or "Panteón" as it is called, lies on the southern side of the village, centered roughly on a line extending from the central plaza. The eastern half of the cemetery is reserved for the anansaya, and the western side for the urinsaya. Today, the burial area for *mistis* (the "Europeanized," people self-identified as "non-Indian" in the Colca Valley) is located roughly in the center, just behind the iron gate in the anansaya sector. The church in Yanque continues a division of spiritual space between the halves, as well as the separate entrances.[9] The positioning of the elite families, the Choquehuanca of the anansaya, and the Checa of the urinsaya is also reinforced by mythohistory.[10] The internal logic of duality continues to play itself out in the Colca Valley. In 1984 the leaders of Madrigal decided that the dual system needed to be maintained because it worked so well as the organizational mechanism for public work on irrigation channels and terracing. In Yanque the clear-cut division on the basis of separate hydraulic systems continues in force. Two separate native communities and political units were recognized as political entities in the mid-1960s by the Ministry of Agriculture: Yanque anansaya and Yanque urinsaya.[11] The sharp division between agricultural systems of Coporaque is likewise maintained. The anthropologist Alfredo Simón Bernal Málaga, born in Coporaque, has stressed the importance of the ritual battles between anansaya and urinsaya residents called the Witite, which continued into the middle of the twentieth century.[12]

The continuation of the dual world in the Andes can also be viewed as the elaboration of the conflict between rural community and the city. The highland community represents order and stability, as well as permanency of place. The modern city represents chaos and disorder, the breakdown of traditional ties of kinship and community. The Danish anthropologist Karsten Paerregaard has studied twentieth-century Colca Valley migration to nearby Arequipa and the national capital of Lima. Migrants face a far different environment from what their ancestors encountered in the early seventeenth century. The scale alone is incomparable. The Lima metropolis of 1613 had a mere 25,000 residents; today it houses several million. Yet those who do emigrate to the cities survive partly by re-creating reciprocal relationships there, and a new urban community with structures paralleling those of the rural countryside. The migrants of Tapay, one of the most "isolated" villages of the Colca Valley on the north side of the river from Cabanaconde and linked to the outside world only by footpath, re-created in Lima the dual structures of saya. Migrants who settled in Lima continue duality identification via annual competition in the soccer match between opposing saya. Other migrants from the valley are attracted to participate in this event, and saya competition of Colca Valley migrants to Lima is several decades old. One elderly informant, for example, told Paerregaard that "the division into moieties is a primitive custom practiced by Tapeños' ancestors and later duplicated by migrants in Lima."[13] Yet the rivalry between saya is variable; for example, if there are insufficient players to form a team, then it is possible for urinsaya players to participate on anansaya teams. Although the modern state and community continue to clash in the urban setting, traditional Andean structures of community contribute to survival.

Another element critical to an understanding of Andean reality is the desire for a better world. Various scholars have explored the role of utopian ideals, especially religious and political, in the historical evolution of the Andean world. The indigenous voices of Felipe Guaman Poma de Ayala and Juan de Santa Cruz Pachacuti Yamqui emphasized Spanish conquest as a cataclysmic shift: the old order was overturned and a new period began. Both authors experienced conquest and alienation and viewed the pre-Spanish world as a better one. And both were products of the new church schools. Christian doctrineros impressed on the minds of the listeners the Last Judgment and coming of the Kingdom of Christ. The notions of utopia and the native Andean concept of a pachacuti coincided with and were reinforced by newly introduced Christian messianism. Franciscans in the Colca Valley and elsewhere were especially fixated on the millenarian nature of their undertaking, and tried to impart that vision to new converts.[14] At the same time the concept of an Inca ruler, an "Inkarrí," associated with cultural innovations and whose return was foretold, is prevalent throughout the Andes. In 1974 a forty-three-year-old informant of Yanque anansaya recounted to Franklin Pease an oral version of the origins in the valley of agriculture with irrigated terraces. He begins with an invocation: "*Inkarripa camachisca pachamama santa tierra.* Because of this we believe until the present time that Inkarrí, it is told that he was like a miraculous god, that when water was needed, Inkarrí would say: 'let there be water at this site.' And the water came. In this instant a little spring of water appeared. When he wanted to construct chacras, that is terraces, they constructed themselves; the stones formed together into walls, they formed themselves into terraces." The informant lamented the present lack of water for Yanque, especially for the anansaya, and longed for the time when water would be abundant again, and when the laborious task of maintaining the terraces and irrigation channels could be completed by order of a miraculous deity.[15]

Some might argue that the sharp division between the world of the *indios* and the world of the *españoles* would ultimately be bridged, as in Mexico, by the evolution of a mixed group. A half millennium of coexistence and an accelerating process of mestizaje should bring that about. But the separation between the two repúblicas was pronounced, and mixture has not been as rapid as in some other parts of the Americas. There are the mistis, but non-Indians are outsiders in the Andean community. The misti exercises political and economic authority. He is the alcalde, appointed by state authorities in the faraway capital. The misti is the merchant, with links to the commercial establishments of Arequipa, and he or she is the teacher, uneasily educating village youth while nostalgically wishing to return to the metropolis as soon as possible. Mistis are engaged in transportation of goods and people in and out of the valley. The misti speaks predominantly Spanish, but is bilingual, even trilingual, speaking Spanish, Quechua, and Aymara. The misti dresses in European clothing, and reads and writes.[16]

The mistis increased in numbers during the course of the nineteenth century, as the political structure of colonialism was breaking down. The "mestizo" in the colonial era was based on a set of criteria based more on birth status than economic class; in the later Bourbon and early national periods, economic status became increasingly important. During the early republic the mistis' position in the valley was based on economic status and association with the church, as well as assuming roles of the local representatives of political authority: the police and appointed administrators. Mistis in the Colca Valley tried to establish ties in the rural districts, uniting priests, merchants, administrators, and landholding interests. The disparate group was bound together by a desire to dominate the local indigenous population, which continued as a dependent group. José María Pérez, a priest of Tapay and Madrigal from 1846 to 1878, provides an example of links established by the mistis. The priest and his brother Manuel Toribio Pérez, from north coastal Piura, entered the Colca Valley with the help of a small inheritance in Arequipa. Manuel married a woman from the north coast and moved to the valley, where the couple ultimately prospered and raised six children. Five of their offspring married villagers, and the priest fathered several children in Tapay.[17] The family exported wool and fruit from the lower valley and gradually secured legal title to their fields. The couple's four sons were born between 1875 and 1883; they spoke Spanish and Quechua and married local girls, thereby gaining access to land. With connections in the district capital of Chivay and in Arequipa, the four brothers became major figures in Tapay, holding various offices, including governor, alcalde mayor, and justice of the peace. As mistis they were bilingual, dressed as Europeans, did not chew coca, rode on horseback, and used cash to buy and sell products. Rather than entering the system of reciprocity, they hired laborers and used oxen or mule teams for plowing their fields. Thus they separated themselves from the common runa, avoiding *ayni* work relationships. But by setting themselves apart from the traditional community, they generated resentment. They resided in Tapay anansaya, more associated with misti residence, while the urinsaya tends to remain traditionally Andean. Further, there is strong competition between the urinsaya, dominated by the Huacallo family, and the anansaya mistis. The predominant urinsaya family may have descended from Marcos Guancallo, kuraka principal identified in the 1604 census. Paerregaard, who by using interviews and parish registers has reconstructed social change in Tapay, concludes that "the Pérez family and hanansaya are characterized by haughtiness and power, whereas the Huacallo family and urinsaya are characterized by stubbornness and revolt."[18]

Race is not a characteristic of the "misti"; culture is. Most likely the misti is a mestizo, but he can be Indian as well. Miscegenation in the valley is modest in spite of half a millennium of contact between the two republics. In 1792 fewer than 10 percent of the valley residents were mestizos, and these were concentrated in a handful of villages. As late as 1940 the percentage of mestizos in Tapay only reached 15.2 percent.[19] The numerical imbalance between Amerindians and outsiders in some sectors of the Americas led to increased miscegenation, but in the Colca Valley mixture was slow. In the central and southern Andes of Peru, the Indian enters the modern era en masse. The population explosion of the twentieth century, in spite of continued high mortality in the valley's villages, especially of infants, is not the result of mixture; rather, it is the consequence of internal regeneration. Mestizaje failed to bridge the two worlds in the valley. The dual world of the present is the world of Indian and non-Indian, and in the Colca Valley the native predominates in numbers, although not in political and economic power.

When asked of their origins in the 1580s, the Collagua and the Cabana related to colonial interrogators that they came from within a mountain. In their search for persistence of pre-Christian beliefs in the same decade, the Spanish discovered that one peak was still believed to be nurturing the people who venerated it, by expelling gold. In the Inca period numerous mitimae households served the great peaks of Condesuyos; 2,000 households were assigned for the cone of Sara Sara, and given 200 female llamas. The peak of Solimana also received a quota of mitimaes. Gómez Hernández received mitimaes and livestock from Arequipa's La Chimba which were designated for service of the mountain crest of Putina.[20] In the 1780s Pascual Guamani, living in the puna above Yura, claimed that the mountains held vast power over him and others in the community.[21] People of the Colca Valley at the end of the twentieth century and beginning of the twenty-first continue revering the forces of the volcanic cones. In Tapay the mountains (*orqos* in Quechua) are designated by sex. Sepregina (5,200 meters) is female, and the snow on her slopes fertilizes the river of her name. That river is the boundary between Tapay's anansaya and urinsaya sections. Tapay villagers envision the peak as "a female urinating in a squatting position."[22] They believe that "at birth every individual is affiliated with a specific orqo. Tapeños conceive of this bond as a godparent-godchild relationship and attribute great importance to it in cases of misfortune." Contemporary villagers believe that sickness is closely related to the forces of the mountains. If one falls ill, the *curandero* is called to contact the orqos to identify the peak associated with the malady. Then the "doctor" prescribes a treatment, often "a visit to the mountain where the deity lives to bring it offerings."[23]

While ascending the summit of Ampato in September 1995, the anthropologist Johan Reinhard and the photographer Stephen Alvarez chanced upon the almost perfectly preserved remains of a young woman, wrapped in a mummy bundle and left with offerings. Textile designs as well as the style of metal and ceramic artifacts suggest the sacrifices date from the late Inca period occupation of the Colca Valley. The remains surfaced partly due to recent ecological change; the nearby Sabancaya Volcano had erupted from its slumber raining gray ash on Ampato's ice-capped summit. Warmer-than-normal temperatures and solar radiation melted away part of the massive glaciated peak of Ampato, exposing treasures that had been encapsulated in ice for half a millennium. The discovery at the summit of Ampato did not cause great surprise, except to outsiders. Numerous gifts were offered at the stone platform at the top of Ampato: gold and silver statues, finely woven colorful textiles, and artifacts made of the revered *Spondylus* shell. Other articles near the mummy included llama bones, corn-filled cloth pouches, and a feather-covered bag containing coca leaves. Mummies of two sacrificed children entombed at a slightly lower

Ampato and Hualca Hualca at sunrise from Yanque (photo by N. D. Cook)

elevation, also buried with numerous objects, were discovered shortly later.[24] During excavations in December 1997, Reinhard and his team uncovered four more human offerings on Ampato, dating from the same period. Other expeditions in 1996 and 1997 centered on the peaks of Sara Sara, north of the Colca canyon, and Pichu Pichu, just southeast of Arequipa. In 1996 at a platform on the summit of Pichu Pichu, two mummified children — a boy and a girl — were discovered. The girl's skull had been molded in conical fashion, in the typical Colla way. On Sara Sara a mummified girl about fifteen years old was found. Buried in the traditional flexed position with knees pressed to her shoulders, she was accompanied by a substantial number of small sacrificial objects.[25]

Textiles, gold and silver articles, stone carvings, shells, coca leaves, llama bones, and chicha beer that would have left no trace, were and continue to be traditional Andean ritual offerings. Sacrifices were made in the fields and irrigation canals to Pachamama, Earth Mother, and in the puna in ceremonies associated with the tending of llamas and alpacas, and they were made to the great snowcapped peaks. The sacrifice of young children was rare and must have occurred only on special occasions. That human sacrifice seems to be associated primarily with the highest mountain summits is emblematic of their significance. Although the sacrifice of young people no longer exists, and binding of the head has been eliminated, the nearby massive Hualca Hualca "still receives offerings from villagers who revere the mountains much as their ancestors did." A Cabanaconde villager in 1995 affirmed during the planting rituals, "We make offerings to Pachamama and the mountain gods, including Ampato, for water and good crops."[26] At the beginning of the twenty-first century, the people of the Colca Valley continue to see themselves as the people of the volcano.

NOTES

Unless otherwise noted, translations of Spanish-language quotations are our own.

ONE *Beneath the Soaring Condor*

1. The first notice of the Colca Valley in the twentieth century stems from a report prepared by U.S. Navy Lt. George Johnson following his 1929 Peruvian assignment: *Peru from the Air*; Robert Shippee, "The Great Wall of Peru and Other Aerial Photographic Studies by the Shippee-Johnson Peruvian Expedition"; Shippee, "Lost Valleys of Peru"; Shippee, "Air Adventures in Peru," and the same author's "A Forgotten Valley of Peru." Johnson was photographer for Shippee; several of the original hundreds of photographs were printed in Julian H. Steward, *Handbook of South American Indians*, 2: plates 4 and 85; in Philip Ainsworth Means, *Fall of the Inca Empire and the Spanish Rule in Peru, 1530–1720*; and in William M. Denevan, *The Cultural Ecology, Archaeology, and History of Terracing and Terrace Abandonment in the Colca Valley of Southern Peru*.

2. There are sharp variations in diurnal temperature, as well as seasonal and annual trends in rainfall. At Chivay (3,633 meters) based on 1973–83 data, the mean daily maximum was 24 degrees Celsius, and the minimum was −2 degrees Celsius. Annual average precipitation was about 385 millimeters. Crop-threatening freezes can occur almost any night of the year. Jonathan Sandor, "Report on Soils in Agricultural Terraces in the Colca Valley," 1:240; and Denevan, *Cultivated Landscapes of Native Amazonia and the Andes*, 188.

3. Cosme Bueno, *Geografía del Perú virreinal*, 86; Tadeo Haenke, *Descripción del Perú*. See also Daniel E. Shea, "The Achoma Archaeology Project," 1:314, 324; and Steve Wernke, "A Reassessment of Collagua and Provincial Inka Ceramic Styles of Arequipa, Peru." There is debate over causes for terrace abandonment; see Denevan, *Cultivated Landscapes of Native Amazonia and the Andes*, 183–84.

4. Juan de Ulloa Mogollón, "Relación de la provincia de los Collaguas," 1:326–33. The terraces predate the Incas; early results indicate terrace construction coinciding with expansion of the Wari civilization (ca. AD 500–1000); see Michael Malpass, "Prehistoric Agricultural Terracing at Chijra, Coporaque," 1:162. Wernke, "A Reassessment

of Collagua and Provincial Inka Ceramic Styles of Arequipa, Peru," points out a growing consensus regarding periodization: First, there is "initial construction and use of segmented, nonirrigated terraces along the upper margins of the valley (ca. 3600–4000 meters above sea level), preliminarily dated to the Middle Horizon Period (ca. AD 600–1000)." Second, from about AD 1000 to 1460, upper terraces were abandoned, and valley residents initiated "construction of platform and valley-side bench terraces" with irrigation systems at lower levels. Third, during roughly the Inca or Late Horizon period (ca. AD 1460–1532), there was intensification; and fourth, with conquest there was "destructuration" and significant abandonment, especially in upper parts of the valley. Sarah O. Brooks indicates the date of initial terrace construction was as early as 2400 BC; see "Prehistoric Agricultural Terraces in the Río Japo Basin, Colca Valley, Peru," 270. See also Santiago Erik Antúñez de Mayolo, *La nutrición en el antiguo Perú*.

5. Bueno, *Geografía del Perú virreinal (siglo XVIII)*, 88. Intensity of volcanic activity varies, with some centuries reasonably quiet and others violent. Bueno in the eighteenth century reported that near Achoma stood "a volcano named Ambato and also Sahuancuna," which, he observed, "throws out smoke and flames that one can clearly see at night" (88). Sandor, "Report on Soils in Agricultural Terraces in the Colca Valley," 241, points out formidable volcanic activity in the Pleistocene and Holocene epochs. Several substantial ash deposits remain in the valley. There may at times be an oversupply of water, rather than drought. For contemporary valley residents' concern about flood and landslides, see the comments of Roberto Benavides, owner of an excavated terrace, in Shea, "The Achoma Archaeology Project," 323–24. Guillet describes an ascent from the valley floor to the village of Lari in 1983 with William M. Denevan. As they neared the top of the embankment, they encountered human remains that they learned had come from a sector of the town cemetery that had recently broken away; see David W. Guillet, *Covering Ground*, 5–6. On the basis of measurements of ice core samples from the Cerro Quelccaya, there were dry periods (about 5 to 20 percent annual reduction in rainfall) in the years AD 540–560, 570–610, 650–730, and 1040–1490. During AD 650 to 850 and AD 1240–55 to 1850–80 — the latter referred to as a "Little Ice Age" — the upper altitude for frost-free crop production was reduced by about 150 meters. See Brooks, "Prehistoric Agricultural Terraces in the Río Japo Basin," 71, 74, 384; Lonnie G. Thompson, Mary E. David, and Ellen Moseley-Thompson, "Glacial Records of Global Climate"; and Denevan, *Cultivated Landscapes of Native Amazonia and the Andes*, 199–200, who points out that "there were two climatic stress periods during the past 1,000 years: first, AD 540–730 (dry) and 650–850 (cold); and second, AD 1040–1490 (dry) and 1240–1880 (cold)."

6. Franklin Pease García Yrigoyen, "Collaguas: Una etnia del siglo XVI," 140, originally considered there to be only one principal ethnic unit in the valley: the Collaguas.

7. Peru, Dirección Nacional de Estadística, *Sexto censo nacional de población levantado el 2 de julio de 1961*.

8. John M. Treacy, *Las chacras de Coporaque* 66–87; Denevan, *Cultivated Landscapes of Native Amazonia and the Andes*, 202–4.

9. Allison C. Paulsen, "Environment and Empire," 121–32, argues that dry periods, especially between 600–1000 and 1400–1532, are associated with the rise of the Wari and Inca empires. Ecological deterioration and population pressure led to massive cultural change. See also John W. Rick, "The Character and Context of Highland Preceramic Society."

10. Edward P. Lanning, *Peru before the Incas*; Luis G. Lumbreras, *The Peoples and Cultures of Ancient Peru*; Michael E. Moseley, *The Incas and Their Ancestors*.

11. Máximo Neira Avendaño, "Los Collaguas," 86–97; the same author's "Prehistoria de la provincia de Caylloma." The archaeologist Steve Wernke, working recently with Willy Yépez and Erika Simborth, surveyed 100 square kilometers in the district, recording 161 sites; "A Reassessment of Collagua and Provincial Inka Ceramic Styles of Arequipa, Peru." Using mapping techniques and collection of surface artifacts, they develop an approximate cultural sequence. They concentrate on the Late Horizon, or Inca period, tracing how the Collagua fit within the context of imperial penetration and control of the valley. They conclude that "the presence of cut stone masonry and large, multi-door *kallanka* [great hall for public ceremonies] structures diagnostic of Inka architecture suggest considerable investment in a decentralized, but coordinated, Inka presence in this part of the valley." In a detailed study of ceramics and labor specialization, Wernke examined almost 4,000 ceramic fragments, confirming findings of Sarah Brooks that there is a modestly distinct Collagua style that can be differentiated from other nearby "regional" styles. He notes four overlapping phases. The sequence is based on form and decoration; the Collagua Inka tend to be "black on red bichromes, and polychromes." Wernke believes that most of these were produced locally in the valley, rather than being imports. Shallow plates with "thin concentric lines inside the rim" and having geometric or motifs, such as birds, camelids, fish, or cultigens, are common. His contention for local production lies in his discovery of potter's wheels at Ullo Ullo.

12. Personal observations, March 1977, based on surface survey of Ullo Ullo. González Holguín defines the Quechua word *ullo* as the male genital organ; I believe the Aymara is the correct one. Wernke, "A Reassessment of Collagua and Provincial Inka Ceramic Styles of Arequipa, Peru," finds in one area of Ullo Ullo, "a U-shaped patio group around a large central structure with a worked stone facade typical of high-status Collagua architecture. The close association between this patio group and the large (29 × 9 meter) Inka kallanka that dominates the central plaza directly to the east also suggests a high-status residential area." Craig Morris, "State Settlements in Tawantinsuyu," 393, points to many settlements elsewhere that can be associated with Inca expansion.

13. Ulloa Mogollón, "Relación de la provincia de los Collaguas," 1:327. The question of "recording" by narrative or picture is imaginatively handled by R. Tom Zuidema, "Guaman Poma between the Arts of Europe and the Andes." See also Gary Urton, *The Social Life of Numbers*; and Catherine J. Julien, *Reading Inca History*.

14. Ulloa Mogollón, "Relación de la provincia de los Collaguas." We consulted the original report in the personal papers of Marcos Jiménez de la Espada in the Royal Acad-

emy of History in 1985. We hoped that the testimony would follow the form of the traditional *interrogatorio*, with separate answers from each witness or deponent. If so, there would be a richness of detail missing in the composite. Unfortunately, even in the original report the interrogatorio form was not followed.

15. Ulloa Mogollón, "Relación de la provincia de los Collaguas," 1:326–27. Other kurakas from the Yanque lower sector (*urinsaya*) at the inquest were Francisco Chacha and Francisco Ingapacta; the upper sector (*anansaya*) was represented by Juan Halanoca and Miguel Nina Taipe. From the Indian grant of Lari Collagua anansaya came Juan Caquia, Felipe Alpaca, and Juan Arqui. Cristóbal Cusi, Marcos Guancallo, and Diego Vaanqui arrived from Lari urinsaya. The kurakas from the two grants of Cabana also contributed; for the anansaya came Luis Ala, Miguel Canauache, and Diego Ala, and for the urinsaya Francisco Anti Ala, Juan Ala, and Pedro Ancas Cabana testified.

16. Ulloa Mogollón, "Relación de la provincia de los Collaguas," 1:327 (for *pucara* quote). Luis Gerónimo de Oré, *Symbolo catholico indiano*, 39r.

17. For a fascinating account of the volcano in Andean cosmology, see Thérèse Bouysse-Cassagne and Pierre Cassagne, "Volcan indien, volcan chrétien." See also J. Earls and I. Silverblatt, "La realidad física y social en la cosmología andina"; and Sabine MacCormack, "Pachacuti."

18. Cestmir Loukotka, *Classification of South American Indian Languages*, 268, 272; Cipriano Muñoz y Manzano, *Bibliografía española de lenguas indígenas de América*, 339, 347; John Rowe, "Inca Culture at the Time of the Spanish Conquest," 185–92; Ulloa Mogollón, "Relación de la provincia de los Collaguas," 1:327 (quote).

19. Catherine J. Julien, *Condesuyo*, places the Collaguas province within the Inca quarter of Condesuyo, and makes strong links between the Cabanaconde and Condesuyos.

20. Johan Reinhard and Stephen Alvarez, "Peru's Ice Maidens," 74.

21. Diego González Holguín, *Vocabulario de la lengua general de todo el Perú llamada Quechua*, defines *apachitas* as "traveler's shrines of piled stones."

22. Ulloa Mogollón, "Relación de la provincia de los Collaguas," 1:329 (quote); Gary Urton, *At the Crossroads of the Earth and the Sky*; Thomas A. Abercrombie, *Pathways of Memory and Power*, 184.

23. Ulloa Mogollón, "Relación de la provincia de los Collaguas," 1:327 (quote); Neira Avendaño, "Excavaciones arqueológicas en las ruinas de Chishra (Chijra), Coporaque," 1:167.

24. Juan de Matienzo, *Gobierno del Perú (1567)*, 81, made the same point regarding Colla head binding. Martín de Murúa, *Historia de los incas, reyes del Perú*, 237 (quote); González Holguín, *Vocabulario de la lengua general de todo el Perú llamada Quechua*; and Bernabé Cobo, *Inca Religion and Customs*, 200–201 (quote).

25. Shea, "Achoma Archaeology Project," 333, describes archaeological evidence of skull deformation in a site near the community.

26. Susan A. Niles, *The Shape of Inca History*; Gary Urton, *The History of a Myth*; Geoffrey W. Conrad and Arthur A. Demarest, *Religion and Empire*.

27. Pedro de Cieza de León, *Crónica del Perú: Primera Parte* [1553], 223–24.

28. Juan de Betanzos, *Suma y narración de los incas*, xi–xvi, then 94 (quote); Rafael Varón Gabai, *Francisco Pizarro and His Brothers*, 193–95.

29. José Toribio Polo, "Luis Gerónimo de Oré," 74–91; Manuel Mendiburu, *Diccionario histórico biográfico del Perú*, 8:247–48; Noble David Cook, "Beyond the *Martyrs of Florida*"; Cook's introduction to Gerónimo de Oré, *Relación de la vida y milagros de San Francisco Solano*.

30. Gerónimo de Oré, *Symbolo catholico indiano*, 41.

31. El Inca Garcilaso de la Vega, *Royal Commentaries of the Incas, and General History of Peru* [1609], 153. Margarita Zamora analyzes veracity in *Language, Authority, and Indigenous History in the "Comentarios reales de los Incas."* Felipe Guaman Poma de Ayala, *El primer nueva corónica y buen gobierno* [ca. 1613], 1:153, reported that Mayta conquered "Condesuyo, Cul(l)ava Conde, Coropuna hasta Arequipa" (Condesuyo, Cabana Conde, Coropuna up to Arequipa).

32. Bernabé Cobo, *History of the Inca Empire* [1653], 119–20.

33. Pease, "Collaguas," 131–67. Guillermo Cock, "Los kurakas de los Collaguas," 100, argues that from the time of Mayta Capac, the Collaguas were confederated vassals of Tawantinsuyu. For Huayna Capac's death, see Noble David Cook, *Born to Die*, 72–83.

34. Pedro de Cieza de León, *El señorío de los incas*, 100. Cobo, *History of the Inca Empire*, 119.

35. Gerónimo de Oré, *Symbolo catholico indiano*, 36–41.

36. Roberto Levillier, *Gobernantes del Perú*, 9:272–78. See María Rostworowski de Diez Canseco, *Historia del Tahuantinsuyu*; Pease, *Del Tawantinsuyu a la historia del Perú*; and John Murra, *Formaciones económicas y políticas del mundo andino*.

37. Paul Kirchoff, "The Social and Political Organization of the Andean Peoples," 5:303; Zuidema, *The Ceque System of Cuzco*, and his *Inca Civilization in Cuzco*; Nathan Wachtel, *Sociedad e ideología*, 36–49; Ulloa Mogollón, "Relación de la provincia de los Collaguas," 1:330.

38. Domingo de Santo Tomás, *Lexicón o vocabulario de la lengua general del Peru* [1560].

39. Betanzos, *Suma y narración de los incas*, 12; Cristóbal de Molina, *Relación de las fábulas y ritos de los Incas*, 6–7. The idea that ancestors might have been animals may have been introduced by Garcilaso de la Vega.

40. Ulloa Mogollón, "Relación de la provincia de los Collaguas," 1:330 (quote).

41. The ayllu has fragmented over time; by the end of the eighteenth century the function of the ayllu had been replaced by European kinship ties, the broader saya structure, and perhaps confraternities. For Lari see Guillet, *Covering Ground*, 197–99.

42. Guaman Poma de Ayala, *Nueva corónica y buen gobierno*; Irene Silverblatt, *Moon, Sun, and Witches*, 4–5; Robert G. Keith, *Conquest and Agrarian Change: The Emergence of the Hacienda System on the Peruvian Coast*, 42–49.

43. John Murra, "Andean Societies before 1532," in *The Cambridge History of Latin America*, 1:63–66. For the north, see Frank Solomon, *Native Lords of Quito in the Age of the Inca*.

44. For the central Peruvian coast, see Rostworowski de Diez Canseco, *Recursos naturales renovables y pesca*. Carlos Sempat Assadourian, *El sistema de la economía colonial*, provides theoretical insight. For exchange mechanisms in the contemporary Colca Valley, see Juvenal Casaverde R., "El trueque en la economía pastoril."

45. Alfred Metraux, *The History of the Incas*, 65–66; Kirchoff, "The Social and Political Organization of the Andean Peoples," 5:302; Santo Tomás, *Lexicón o vocabulario de la lengua general del Peru.*

46. Santo Tomás, *Lexicón o vocabulario de la lengua general del Peru.*

47. Antonio Ricardo, *Vocabulario y phrasis en la lengua general de los indios del Perú, llamada Quichua* [1586].

48. Ludovico Bertonio, *Vocabulario de la lengua Aymara* [1612].

49. Pedro Sarmiento de Gamboa, *Segunda parte de la historia general, llamada Indica* [1572], 50. Sarmiento de Gamboa, who came to Peru in the 1550s during the administration of Viceroy Conde de Nieva, provides one of the most complete accounts of Inca politics. See Raúl Porras Barrenechea, *Los cronistas del Perú (1528–1650) y otros ensayos*, 362–75. Pease considers him, along with Cristóbal de Molina, one of the four most important sources; see Pease G. Y., *Las crónicas y los Andes*, 35–39, 103–5.

50. Garcilaso de la Vega, *Royal Commentaries of the Incas, and General History of Peru*, 1:84, 263; Molina, *Fábulas y ritos de los incas*, 47–48. Molina's contribution is analyzed in Porras Barrenechea, *Los cronistas del Perú (1528–1650) y otros ensayos*, 349–61; and in Pease, *Las crónicas y los Andes*, 36.

51. Adolph F. A. Bandelier, *The Islands of Lake Titicaca and Koati*, 339; Alonso Ramos Gavilán, *Historia del santuario de nuestra señora de Copacabana* [1621], 67.

52. Claude Levi-Strauss, *The Elementary Structures of Kinship*, 69; Robin Fox, *Kinship and Marriage*, 182; George Peter Murdock, *Social Structure*, 124–25; Salvador Palomino Flores, "Duality in the Socio-cultural Organization of Several Andean Populations."

53. Personal observations are based on research in the Yanque parish registers.

54. Ulloa Mogollón, "Relación de la provincia de los Collaguas," 1:330; Antonine Tibesar, *Franciscan Beginnings in Colonial Peru.*

55. Fernando de Armas Medina, *Cristianización del Perú (1532–1600)*; MacCormack, *Religion in the Andes*; Nicholas Griffiths, *The Cross and the Serpent.*

56. Ulloa Mogollón, "Relación de la provincia de los Collaguas," 1:330; Ramos Gavilán, *Historia del santuario de nuestra señora de Copacabana*, 85; Silverblatt, *Moon, Sun, and Witches*, 21–31. See also Verónica Salles-Reese, *From Viracocha to the Virgin of Copacabana.*

57. Ulloa Mogollón, "Relación de la provincia de los Collaguas," 1:330.

58. Ibid. Several apachitas still exist; an important one was located in the 1980s (personal observation) not far from the summit of the steep road leading up to Yanque as one crosses the river from the Ullo Ullo fields on the canyon's north slope.

59. For population see Noble David Cook, *The People of the Colca Valley*, 82–86; Treacy, *Las chacras de Coporaque*, 165–74, provides valuable insight into the relation of population size and carrying capacity.

60. Pease, "Collaguas: Una etnia del siglo XVI," 148–56.

1. Betanzos, *Suma y narración de los incas*, 253. The chapter epigraph is from Archivum Sancti Isidori Hibernorum, Rome, Leg. 2/10, "Memorial de las doctrinas de la provincia de los Collaguas," thanks to Antonine Tibesar.

2. MacCormack, *Religion in the Andes*, 308–10, 363–64.

3. Juan de Santa Cruz Pachacuti Yamqui, *Historia de los Incas*, 215–16.

4. Murúa, *Historia de los incas, reyes del Perú*, 135.

5. Cook, *Born to Die*, 81, 92.

6. Cook, *The People of the Colca Valley*, 50–51.

7. Betanzos, *Suma y narración de los incas*, 137.

8. MacCormack, *Religion in the Andes*, 284; see the same author's "Pachacuti."

9. John Hemming, *The Conquest of the Incas*. For a vividly written sixteenth-century version, see Pedro de Cieza de León, *The Discovery and Conquest of Peru*.

10. José de la Puente Brunke, *Encomienda y encomenderos en el Perú*, 19–22; Noble David Cook, *Demographic Collapse: Indian Peru, 1520–1620*, and the same author's "Population Data for Indian Peru"; Alejandro Málaga Medina, "Consideraciones económicas sobre la visita de la provincia de Arequipa," 302; Julien, *Condesuyo*, xii.

11. Patricia Seed, *Ceremonies of Possession in Europe's Conquest of the New World, 1492–1640*, argued the *requerimiento* was the principal act to signify possession that the Spanish used, but in terms of people and their permanent control, the act here described is more appropriate.

12. AGI, Justicia 397.

13. Charles Gibson, *Tlaxcala in the Sixteenth Century*; Adolfo Luis González Rodríguez, *La encomienda en Tucumán*.

14. Hemming, *The Conquest of the Incas*, 184.

15. Waldemar Espinosa Soriano, "Los señores étnicos de Chachapoyas y la alianza hispano-chacha," and the same author's "Los Huancas, aliados de la conquista"; Hemming, *The Conquest of the Incas*, 169–234.

16. AGI, Justicia 397.

17. Cieza de León, *Discovery and Conquest of Peru*, gives a fine description based on interviews with participants; Hemming, *The Conquest of the Incas*, presents a modern version.

18. Alexandra Parma Cook and Noble David Cook, *Good Faith and Truthful Ignorance*, 11–13. The chronicler Gonzalo Fernández de Oviedo wrote that the group from Chile "departed the said city of Arequipa [still not founded] on 12 March 1537" on their way to Cuzco; from Alejandro Málaga Medina, *Historia general de Arequipa*, 215–18, cited by Edgardo Rivera Martínez, *Imagen y leyenda de Arequipa*, 52.

19. AGI, Justicia 397.

20. Santiago Martínez, *Fundadores de Arequipa*, 357–59.

21. Steve J. Stern, *Peru's Indian Peoples and the Challenge of Spanish Colonialism*, outlines the way Andeans quickly learned how to use the Spanish legal system. Lockhart, *Spanish*

Peru, 1532–1560, 18, notes that the Basque Lope de Idiáquez went to Peru after holding a position in Santa Marta, in northern Colombia; BP, no. 77.

22. Juan Pérez de Tudela y Bueso, *Documentos relativos a don Pedro de la Gasca y a Gonzalo Pizarro,* 1:148–49 (Bautistiano quote from AGI, Patronato 120, no. 2, ramo 9).

23. Martínez, *Fundadores de Arequipa,* 240–42; Puente Brunke, *Encomienda y encomenderos en el Perú,* 419; Rafael Loredo, *Los Repartos,* 194–204; Cieza de León, *Discovery and Conquest of Peru,* 413–17.

24. Keith A. Davies, *Landowners in Colonial Peru,* 7–12.

25. Davies, *Landowners in Colonial Peru,* 13–18; Víctor Sánchez-Moreno Bayarri, *Arequipa colonial y las fuentes de su historia.*

26. Loredo, *Los Repartos,* 194, 201–2; Málaga Medina, "Consideraciones económicas sobre la visita de la provincia de Arequipa," 301–2.

27. Varón Gabai, *Francisco Pizarro and his Brothers,* 266; Loredo, *Los repartos,* 194, 200.

28. AGI, Justicia 397; Hemming, *The Conquest of the Incas.*

29. AGI, Justicia 397.

30. Ibid. (quote); Lockhart, *Spanish Peru, 1532–1560,* 18; in later testimony Juan de Arbes said that the Indians given to Miguel de Vergara that "were of Lope de Idiáquez" were really his because they first belonged to his father, Cristóbal Pérez, AGI, Justicia 399.

31. Cieza de León, *Discovery and Conquest of Peru,* and Cook and Cook, *Good Faith and Truthful Ignorance,* cover this complex period. See also Pérez de Tudela y Bueso, *Crónicas del Perú;* and Juan Cristóbal Calvete de Estrella, *La rebelión de Pizarro en el Perú y vida de don Pedro Gasca,* 4:227–409, 5:1–147.

32. Teodoro Hampe-Martínez, *Don Pedro de la Gasca 1493–1567.*

33. AGI, Justicia 397, Patronato 109, Patronato 120, no. 2, ramo 9; Cook and Cook, *Good Faith and Truthful Ignorance,* 25–27; Pérez de Tudela y Bueso, *Documentos relativos a don Pedro de la Gasca y a Gonzalo Pizarro,* 1:260–62, 2:66–67.

34. AGI, Patronato 109; Agustín de Zárate, *Historia del descubrimiento y conquista del Perú,* 307–12; Cook and Cook, *Good Faith and Truthful Ignorance,* 28–29; Hemming, *The Conquest of the Incas,* 271–72.

35. Varón Gabai, *Francisco Pizarro and his Brothers,* 266.

36. Cieza de León, *The Discovery and Conquest of Peru,* 341.

37. Gerónimo de Oré, *Symbolo catholico indiano,* 41; Málaga Medina, "Consideraciones económicas sobre la visita de la provincia de Arequipa," 301.

38. BNL, C 341.

39. Tibesar, *Franciscan Beginnings in Colonial Peru,* 10–14; Diego de Mendoza, *Chronica de la Provincia de San Antonio de los Charcas* [Madrid, 1664], 51.

40. Tibesar, *Franciscan Beginnings in Colonial Peru,* 43. ASFL, reg. 15, parte 5, "Parecer de los doctrineros de los Collaguas."

41. Diego de Córdoba y Salinas, *Chronica franciscana de las provincias del Perú* [1651], 330.

42. BNL, B 124, f. 200r; Juan de Chaves died about 1618.

43. Archivum Sancti Isidori Hibernorum, Rome, Leg. 2/10, "Memorial de las doctrinas de la provincia de los Collaguas"; ASFL, reg. 15, parte 5, "Parecer acerca de los doctrineros de los Collaguas."

1. Lockhart, *Men of Cajamarca*, 175–89, provides a balanced evaluation of Gonzalo Pizarro's career; Zárate, *Historia del Descubrimiento y conquista del Perú*, 374–75, describes his execution. Martínez, *Fundadores de Arequipa*, 191–93; and Mendiburu, *Diccionario histórico biográfico del Perú*, 5:313–14, both report Fuentes was killed at Huarina. Someone else must have been given temporary control of the encomienda in the brief interim.

   The chapter epigraph is from the Archivo Histórico Nacional, Madrid, Diversos de Indias 152, cited by Puente Brunke, *Encomienda y encomenderos*, 80.

2. AGI, Lima 144.

3. Of an original 1,800 to 2,000 "Indians" in the Machaguay señorío in 1540, there were only about 900 in 1548, with 400 under Juan de la Torre, and 500 with Hernando de Silva.

4. BP, 409, f. 105r; AGI, Justicia 397, f. 142r–43r.

5. Cook, *Tasa de la visita general de Francisco de Toledo* [1571–75], 234–35. The viceroy the Marqués de Cañete gave the encomienda to Juan de Hinojosa; when inspected in 1573 it was under the control of his son, by the same name, in "second life" (i.e., the second generation allowed by the grant).

6. AGI, Lima 144; Luis J. Garraín Villa, *Llerena en el siglo XVI*, 50.

7. AGI, Patronato 109; Cook and Cook, *Good Faith and Truthful Ignorance*, 37–41.

8. AGI, Lima 144.

9. Ibid.; Martínez, *Fundadores de Arequipa*, 1–11. The girl's family provided an 8,000-peso dowry—a relatively small amount—suggesting the match was much desired by De la Torre; their marriage was celebrated 16 August 1577.

10. AGI, Lima 144.

11. Martínez, *Fundadores de Arequipa*, 11–12.

12. Cook and Cook, *Good Faith and Truthful Ignorance*, 12–18.

13. Ibid., 18–28.

14. Lockhart, *Men of Cajamarca*, 300–305; Cook and Cook, *Good Faith and Truthful Ignorance*, 36–37.

15. One of Noguerol's Peruvian majordomos was Alonso de Galleguillos. In the encomendero's testament, opened (1 October 1581) in Medina del Campo, Spain, he set up a mechanism designed in part to collect revenues owed him, as well as to provide some restitution to his charges, tributaries in the Colca Valley who might have suffered under his authority. BNL, B 1173; Guillermo Lohmann Villena, "La restitución por conquistadores y encomenderos"; Cook and Cook, *Good Faith and Truthful Ignorance*, 138–40.

16. AGI, Justicia 448. Noguerol's legal problems were compounded by charges of bigamy; see Cook and Cook, *Good Faith and Truthful Ignorance*.

17. Cook and Cook, *Good Faith and Truthful Ignorance*, 127–29.

18. AGI, Justicia 399.

19. Ibid.

20. All quotes in this section are from ibid., 471; BP no. 1960; LCA, 1:73v.

21. AGI, Justicia 399, 471.

22. AGI, Justicia 399; Escribanía de Cámara 499A.

23. Cook, *Tasa de la visita general de Francisco de Toledo*, 107, 122, 137, 152, 155, 162, 169. See Rostworowski de Diez Canseco, "Repartimiento de doña Beatriz Coya, en el valle de Yucay"; and her *Doña Francisca Pizarro*.

24. AGI, Justicia 399.

25. ANP, Derecho Indígena y Encomiendas, leg. 1, cuad. 10; Víctor Barriga, *Documentos para la historia de Arequipa*, 3:136–39, 173–75, 200–13, 219–32; AGI, Martínez, *Fundadores de Arequipa*, 307.

26. Davies, *Landowners in Colonial Peru*, 49; Barriga, *Documentos para la historia de Arequipa*, 3:136–39, 173–75, 200–13, 219–32.

27. AGI, Patronato 114 ("who in his language" quote); Lima 471 ("for love" quote).

28. AGI, Patronato 114; Escribanía de Cámara 499A.

29. AGI, Patronato 114; Escribanía de Cámara 499A.

30. AGI, Justicia 471; Martínez, *Fundadores de Arequipa*, 217–20, 224–45, 411.

31. AGI, Justicia 471.

32. Ibid.; Martínez, *Fundadores de Arequipa*, 222.

33. AGI, Justicia 471; RAH, Madrid, A/47, 4804.

34. Pérez de Tudela y Bueso, *Documentos relativos a don Pedro de la Gasca y a Gonzalo Pizarro*, 1:148–449.

35. AGI, Patronato 2, ramo 9; Lima 144; Justicia 471; Pérez de Tudela y Bueso, *Documentos relativos a don Pedro de la Gasca y a Gonzalo Pizarro*, 2:148–49; Martínez, *Fundadores de Arequipa*, 255; Davies, *Landowners in Colonial Peru*, 68.

36. AGI, Patronato 2, ramo 9; Justicia 471; Martínez, *Fundadores de Arequipa*, 255.

37. Cook, *Demographic Collapse*, 247–55. See Sempat Assadourian, "La despoblación indígena en el Perú y Nueva España durante el siglo XVI y la formación de la economía colonial"; and the same author's "La crisis demográfica del siglo XVI y la transición del Tawantinsuyu al sistema mercantil colonial."

38. AGI, Justicia 432 (quote); Loredo, *Los repartos*, 194–204.

39. Zárate, *Historia del descubrimiento y conquista del Perú*, 105–6.

40. BP, 1960, f. 13.

41. Noble David Cook, *The People of the Colca Valley*; the same author's *Born to Die*, 112–13.

42. RAH, no. 9-4664; this incomplete copy of the tribute assessment was published by Rostworowski de Diez Canseco, "La tasa ordenada por el Licenciado Pedro de la Gasca (1549)."

43. Rostworowski de Diez Canseco, "La tasa ordenada por el Licenciado Pedro de la Gasca (1549)."

44. Ibid.

45. Puente Brunke, *Encomienda y encomenderos en el Perú*, 242.

46. Hemming, *The Conquest of the Incas*, 385.

47. Ibid., 386; Karen Spalding, *Huarochirí*, 149. The cabildo of Arequipa accepted Ribera's

account 28 March 1555, LCA, f. 274–78. See Francisco de Zabálburu and José Sancho Rayon, *Nueva colección de documentos inéditos para la historia de España y sus Indias*, esp. vol. 6.

48. Rowe, "The Incas under Spanish Colonial Institutions," 156; Spalding, *Huarochirí*, 148–49; Renzo Honores, "El *ius commune* en los Andes."

49. AGI, Indiferente General 1624; Spalding, *Huarochirí*, 149–50; Matienzo, *Gobierno del Perú (1567)*, 98.

50. AGI, Indiferente General 1624; Spalding, *Huarochirí*, 149–50; Matienzo, *Gobierno del Perú (1567)*, 98.

51. Spalding, *Huarochirí*, 148–56, examines thoroughly the question of perpetuity; see Ismael Sánchez Bello, "El gobierno del Perú, 1550–1564."

52. Hemming, *The Conquest of the Incas*, 399.

53. The Taki Onqoy movement plays a central role in the historiographical debate on the 1560s as a watershed in early colonial Andean region. Spalding, *Huarochirí*, 246–48; and Stern, *Peru's Indian Peoples and the Challenge of Spanish Colonialism*, 51–76, emphasize the impact on the mind of the colonial bureaucracy. See Luis Millones, "Nuevos aspectos del Taki Onqoy."

54. Millones, *El retorno de los huacas*, 178, 191; MacCormack, *Religion in the Andes*, 181–204, provides important analysis of the movement, and of the purification ritual of Citua, which also relates to sickness.

55. Griffiths, *The Cross and the Serpent*, 8–13; MacCormack, *Religion in the Andes*, 181–204.

FOUR *Constructing an "Andean Utopia"*

1. Lohmann Villena, *El corregidor de indios en el Perú bajo los Austrias*; Bravo Guerreira, "Polo de Ondegardo y Guaman Poma."

2. Henry E. Huntington Library and Art Gallery, *From Panama to Peru*, 540–41.

3. Vargas Ugarte, *Historia general del Perú*, 2:129.

4. BNL, B 478; Málaga Medina, "Los Collaguas en la historia de Arequipa en el siglo XVI," 101, 118.

5. Levillier, *Gobernantes del Perú*, 3:117–18; Lohmann Villena, *El corregidor de indios*; Spalding, *Huarochirí*, 222.

6. BNL, B 478; Málaga Medina, "Los Collaguas en la historia de Arequipa en el siglo XVI," 116–18.

7. Vargas Ugarte, *Historia general del Perú*, 2:129–75.

8. Bartolomé de las Casas, *Obras escogidas*, 1:16–24. See also Lewis Hanke, *The Spanish Struggle for Justice in the Conquest of America*, 54–58.

9. Levillier, *Don Francisco de Toledo: Supremo organizador del Perú*, 78.

10. Ibid., 98–100.

11. Ibid., 129.

12. Levillier, *Don Francisco de Toledo: Supremo organizador del Perú*, 2:3–4.

13. A version of Toledo's ordinances for Indian towns that was issued in Arequipa is

published in Lohmann Villena, *Francisco de Toledo*, 2:217–66. That edition used the document in BNL, B 511; we use BNL, A 589.

14. BNL, A 589.

15. Ibid. In the Republican era, the principal local official came to be called the *varayoc*.

16. Ibid.

17. Ibid.

18. Ibid.

19. Ibid. See for the Indian notaries, Kathyrn Burns, "Notaries, Truth, and Consequences"; and Susan Kellogg and Matthew Restall, *Dead Giveaways*.

20. BNL, A 589; in this case one *topo* (see chapter 6 for details on this unit of quantity) of land.

21. ANP, Residencias 4, cuad. 8, f. 484.

22. BNL, A 589. Examination of potential doctrineros for language competency was institutionalized. On 21 June 1594 Viceroy García Hurtado de Mendoza recognized the approval of fifteen Franciscans who had passed the examination administered by the Augustinian friar Juan Martínez, a professor of Quechua at the Universidad de los Reyes in Lima; ASFL, reg. 9, 601r–602v.

23. ASFL, reg. 14. As measured by the ability to sign legal papers, at least some native residents learned to read and write. In a document of 8 December 1585, Colca Valley kurakas Juan Caquia, Juan Suyo, Felipe Alpaca, Luis Ala, and Agustín Casa signed; ASFL, reg. 15, 462v.

24. Hemming, *The Conquest of the Incas*, 441–56; Peter Bakewell, *Miners of the Red Mountain*, 61–80.

25. Archivum Sancti Isidori Hibernorum, Rome, Leg. 2/10, "Memorial de las doctrinas de la provincia de los Collaguas."

26. Tibesar, *Franciscan Beginnings in Colonial Peru*, 39–40; from Rich Collection 82, f. 71b, New York Public Library.

27. AGI, Lima 28A.

28. Vargas Ugarte, *Concilios Limenses*, 1:249–50.

29. Matienzo, *Gobierno del Perú (1567)*, 48–52.

30. The process is described in AGI, Lima 28A, 29; and BNL, B 511C. In Huarochirí the first official, Lorenzo de Figueroa, was unable to complete the resettlement process. Only after the corregidor Diego Dávila Brizeño applied ten years of constant pressure was it completed there; see Spalding, *Huarochirí*, 81.

31. Vargas Ugarte, *Concilios Limenses*, 1:249; AGI, Lima 28A.

32. AGI, Lima 29.

33. On 22 and 25 January 1574 Rodrigo de Cantos Andrada, inspector of Lima and Huamanga, condemned and fined "certain caciques and indios principales of the repartimiento of Huarochirí for returning to their old villages." The fine was applied to the costs of the visita; from AGI, Contaduría 1785.

34. Málaga Medina, "Los Collaguas en la historia de Arequipa en el siglo XVI," 101. Málaga reconstructed the names of the ayllus from a badly damaged document in the ANP. Information on Yanque was not available. Personal communication, June 1991.

35. Pease, "Collaguas: Una etnia del siglo XVI," 153–56.

36. Field research conducted in the Colca Valley, 1977.

37. Carlos A. Romero, "Libro de la visita general del Virrey Francisco de Toledo," 117–20.

38. Levillier, *Francisco de Toledo*, 1:129–30.

39. Romero, "Libro de la visita general del Virrey Francisco de Toledo," 121–24; Lohmann Villena, *Francisco de Toledo*, 1:6.

40. Romero, "Libro de la visita general del Virrey Francisco de Toledo," 129–35.

41. Cook, *Tasa de la visita general de Francisco de Toledo*, 217–27.

FIVE *Social and Political Structure*

1. María A. Benavides, "Dualidad social e ideológica en la provincia de Collaguas, 1570–1731."

2. Thomas C. Patterson, *The Inca Empire*, 42–68, stresses the ayllu, while Zuidema, *The Ceque System of Cuzco*, views the moiety as the key element.

3. Garcilaso de la Vega, *Royal Commentaries of the Incas, and General History of Peru*, 44.

4. Cobo, *History of the Inca Empire*, 195–99.

5. Ulloa Mogollón, "Relación de la provincia de los Collaguas," 1:329; Blas Valera, as quoted by Garcilaso de la Vega, *Royal Commentaries of the Incas, and General History of Peru*, 263.

6. Personal observations based on field research; Benavides, "Dualidad social e ideológica en la provincia de Collaguas, 1570-1731," 137, 145, 150–51; David Guillet, "Terracing and Irrigation in the Peruvian Highlands." Treacy, *Las chacras de Coporaque*, 215, notes a clear delineation between agricultural fields of the two halves in modern Coporaque.

7. Noble David Cook, "Eighteenth-Century Population Change in Andean Peru," 248–50.

8. APY, Visitas, Coporaque Urinsaya 1604.

9. Cook, *The People of the Colca Valley*, 75–89.

10. Vargas Ugarte, *Concilios Limenses*, First Church Council, no. 17.

11. Ibid.

12. Vargas Ugarte, *Concilios Limenses*, Second Church Council, no. 28; no. 15 required the doctrineros to keep careful record of the parishioners.

13. Ibid., 1:245, no. 37.

14. BNL, A 589, B 511.

15. According to Garcilaso de la Vega, *Royal Commentaries of the Incas, and General History of Peru*, 206, "It was not lawful for those of different provinces to intermarry, or even those of different towns. All were to marry within their own towns and their own families like the tribes of Israel, so as not to confuse and mix lineages and tribes."

16. Vargas Ugarte, *Concilios Limenses*, Second Church Council, 1:248, no. 62.

17. Cook, *The People of the Colca Valley*, 82.

18. W. E. Carter, "Trial Marriage in the Andes?"

19. BNL, A 589, B 511.

20. Ibid.; Silverblatt, *Moon, Sun, and Witches*, stresses the inferior position of the woman under the colonial regime.

21. BNL, A 589, B 511.

22. Ibid.; see also Espinosa Soriano, "El alcalde mayor indígena en el virreinato del Perú."

23. APY, Visitas 1604. Silverblatt, *Moon, Sun, and Witches*, points out resistance to domination; while Luis Martín, *Daughters of the Conquistadores*, stresses the flexible roles Spanish women exercised in spite of culturally condoned subservience to males. The concept of *yanantin* described by Tristan Platt is summarized by Enrique Mayer: "Equal things but in mirror image to each other are in a *yanantin* relationship; for example, left and right hands are the same but in mirror image to each other. Husband and wife are also conceptualized in a *yanantin* relationship." Enrique Mayer, "Beyond the Nuclear Family," 77.

24. BNL, A 589, B 511.

25. Ibid.

26. Ibid.

27. Ibid.

28. Ibid.

29. Ibid.

30. APY, Visitas, Lari 1604–1605.

31. Robert D. Wood, *"Teach Them Good Customs,"* provides a useful overview of the educational role of the regulars; BNL, A 589.

32. Wood, *"Teach Them Good Customs,"* 106–7.

33. BNL, A 589.

34. APY, Visita de Yanque Urinsaya 1604; AGI, Lima 309. For the bishop, see Kenneth Mills, *Idolatry and Its Enemies*, 140–46.

35. LCA, vol. 2.

36. BNL, A 589.

37. ANP, Residencias 5, cuad. 9.

38. Ulloa Mogollón, "Relación de la provincia de los Collaguas," 1:331; Diego de Ocaña, *A través de la América del Sur*, 216 (quote). Failure to maintain and build the educational and transportation infrastructure plagued, and continues to plague, Peruvian authorities. Shift of thermal springs is beyond the power of a bureaucracy's control, but not so schools and teachers. Local officials, members of the Consejo Provincial de Caylloma, were chastised in a report of 3 November 1896. Only two districts in the entire province had schools for primary instruction, because they did not press for them, nor was it budgeted. BNL, D 6257.

39. Ulloa Mogollón, "Relación de la provincia de los Collaguas," 1:328.

40. Ibid., 1:330.

41. AGI, Lima 305.

42. BNL, A 589, B 511.

43. BNL, A 589, B 511; Málaga Medina, "Los Collaguas en la historia de Arequipa en el siglo XVI," 120.

44. BNL, A 589, B 511.

45. Ibid.

46. Ibid.

47. Ibid.

48. Ibid.

49. APY, Visitas, Coporaque Urinsaya 1604.

50. BNL, A 589, B 511; Ulloa Mogollón, "Relación de la provincia de los Collaguas."

51. BNL, A 589, B 511.

52. APY, Visitas, Coporaque Urinsaya 1604.

53. BNL, A 589, B 511.

54. BNL, B 511.

55. APY, Visitas 1615.

56. APY, Visitas, Cabanaconde Urinsaya, 1645.

SIX *Tribute and the Domestic Economy*

1. Puente Brunke, *Encomienda y encomenderos en el Perú*, 13–30; Cook, "Population Data for Indian Peru," 73–75, 115–16.

2. AGI, Indiferente General 748; Contaduría 1822; Justicia 448.

3. APY, Visitas 1604. For the tomín payment, see Cook, *Tasa de la visita general de Francisco de Toledo*.

4. AGI, Contaduría 1786, published in Cook, *Tasa de la visita general de Francisco de Toledo*; the quoted cloth description is from Spalding, *Huarochirí*, 133.

5. ANP, Residencias 4, cuad. 8. The six-month payment period was called a *tercio*.

6. AGI, Contaduría 1786.

7. AGI, Justicia 448.

8. Ibid.

9. Ibid.

10. BNL, B 415.

11. BNL, B 415; ANP, Residencias 4, cuad. 6.

12. ANP, Residencias 4, cuad. 8; Juan Carlos Crespo, "Los Collaguas en la visita de Alonso Fernández de Bonilla," 55–56.

13. Ibid.

14. AGI, Justicia 448.

15. Nathan Wachtel, *Sociedad e ideología*, 130–48, explores similar themes.

16. Manuel Burga, *De la encomienda a la hacienda capitalista*; Luis Miguel Glave and María Isabel Remy, *Estructura agraria y vida rural en una región andina*.

17. González Holguín, *Vocabulario de la lengua general de todo el Perú llamada Quechua*; Murra, *The Economic Organization of the Inka State*, 30; David J. Robinson, "Estudio," in *Collaguas II: Lari Collaguas*, lviii–lix.

18. John V. Murra, "Introducción," in Felipe Guaman Poma de Ayala, *El primer nueva corónica y buen gobierno*, 1:xv; Mayer, "Beyond the Nuclear Family," 60–61.

19. Ulloa Mogollón, "Relación de la provincia de los Collaguas," 1:328; Treacy, *Las chacras de Coporaque*, 168–73; Santiago Erik Antúñez de Mayolo, *La nutrición en el antiguo Perú*; Fernando Rozas Bonuccelli, *Plantas alimenticias en el antiguo Perú*; APY, Visita de Lari Collaguas, 1604–1605.

20. The examples are from Pease, *Collaguas I*.

21. Treacy, *Las chacras de Coporaque*, 100, 134.

22. Ibid., 102–3, 138; for Yanque, field observations.

23. BNL, A 589, B 511.

24. Treacy, *Las chacras de Coporaque*, 141–55. Recent construction of new terraces and repair of old ones in Coporaque allowed John Treacy to calculate the labor input in work hours to complete the job. The equipment used is "modern" but not mechanical. Thirty adults working six hours daily can restore a hectare in fewer than ten weeks, and construct a new one of the same size in twelve. A workforce of sixty can construct one in six weeks.

25. Ibid., 195–207.

26. González Holguín, *Vocabulario de la lengua general de todo el Perú llamada Quechua* (quoted definition). See also ibid., 187–89. For the agricultural calendar, see MacCormack, "Time, Space, and Ritual Action."

27. Pease, *Collaguas I*, 439.

28. Ibid., 216.

29. LCA, vol. 1, 27 May 1552. See Alfred W. Crosby, *The Colombian Exchange*, and the same author's *Ecological Imperialism*; and Elinor G. K. Melville, *A Plague of Sheep*.

30. LCA, vol. 6, 13 August 1590.

31. BNL, A 589, B 511.

32. Karsten Paerregaard, *Linking Separate Worlds*, 34–35, 52.

33. Crespo, "Los Collaguas en la visita de Alonso Fernández de Bonilla," 54; Treacy, *Las chacras de Coporaque*, 171–72; AGI, Contaduría 1786.

34. Jorge A. Flores Ochoa, *Pastores de puna*. See also chapters by Glynn Custred, "Las punas de los Andes Centrales"; and Daniel W. Gade, "Llama, alpaca y vicuña."

35. BNL, A 589, B 511.

36. Ibid. For an excellent description of the chaco see Cieza de León, *The Discovery and Conquest of Peru*, 164–65, 167.

37. Pease, *Collaguas I*.

38. Ibid.

39. Ibid., 423.

40. Casaverde, "El trueque en la economía pastoril," 171–92.

41. Ulloa Mogollón, "Relación de la provincia de los Collaguas," 1:328.

42. Nathan Wachtel, *Vision of the Vanquished*.

1. Rostworowski de Diez Canseco, *Historia del Tahuantinsuyu*, 235–38; Cook, "Population Data for Indian Peru," 73–75; Cook, *Demographic Collapse*, 112–14, 247–48; Puente Brunke, *Encomienda y encomenderos en el Perú*, 13–30.

2. Tibesar, *Franciscan Beginnings in Colonial Peru*, 68; LCA, vol. 1, f. 157v (quote).

3. LCA, vol. 1, meeting of 22 October 1550; AGI, Contaduría 1785.

4. AGI, Contaduría 1822, 1636 residencia de Pedro Sánchez de Coz.

5. AGI, Lima 28A, expediente 63-G.

6. Jeffrey A. Cole, *The Potosí Mita*; Bakewell, *Miners of the Red Mountain*; Enrique Tandeter, "Forced and Free Labour in Late Colonial Potosí."

7. Spalding, *Huarochirí*, 164–67.

8. Lohmann Villena, *Francisco de Toledo*, 2:377–78, 283 (quote).

9. ANP, Derecho Indígena y Encomiendas, leg. 23, cuad. 630; BNL, B 415; LCA, vol. 6; Málaga Medina, "Los Collaguas en la historia de Arequipa en el siglo XVI," 114; Lohmann Villena, *Toledo*, 2:361–62.

10. BNL, B 415 (quotes); AGI, Lima 111.

11. BNL, B 415.

12. Ibid.

13. Ibid.

14. BNL, B 115.

15. BNL, B 415; Málaga Medina, "Los Collaguas en la historia de Arequipa en el siglo XVI," 121.

16. AGI, Lima 272.

17. AGI, Lima 111. The impact of the mercury amalgamation process on the health of the laborers at Caylloma can be compared to conditions at Huancavelica; see Kendall W. Brown, "Workers' Health and Colonial Mercury Mining at Huancavelica, Peru."

18. Nicolas P. Cushner, *Farm and Factory*; de Ocaña, *A través de la América del Sur*, 216.

19. AGI, Lima 144.

20. Ibid. Those present on 5 March were from Yanque Collaguas: Don Bernabé Taco, Don Francisco Guaman Yanqui, and Don Martín Chacha. Also there were kurakas principales of Lari Collaguas of Alonso Picado — Don Bartolomé Guanqui, Don Felipe Condo, and Don Francisco Chavi — as well as kurakas of Lari, Don Juan de Sandoval and Don Miguel Ala, of the repartimiento de Don Rodrigo de Mendoza.

21. Ibid.

22. AGI, Lima 144 (quotes); APY, Visitas, Lari anansaya, 1604–1605.

23. AGI, Lima 144.

24. Ibid.

25. Ibid.

26. Ibid.

27. AGI, Lima 95; Lima 144; Lima 571.

28. AGI, Lima 95.

29. AGI, Lima 95; Lima 144; Lima 571.

30. ASFL, reg. 15.

31. Ulloa Mogollón, "Relación de la provincia de los Collaguas," 1:331–32 (quote); Francisco Xavier Echeverría, "Memoria de la Santa Iglesia de Arequipa," 4:91.

32. BP, 2816, f. 338.

33. Bueno, *Geografía del Perú virreinal (siglo XVIII)*.

34. AGI, Lima 572.

35. AGI, Escribanía de Cámara 568A.

36. Ibid.

37. Mendoza, *Chronica de la Provincia de San Antonio de los Charcas*, 125–26 (quotes); Echeverría, "Memoria de la Santa Iglesia de Arequipa," 4:91–94.

38. BP, 409, f. 230v–31r; Ulloa Mogollón, "Relación de la provincia de los Collaguas," 1:332; Pease, "Collaguas: Una etnia del siglo XVI," 143.

39. AGI, Lima 28A; Lima 30, no. 2; Lima 571; Barriga, *Documentos para la historia de Arequipa*, 1:384–85, 390–91; 2:253.

40. Barriga, *Documentos para la historia de Arequipa*, 1:392–402.

41. Ibid., 1:395–96.

42. Ibid., 1:397.

43. Ibid., 1:401.

44. AGI, Lima 571; BP, 409, 230v–31r; Pérez de Tudela y Bueso, *Documentos relativos a don Pedro de la Gasca y a Gonzalo Pizarro*, 1:460.

45. LCA, vol. 2, 28 June 1560.

46. Stonemason Simón Bernabé received thirty-five pesos from the kuraka of Yanque anansaya for a significant part of the construction on 10 October 1801. APY, Libros Varios de la Iglesia, Libro de Fábrica, 1690–1731.

47. AGI, Contaduría 1786.

48. Noble David Cook, "La población de la parroquia de Yanahuara, 1738–47." Examples based on research in the Yanahuara parish archive.

49. BNM, 3032; for published text see Noble David Cook, *Padrón de los indios de Lima en 1613*.

50. Ibid.

EIGHT *Indoctrination and Resistance*

1. Griffiths, *The Cross and the Serpent*, 6–8.

2. Armas Medina, *Cristianización del Perú (1532–1600)*, 487–518. The Franciscans kept close track of whether there was papal authorization for them to administer the sacraments in the Indies; the bull of Pius V, Rome, 24 March 1567, is a good example, in ASFL, reg. 13, 536v–45v.

3. Mendoza, *Chronica de la Provincia de San Antonio de los Charcas*, 41–42, 49–51; BNM, 2950. Emilio Lissón y Chaves, *La Iglesia de España en el Perú*, 4:139–47, based on AGI, Lima 320, reports that in 1595 the Franciscan monastery in Arequipa housed four-

teen to sixteen religious. Of those, eight or nine performed Mass, and there were two to three *frailes del coro*, with four lay brothers. The principal house in Lima held 90, including 20 to 24 novices.

4. Tibesar, *Franciscan Beginnings in Colonial Peru*, 35–50, 68.

5. AGI, Charcas 142.

6. Tibesar, *Franciscan Beginnings in Colonial Peru*, 48, 65–68.

7. Vargas Ugarte, *Concilios Limenses*, "Constituciones de los naturales," First Council, nos. 2, 3, 5, 6, 11.

8. Ibid., "Constituciones de los españoles," First Council, nos. 38, 79.

9. Ibid., Second Council, nos. 28, 32.

10. AGI, Lima 30, no. 2, f. 100–101.

11. Vargas Ugarte, *Concilios Limenses*, Sixth Council, 2:18–19, no. 15.

12. Ibid., Second Council, 1:253–55, nos. 100–110.

13. Ibid., Third Council, 1:345, nos. 4, 5.

14. Ibid., Third Council, 1:339, 351, nos. 17, 39.

15. Ibid., Third Council, 1:348, no. 11.

16. Ibid., Third Council, 1:358, 373, no. 1, 4.

17. Enrique Fernández, *Monumenta peruana VIII (1603–1604)*, 214–15; Joanne Rappaport and Tom Cummins, "Between Images and Writing"; Urton, "From Knots to Narratives."

18. AGI, Contaduría 1785.

19. AGI, Indiferente General 857.

20. BNL, C 341.

21. ASFL, reg. 13, 15. The friars could not collect a stipend for their work, rather a "gift." The amount set by Toledo was 400 pesos yearly for the thirteen Franciscans in the Yanque and Lari doctrinas, plus 400 for the friar in La Chimba of Arequipa for the Indians of the Lari encomiendas, and another 250 pesos for those of Yanque in La Chimba, ASFL, reg. 9, 375r–77r.

22. BNM, 2950, 81v–82v.

23. ASFL, reg. 13, 220–21; AGI, Lima 131.

24. ASFL, reg. 13, 497r–98r; AGI, Lima 131.

25. ASFL, reg. 13, 497r–500v.

26. ASFL, reg. 13, 497r–99v (quotes); AGI, Lima 131.

27. ASFL, reg. 13, 323r, 497r–500v (quotes); AGI, Lima 318; Vargas Ugarte, *Historia de la Iglesia en el Perú*, 2:206.

28. ASFL, reg. 13, 618r–v.

29. ASFL, reg. 13, 323r (quote); AGI, Lima 131.

30. AGI, Lima 135.

31. Ibid. Bishop Pedro Perea wrote the monarch (31 January 1627) that the Franciscans held the doctrinas of Yanque, Callalli, Tute, Tisco, Chivay, Sibayo, and Achoma; while the seculars administered Lluta, Caylloma, Lari, Madrigal, Maca, Cabana, Pinchollo, and Guambo. See AGI, Lima 309.

32. AGI, Lima 326.

33. Ibid.

34. AGI, Lima 312 (quotes); Vargas Ugarte, *Historia de la Iglesia en el Perú*, 2:175, 2:431.

35. AGI, Lima 309; the bishop frequently reported his activities to the monarch. When he learned of the king's economic needs to protect Christianity, he sent a circular to all clergy in the diocese, requesting contributions. At least one Colca Valley curate complied. Licentiate Antonio de Castro Cigales, priest of Maca and Ichupampa, gave 100 pesos. One wonders if his parishioners understood the purpose. See also Vargas Ugarte, *Historia de la Iglesia en el Perú*, 2:438.

36. Lissón y Chaves, *La Iglesia de España en el Perú*. 4:346–47; Vargas Ugarte, *Historia de la Iglesia en el Perú*, 2:440.

37. AGI, Lima 309; Lima 312; Vargas Ugarte, *Historia de la Iglesia en el Perú*, 2:175, 431, 435–38; Kenneth Mills, *Idolatry and Its Enemies*, 137–64, traces the career of Bishop Villagómez.

38. AGI, Lima 305.

39. Vargas Ugarte, *Concilios Limenses*, 2:242–46; Pease, *Collaguas I*.

40. Luis Gerónimo de Oré, *Ritvale, sev manvale Pervanum et forma brevis . . .* (quote on 58); Pease, *Collaguas I*.

41. Vargas Ugarte, *Concilios Limenses*, First Council nos. 15, 16, 18; quote from Third Council.

42. Personal observations, parish registers of Yanque.

43. Oré, *Ritvale, sev manvale Pervanum et forma brevis*, 254.

44. Vargas Ugarte, *Concilios Limenses*, First Council, no. 25.

45. Enrique T. Bartra, "Los autores del Catecismo del Tercer Concilio Limense," and the same author's *Tercer Concilio Limense*, 61; BNL, C 341, 28r, 55v; AGI, Lima 126.

46. The cofradías were adopted quickly by Amerindians. The Spanish elite were active in cofradías in Arequipa. In 1582 Colca Valley figures who were members of the Cofradía de la Caridad in Arequipa included Juan de la Torre, Francisco de la Torre, and Gonzalo Gómez de Buitrón. AGI, Lima 126.

47. Tibesar, *Franciscan Beginnings in Colonial Peru*, 66; Ulloa Mogollón, "Relación de la provincia de los Collaguas," 1:332; APY, Libros Varios de la Iglesia de Yanque.

48. Tibesar, *Franciscan Beginnings in Colonial Peru*, 35–40.

49. Ulloa Mogollón, "Relación de la provincia de los Collaguas," 1:332.

50. ANP, Residencias 5, cuad. 9.

51. AGI, Lima 30. For visual images of the churches, see Luis Enrique Tord, *Templos coloniales del Colca-Arequipa*.

52. Griffiths, *The Cross and the Serpent*, 8–13; MacCormack, *Religion in the Andes*, 181–204.

53. AGI, Lima 29; Lima 30; Vargas Ugarte, *Concilios Limenses*, 1:253–55.

54. ANP, Residencias 5, cuad. 9.

55. BNM, 2950.

56. Systematic analysis of the relation of art and architecture to the religious experience of the valley's people warrants fresh attention. See Valerie Fraser, *The Architecture of Conquest*.

57. AGI, Lima 326.

58. Ibid.; Mills, *Idolatry and Its Enemies*, provides a fine analysis of the process in mid-seventeenth-century Peru.

59. The term *transculturation* was coined by the Cuban sociologist Fernando Ortiz, and was brought into wider usage by the anthropologist Melville J. Herskovits, in *Man and His Works*, 529.

NINE *Crisis in "República de los Españoles"*

1. The quotations in this chapter's first two epigraphs can be found in Victor M. Barriga, *Los terremotos en Arequipa, 1582–1868*, 47, 149.

2. Richard L. Kagan, *Urban Images of the Hispanic World, 1493–1793*; Jay Kinsbruner, *The Colonial Spanish-American City*, 23–45.

3. Loredo, *Los repartos*, 194, 201–2; Málaga Medina, "Consideraciones económicas sobre la visita de la provincia de Arequipa," 301–2.

4. Cook, *Tasa de la visita general de Francisco de Toledo*, 220–21.

5. AGI, Contaduría 1786; Cook, "Population Data for Indian Peru," 112; Lohmann Villena, "La restitución por conquistadores y encomenderos"; Martínez, *Fundadores de Arequipa*, 224–25, 412–13; ANP, Residencias 5, cuad. 9. Francisco and Mariana's son Francisco Retamoso de la Cuba married Doña Violante de la Torre Padilla, granddaughter of one of the Arequipa founders, Juan de la Torre.

6. The 1575 suit was brought by Francisco de San Millán on behalf of the widow of Miguel Cornejo, Leonor Méndez. See Archivo Departamental de Arequipa, Corregimientos (Causas Ordinarias), 1 (1575); 3 (1611); 4 (1621); cited by Puente Brunke, *Encomienda y encomenderos en el Perú*, 282–83, 416, 419; and Martínez, *Fundadores de Arequipa*, 411–13.

7. AGI, Patronato 2, ramo 9 (quotes); Lima 144; Justicia 471; Martínez, *Fundadores de Arequipa*, 255–57; Schäfer, *Consejo Real y Supremo de las Indias*, 480, 530; see Davies, *Landowners in Colonial Peru*, 68.

8. AGI, Lima 144 (quote); Patronato 124.

9. AGI, Lima 144 (quotes); Patronato 124.

10. AGI, Patronato 120; Lima 3, 6, 1061; Contaduría 1822; Puente Brunke, *Encomienda y encomenderos en el Perú*, 419; Martínez, *Fundadores de Arequipa*, 257; Schäfer, *El Consejo Real y Supremo de las Indias*, 481.

11. AGI, Lima 202, no. 8.

12. BP, no. 409, f. 105r; AGI, Justicia 397, 142r–43r.

13. Ibid.; the documents provide rich detail of the stormy relation between father and son.

14. BNM, 3044.

15. AGI, Lima 144; Patronato 124.

16. AGI, Patronato 124.

17. LCA, vol. 6; AGI, Lima 144 (quotes); Patronato 124.

18. LCA, vol. 6; AGI, Lima 144 (quotes); Patronato 124.

19. AGI, Patronato 124 (quotes); Contaduría 1822.

20. AGI, Escribanía de Cámara 499A.

21. Ibid.

22. Pablo E. Pérez-Mallaina and Bibiano Torres Ramírez, *La Armada del Mar del Sur*, 2–3, 243–45, 248.

23. AGI, Escribanía de Cámara 499A.

24. Ibid.

25. AGI, Patronato 143, no. 1, ramo 3; Escribanía de Cámara 499A; Martínez, *Fundadores de Arequipa*, 307.

26. AGI, Indiferente General 2093, no. 4. Diego Hernández de la Cuba Maldonado was about sixty-six years old when he died; see Martínez, *Fundadores de Arequipa*, 308–15.

27. AGI, Lima 144; Contaduría 1822; Escribanía de Cámara 499A.

28. AGI, Lima 144; Contaduría 1822; Escribanía de Cámara 499A; Martínez, *Fundadores de Arequipa*, 310.

29. AGI, Patronato 143, no. 1, ramo 3, 7 April 1606.

30. AGI, Lima 95; Lima 116; Patronato 143, no. 1, ramo 3 (quote); Contaduría 1822; Puente Brunke, *Encomienda y encomenderos en el Perú*, 255.

31. Francisco Noguerol de Ulloa was a colorful character, whose trials and tribulations are the subject of Cook and Cook, *Good Faith and Truthful Ignorance*.

32. ANP, Residencias 5, cuad. 9.

33. Ibid. (quotes); Anastasio Rojo Vega, *Enfermos y sanadores en la Castilla del siglo XVI*, 72.

34. ANP, Residencias 5, cuad. 9.

35. Ibid.

36. AGI, Justicia 480 (quote); Crespo, "Los Collaguas en la visita de Alonso Fernández de Bonilla," 58.

37. AGI, Indiferente General 2097, no. 153.

38. AGI, Lima 131.

39. AGI, Lima 95.

40. Barriga, *Los terremotos en Arequipa*, v–vi.

41. AGI, Lima 30, cuad. 6.

42. Barriga, *Los terremotos en Arequipa*, 4.

43. Ibid., 20.

44. ANP, Residencias 5, cuad. 9; Barriga, *Los terremotos en Arequipa*, 32–33.

45. Barriga, *Los terremotos en Arequipa*, 37–39.

46. Ibid., 35–36.

47. BNL, B 415; Barriga, *Los terremotos en Arequipa*, 37–43.

48. Barriga, *Los terremotos en Arequipa*, 47 (quote); Pease, *Collaguas I*, 343.

49. Barriga, *Los terremotos en Arequipa*, 47.

50. Mendoza, *Chronica de la Provincia de San Antonio de los Charcas*, 131–32.

51. AGI, Lima 111.

52. Barriga, *Los terremotos en Arequipa*, 84–85.

53. Ibid., 85–86, 90.

54. AGI, Lima 135.

55. AGI, Indiferente General 748; Barriga, *Los terremotos en Arequipa*, 91 (quote), 156.
56. Barriga, *Los terremotos en Arequipa*, 163.
57. Ibid., 149.
58. Ibid., 135–92.
59. APY, Visitas, Lari anansaya, 1604–5.
60. From Cook, "Population Data for Indian Peru."
61. AGI, Lima 116; Cook, *The People of the Colca Valley*, 81–88.
62. Ulloa Mogollón, "Relación de la provincia de los Collaguas"; Haenke, *Descripción del Perú*, 278.

EPILOGUE   Andean Counterpoint

1. Treacy, *Las chacras de Coporaque*, 243–44.
2. Thomas M. Davies, *Indian Integration in Peru*, 17–19, 29–30, provides the legal background for nineteenth-century legislation involving Indian communities.
3. Davies, *Indian Integration in Peru*, 32; ANP, Archivo Histórico del Ministerio de Hacienda, Caylloma, no, 0284, no. 0286. See Mark Thurner, *From Two Republics to One Divided*; and Florencia E. Mallon, *The Defense of Community in Peru's Central Highlands*.
4. Stern, *Peru's Indian Peoples and the Challenge of Spanish Colonialism.* Spalding, *Huarochirí*, 47, 54–55, discusses the concept; she suggests that it referred to the entire district: "The colonial province of Huarochirí was the more populous and important northern half of the old Inca province of Yauyos; it was the upper moiety of the old province and the residence of the principal kuraka." Billie Jean Isbell, *To Defend Ourselves*, 198–203, devotes considerable attention to outlining the contemporary importance of dual organization in the community of Chuschi, as well as male–female oppositions.
5. Brooke Larson, *Colonialism and Agrarian Transformation in Bolivia* (1988 ed.), 148–59. Larson recognized the problem as she entered into its internal complexities for the Bolivian community of Tapacarí, where anansaya and urinsaya were important, as she delineated the importance of rivalry between kurakas of the halves for two decades in the eighteenth century. See also Thomas A. Abercrombie, *Pathways of Memory and Power*.
6. John M. Baines, *Revolution in Peru*, 17–28.
7. José María Arguedas, *Yawar fiesta*; *Los ríos profundos*; *El sexto* comprise the most important novels. For anthropology, see his *Dioses y hombres de Huarochirí*; and *Las comunidades de España y del Perú*.
8. Ciro Alegría, *El mundo es ancho y ajeno*. Brooke Larson, in a revised (1998) edition of her work on Cochabamba, 322–90, provides an illuminating evaluation of ethnohistorical scholarship on the Andes in the past two decades.
9. Benavides, "Dualidad social e ideológica en la provincia de Collaguas, 1570–1731," 138–45.
10. Pease, *Del Tawantinsuyu a la historia del Perú*, 155–56.

11. Benavides, "Dualidad social e ideológica en la provincia de Collaguas, 1570–1731," 145, 150.

12. Treacy, *Las chacras de Coporaque*, 212–24; Benavides, "Dualidad social e ideológica en la provincia de Collaguas, 1570–1731," 150; Alfredo Simón Bernal Málaga, "Danzas de las etnias collaguas y colonias." The ritual battle dances frequently resulted in one or more deaths each season.

13. Paerregaard, *Linking Separate Worlds*, 221–22.

14. Mallon, *Peasant and Nation*, 324–25, 328; Alberto Flores Galindo, *Buscando un Inca*; Burga, *Nacimiento de una utopía*; Juan Ossio, *Ideología mesiánica del mundo andino*; Millones, *El retorno de las huacas*; Pease, *Del Tawantinsuyu a la historia del Perú*, 151–59; MacCormack, *Religion in the Andes*, 282–87.

15. Pease, *Del Tawantinsuyu a la historia del Perú*, 151. See also Pease, *Los últimos incas del Cuzco*, 117–30.

16. Montoya suggests that the origin of the term is a simple Quechua transliteration of *mestizo*. See Rodrigo Montoya, "Identidad étnica y luchas agrarias en los Andes peruanos," 251.

17. Paerregaard, *Linking Separate Worlds*, 163–64.

18. Ibid., 173 (quote), 167–79.

19. AGI, Indiferente General 1525. According to the 1792 count, there were 16,554 Indians, 240 Spaniards, 1,417 mestizos, 335 "free colored," and 29 slaves in the province of Caylloma. For 1843, there were in the province 19,343 Indians, and 2,097 *castas*, a category that included "all others" — Spaniards, mestizos, mulattoes, blacks. In 1940, the Indian population was listed as 22,243; the "other" category, 5,291. In 1940, if one eliminates the villages of Lluta, Huanca, Chivay, and Caylloma, where the Spaniards and mestizos are concentrated, then the percentage of Indians remains very high; see Cook, *The People of the Colca Valley*, 36–43. Paerregaard, *Linking Separate Worlds*, 33–36, examined the parish registers for the relatively isolated community of Tapay. He found that of 190 deaths between 1792 and 1802, 19 were "mestizos" and 10 "Spaniards." See also Nelson Manrique, *Colonialismo y pobreza campesina*, 202–3.

20. Julien, *Condesuyo*, 126.

21. Griffiths, *The Cross and the Serpent*, 233–35.

22. Paerregaard, *Linking Separate Worlds*, 206.

23. Ibid., 207.

24. Johan Reinhard and Stephen Alvarez, "Peru's Ice Maidens" 74.

25. Johan Reinhard, "Research Update," 128–35.

26. Reinhard and Alvarez, "Peru's Ice Maidens," 70, 74.

BIBLIOGRAPHY

Abbreviations Used in the Notes

AGI   Archivo General de Indias (Seville)
ANP   Archivo Nacional del Perú (Lima)
APY   Archivo Parroquial (Yanque)
BNL   Biblioteca Nacional (Lima)
BNM   Biblioteca Nacional (Madrid)
BP   Biblioteca del Palacio Real (Madrid)
LCA   Libros de Cabildos (Arequipa)
RAH   Real Academia de la Historia (Madrid)

Sources Cited

Abercrombie, Thomas A. *Pathways of Memory and Power: Ethnography and History among an Andean People*. Madison: University of Wisconsin Press, 1998.

Acosta, José de. *Historia natural y moral de las Indias* [1590]. Madrid: Historia 16, 1987.

Alegría, Ciro. *El mundo es ancho y ajeno*. Santiago de Chile: Ediciones Ercilla, 1941.

Andrien, Kenneth J. *The Kingdom of Quito, 1690–1830: The State and Regional Development*. Cambridge: Cambridge University Press, 1995.

Antúnez de Mayolo, Santiago Erik. *La nutrición en el antiguo Perú*. Lima: Banco Central de Reserva, 1981.

Arguedas, José María. *Las comunidades de España y del Perú*. Lima: Universidad Nacional Mayor de San Marcos, 1968.

———. *Dioses y hombres de Huarochirí*. Lima: Museo Nacional de la Historia, 1966.

———. *Los ríos profundos*. Buenos Aires: Losada, 1958.

———. *El sexto*. Lima: Mejía Baca, 1961.

———. *Yawar fiesta*. Lima, 1941.

Armas Medina, Fernando de. *Cristianización del Perú (1532–1600)*. Seville: Escuela de Estudios Hispanoamericanos, 1953.

Ascher, Marcia, and Robert Ascher. *The Code of the Quipo: A Study in Media, Mathematics, and Culture*. Ann Arbor: University of Michigan Press, 1981.

Baines, John M. *Revolution in Peru: Mariátegui and the Myth*. Tuscaloosa: University of Alabama Press (published for the Latin American Studies Program), 1972.

Bakewell, Peter. *Miners of the Red Mountain: Indian Labor in Potosí, 1545–1650*. Albuquerque: University of New Mexico Press, 1984.

Bandelier, Adolph F. A. *The Islands of Lake Titicaca and Koati*. New York: Hispanic Society, 1910.

Barriga, Víctor M., ed. *Documentos para la historia de Arequipa*. 3 vols. Arequipa: La Colmena, 1939–55.

————, ed. *Memorias para la historia de Arequipa*. 4 vols. Arequipa: La Colmena, 1941–52.

————, ed. *Los terremotos en Arequipa, 1582–1868*. Arequipa: La Colmena, 1951.

Bartra, Enrique T. "Los autores del Catecismo del Tercer Concilio Limense." *Mercurio Peruano* 470(1967):359–72.

————. *Tercer Concilio Limense, 1582–1583*. Lima: Facultad de Teología Pontificia y Civil, 1982.

Benavides, María A. "Análisis del uso de tierras registrado en las visitas de los siglos XVI y XVII a la provincia de Yanquecollaguas, Arequipa." In *The Cultural Ecology, Archaeology, and History of Terracing and Terrace Abandonment in the Colca Valley of Southern Peru: Technical Report to the National Science Foundation and the National Geographic Society*, edited by William M. Denevan, pp. 1:493–508. Madison: University of Wisconsin Press, 1986.

————. "Apuntes históricos y etnográficos del valle del río Colca (Arequipa, Peru) 1575–1980." *Boletín de Lima* 50(1987):7–20.

————. "Cambios en el paisaje agroecológico de la provincia de Collaguas: Un análisis de documentos en los archivos de Arequipa, Perú." *Revista Archivo Arzobispal de Arequipa* 2(1995):15–46.

————. "Cambios en la tenencia y el uso de tierras desde el siglo XVI hasta el presente en el valle del Colca (Caylloma, Arequipa)." In *The Cultural Ecology, Archaeology, and History of Terracing and Terrace Abandonment in the Colca Valley of Southern Peru: Technical Report to the National Science Foundation and the National Geographic Society*, edited by William M. Denevan, pp. 1:509–524. Madison: University of Wisconsin Press, 1986.

————. "Coporaque in the 1591 Visita of Yanquecollaguas Urinsaya." In *The Cultural Ecology, Archaeology, and History of Terracing and Terrace Abandonment in the Colca Valley of Southern Peru: Technical Report to the National Science Foundation and the National Geographic Society*, edited by William M. Denevan, pp. 1:390–405. Madison: University of Wisconsin Press, 1986.

————. "Coporaque in the 1604 Visita of Yanquecollaguas Urinsaya." In *The Cultural Ecology, Archaeology, and History of Terracing and Terrace Abandonment in the Colca Valley of Southern Peru: Technical Report to the National Science Foundation and the National Geographic Society*, edited by William M. Denevan, pp. 1:406–25. Madison: University of Wisconsin Press, 1986.

————. "Coporaque in the 1615–1617 Visita of Yanquecollaguas Urinsaya." In *The Cultural*

Ecology, Archaeology, and History of Terracing and Terrace Abandonment in the Colca Valley of Southern Peru: Technical Report to the National Science Foundation and the National Geographic Society, edited by William M. Denevan, pp. 1:509–24. Madison: University of Wisconsin Press, 1986.

————. "Coporaque Toponyms: Comparison and Analysis of Place Names in the 16th, 17th, and 20th Centuries." In *The Cultural Ecology, Archaeology, and History of Terracing and Terrace Abandonment in the Colca Valley of Southern Peru: Technical Report to the National Science Foundation and the National Geographic Society*, edited by William M. Denevan, pp. 1:450–492. Madison: University of Wisconsin Press, 1986.

————. "La división social y geográfica hanansaya/urinsaya en el valle del Colca y la provincia de Caylloma." In *The Cultural Ecology, Archaeology, and History of Terracing and Terrace Abandonment in the Colca Valley of Southern Peru: Technical Report to the National Science Foundation and the National Geographic Society*, edited by William M. Denevan, pp. 2:46–53. Madison: University of Wisconsin Press, 1988.

————. "Dualidad social e ideológica en la provincia de Collaguas, 1570–1731." *Historia y Cultura* 21(1991–92):127–60.

————. "Grupos de poder en el valle del Colca (Arequipa). Siglos XVI–XX." In *Sociedad andina: Pasado y presente*, edited by Ramiro Matos Mendieta, pp. 151–78. Lima: FOMCIENCIAS, 1988.

————. "Land Tenure in the Colca Valley, 16th to 20th Centuries." In *The Cultural Ecology, Archaeology, and History of Terracing and Terrace Abandonment in the Colca Valley of Southern Peru: Technical Report to the National Science Foundation and the National Geographic Society*, edited by William M. Denevan, pp. 2:54–66. Madison: University of Wisconsin Press, 1988.

————. "Two Traditional Andean Peasant Communities under the Stress of Market Penetration: Yanque and Madrigal in the Colca Valley, Peru." M.A. thesis, University of Texas, Austin, 1983.

————. "The Yanque Parish Archive." In *The Cultural Ecology, Archaeology, and History of Terracing and Terrace Abandonment in the Colca Valley of Southern Peru: Technical Report to the National Science Foundation and the National Geographic Society*, edited by William M. Denevan, pp. 2:25–37. Madison: University of Wisconsin Press, 1988.

Bennett, Wendell C., and Junius B. Bird. *Andean Culture History*. New York: Museum of Natural History, 1960.

Bernal Málaga, Alfredo Simón. "Danzas de las etnias Collaguas y Colonias: Un estudio de la cuenca del Colca, Caylloma." M.A. thesis, Universidad Nacional de San Agustín, Arequipa, 1983.

Bertonio, Ludovico. *Vocabulario de la lengua Aymara* [1612]. La Paz: Tipografía Bosco, 1956.

Betanzos, Juan de. *Suma y narración de los incas* [1551], edited by María del Carmen Martín Rubio. Madrid: Atlas, 1987.

Bolton, Ralph, and Enrique Mayer, eds. *Andean Kinship and Marriage*. Washington, D.C.: Special Publication of the American Anthropological Association no. 7, 1977.

Boone, Elizabeth Hill, and Tom Cummins, eds. *Native Traditions in the Postconquest World*. Washington, D.C.: Dumbarton Oaks, 1998.

Bouysse-Cassagne, Thérèse. *La identidad aymara: Aproximación histórica*. La Paz: HISBOL, 1987.

———. *Lluvias y cenizas: Dos Pachacuti en la historia*. La Paz: HISBOL, 1988.

———. "Pertinencia étnica, status económico y lenguas en Charcas a fines del siglo XVI." In *Tasa de la visita general de Francisco de Toledo*, edited by Noble David Cook, pp. 312–28. Lima: Universidad Nacional Mayor de San Marcos, 1975.

Bouysse-Cassagne, Thérèse, and Pierre Cassagne. "Volcan indien, volcan chrétien: A propos de l'éruption du Huaynaputina en l'an 1600. Pérou méridional." *Journal de la Société des Américanistes* 70(1984):43–68.

Bowser, Frederick P. *The African Slave in Colonial Peru: 1524–1650*. Stanford, Calif.: Stanford University Press, 1974.

Briggs, Lucy T., et al., eds. *Identidades andinas y lógicas del campesinado*. Lima: Mosca Azul, 1986.

Brooks, Sarah O. "Prehistoric Agricultural Terraces in the Río Japo Basin, Colca Valley, Peru." Ph.D. dissertation, University of Wisconsin, Madison, 1998.

Brooks, Sarah, and M. Olivares Ayala. "The pre-Inca Huarancante Canal, Colca Valley, Peru." Paper presented at the 26th Annual Midwest Conference on Andean and Amazonian Archaeology, Anthropology, and Ethnohistory, University of Illinois, Urbana-Champaign, 1998.

Browman, David L. "Pastoral Nomadism in the Andes." *Current Anthropology* 15(1974):188–96.

Brown, Kendall W. "Workers' Health and Colonial Mercury Mining at Huancavelica, Peru." *Americas* 57:4(2001):467–96.

Bueno, Cosme. *Geografía del Perú virreinal (siglo XVIII)*. Lima: Daniel Valcárcel, 1951.

Burga, Manuel. *De la encomienda a la hacienda capitalista: El valle de Jequetepeque del siglo XVI a XX*. Lima: Instituto de Estudios Peruanos, 1976.

———. *Nacimiento de una utopía: Muerte y resurrección de los incas*. Lima: Instituto de Apoyo Agrario, 1988.

Burns, Kathryn. *Colonial Habits: Convents and the Spiritual Economy of Cuzco, Peru*. Durham, N.C.: Duke University Press, 1999.

———. "Notaries, Truth, and Consequences." *American Historical Review* 110(2005):250–79.

Cabello de Balboa, Miguel. *Miscelánea antártica: Una historia del Perú antiguo* [1586]. Lima: Universidad Nacional Mayor de San Marcos, 1951.

Cahill, David. "Taxonomy of a Colonial 'Riot': The Arequipa Disturbances of 1780." In *Reforms and Insurrection in Bourbon New Granada and Peru*, edited by John R. Fisher, Allan J. Kuethe, and Anthony McFarlane, pp. 255–91. Baton Rouge: Louisiana State University Press, 1990.

Calvete de Estrella, Juan Cristóbal. *La Rebelión de Pizarro en el Perú y vida de don Pedro Gasca*. In *Crónicas del Perú*, edited by Juan Pérez de Tudela y Bueso, pp. 4:227–409, 5:1–147. Madrid: Atlas, 1964–65.

Campbell, Leon G. "Ideology and Factionalism during the Great Rebellion, 1780–1782." In

Resistance, Rebellion, and Consciousness in the Andean Peasant World, 18th to 20th Centuries, edited by Steve J. Stern, pp. 110–42. Madison: University of Wisconsin Press, 1987.

Cardich, Agusto. "The Fluctuating Upper Limits of Cultivation in the Central Andes and Their Impact on Peruvian Prehistory." In *Advances in World Archaeology*, pp. 4:293–333. New York: Academic Press, 1985.

Carter, W. E. "Trial Marriage in the Andes?" In *Andean Kinship and Marriage,* edited by Ralph Bolton and Enrique Mayer, pp. 177–216. Washington, D.C.: Special Publication of the American Anthropological Association no. 7, 1977.

Casaverde R., Juvenal. "El trueque en la economía pastoril." In *Pastores de puna: Uywami-chiq punarunakuna,* edited by Jorge A. Flores Ochoa, pp. 171–92. Lima: Instituto de Estudios Peruanos, 1977.

Castelli, Amalia, Marcia Koth de Paredes, and Mariana Mould de Pease, eds. *Etnohistoria y antropología andina.* Lima: Centro de Proyección Cristiana, 1981.

Cieza de León, Pedro de. *Crónica del Perú: Primera Parte* [1553]. Lima: Pontificia Universidad Católica del Perú, 1986.

———. *Crónica del Perú: Tercera Parte* [1551–54], edited by Francesca Cantú. Lima: Pontificia Universidad Católica del Perú, 1987.

———. *The Discovery and Conquest of Peru: Chronicles of the New World Encounter,* translated and edited by Alexandra Parma Cook and Noble David Cook. Durham, N.C.: Duke University Press, 1998.

———. *Obras completas* [1551–54]. 2 vols. Madrid: Consejo Superior de Investigaciones Científicas, 1984–85.

———. *El señorío de los incas.* Lima: Instituto de Estudios Peruanos, 1967.

Cobo, Bernabé. *History of the Inca Empire* [1653], translated and edited by Ronald Hamilton. Austin: University of Texas Press, 1979.

———. *Inca Religion and Customs,* translated and edited by Ronald Hamilton. Austin: University of Texas Press, 1990.

Cock, Guillermo. "Ayllu, territorio y frontera en los Collaguas." In *Etnohistoria y antropología andina,* edited by Marcia Koth de Paredes and Amalia Castelli, pp. 29–32. Lima: Centro de Proyección Cristiana, 1978.

———. "El ayllu en la sociedad andina: Alcances y perspectivas." In *Etnohistoria y antropología andina,* edited by Amalia Castelli, Marcia Koth de Paredes, and Mariana Mould de Pease, pp. 231–56. Lima: Centro de Proyección Cristiana, 1981.

———. "Los kurakas de los Collaguas: Poder político y poder económico." *Historia y Cultura* 10(1976/77):95–118.

Cole, Jeffrey A. *The Potosí Mita, 1573–1700: Compulsory Indian Labor in the Andes.* Stanford, Calif.: Stanford University Press, 1985.

Conrad, Geoffrey W., and Arthur A. Demarest. *Religion and Empire: The Dynamics of Aztec and Inca Expansionism.* Cambridge: Cambridge University Press, 1984.

Cook, Alexandra Parma, and Noble David Cook. *Good Faith and Truthful Ignorance: A Case of Transatlantic Bigamy.* Durham, N.C.: Duke University Press, 1991.

Cook, Noble David. "Beyond the *Martyrs of Florida*: The Versatile Career of Luis Gerónimo de Oré." *Florida Historical Quarterly* 71(1992):169–87.

Cook, Noble David. *Born to Die: Disease and New World Conquest, 1492–1650.* Cambridge: Cambridge University Press, 1998.

———. "Cabanas y Collaguas en la era prehispánica." In *Arqueología, antropología e historia en los Andes: Homenaje a María Rostworowski,* edited by Rafael Varón Gabai and Javier Flores Espinosa, pp. 379–98. Lima: Instituto de Estudios Peruanos, 1997.

———. *Demographic Collapse: Indian Peru, 1520–1620.* Cambridge: Cambridge University Press, 1981.

———. "Eighteenth-Century Population Change in Andean Peru: The Parish of Yanque." In *Studies in Spanish American Population History,* edited by David J. Robinson, pp. 243–70. Boulder, Colo.: Westview Press, 1981.

———. "Libro de cargos del tesorero Alonso Riquelme con el rescate de Atahualpa." *Humanidades* 2(1969):41–88.

———. *The People of the Colca Valley: A Population Study.* Boulder, Colo.: Westview Press, 1982.

———. "La población de la parroquia de Yanahuara, 1738–47." In *Collaguas I,* edited by Franklin Pease, pp. 13–34. Lima: Pontificia Universidad Católica del Perú, 1977.

———. "Population Data for Indian Peru: Sixteenth and Seventeenth Centuries." *Hispanic American Historical Review* 62(1982):73–120.

———, ed. *Padrón de los indios de Lima en 1613.* Lima: Universidad Nacional Mayor de San Marcos, 1968.

———, ed. *Tasa de la visita general de Francisco de Toledo* [1571–75]. Lima: Universidad Nacional Mayor de San Marcos, 1975.

Cook, Noble David, and Franklin Pease. "New Research Opportunities in Los Collaguas, Peru." *Latin American Research Review* 10(1975):201–2.

Córdoba y Salinas, Diego de. *Chronica franciscana de las provincias del Perú* [1651]. Washington, D.C.: Academy of American Franciscan History, 1957.

Córdova Aguilar, Hildegardo, Luis Gonzales Ilizarbe, and Carlos Guevara Tello. "Agriculture in Coporaque." In *The Cultural Ecology, Archaeology, and History of Terracing and Terrace Abandonment in the Colca Valley of Southern Peru: Technical Report to the National Science Foundation and the National Geographic Society,* edited by William M. Denevan, pp. 1:60–87. Madison: University of Wisconsin Press, 1986.

Costa, Luis Miguel. "Patronage and Bribery in Sixteenth-Century Peru: The Government of Viceroy Conde del Villar and the Visita of Licentiate Alonso Fernández de Bonilla." Ph.D. dissertation, Florida International University, Miami, 2005.

Covey, R. A. "Inka Administration of the Far South Coast of Peru." *Latin American Antiquity* 11:2(2000): 119–38.

Crespo, Juan Carlos. "Los Collaguas en la visita de Alonso Fernández de Bonilla." In *Collaguas I,* edited by Franklin Pease, pp. 53–92. Lima: Pontificia Universidad Católica del Perú, 1977.

Crosby, Alfred W. *The Colombian Exchange: Biological and Cultural Consequences of 1492.* Westport, Conn.: Greenwood Press, 1972.

———. *Ecological Imperialism: The Biological Expansion of Europe, 900–1900.* Cambridge: Cambridge University Press, 1986.

Cuadros, Juan José. "El control ecológico vertical en la economía de los Collaguas." M.A. thesis, Universidad Nacional de San Agustín, Arequipa, 1973.

———. "Informe etnográfico de Collaguas (1974–1975)." In *Collaguas I*, edited by Franklin Pease, pp. 35–52. Lima: Pontificia Universidad Católica del Perú, 1977.

Cushner, Nicholas P. *Farm and Factory: Jesuits in the Development of Agrarian Capitalism in Colonial Quito, 1600–1767*. New York: SUNY Press, 1982.

Custred, Glynn. "Las punas de los Andes Centrales." In *Pastores de puna: Uywamichiq punarunakuna*, edited by Jorge A. Flores Ochoa, pp. 55–85. Lima: Instituto de Estudios Peruanos, 1977.

D'Altroy, Terence N. *Provincial Power in the Inka Empire*. Washington, D.C.: Smithsonian Institution Press, 1992.

Davies, Keith A. *Landowners in Colonial Peru*. Austin: University of Texas Press, 1984.

Davies, Thomas M. *Indian Integration in Peru: A Half Century of Experience, 1900–1948*. Lincoln: University of Nebraska Press, 1974.

Denevan, William M. "Comments on the 1931 Shippee-Johnson Expedition to the Colca Valley." In *The Cultural Ecology, Archaeology, and History of Terracing and Terrace Abandonment in the Colca Valley of Southern Peru: Technical Report to the National Science Foundation and the National Geographic Society*, edited by William M. Denevan, pp. 2:87–90. Madison: University of Wisconsin Press, 1988.

———. *Cultivated Landscapes of Native Amazonia and the Andes*. Oxford: Oxford University Press, 2001.

———. "Introduction: The Río Colca Abandoned Terrace Project." In *The Cultural Ecology, Archaeology, and History of Terracing and Terrace Abandonment in the Colca Valley of Southern Peru: Technical Report to the National Science Foundation and the National Geographic Society*, edited by William M. Denevan, pp. 1:8–46. Madison: University of Wisconsin Press, 1986.

———. "Measurement of Abandoned Terracing from Air Photos: Colca Valley, Peru." *Yearbook, Conference of Latin Americanist Geographers*, 14(1988): 20–30.

———, ed. *The Cultural Ecology, Archaeology, and History of Terracing and Terrace Abandonment in the Colca Valley of Southern Peru: Technical Report to the National Science Foundation and the National Geographic Society*. 2 vols. Madison: University of Wisconsin Press, 1986–88.

———, ed. *The Native Population of the Americas in 1492*. 2nd ed. Madison: University of Wisconsin Press, 1992.

Denevan, William M., and Laurua Hartwig. "Measurement of Terrace Abandonment in the Colca Valley." In *The Cultural Ecology, Archaeology, and History of Terracing and Terrace Abandonment in the Colca Valley of Southern Peru: Technical Report to the National Science Foundation and the National Geographic Society*, edited by William M. Denevan, pp. 1:99–115. Madison: University of Wisconsin Press, 1986.

Denevan, William M., John M. Treacy, and Jon Sandor. "Physical Geography of the Coporaque Region." In *The Cultural Ecology, Archaeology, and History of Terracing and Terrace Abandonment in the Colca Valley of Southern Peru: Technical Report to the National Sci-*

ence Foundation and the National Geographic Society, edited by William M. Denevan, pp. 1:47–59. Madison: University of Wisconsin Press, 1986.

Deústua, José. "Acceso a recursos en Yanque-Collaguas en 1591: Una experiencia estadística." In *Etnohistoria y antropología andina*, edited by Marcia Koth de Paredes and Amalia Castelli, pp. 41–52. Lima: Centro de Proyección Cristiana, 1978.

Dick, R. P., J. A. Sandor, and N. S. Eash. "Soil Enzyme Activities after 1500 Years of Terrace Agriculture in the Colca Valley, Peru." *Agriculture, Ecosystems and Environment* 50(1994): 123–31.

Dobyns, Henry F. "An Outline of Andean Epidemic History to 1720." *Bulletin of the History of Medicine* 37(1963):493–515.

Earls, John, and Silverblatt, Irene. "La realidad física y social en la cosmología andina." *Proceedings of the 42nd International Congress of Americanists* 4(1976):299–325.

Eash, Neal S. "Natural and Ancient Agricultural Soils in the Colca Valley, Peru." M.A. thesis. Iowa State University, Ames, 1989.

Echeverría, Francisco Xavier. "Memoria de la Santa Iglesia de Arequipa." In *Memorias para la historia de Arequipa*, edited by Víctor M. Barriga, pp. 4:80–104. Arequipa: La Colmena, 1952.

Elliott, John. *Imperial Spain, 1469–1716*. New York: Mentor Books, 1966.

Espinosa Soriano, Waldemar. "El alcalde mayor indígena en el virreinato del Perú." *Anuario de Estudios Americanos* 17(1960):183–300.

———. "Los Huancas, aliados de la conquista." *Anales Científicos de la Universidad del Centro del Perú* 1(1972):5–407.

———. "Los señores étnicos de Chachapoyas y la alianza hispano-chacha." *Revista Histórica* 30(1967):224–332.

———, ed. *Visita hecha a la provincia de Chucuito por Garcí Diez de San Miguel en el año 1567*. Lima: Talleres Gráficos Quirós, 1964.

Estete, Miguel de. *Relación de la conquista del Perú* [ca. 1533], edited by Horacio H. Urteaga. Lima: Sanmartí, 1924.

Fagan, Brian. *Floods, Famines, and Emperors: El Niño and the Fate of Civilizations*. New York: Basic Books, 1999.

Fernández, Enrique, ed. *Monumenta Peruana VIII (1603–1604)*. Rome: Institutum Historicum Societatis Iesu, 1986.

Fisher, John R. *Government and Society in Colonial Peru: The Intendant System, 1784–1814*. London: University of London, 1970.

———. *Silver Mines and Silver Miners in Colonial Peru, 1776–1824*. Liverpool: Centre for Latin-American Studies, 1977.

Fisher, John R., Allan J. Kuethe, and Anthony McFarlane, eds. *Reforms and Insurrection in Bourbon New Granada and Peru*. Baton Rouge: Louisiana State University Press, 1990.

Flores Galindo, Alberto. *Buscando un Inca: Identidad y utopía en los Andes*. Lima: Instituto de Apoyo Agrario, 1987.

Flores Ochoa, Jorge A., ed. *Pastores de puna: Uywamichiq punarunakuna*. Lima: Instituto de Estudios Peruanos, 1977.

Fox, Robin. *Kinship and Marriage*. Middlesex, England: Penguin, 1973.

Fraser, Valerie. *The Architecture of Conquest: Building in the Viceroyalty of Peru, 1535–1635*. Cambridge: Cambridge University Press, 1990.

Fuentes, Manuel Atanasio, ed. *Memorias de los virreyes que han governado el Perú durante el tiempo del coloniaje español*. 6 vols. Lima: F. Bailly, 1859.

Gade, Daniel W. "Llama, alpaca y vicuña: Ficción y realidad." In *Pastores de puna: Uywamichiq punarunakuna*, edited by Jorge A. Flores Ochoa, pp. 113–20. Lima: Instituto de Estudios Peruanos, 1977.

Gade, Daniel W., and Mario Escobar. "Village Settlement and the Colonial Legacy in Southern Peru." *Geographical Review* 72(1982):430–49.

Galdos Rodríguez, Guillermo. *Comunidades prehispánicas de Arequipa*. Arequipa: Bustamante, 1987.

———. "Expansión de los Collaguas hacia el valle de Arequipa." *El Derecho* (Arequipa) 63(1984):81–152.

———. *Kuntisuyu: Lo que encontraron los españoles*. Arequipa: Bustamante, 1985.

Garcilaso de la Vega, El Inca. *Royal Commentaries of the Incas, and General History of Peru* [1609], translated and edited by Harold V. Livermore. Austin: University of Texas Press, 1966.

Garraín Villa, Luis J. *Llerena en el siglo XVI: La emigración a Indias*. Madrid: Ediciones Tuero, 1991.

Gelles, Paul H. "Channels of Power, Fields of Contention: The Politics and Ideology of Irrigation in an Andean Peasant Community." Ph.D. dissertation, Harvard University, Cambridge, Mass., 1990.

———. "Channels of Power, Fields of Contention: The Politics and Ideology of Irrigation in an Andean Peasant Community." In *Irrigation at High Altitudes: The Social Organization of Water Control Systems in the Andes*, pp. 233–73, edited by William P. Mitchell and David Guillet. Society for Latin American Anthropology Publication Series 12, 1994.

———. "Equilibrium and Extraction: Dual Organization in the Andes." *American Ethnologist* 22:4(1995): 710–42.

———. *Los hijos de Hualca Hualca: Historia de Cabanaconde*. Arequipa: Centro de Apoyo y Promoción al Desarrollo Agrario, 1988.

———. "Irrigation as a Cultural System: Introductory Remarks." In *Culture and Environment: A Fragile Coexistence*. Proceedings of the Twenty-fourth Annual Conference of the Archaeological Association of the University of Calgary, edited by Ross W. Jamieson, Sylvia A. Abonyi, and Neil A. Mirau, pp. 329–332. Calgary: University of Calgary Archaeological Association, 1993.

———. "The Political Ecology of Irrigation in an Andean Peasant Community." In *Canals and Communities: Small-Scale Irrigation Systems*, edited by Jonathan B. Mabry, pp. 88–115. Tucson: University of Arizona Press, 1996.

———. *Water and Power in Highland Peru: The Cultural Politics of Irrigation and Development*. New Brunswick, N.J.: Rutgers University Press, 2000.

Gibson, Charles. *Tlaxcala in the Sixteenth Century*. Stanford, Calif.: Stanford University Press, 1967.

Glave, Luis Miguel, and María Isabel Remy. *Estructura agraria y vida rural en una región an-*

dina: *Ollantaytambo entre los siglos XVI y XIX*. Cuzco: Centro de Estudios Regionales Andinos "Bartolomé de las Casas," 1983.

Gómez Rodríguez, Juan de la Cruz. "Historia agraria colonial en la provincia de Caylloma." In *Etnohistoria y antropología andina*, edited by Marcia Koth de Paredes and Amalia Castelli, pp. 17-28. Lima: Centro de Proyección Cristiana, 1978.

―――. "La reforma agraria en Caylloma." M.A. thesis, Pontificia Universidad Católica del Perú, Lima, 1978.

González, Fernando Luis. "Fences, Fields and Fodder: Enclosures in Lari, Valley del Colca, Southern Peru." M.A. thesis, University of Wisconsin, Madison, 1995.

González Holguín, Diego. *Gramatica y arte nveva dela lengva general de todo el Peru, llamada lengua Qquichua, o lengua del Inca*. Lima: Francisco del Canto, 1607.

―――. *Vocabulario de la lengua general de todo el Perú llamada Quechua* [1608]. Lima: Universidad Nacional Mayor de San Marcos, 1952.

González Rodríguez, Adolfo Luis. *La encomienda en Tucumán*. Seville: Diputación Provincial, 1984.

Griffiths, Nicholas. *The Cross and the Serpent: Religious Repression and Resurgence in Colonial Peru*. Norman: University of Oklahoma Press, 1996.

Gross, Daniel R., ed. *Peoples and Cultures of Native South America*. Garden City, N.Y.: Doubleday, 1973.

Guerreira, Bravo. "Polo de Ondegardo y Guaman Poma—Dos mentalidades ante un problema: La condición del indígena en el Perú en el siglo XVI." In *Homenaje a Gonzalo Fernández de Oviedo*, edited by Francisco de Solano and Fermín del Pino, pp. 2:275-89. Madrid: Instituto Gonzalo Fernández de Oviedo, 1983.

Guevara-Gil, Armando, and Frank Salomon. "A 'Personal Visit': Colonial Political Ritual and the Making of the Indians in the Andes." *Colonial Latin American Review* 3:1-2(1994):3-36.

Guillet, David. *Agrarian Reform and Peasant Economy in Southern Peru*. Columbia: University of Missouri Press, 1979.

―――. "Agricultural Intensification and Deintensification in Lari, Colca Valley, Southern Peru." *Research in Economic Anthropology* 8(1987):201-24.

―――. "Contemporary Agricultural Terracing in Lari, Colca Valley, Peru: Implications for Theories of Terrace Abandonment and Programs of Terrace Restoration." *British Archaeological Reports, International Series* 359(1987):193-206.

―――. *Covering Ground: Communal Water Management and the State in the Peruvian Highlands*. Ann Arbor: University of Michigan Press, 1992.

―――. "Terracing and Irrigation in the Peruvian Highlands." *Current Anthropology* 28(1987):409-30.

Gutiérrez, Ramón, Cristina Esteras, and Alejandro Málaga Medina. *El Valle del Colca (Arequipa): Cinco Siglos de Arquitectura y Urbanismo*. Buenos Aires: Libros de Hispanoamérica, Instituto Argentino de Investigaciones en Historia de la Arquitectura y del Urbanismo, 1986.

Haenke, Tadeo. *Descripción del Perú*. Lima: Lucero, 1901.

Hampe Martínez, Teodoro. *Don Pedro de la Gasca 1493–1567: Su obra política en España y América*. Lima: Pontificia Universidad Católica del Perú, 1989.

Hanke, Lewis. *The Spanish Struggle for Justice in the Conquest of America*. Boston: Little, Brown and Company 1965.

Harrison, Regina. *Signs, Songs, and Memory in the Andes: Translating Quechua Language and Culture*. Austin: University of Texas Press, 1989.

Hemming, John. *The Conquest of the Incas*. London: Sphere Books, 1972.

Henry E. Huntington Library and Art Gallery. *From Panama to Peru: The Conquest of Peru by the Pizarros. The Rebellion of Gonzalo Pizarro and the Pacification by La Gasca*. London: Magee Brothers, 1925.

Heras, Julián. *Aporte de los franciscanos a la evangelización del Perú*. Lima: Editora Latina, 1992.

———. "Los franciscanos en el valle del Colca (Arequipa) dos siglos y medio de evangelización." In *La evangelización del Perú, siglos XVI–XVII*, pp. 379–449. Arequipa: Actas del Congreso Peruano de Historia Eclesiástica, 1990.

Herskovits, Melville J. *Man and His Works: The Science of Cultural Anthropology*. New York: Knopf, 1948.

Honores, Renzo. "El *ius commune* en los Andes: Una aproximación a los informes del licenciado Polo Ondegardo (c. 1517–1575)." M.A. thesis, Pontificia Universidad Católica del Perú, Lima, 2005.

Hurley, William. "Highland Peasants and Rural Development in Southern Peru: The Colca Valley and the Majes Project." Ph.D. dissertation, Oxford University, 1978.

Hyslop, John. *The Inca Road System: Survey and general analysis*. Orlando, Fla.: Academic Press, 1984.

———. *Inca Settlement Planning*. Austin: University of Texas Press, 1990.

Isbell, Billie Jean. *To Defend Ourselves: Ecology and Ritual in an Andean Village*. Prospect Heights, Ill.: Waveland Press, 1978.

Jacobsen, Nils. *Mirages of Transition: The Peruvian Altiplano, 1780–1930*. Berkeley: University of California Press, 1993.

Jamieson, Ross W., Sylvia A. Abonyi, and Neil A. Mirau, eds. *Culture and Environment: A Fragile Coexistence. Proceedings of the Twenty-fourth Annual Conference of the Archaeological Association of the University of Calgary*. Calgary: University of Calgary Archaeological Association, 1993.

Jiménez de la Espada, Marcos, ed. *Relaciones geográficas de Indias, Perú*. 3 vols. Rev. ed. Madrid: Atlas, 1965.

Johnson, George R. *Peru from the Air*. New York: American Geographical Society, Special Publications no. 12, 1930.

Julien, Catherine J. *Condesuyo: The Political Division of Territory under Inca and Spanish Rule*. Bonn, Germany: Estudios Americanistas de Bonn, BAS 19, 1991.

———. "Finding a Fit: Archaeology and Ethnohistory of the Incas." In *Provincial Inca*, edited by M. Malpass, pp. 177–233. Iowa City: University of Iowa Press, 1993.

———. *Hatunqolla: A View of Inca Rule from the Lake Titicaca Region*. Berkeley: University of California Press, 1983.

Julien, Catherine J. "How Inca Decimal Administration Worked." *Ethnohistory* 35:3(1988): 257–77.

————. *Reading Inca History*. Iowa City: University of Iowa Press, 2000.

Kagan, Richard L. *Urban Images of the Hispanic World, 1493–1793*. New Haven, Conn.: Yale University Press, 2000.

Keatinge, Richard W., ed. *Peruvian Prehistory: An Overview of pre-Inca and Inca Society*. Cambridge: Cambridge University Press, 1988.

Keith, Robert G. *Conquest and Agrarian Change: The Emergence of the Hacienda System on the Peruvian Coast*. Cambridge, Mass.: Harvard University Press, 1976.

Kellogg, Susan, and Matthew Restall, eds. *Dead Giveaways: Indigenous Testaments of Colonial Mesoamerica and the Andes*. Salt Lake City: University of Utah Press, 1998.

Kinsbruner, Jay. *The Colonial Spanish-American City: Urban Life in the Age of Atlantic Capitalism*. Austin: University of Texas Press, 2005.

Kirchoff, Paul. "The Social and Political Organization of the Andean Peoples." In *Handbook of South American Indians*, edited by Julian H. Steward, pp. 5:293–311. 7 vols. Washington, D.C.: Bureau of American Ethnology Bulletins, no. 143, 1946–59.

Koth de Paredes, Marcia, and Amalia Castelli, eds. *Etnohistoria y antropología andina*. Lima: Centro de Proyección Cristiana, 1978.

Kubler, George. "The Quechua in the Colonial World." In *Handbook of South American Indians*, edited by Julian H. Steward, pp. 2:331–410. 7 vols. Washington, D.C.: Bureau of American Ethnology Bulletins, no. 143, 1946–59.

Lanning, Edward P. *Peru before the Incas*. Englewood Cliffs, N.J.: Prentice Hall, 1967.

Larson, Brooke. *Colonialism and Agrarian Transformation in Bolivia: Cochabamba, 1550–1900*. Princeton, N.J.: Princeton University Press, 1988. 2nd ed. Durham, N.C.: Duke University Press, 1998.

Las Casas, Bartolomé de. *Obras escogidas*, edited by Juan Pérez de Tudela Bueso. 2 vols. Madrid: Biblioteca de Autores Españoles, 1957.

Lastres, Juan B. *Historia de la medicina peruana*. 3 vols. Lima: Universidad Nacional Mayor de San Marcos, 1951.

Leguia y Martínez, Germán. *Historia de Arequipa*. 2 vols. Lima: El Lucero, 1913.

Leone, Mark P., ed. *Contemporary Archaeology: A Guide to Theory and Contributions*. Carbondale: Southern Illinois University Press, 1972.

Levillier, Roberto. *Don Francisco de Toledo: Supremo organizador del Perú*. Madrid: Espasa-Calpe, 1935.

————. *Don Francisco de Toledo, supremo organizador del Perú: Informaciones sobre los incas (1570–1572)*. Buenos Aires: [Imprenta Porter hnos.], 1940.

————, ed. *Gobernantes del Perú: Cartas y papeles, siglo XVI*. 14 vols. Madrid: Juan Pueyo, 1925.

Lévi-Strauss, Claude. *The Elementary Structures of Kinship*. Boston: Beacon Press, 1969.

Linares Delgado, L. R. "Cronología y relaciones culturales pre-hispánicas del Valle del Chili: Arequipa." Licentiate thesis, Universidad Católica Santa María, Arequipa, 1989.

Linares Málaga, Eloy. *Visita guiada para conocer el cañón más profundo del mundo*. Arequipa: Museo de la Universidad Nacional de San Agustín, 1983.

Lissón y Chaves, Emilio. *La Iglesia de España en el Perú*. 4 vols. Seville: [Católica Española], 1943–46.

Lockhart, James. *Men of Cajamarca: A Social and Biographical Study of the First Conquerors of Peru*. Austin: University of Texas Press, 1972.

———. *Spanish Peru, 1532–1560: A Colonial Society*. Madison: University of Wisconsin Press, 1968.

Lohmann Villena, Guillermo. *El corregidor de indios en el Perú bajo los Austrias*. Madrid: Ediciones Cultura Hispánica, 1957.

———. *Las minas de Huancavelica en los siglos XVI y XVII*. Seville: Escuela de Estudios Hispanoamericanos, 1949.

———. "La restitución por conquistadores y encomenderos: Un aspecto de la incidencia Lascasiana en el Perú." *Anuario de Estudios Americanos* 23(1966):21–89.

———, ed. *Francisco de Toledo: Disposiciones gubernativas para el virreinato del Perú, 1569–80*. 2 vols. Seville: Escuela de Estudios Hispanoamericanos, 1986–89.

López de Velasco, Juan. *Geografía y descripción universal de las Indias* [1568]. Madrid: Fortanet, 1894.

Loredo, Rafael. *Los repartos*. Lima: Miranda, 1958.

Loukotka, Cestmir. *Classification of South American Indian Languages*. Los Angeles: University of California, 1968.

Lumbreras, Luis G. *The Peoples and Cultures of Ancient Peru*. Washington, D.C.: Smithsonian Institution, 1974.

Mabry, Jonathan B., ed. *Canals and Communities: Small-Scale Irrigation Systems*. Tucson: University of Arizona Press, 1996.

MacCormack, Sabine. "Pachacuti: Miracles, Punishments, and Last Judgment. Visionary Past and Prophetic Future in Early Colonial Peru." *American Historical Review* 93(1988):960–1006.

———. *Religion in the Andes: Vision and Imagination in Early Colonial Peru*. Princeton, N.J.: Princeton University Press, 1991.

———. "Time, Space, and Ritual Action: The Inka and Christian Calendars in Early Colonial Peru." In *Native Traditions in the Postconquest World*, edited by Elizabeth Hill Boone and Tom Cummins, pp. 295–343. Washington, D.C.: Dumbarton Oaks, 1998.

Málaga, Alfredo Simón Bernal. "Danzas de las etnias collaguas y colonias: Un estudio en la cuenca del Colca, Caylloma." M.A. thesis, Universidad Mayor de San Agustín, Arequipa, 1983.

Málaga Medina, Alejandro. "Los Collaguas en la historia de Arequipa en el siglo XVI." In *Collaguas I*, edited by Franklin Pease, pp. 93–130. Lima: Pontificia Universidad Católica del Perú, 1977.

———. "Consideraciones económicas sobre la visita de la provincia de Arequipa." In *Tasa de la visita general de Francisco de Toledo*, edited by Noble David Cook, pp. 299–311. Lima: Universidad Nacional Mayor de San Marcos, 1975.

———. *Historia general de Arequipa* . Arequipa: Fundación M. J. Bustamante de la Fuente, 1990.

———. "Las reducciones en el Perú (1532–1600)." *Historia y Cultura* 8(1974):141–72.

Málaga Medina, Alejandro. *Reducciones toledanas en Arequipa (pueblos tradicionales)*. Arequipa: PUBLIUNSA, 1989.

Málaga Medina, Alejandro, and Eusebio Quiroz. "La rebelión de Túpac Amaru en Arequipa." *Historia* (Arequipa), 2(1983):98–137.

Mallon, Florencia E. *The Defense of Community in Peru's Central Highlands: Peasant Struggle and Capitalist Transition, 1860–1940*. Princeton, N.J.: Princeton University Press, 1983.

———. *Peasant and Nation: The Making of Postcolonial Mexico and Peru*. Berkeley: University of California Press, 1995.

Malpass, Michael. "Prehistoric Agricultural Terracing at Chijra, Coporaque." In *The Cultural Ecology, Archaeology, and History of Terracing and Terrace Abandonment in the Colca Valley of Southern Peru: Technical Report to the National Science Foundation and the National Geographic Society*, edited by William M. Denevan, pp. 1:150–66. Madison: University of Wisconsin Press, 1986.

Malpass, Michael A., and P. de la Vera Cruz Chávez. "Ceramic Sequence from Chijra, Colca Valley, Peru." In *The Cultural Ecology, Archaeology, and History of Terracing and Terrace Abandonment in the Colca Valley of Southern Peru: Technical Report to the National Science Foundation and the National Geographic Society*, edited by William M. Denevan, pp. 2:204–33. Madison: University of Wisconsin Press, 1988.

———. "Cronología y secuencia de la cerámica de Chijra, valle del Colca." *Gaceta Arqueológica Andina* 18/19(1990):41–57.

Manrique, Nelson. *Colonialismo y pobreza campesina: Caylloma y el valle del Colca, siglos XVI–XX*. Lima: DESCO, 1985.

Mariátegui, José Carlos. *7 ensayos de interpretación de la realidad peruana*. Caracas: Biblioteca Ayacucho, 1979.

Márquez, M. G., and R. B. Montoro. "Arqueología del valle de Majes." *Gaceta Arqueológica Andina* 18/19(1990):25–40.

Marsilli, María N. "God and Evil in the Gardens of the Andean South: Mid-colonial Rural Religion in the Diocese of Arequipa." Ph.D. dissertation, Emory University, Atlanta, 2002.

———. " 'I Heard It through the Grapevine': Analysis of an Anti-secularization Initiative in the Sixteenth-Century Arequipan Countryside, 1584–1600." *Americas* 61(2005): 647–72.

Martin, Deborah. "Archaeology of Terraces and Settlement at Chilacota, Coporaque." In *The Cultural Ecology, Archaeology, and History of Terracing and Terrace Abandonment in the Colca Valley of Southern Peru: Technical Report to the National Science Foundation and the National Geographic Society*, edited by William M. Denevan, pp. 221–34. Madison: University of Wisconsin Press, 1986.

Martín, Luis. *Daughters of the Conquistadores: Women of the Viceroyalty of Peru*. Albuquerque: University of New Mexico Press, 1983.

Martínez, Santiago. *Fundadores de Arequipa*. Arequipa: Tipografía La Luz, 1936.

Masuda, Shozo, Izumi Shimada, and Craig Morris, eds. *Andean Ecology and Civilization: An Interdisciplinary Perspective on Andean Ecological Complementarity*. Tokyo: University of Tokyo Press, 1985.

Matienzo, Juan de. *Gobierno del Perú (1567)*, edited by Guillermo Lohmann Villena. Paris: Institut Français d'Etudes Andines, 1967.

Matto de Turner, Clorinda. *Birds without a Nest: A Story of Indian Life and Priestly Oppression in Peru*. Austin: University of Texas Press, 1996.

Mayer, Enrique. "Beyond the Nuclear Family." In *Andean Kinship and Marriage*, edited by Ralph Bolton and Enrique Mayer, pp. 60–80. Washington, D.C.: Special Publication of the American Anthropological Association no. 7, 1977.

————. *A Tribute to the Household: Domestic Economy and the Encomienda in Colonial Peru*. Austin: University of Texas Institute of Latin American Studies, 1982.

McCamant, Kris Ann. "The Organization of Agricultural Production in Coporaque, Peru." M.A. thesis. Berkeley: University of California, 1986.

Means, Philip Ainsworth. *Biblioteca andina*. Detroit: Blaine Ethridge, 1973.

————. *Fall of the Inca Empire and the Spanish Rule in Peru, 1530–1720*. New York: Charles Scribner's Sons, 1932.

Melville, Elinor G. K. *A Plague of Sheep: Environmental Consequences of the Conquest of Mexico*. New York: Cambridge University Press, 1994.

Mendiburu, Manuel. *Diccionario histórico biográfico del Perú*. 12 vols. Lima: Imprenta "Enrique Palacios," 1931–34.

Mendoza, Diego de. *Chronica de la Provincia de San Antonio de los Charcas* [Madrid, 1664]. La Paz: Editorial Casa Municipal de la Cultura Franz Tamayo, 1976.

Menzel, Dorothy. "Archaism and Revival on the South Coast of Peru." In *Peoples and Cultures of Native South America*, edited by Daniel R. Gross, pp. 19–27. Garden City, N.Y.: Doubleday, 1973.

————. "The Inca Occupation of the South Coast of Peru." *Southwestern Journal of Anthropology* 15(1959):125–42.

Metraux, Alfred. *The History of the Incas*. New York: Schocken Books, 1970.

Miller, Naomi, and Kathyrn L. Gleason, eds. *The Archaeology of Garden and Field*. Philadelphia: University of Pennsylvania Press, 1994.

Millones, Luis. "Los ganados del señor: Mecanismos de poder en las comunidades andinas en los siglos XVIII y XIX." *América Indígena* 39(1979):107–43.

————. "Nuevos aspectos del Taki Onqoy." In *Ideología mesiánica del mundo andino*, edited by Juan Ossio, pp. 95–101. Lima: Ignacio Prado Pastor, 1973.

————, ed. *El retorno de las huacas: Estudios y documentos sobre el Taki Onqoy. Siglo XVI*. Lima: Instituto de Estudios Peruanos, 1990.

Mills, Kenneth. *Idolatry and Its Enemies: Colonial Andean Religion and Extirpation, 1640–1750*. Princeton, N.J.: Princeton University Press, 1997.

Mitchell, William P., and David Guillet, eds. *Irrigation at High Altitudes: The Social Organization of Water Control Systems in the Andes*. Arlington, Va.: Society for Latin American Anthropology Publication Series 12, 1994.

Molina, Cristóbal de. *Relación de las fábulas y ritos de los incas* [ca. 1575]. Lima: Sanmartí, 1916.

Montoya, Rodrigo. "Identidad étnica y luchas agrarias en los Andes peruanos." In *Identidades andinas y lógicas del campesinado*, edited by Lucy T. Briggs, et al, pp. 247–78. Lima: Mosca Azul, 1986.

Mörner, Magnus, and Efraín Trelles. "A Test of Causal Interpretations of the Túpac Amaru Rebellion." In *Resistance, Rebellion, and Consciousness in the Andean Peasant World, 18th to 20th Centuries*, edited by Steve J. Stern, pp. 94–109. Madison: University of Wisconsin Press, 1987.

Morris, Craig. "State Settlements in Tawantinsuyu: A strategy of compulsory urbanism." In *Contemporary Archaeology: A Guide to Theory and Contributions*, edited by M. P. Leone, pp. 393–401. Carbondale: Southern Illinois University, 1972.

Moseley, Michael E. *The Incas and Their Ancestors: The Archaeology of Peru*. New York: Thames and Hudson, 1992.

Muñoz y Manzano, Cipriano. *Bibliografía española de lenguas indígenas de América*. Madrid: Atlas, 1977.

Murdock, George Peter. *Social Structure*. New York: Macmillan, 1967.

Murra, John. "Andean Societies before 1532." In *The Cambridge History of Latin America*, edited by Leslie Bethell, pp. 1:59–90. 11 vols. Cambridge: Cambridge University Press, 1984–95.

———. *The Economic Organization of the Inka State*. Greenwich, Conn.: JAI Press, 1980.

———. *Formaciones económicas y políticas del mundo andino*. Lima: Instituto de Estudios Peruanos, 1975.

———. "Los olleros del Inka: Hacia una historia y arqueología del Qollasuyu." In *Historia, problema y promesa: Homenaje a Jorge Basadre*, edited by F. Miro Quesada, F. Pease G. Y. and D. Sobrevilla, pp. 415–23. Lima: Pontificia Universidad Católica del Perú, 1978.

———, ed. *Visita de la provincia de León de Huánuco* [1562]. 2 vols. Lima: Villanueva, 1967, 1972.

Murra, John, and Mercedes López-Baralt, eds. *Las cartas de Arguedas*. Lima: Pontificia Universidad Católica del Perú, 1996.

Murúa, Martín de. *Historia de los incas, reyes del Perú*, edited by Horacio H. Urteaga and Carlos A. Romero. Lima: Sanmartí, 1925.

Navarrete, Martín Fernández de, ed. *Colección de documentos inéditos para la historia de España*. 112 vols. Madrid, 1842–95.

Neira Avendaño, Máximo. "Los Collaguas." Ph.D. dissertation, Universidad de Arequipa, 1961.

———. "Excavaciones arqueológicas en las ruinas de Chishra (Chijra), Coporaque." In *The Cultural Ecology, Archaeology, and History of Terracing and Terrace Abandonment in the Colca Valley of Southern Peru: Technical Report to the National Science Foundation and the National Geographic Society*, edited by William M. Denevan, pp. 1:167–97. Madison: University of Wisconsin Press, 1986.

———. "Prehistoria de la provincia de Caylloma." *Humanitas* (Arequipa) 2(1964):177–99.

Niles, Susan A. *The Shape of Inca History: Narrative and Architecture in an Andean Empire*. Iowa City: University of Iowa Press, 1999.

Ocaña, Diego de. *A través de la América del Sur*. Madrid: Historia 16, 1987.

Oré, Luis Gerónimo de. *Relación de la vida y milagros de San Francisco Solano*, edited by Noble David Cook. Lima: Pontificia Universidad Católica del Perú, 1998.

————. *Ritvale, sev manvale Pervanum et forma brevis . . .*, *1607*. Naples: Iacobum Carlinum y Constantinum Vitalem, 1607.

————. *Symbolo catholico indiano*. Lima: Ricardo, 1598.

Ossio, Juan, ed. *Ideología mesiánica del mundo andino*. Lima: Ignacio Prado Pastor, 1973.

Pachacuti Yamqui, Juan de Santa Cruz. *Historia de los incas*. Lima: Sanmartí, 1927.

Paerregaard, Karsten. *Linking Separate Worlds: Urban Migrants and Rural Lives in Peru*. Oxford: Berg, 1997.

Palomino Flores, Salvador. "Duality in the Socio-cultural Organization of Several Andean Populations." *Folk* 13(1971):65–88.

Pärssinen, Martti, and A. Siiriäinen. "Inka-style Ceramics and Their Chronological Relationship to the Inka Expansion in the Southern Lake Titicaca Area (Bolivia)." *Latin American Antiquity* 8:3(1997):255–71.

Patterson, Thomas C. *The Inca Empire: The Formation and Disintegration of a Pre-Capitalist State*. Oxford: Berg, 1991.

Paulsen, Allison C. "Environment and Empire: Climatic Factors in Prehistoric Andean Culture Change." *World Archaeology* 8(1976):121–32.

Pease García Yrigoyen, Franklin. "Ayllu y parcialidad: Reflexiones sobre el caso de Collaguas." In *Etnohistoria y antropología andina*, edited by Amalia Castelli, Marcia Koth de Paredes, and Mariana Mould de Pease, pp. 19–34. Lima: Centro de Proyección Cristiana, 1981.

————. "Collaguas: Una etnia del siglo XVI. Problemas iniciales." In *Collaguas I*, edited by Franklin Pease, pp. 131–67. Lima: Pontificia Universidad Católica del Perú, 1977.

————. *Las crónicas y los Andes*. Lima: Fondo de Cultura Económica, 1995.

————. *El dios creador andino*. Lima: Mosca Azul, 1973.

————. "Inkarrí en Collaguas." In *Etnohistoria y antropología andina*, edited by Marcia Koth de Paredes and Amalia Castelli, pp. 237–40. Lima: Centro de Proyección Cristiana, 1978.

————. *Del Tawantinsuyu a la historia del Perú*. Lima: Instituto de Estudios Peruanos, 1978.

————. *Los últimos incas del Cuzco*. Lima: Villanueva, 1972.

————, ed. *Collaguas I*. Lima: Pontificia Universidad Católica del Perú, 1977.

Pérez de Tudela y Bueso, Juan, ed. *Crónicas del Perú*. 5 vols. Madrid: Atlas, 1964–65.

————, ed. *Documentos relativos a don Pedro de la Gasca y a Gonzalo Pizarro*. 2 vols. Madrid: Real Academia de la Historia, 1964.

Pérez-Mallaina, Pablo E., and Bibiano Torres Ramírez. *La Armada del Mar del Sur*. Seville: Escuela de Estudios Hispanoamericanos, 1987.

Peru. Dirección Nacional de Estadística. *Censo nacional de población y ocupación, 1940*. 9 vols. Lima: Imprenta Torres Aguirre, 1944–49.

————. *Resumen del censo general de habitantes del Perú hecho en 1876*. Lima: Imprenta del Estado, 1878.

————. *Sexto censo nacional de población levantado el 2 de julio de 1961: Resultados de primera prioridad*. Lima: [n.p.], 1964.

Polo, José Toribio. "Apuntes sobre las epidemias del Perú." *Revista Histórica* 2(1907):50–109.

————. "Luis Gerónimo de Oré." *Revista Histórica* 2(1913):74–91.

Poma de Ayala, Felipe Guaman. *El primer nueva corónica y buen gobierno* [ca. 1613], edited by John V. Murra and Rolena Adorno. 3 vols. Mexico City: Siglo Veintiuno, 1980.

Porras Barrenechea, Raúl. *Los cronistas del Perú (1528–1650) y otros ensayos*, edited by Franklin Pease G. Y. Lima: Banco de Crédito del Perú, 1986.

————, ed. *Cartas del Perú (1524–1543)*. Lima: Sociedad de Bibliófilos Peruanos, 1959.

————, ed. *Las relaciones primitivas de la conquista del Perú*. 2nd ed. Lima: Minerva, 1967.

Puente Brunke, José de la. *Encomienda y encomenderos en el Perú: Estudio social y político de una institución colonial*. Seville: Diputación Provincial, 1992.

Quiroz, Eusebio. "La rebelión de 1780 en Arequipa." In *La emancipación americana en Bolivia y Perú*, edited by Carlos Urquizo Sossa, pp. 3:13–87. La Paz, 1976.

Raleigh, Charles P. "Demographic Analysis of the 1591 Colca Valley Census." In *The Cultural Ecology, Archaeology, and History of Terracing and Terrace Abandonment in the Colca Valley of Southern Peru: Technical Report to the National Science Foundation and the National Geographic Society*, edited by William M. Denevan, pp. 1:525–41. Madison: University of Wisconsin Press, 1986.

Ramírez, Susan Elizabeth. *To Feed and Be Fed: The Cosmological Bases of Authority and Identity in the Andes*. Stanford, Calif.: Stanford University Press, 2005.

Ramos Gavilán, Alonso. *Historia del santuario de nuestra señora de Copacabana* [1621]. Lima: Ignacio Prado Pastor, 1988.

Rappaport, Joanne, and Tom Cummins. "Between Images and Writing: The Ritual of the King's *Quillca*." *Colonial Latin American Review* 7(1998):7–32.

Reinhard, Johan. "Research Update: New *Mummies*." *National Geographic* 194:1(July 1998): 128–35.

Reinhard, Johan, and Stephen Alvarez. "Peru's Ice Maidens: Unwrapping the Secrets." *National Geographic* 189:6(June 1996):62–81.

Rénique, José Luis, and Trelles, Efraín. "Aproximación demográfica, Yanque-Collaguas 1591." In *Collaguas I*, edited by Franklin Pease, pp. 169–89. Lima: Pontificia Universidad Católica del Perú, 1977.

Rensch, Carolyn. "A Portrait of Yanque, Peru: The Changing Roles and Status of Women." M.A. thesis, University of Texas, Austin, 1983.

Ricardo, Antonio. *Vocabulario y phrasis en la lengua general de los indios del Perú, llamada Quichua* [1586]. Lima: Universidad Nacional Mayor de San Marcos, 1951.

Rick, John W. "The Character and Context of Highland Preceramic Society." In *Peruvian Prehistory: An Overview of pre-Inca and Inca Society*, edited by Richard W. Keatinge, pp. 3–40. Cambridge: Cambridge University Press, 1988.

Rivera Martínez, Edgardo, ed. *Imagen y leyenda de Arequipa: Antología 1540–1990*. Lima: Fundación M. J. Bustamante de la Fuente, 1990.

Robinson, David J., ed. *Collaguas II: Lari Collaguas. Economía, sociedad y población, 1604–1605*. Lima: Pontificia Universidad Católica del Perú, 2003.

————, ed. *Collaguas III: Yanque Collaguas: Sociedad, economía y población, 1604–1617*. Lima: Pontificia Universidad Católica del Perú, 2006.

————, ed. *Studies in Spanish American Population History*. Boulder, Colo.: Westview Press, 1981.

Rojo Vega, Anastasio. *Enfermos y sanadores en la Castilla del siglo XVI*. Valladolid, Spain: Universidad de Valladolid, 1993.

Romero, Carlos A. "Libro de la visita general del Virrey Francisco de Toledo." *Revista Histórica* 7(1924):115–216.

Rostworowski de Diez Canseco, María. *Curacas y sucesiones: Costa norte*. Lima: Imprenta Minerva, 1961.

———. *Doña Francisca Pizarro: Una ilustre mestiza, 1534–1598*. Lima: Instituto de Estudios Peruanos, 1989.

———. *Etnia y sociedad: Costa peruana prehispánica*. Lima: Instituto de Estudios Peruanos, 1977.

———. *Historia del Tahuantinsuyu*. Lima: Instituto de Estudios Peruanos, 1988.

———. *History of the Inca Realm*. New York: Cambridge University Press, 1999.

———. *Recursos naturales renovables y pesca: Siglos XVI y XVII*. Lima: Instituto de Estudios Peruanos, 1981.

———. "Repartimiento de doña Beatriz Coya, en el valle de Yucay." *Historia y Cultura* 4(1970):153–267.

———. "La tasa ordenada por el Licenciado Pedro de la Gasca (1549)." *Revista Histórica* 34(1985):53–102.

Rowe, John Howland. "Inca Culture at the Time of the Spanish Conquest." In *Handbook of South American Indians*, edited by Julian H. Steward, 2:183–330. 7 vols. Washington, D.C.: Bureau of American Ethnology Bulletins, no. 143, 1946–59.

———. "The Incas under Spanish Colonial Institutions." *Hispanic American Historical Review* 37(1957):155–99.

Rozas Bonuccelli, Fernando. *Plantas alimenticias en el antiguo Perú*. Lima: CONCYTEC, 1989.

Salinas y Cordova, Fray Buenaventura de. *Memorial de las historias del Nvevo Mvndo Perv* [1630]. Lima: Universidad Nacional Mayor de San Marcos, 1957.

Salles-Reese, Verónica. *From Viracocha to the Virgin of Copacabana: Representation of the Sacred at Lake Titicaca*. Austin: University of Texas Press, 1997.

Salomon, Frank. "Ancestor Cults and Resistance to the State in Arequipa, ca. 1748–1754." In *Resistance, Rebellion, and Consciousness in the Andean Peasant World, 18th to 20th Centuries*, edited by Steve J. Stern, pp. 148–65. Madison: University of Wisconsin Press, 1987.

———. *Native Lords of Quito in the Age of the Inca*. Cambridge: Cambridge University Press, 1986.

Sánchez-Albornoz, Nicolás. *El indio en el Alto Perú a fines del siglo XVII*. Lima: Seminario de Historia Rural Andina, 1973.

———. *Indios y tributos en el Alto Perú*. Lima: Instituto de Estudios Peruanos, 1978.

———, ed. *Población y mano de obra en América Latina*. Madrid: Alianza Americana, 1985.

Sánchez Bello, Ismael. "El gobierno del Perú, 1550–1564." *Anuario de Estudios Americanos* 17(1960):407–524.

Sánchez-Moreno Bayarri, Víctor. *Arequipa colonial y las fuentes de su historia: Estudio crítico*. Lima: Aserprensa, 1987.

Sandor, Jonathan A. "Initial Investigation of Soils in Agricultural Terraces in the Colca Valley, Peru." *British Archaeological Reports, International Series* 359(1987):163–92.

Sandor, Jonathan A. "Long-term Effects of Prehistoric Agriculture on Soils: Examples from New Mexico and Peru." In *Soils in Archaeology: Landscape Evolution and Human Occupation*, edited by V. T. Holliday, pp. 217-45. Washington, D.C.: Smithsonian Institution Press, 1992.

――――. "Report on Soils in Agricultural Terraces in the Colca Valley." In *The Cultural Ecology, Archaeology, and History of Terracing and Terrace Abandonment in the Colca Valley of Southern Peru: Technical Report to the National Science Foundation and the National Geographic Society*, edited by William M. Denevan, pp. 1:235-75. Madison: University of Wisconsin Press, 1986.

――――. "Soil Conservation and Redevelopment of Agricultural Terraces in the Colca Valley, Peru." *Journal of the Washington Academy of Sciences* 77(1987):149-54.

Sanford, Patricia R. "Pollen Analysis of Agricultural Terrace Soils from Coporaque." In *The Cultural Ecology, Archaeology, and History of Terracing and Terrace Abandonment in the Colca Valley of Southern Peru: Technical Report to the National Science Foundation and the National Geographic Society*, edited by William M. Denevan, pp. 1:276-90. Madison: University of Wisconsin Press, 1986.

Santillán, Hernando de. *Relación de su gobierno* [1563]. Lima: Sanmartí, 1927.

Santisteban Ochoa, Julián. *Los obrajes en el virreinato del Perú*. Lima: Museo Nacional de Historia, 1964.

Santo Tomás, Domingo de. *Grammática o arte de la lengua general de los indios de los reynos del Perú*. Lima: Universidad Nacional Mayor de San Marcos, 1951.

――――. *Lexicón o vocabulario de la lengua general del Peru* [1560]. Lima: Universidad Nacional Mayor de San Marcos, 1951.

Sarmiento de Gamboa, Pedro. *Segunda parte de la historia general, llamada Indica* [1572]. Buenos Aires: Emecé, 1942.

Schäfer, Ernst. *El Consejo Real y Supremo de las Indias*. 2 vols. Seville: Imp. M. Carmona, 1935-47.

Seed, Patricia. *Ceremonies of Possession in Europe's Conquest of the New World, 1492-1640*. Cambridge: Cambridge University Press, 1995.

Seltzer, Geoffrey O., and Christine A. Hastorf. "Climatic Change and Its Effect on Prehispanic Agriculture in the Central Peruvian Andes." *Journal of Field Archaeology* 17(1990):397-414.

Sempat Assadourian, Carlos. "La crisis demográfica del siglo XVI y la transición del Tawantinsuyu al sistema mercantil colonial." In *Población y mano de obra en América Latina*, edited by Nicolás Sánchez-Albornoz, pp. 69-93. Madrid: Alianza Americana, 1985.

――――. "La despoblación indígena en el Perú y Nueva España durante el siglo XVI y la formación de la economía colonial." *Historia Mexicana* 38(1989):419-53.

――――. *El sistema de la economía colonial: Mercado interno, regiones y espacio económico*. Lima: Instituto de Estudios Peruanos, 1982.

Shea, Daniel E. "The Achoma Archaeology Project." In *The Cultural Ecology, Archaeology, and History of Terracing and Terrace Abandonment in the Colca Valley of Southern Peru: Technical Report to the National Science Foundation and the National Geographic Society*, edited by William M. Denevan, pp. 1:313–62. Madison: University of Wisconsin Press, 1986.

———. "Discussion of the Prehistoric Settlement at Achoma." In *Achoma Archaeology: A Study of Terrace Irrigation in Peru*, edited by Daniel E. Shea, pp. 49–58. Beloit, Wisc.: Logan Museum of Anthropology, 1997.

———. "An Hypothesis Concerning Terrace Construction in the Colca Valley." In *The Cultural Ecology, Archaeology, and History of Terracing and Terrace Abandonment in the Colca Valley of Southern Peru: Technical Report to the National Science Foundation and the National Geographic Society*, edited by William M. Denevan, pp. 1:376–85. Madison: University of Wisconsin Press, 1986.

———. "Preliminary Discussion of Prehistoric Settlement at Achoma." In *The Cultural Ecology, Archaeology, and History of Terracing and Terrace Abandonment in the Colca Valley of Southern Peru: Technical Report to the National Science Foundation and the National Geographic Society*, edited by William M. Denevan, pp. 1:363–75. Madison: University of Wisconsin Press, 1986.

———. "Preliminary Discussion of Prehistoric Settlement and Terracing at Achoma in the Colca Valley, Peru." *British Archaeological Reports, International Series* 359(1987): 67–88.

———, ed. *Achoma Archaeology: A Study of Terrace Irrigation in Peru*. Beloit, Wisc.: Logan Museum of Anthropology, 1997.

Shippee, Robert. "Air Adventures in Peru." *National Geographic Magazine* 63:1(1933):80–120.

———. "A Forgotten Valley of Peru." *National Geographic Magazine* 65:1(1934):110–32.

———. "The Great Wall of Peru and Other Aerial Photographic Studies by the Shippee-Johnson Peruvian Expedition." *Geographical Review* 22(1932):1–29.

———. "Lost Valleys of Peru: Results of the Shippee-Johnson Peruvian Expedition." *Geographical Review* 22(1932):562–81.

Silverblatt, Irene. *Moon, Sun, and Witches: Gender Ideologies and Class in Inca and Colonial Peru*. Princeton, N.J.: Princeton University Press, 1987.

Smith, C. T. "Depopulation of the Central Andes in the 16th Century." *Current Anthropology* 11(1970):453–64.

Spalding, Karen. *De indio a campesino: Cambios en la estructura social del Perú colonial*. Lima: Instituto de Estudios Peruanos, 1974.

———. *Huarochirí: An Andean Society under Inca and Spanish Rule*. Stanford, Calif.: Stanford University Press, 1984.

Stanish, Charles. *Ancient Andean Political Economy*. Austin: University of Texas Press, 1992.

———. "A Late Pre-Hispanic Ceramic Chronology for the Upper Moquegua Valley, Peru." Chicago: Fieldiana 16 (n.s.), Field Museum of Natural History, 1991.

Stern, Steve J. "The Age of Andean Insurrection, 1742–1782: A Reappraisal." In *Resistance, Rebellion, and Consciousness in the Andean Peasant World: 18th to 20th Centuries*, edited by Steve J. Stern, pp. 34–93. Madison: University of Wisconsin Press, 1987.

———. *Peru's Indian Peoples and the Challenge of Spanish Colonialism: Huamanga to 1640*. Madison: University of Wisconsin Press, 1982.

Stern, Steve J., ed. *Resistance, Rebellion, and Consciousness in the Andean Peasant World: 18th to 20th Centuries*. Madison: University of Wisconsin Press, 1987.

Steward, Julian H., ed. *Handbook of South American Indians*. 7 vols. Washington, D.C.: Bureau of American Ethnology Bulletins, no. 143, 1946–59.

Szeminski, Jan. "Why Kill the Spaniard? New Perspectives on Andean Insurrectionary Ideology in the 18th Century." In *Resistance, Rebellion, and Consciousness in the Andean Peasant World, 18th to 20th Centuries*, edited by Steve J. Stern, pp. 166–92. Madison: University of Wisconsin Press, 1987.

Tandeter, Enrique. "Forced and Free Labour in Late Colonial Potosí." *Past and Present* 93(1981):98–136.

Thompson, Lonnie G., Mary E. David, and Ellen Moseley-Thompson. "Glacial Records of Global Climate: A 1500-Year Tropical Ice Core Record of Climate." *Human Ecology* 22(1994):83–95.

Thurner, Mark. *From Two Republics to One Divided: Contradictions of Postcolonial Nationmaking in Andean Peru*. Durham, N.C.: Duke University Press, 1997.

Tibesar, Antonine, O.F.M. *Franciscan Beginnings in Colonial Peru*. Washington, D.C.: Academy of American Franciscan History, 1953.

Tord, Luis Enrique. *Templos coloniales del Colca-Arequipa*. Lima: Papelera Atlas, 1983.

Torres de Mendoza, L., ed. *Colección de documentos inéditos relativos al descubrimiento, conquista y colonización de las posesiones españolas en América y Oceanía*. 42 vols. Madrid: M. B. de Quirós, 1864–84.

Treacy, John M. "Agricultural Terraces in Peru's Colca Valley: Promises and Problems of an Ancient Technology." In *Fragile Lands of Latin America: Strategies for Sustainable Development*, edited by John O. Browder, pp. 209–29. Boulder, Colo.: Westview Press, 1989.

———. "Building and Rebuilding Agricultural Terraces in the Colca Valley of Peru." *Yearbook, Conference of Latin Americanist Geographers* 13(1987):51–57.

———. *Las chacras de Coporaque: Andenería y riego en el Valle del Colca*. Lima: Instituto de Estudios Peruanos, 1994.

———. "An Ecological Model for Estimating Prehistoric Population at Coporaque." In *The Cultural Ecology, Archaeology, and History of Terracing and Terrace Abandonment in the Colca Valley of Southern Peru: Technical Report to the National Science Foundation and the National Geographic Society*, edited by William M. Denevan, pp. 1:88–98. Madison: University of Wisconsin Press, 1986.

———. "Teaching Water: Hydraulic Management and Terracing in Coporaque, in the Colca Valley, Peru." In *Irrigation at High Altitudes: The Social Organization of Water Control Systems in the Andes*, edited by William P. Mitchell and David Guillet, pp. 99–114. Arlington, Va.: Society for Latin American Anthropology Publication Series 12, 1994.

Treacy, John M., and William M. Denevan. "The Creation of Cultivable Land through Terracing." In *The Archaeology of Garden and Field*, edited by Naomi F. Miller and Kathryn L. Gleason, pp. 91–110. Philadelphia: University of Pennsylvania Press, 1994.

———. "Survey of Abandoned Terraces, Canals, and Houses at Chijra, Coporaque." In *The Cultural Ecology, Archaeology, and History of Terracing and Terrace Abandonment in the Colca Valley of Southern Peru: Technical Report to the National Science Foundation and the National Geographic Society*, edited by William M. Denevan, pp. 1:198–220. Madison: University of Wisconsin Press, 1986.

Trelles Arestegui, Efraín. *Lucas Martínez Vegazo: Funcionamiento de una encomienda peruana inicial*. Lima: Pontificia Universidad Católica del Perú, 1983.

Ugarte y Ugarte, Eduardo. "Los caciques de Chucuito y Arequipa contra la perpetuidad de la encomienda." *Hombre y Mundo* (Arequipa) 1(1966):30–50.

Ulloa Mogollón, Juan de. "Relación de la provincia de los Collaguas (1586)." In *Relaciones geográficas de Indias, Perú*, edited by Marcos Jiménez de la Espada, pp. 1:326–33. 3 vols. Madrid: Atlas, 1965.

Urquizo Sossa, Carlos, ed. *La emancipación americana en Bolivia y Perú*. La Paz: Editorial Casa Municipal de la Cultura Franz Tamayo, 1976.

Urton, Gary. *At the Crossroads of the Earth and the Sky: An Andean Cosmology*. Austin: University of Texas Press, 1981.

————. *The History of a Myth: Pacariqtambo and the Origin of the Inkas*. Austin: University of Texas Press, 1990.

————. "From Knots to Narratives: Reconstructing the Art of Historical Record Keeping in the Andes from Spanish Transcriptions of Inka *Khipus*." *Ethnohistory* 45(1998):409–38.

————. *The Social Life of Numbers: A Quechua Ontology of Numbers and Philosophy of Arithmetic*. Austin: University of Texas Press, 1997.

U.S., Library of Congress. *The Harkness Collection in the Library of Congress: Calendar of Manuscripts Concerning Peru, 1531–1651*. Washington, D.C., 1932.

Valderrama Fernández, Ricardo, and Carmen Escalante Gutiérrez. *Del Tata Mallku a la Mama Pacha: Riego, sociedad y ritos en los Andes Peruanos*. Lima: DESCO, 1988.

————. *La doncella sacrificada: Mitos del Valle del Colca*. Lima: Universidad Nacional de San Agustín and Instituto Francés de Estudios Andinos, 1997.

————. "Sistemas de riego y organización social en el valle del Colca — Caso Yanque." *Allpanchis* 27(1986):179–202.

Van Buren, M. "Community and Empire in Southern Peru: The Site of Torata Alta under Spanish Rule." Ph.D. dissertation, University of Arizona, Tucson, 1993.

Vargas Ugarte, Rubén. *Historia de la Iglesia en el Perú*. 5 vols. Vol. 1, Lima: Imprenta Santa María, 1954. Vols. 2–5, Burgos: Imprenta de Aldecoa, 1959–62.

————. *Historia general del Perú*. 10 vols. Lima: Editor Carlos Milla Batres, 1981–84.

————, ed. *Concilios Limenses*. 3 vols. Lima: Tipografía Peruana, 1954.

Varón Gabai, Rafael. *Curacas y encomenderos: Acomodamiento nativo en Huaraz, siglos XVI y XVII*. Lima: P. L. Villanueva, 1980.

————. *Francisco Pizarro and His Brothers: The Illusion of Power in Sixteenth-Century Peru*. Norman: University of Oklahoma Press, 1997.

Vázquez de Espinosa, Antonio. *Compendio y descripción de las Indias occidentales*. Washington, D.C.: Smithsonian Miscellaneous Collections, vol. 108, 1948.

Vera Cruz Chávez, Pablo de la. "Cronología y corología de la cuenca del río Camaná — Majes — Colca — Arequipa." Licentiate thesis. Universidad Católica Santa María, Arequipa, 1989.

Vera Cruz Chávez, Pablo de la. "Estudio arqueológico en el Valle de Cabanaconde, Arequipa." B.A. thesis. Universidad Católica Santa María, Arequipa, 1988.

Villagómez, Pedro de. *Carta pastoral de exhortación e instrucción contra las idolatrías de los indios del arzobispado de Lima* [1649]. Lima: Sanmartí, 1919.

Wachtel, Nathan. *Sociedad e ideología: Ensayos de historia y antropología andinas.* Lima: Instituto de Estudios Peruanos, 1973.

———. *Vision of the Vanquished: The Spanish Conquest of Peru through Indian Eyes, 1530–1570.* Hassocks, Sussex, England: Harvester Press, 1977.

Waugh, Richard, and John M. Treacy. "Hydrology of the Coporaque Irrigation System." In *The Cultural Ecology, Archaeology, and History of Terracing and Terrace Abandonment in the Colca Valley of Southern Peru: Technical Report to the National Science Foundation and the National Geographic Society*, edited by William M. Denevan, pp. 1:116–49. Madison: University of Wisconsin Press, 1986.

Webber, Ellen R. "Cows in the Colca: Household Cattle Raising in Achoma, Peru." M.A. thesis, University of Wisconsin, Madison, 1993.

Weibel, Max. "El cañón de Colca: La cisura de erosión más profunda de los Andes." *Boletín de Lima* 13(1981):41–45.

Wernke, Steven Arlyn. "An Archaeo-history of Andean Community and Landscape: The Late Prehispanic and Early Colonial Colca Valley, Peru." Ph.D. dissertation, University of Wisconsin, Madison, 2003.

———. "A Reassessment of Collagua and Provincial Inka Ceramic Styles of Arequipa, Peru." Paper presented at the 66th Annual Meeting of the Society for American Archaeology, 18–22 April 2001, New Orleans.

Wheeler, Jane C. "Faunal Remains from Archaeological Excavations at Coporaque." In *The Cultural Ecology, Archaeology, and History of Terracing and Terrace Abandonment in the Colca Valley of Southern Peru: Technical Report to the National Science Foundation and the National Geographic Society*, edited by William M. Denevan, pp. 1:291–312. Madison: University of Wisconsin Press, 1986.

Whitaker, Arthur P. *The Huancavelica Mercury Mine.* Cambridge, Mass.: Harvard University Press, 1941.

Wightman, Ann M. *Indigenous Migration and Social Change: The Forasteros of Cuzco, 1570–1720.* Durham, N.C.: Duke University Press, 1990.

Wood, Robert D. *"Teach Them Good Customs": Colonial Indian Education and Acculturation in the Andes.* Culver City, Calif.: Labyrinthos, 1986.

Zabálburu, Francisco, and José Sancho Rayón, eds. *Nueva colección de documentos inéditos para la historia de España y sus Indias.* 6 vols. Madrid: [n.p.], 1894–96.

Zamora, Margarita. *Language, Authority, and Indigenous History in the "Comentarios reales de los incas."* Cambridge: Cambridge University Press, 1988.

Zárate, Agustín de. *Historia del descubrimiento y conquista del Perú* [1555], edited by Franklin Pease G. Y. and Teodoro Hampe Martínez. Lima: Pontificia Universidad Católica del Perú, 1995.

Zavala, Silvio. *La encomienda indiana.* Madrid: Centro de Estudios Históricos, 1935.

———. *El servicio personal de los indios en el Perú*. 3 vols. Mexico City: El Colegio de México, 1978–80.

Zimmerer, Karl S. *Changing Fortunes: Biodiversity and Peasant Livelihood in the Peruvian Andes*. Berkeley: University of California Press, 1996.

Zuidema, R. Tom. *The Ceque System of Cuzco: The Social Organization of the Capital of the Inca*. Leiden, Netherlands: Brill, 1964.

———. "Guaman Poma between the Arts of Europe and the Andes." *Colonial Latin American Review* 3:1–2(1994):37–85.

———. *Inca Civilization in Cuzco*. Austin: University of Texas Press, 1990.

INDEX

Inca penetration of, 14–18; under Inca rule, 18–20, 23–27, 45, 122, 127–28, 153, 245, 249–250; linguistic differences in, 11, 12; *mitayos* from, 156, 158–63, 166–67, 171, 178–80, 231, 236–41; population of, 26, 65–66, 74, 109, 153–54, 227, 241, 242, 245; pre-Inca, 7–8, 141, 263 n.11; during republican period, 251, 252, 256–57; resistance in, 49, 75, 96–97, 139, 207–11, 247; Toledo ordinances and, 84–90, 113–17, 146, 150–51, 176, 187, 206, 248, 251; *visita general* and, 100–103, 128, 149, 242. *See also* Agriculture; Andean culture, social organization of; Barter; *Doctrinas*; Duality; *Kurakas*; *Obrajes*; *Reducciones*; Terraces; *Visitas*

Collagua, 6, 104, 127–28; *encomienda*, 30, 38–39, 40, 54–56, 67–68, 102–3, 107, 132–35, 136–37, 141, 149, 151–52, 228, 236–37; Gonzalo Pizarro and, 45–46, 51, 228; *mita de plaza* in Arequipa and, 38, 103, 154–55, 156, 159, 160–63; origin myth of, 3, 10–11, 105, 257; restitution of Franciscans and, 190–195; skull deformation of, 13–14, 116

Collaguas, Los (*corregimiento*), 6, 80–82, 94, 229–33, 240–41

Collaguata (Cullahuata), 10, 13, 49

Colmenares, Gaspar de, 129

Colonial administration, 79–90, 92–104, 122–30, 139, 153–54, 180, 215–33, 247–49, 251–52. *See also* Tribute

Conchucos, 208

Concubinage, 100, 111, 118, 201

Conopas, 12, 49, 249

Conquest of Peru, 31, 33, 131

Contreras, Doña Catalina de, 54, 221, 222

Conversion, 39, 46–49, 83, 110, 128, 149, 178, 181–82, 188, 204, 246. *See also* Colca Valley, conversion in

Coporaque, 10, 15, 93–94, 108, 113, 121, 127, 129, 140, 141–46, 177, 238, 245, 254; church in, 205–6, 209–10

Córdoba, Juan de, 175

Córdoba y Salinas, Fray Diego de, 47

Coro Inga, Diego, 9, 85, 87–89, 208, 229, 230

Corregidores, 59, 80–82, 86, 89, 120, 121–22, 197, 208–9, 222, 226, 227, 228–30; abuses by, 156, 165, 167, 231, 232–33; *doctrinas* and, 111, 190–92, 198; *kurakas* and, 90, 125, 126, 128, 132, 137, 206; *mita* and, 159, 160, 161, 162–63, 175–76, 237–38, 239–41; *reducciones* and, 92–100, 147–48, 272 n.30

Corregimiento, 80–82, 132

Corruption, 61–62, 63, 72, 137–38, 163–69, 232, 233. See also *Residencia*

Corsairs, 219, 222, 224, 226, 232

Council of the Indies, 42, 43, 52, 60, 62, 70, 71, 118, 164, 194, 210, 225, 228

Crops. *See* Agriculture

Cruz, Baltasar de la, 194

Cuba, Antonio de la, 226, 227

Cuba, Doña María de la, 225–26, 232

Cuba Maldonado, Diego. *See* Hernández de la Cuba Maldonado, Diego

Cuba Maldonado, Doña Mariana de la, 218

Cuba Maldonado, Gerónimo de la, 225–28, 232, 234

Cuzco, 11, 30, 37–38, 42, 47, 72, 74, 106–7, 124, 198, 225, 226, 238; Colca Valley and, 31–32, 95, 189, 192–93, 194–95, 196; uprising in, 33–35

Dávalos de Ribera, Don Juan, 227

Dávalos Santillán, Doña Elvira, 226–227

Dávila, Gerónimo, 241

Disease. *See* Epidemics; Hospitals; Physicians

Doctrinas (Indian parishes), 9–10, 79, 89–90, 102, 103, 135, 149, 150, 182–207, 246–47; churches in, 106, 108, 170, 173, 178, 190, 196, 205–7, 209–10, 231; outdoor chapel in, 206; pastoral *visitas* of, 196–98, 210

Women, 87, 101–2, 103, 112–13, 125, 127,
130, 146–47, 156–57, 274 n.23; under
Incas, 14, 15, 16, 18, 20, 24, 258; marriage
and, 110–12, 223; prostitution and, 86,
176; Spanish, 35, 52–54, 58–60, 61, 62–
63, 64, 159, 163, 218–19, 220, 221, 223–24,
225–27, 231. *See also* Concubinage

Yanahuara (La Chimba), 103, 135, 160, 161,
177, 178–79, 218, 223, 230, 240, 246, 258
Yanantin, 113, 274 n.23

Yanque, 9, 82, 94, 105, 108–9, 163, 177, 199–
200, 205, 229, 230, 239, 255–56; La Brota,
8, 12, 94–96; church in, 206–7, 210; *sayas*
in, 96, 106, 107–8, 129–30, 142, 151–52,
206, 254
Yanque Collaguas. *See* Collagua
Yanque *Viejo*. *See* Ullo Ullo
Yanquinicho, 32, 35
Ybáñez de Yruegas, Pedro, 164

Zapata, Friar Luis de, 182

Noble David Cook is professor in and chair of the Department
of History at Florida International University. He is the author of
"Born to Die": Disease and New World Conquest, 1492–1650 (1998); (with
Alexandra Parma Cook) Good Faith and Truthful Ignorance: A Case of
Transatlantic Bigamy (Duke, 1991); The People of the Colca Valley: A
Population Study (1982); and Demographic Collapse: Indian Peru, 1520–1620
(1981). His edited works include (with Alexandra Parma Cook) The
Discovery and Conquest of Peru: Chronicles of the New World Encounter, by
Pedro de Cieza de León (Duke, 1998), and (with W. George Lovell)
"Secret Judgments of God": Old World Disease in Colonial Spanish
America (1992).

Alexandra Parma Cook is an independent scholar. She is the author
(with Noble David Cook) of Good Faith and Truthful Ignorance: A Case
of Transatlantic Bigamy (Duke, 1991). She translated and coedited (with
Noble David Cook) The Discovery and Conquest of Peru: Chronicles of the
New World Encounter, by Pedro de Cieza de León (Duke, 1998).

Library of Congress Cataloging-in-Publication Data
Cook, Noble David.
People of the volcano : Andean counterpoint in the Colca Valley of
Peru / Noble David Cook, with Alexandra Parma Cook.
p. cm.
Includes bibliographical references and index.
ISBN-13: 978-0-8223-3988-5 (cloth : alk. paper)
ISBN-13: 978-0-8223-3971-7 (pbk. : alk. paper)
1. Colla Indians—Peru—Colca River Valley (Arequipa)—History—
Sources. 2. Colla Indians—Peru—Colca River Valley (Arequipa)—
Social life and customs. 3. Colla Indians—Peru—Colca River Valley
(Arequipa)—Census. 4. Colca River Valley (Arequipa, Peru)—
History—Sources. 5. Colca River Valley (Arequipa, Peru)—Social life
and customs. I. Cook, Alexandra Parma. II. Title.
F3430.1.C6C66 2007
985'.32—dc22   2006035584